Cam Brewer, Herb Hammond, and Sean Markey offer an ecosystem-based approach to city planning. *They* build their approach on the emerging science of urban ecology. *Nature-First Cities: Restoring Relationships with Ecosystems and with Each Other* is a timely, important work.

FREDERICK STEINER, author of *Making Plans: How to Engage with Landscape, Design, and the Urban Environment*

EST. ◆ 1907

FRIESENS
IDEAS CRAFTED IN PRINT
— EMPLOYEE-OWNED —

Vault

Pr
ori
an
thr
sca

Title: Nature-First Cities

Docket: 301308

PRODUCTION SPECIFICATIONS

Trim size:	6 x 9	
Page count:	258	
Text:	Finch Offset FSC, 60 lb. *— HP 7250 Inkjet*	
Insert:		
Cover:	Kallima C1S FSC, 10 pt. *— YB HP 50000*	
Board:		
Endsheet:		
Dustjacket:	*Soft Cover Sewn w/ Flaps*	
Binding:		
Specialty	*Coloured images*	

Mo
lanc
inte
Can
natu
mor
vibra

Imag
the q
Fence
book
priori
and w

Cam Brewer, Herb Hammond,
and Sean Markey

N̄ature-First
CITIES

Restoring Relationships with
Ecosystems and with Each Other

UBCPress · Vancouver

Printed in Canada on FSC-certified ancient-forest-free paper (100% post-consumer recycled) that is processed chlorine- and acid-free.

UBC Press is a Benetech Global Certified Accessible™ publisher. The epub version of this book meets stringent accessibility standards, ensuring it is available to people with diverse needs.

Library and Archives Canada Cataloguing in Publication

Title: Nature-first cities: restoring relationships with ecosystems and with each other / Cam Brewer, Herb Hammond, and Sean Markey.
Names: Brewer, Cam (Cameron B.), author. | Hammond, Herb, author. | Markey, Sean Patrick, author.
Description: Includes bibliographical references and index.
Identifiers: Canadiana (print) 20240361504 | Canadiana (ebook) 20240361539 | ISBN 9780774868648 (softcover) | ISBN 9780774868662 (EPUB) | ISBN 9780774868655 (PDF)
Subjects: LCSH: Urban ecology (Sociology) | LCSH: City planning—Environmental aspects. | LCSH: Sustainable urban development. | LCSH: Nature. | LCSH: Climate change mitigation.
Classification: LCC HT241 .B74 2024 | DDC 307.76—dc23

UBC Press gratefully acknowledges the financial support for our publishing program of the Government of Canada, the Canada Council for the Arts, and the British Columbia Arts Council.

This book has been published with the help of a grant from the Canadian Federation for the Humanities and Social Sciences, through the Scholarly Book Awards, using funds provided by the Social Sciences and Humanities Research Council of Canada. We also acknowledge support from Furthermore, a program of the J.M. Kaplan Fund, and the SFU Publications Fund.

Furthermore:
a program of the J.M. Kaplan Fund

UBC Press is situated on the traditional, ancestral, and unceded territory of the xʷməθkʷəy̓əm (Musqueam) people. This land has always been a place of learning for the xʷməθkʷəy̓əm, who have passed on their culture, history, and traditions for millennia, from one generation to the next.

UBC Press
The University of British Columbia
www.ubcpress.ca

Contents

Illustrations

Foreword

Faisal Moola and David Suzuki

For most of human history, people were nomadic hunter-gatherers, following animals and plants through the seasons and on long-distance migrations carrying all that they owned with them. Ten thousand years ago the Agricultural Revolution began a profound shift in human social evolution since, with a reliable source of food, we could settle in places and build permanent structures. But for most of the rest of our existence, we lived in rural villages centred on agriculture. Today the world's population has become concentrated in urban areas, including high-density megacities such as Tokyo (37 million), Delhi (28 million), Mexico City (21 million), and Cairo (20 million). Rapid urbanization is both a response to and a driver of massive economic and social change happening across the planet. For example, over 60 percent of world GDP is generated in just 600 global cities. This includes not only international financial hubs such as New York City and London but also emerging powerhouse markets in the developing world, such as São Paulo and Lagos.[1]

Despite being a vast nation of mountains, forests, prairies, and ice, Canada, like many other countries, is truly an urban society. Over 82 percent of Canadians now reside in cities and suburbs, and according to the United Nations Canada is among the top urbanized nations on the planet, ahead of France, Spain, Germany, Mexico, Italy, and most other countries.[2]

The significance of urbanization in Canada parallels the unprecedented shifts in global population and human land use that have been under way for decades. The Greater Toronto and Hamilton Area alone generates about a fifth of Canada's total annual economic activity – well ahead of the oil and gas sector that dominates the business news headlines and the attention of our politicians.

Although many people move to cities as a matter of choice to seek a better life and greater opportunities, war, political conflict, and climate change are driving the mass migration of people from rural to urban areas. As noted by Neil Adger and his coauthors, the "involuntary migration to cities, whether from conflict or from environmental catastrophes, is a matter of survival" and a primary means of adaptation in an increasingly uncertain and insecure world.[3] Tragically, new migrants to cities often face poverty and live with chronic housing insecurity.

Although the staggering ascendancy of urbanization has been examined by other authors previously, *Nature-First Cities: Restoring Relationships with Ecosystems and with Each Other* challenges the dominant perception of cities as either booming metropolises or impoverished slums inhospitable to nature and wildlife. As Cam Brewer, Herb Hammond, and Sean Markey argue in this book, urbanized geographies too often have been dismissed as "landscapes of regret," unsuitable for nature conservation because of their degree of fragmentation and ecological degradation from urban sprawl and unsustainable infrastructure development.[4] Indeed, in cities around the world, local woodlands, wetlands, and farmlands continue to be cut down, drained, dug up, and paved over to make way for yet more freeways, parking lots, and sprawling housing developments, with calamitous consequences for native biodiversity.

Despite the explosive pace and scale of urbanization across the planet, the authors of *Nature-First Cities* make the compelling case that our cities and suburbs hold out great hope as "landscapes of opportunity" for human and nonhuman biodiversity alike.[5] Urbanized regions contain important remnant habitats for wildlife, such as pollinators and songbirds; support essential ecosystem services such as flood control, carbon sequestration and storage, and protection from soil erosion, pests, and diseases; and provide recreational opportunities. As shown in this book, urban green space, including green infrastructure technologies integrated into the built environment (e.g., green walls and roofs, rain gardens, and engineered wetlands), also extend the life span of and/or replace many types of traditional infrastructure, such as stormwater management, and thereby save tens of millions of dollars for cash-strapped municipal governments.

An important focus of *Nature-First Cities* is on the physical and mental health benefits of green space for urban dwellers. People living in urban areas are less active, suffer from greater stress levels, and are exposed to poorer air quality in neighbourhoods that lack street trees, city parks, and other forms of urban greening.[6] As discussed in this book, urban greening strategies are therefore a critical preventative public health-care intervention since they reduce exposure to deadly air pollution and extreme heat, ameliorate stress, and promote greater physical activity along with other health benefits. Despite these benefits, there is great socio-economic disparity in the amount of, quality of, and access to green space in Canadian and other cities. Whereas the urban tree canopy is high in wealthier and whiter neighbourhoods, lower-income and racialized communities are often effectively deforested, thereby suffering from great inequity in environmental benefits and burdens of urban planning policies. As noted by University of Toronto professor Stephen Bede Scharper, "urban tree lines often follow the fault lines of social, economic, political, and ecological disparity. Just as we experience racial and economic inequality, we also experience unequal ecologies, places where people experience both economic and ecological marginalization."[7]

People have long recognized the importance of green spaces in cities. There are records of Egyptian gardens dating back 3,600 years, and in ancient Rome the architect and engineer Vitruvius wrote an urban design manual in 27 BC that outlined the key ecological principles of good landscape design. As noted in *Nature-First Cities,* although public parks were established as early as the sixteenth century in cities across Europe and the Middle East, it was not until the twentieth century that a popular urban parks movement was created to improve the physical aspects of cities suffering from urban disease and decay. For example, following a deadly cholera outbreak in 1833, the English Parliament established a Select Committee on Public Works that recommended that every city and town in the country establish a public park. In 1847, the country's first urban park was opened to the public in Birkenhead near Liverpool. A young landscape architect by the name of Frederick Law Olmsted who visited the park was so inspired by the experience that he went on to create dozens of new urban parks in cities across North America, including the most famous urban park in the world: Central Park in New York City.[8]

Unlike the private gardens and palatial estates of the aristocrats and industrialists of the time, Olmsted's designs were much more naturalistic and based on a design philosophy called "Greensward," an English term for a large, unbroken swath of land.[9] Another key design element for Olmsted was his desire that urban parks contribute to the improved health and mental well-being of urban dwellers: "Two classes of improvements were to be planned for this purpose; one directed to secure pure and wholesome air, to act through the lungs; the other to secure an antithesis of objects of vision to those of the streets and houses which should act remedially, by impressions on the mind and suggestions to the imagination."[10] *Nature-First Cities* builds on the foundational principles of landscape ecology and green infrastructure advanced by earlier green planning visionaries such as Frederick Law Olmsted, Ebenezer Howard, and Cornelia Hahn Oberlander. The authors advocate for a nature-first approach to how we plan, develop, and restore our cities, which they call nature-directed stewardship (NDS). Central to this innovative approach to urban planning is the need to protect both existing green spaces within and at the edges of our growing urban communities and to design our cities and suburbs with nature in mind. Unlike earlier green planning ideas, which advocated for more urban parks but failed to address the ecological conditions of unprotected surrounding areas, NDS operates at multiple scales, from site-level interventions (e.g., building a rain garden in a front yard) to neighbourhood-wide efforts (e.g., converting city back alleys into verdant ecological corridors) to watershed-level decisions (e.g., establishing new municipal parks). This spatially integrated approach to urban planning (managing simultaneously for land, air, water, wildlife, and people across space and time) is reflective of the interconnected and interdependent biocultural approaches used by Indigenous Peoples for millennia.

The principles of NDS are already being employed in cities across the world, and the authors describe these principles through a series of case studies. They include the protection of urban waterways in Melbourne, cooperative watershed management in Portland, and a regional protected areas network in Durban, South Africa. An entire chapter of the book is devoted to the lessons learned from NDS planning in Vancouver's Still Creek watershed, with which the authors have been personally involved. Once blanketed in old-growth forest, 81 percent of the Still Creek watershed is now covered in concrete and asphalt, such as roads and other major transportation corridors, roofs, driveways, paved yards, and other impermeable surfaces inhospitable to biodiversity. The authors' NDS restoration network plan for the watershed proposes a range of actions, including daylighting buried salmon streams and converting surfaces from impermeable to permeable to restore the natural flow and dispersal of water throughout the watershed. The overarching vision is to eventually restore the ecological integrity of the Still Creek watershed from its current degraded ecological condition to its earlier pre-urban character, including the full range of its natural composition, structure, and function.

Urban planning policy and practice, such as the day-to-day management of parks and other green spaces, have long reinforced the misguided belief that management expertise should be informed exclusively by Western science. As noted by Indigenous scholar Andrea Reid, Western science has not only taken precedence over Indigenous knowledge systems in conservation and other areas of public policy but also tended to reinforce embedded power imbalances to the detriment of local communities.[11] "This only serves to strengthen Western science for its own ends and to concentrate power in administrative centers, rather than in communities."[12] The authors of *Nature-First Cities* have recognized this perverse outcome of traditional urban greening by advocating for community-led approaches to NDS design and implementation, including Indigenous-led approaches. Members of the public are already getting involved in greening their communities. For example, several years ago the David Suzuki Foundation and more than a dozen local community groups launched a cheeky new campaign to create Canada's first "Homegrown National Park" in downtown Toronto. This crowd-sourced green urban corridor is located along one of the city's most notable "lost rivers," which now lies buried beneath asphalt and concrete. The project aims to protect, restore, and create urban green space and other green infrastructure by planting native trees and shrubs, cultivating bird and pollinator-friendly gardens, growing food in backyards and on balconies, and encouraging people to spend time outdoors in support of improved health and well-being. The David Suzuki Foundation has since partnered with municipalities, such as the City of Markham, to scale-up the project rapidly by greening interventions along major infrastructure corridors – rail, hydro, and road.

Continuing to ignore the natural and green infrastructure needs of our towns and cities – such as protecting wetlands and forests, establishing local parks, and creating naturalized schoolgrounds – is shortsighted. As described in *Nature-First Cities,* urban green space and green infrastructure complement traditional infrastructure; provide many ecological, economic, and social benefits; and contribute to the health and well-being of urban dwellers. Isn't it time that we protected, restored, and enhanced the nature in our own neighbourhoods?

Preface

The book that you hold in your hands is about restoration – restoration of our relationships with nature and with each other. It is about the imperative of mending these relationships for their own sake and in order to address the threats of climate and biodiversity collapse. And it is about rebuilding these relationships on the understanding that we are not separate from nature or from each other.

The climate emergency and biodiversity crisis are humanity's doing – and perhaps undoing. That (un)doing is excused in our dominant Western culture by a "framing story" that celebrates the exploitation of nature and excuses its unequal distribution of benefits and burdens.[1] Unravelling natural ecosystems, the climate emergency, and the looming biodiversity crisis are discounted by those most responsible, while those least responsible shoulder existential consequences. In this way, a lack of equity inflames the ecological and social crises.

Restoration offers a new framing story: a story about protection, regeneration, and reciprocity; a story about a new accord in which human beings, both inside and outside urban areas, assume a respectful and grateful role as a part of nature. Nature directs us to recognize and affirm essential ecosystem processes – such as climate moderation, carbon sequestration and storage, water purification, biological diversification, flood and drought regulation, and spiritual and physical healing – as ecosystem benefits that are intrinsic to nature and essential to our survival. Seen in this way, nature provides ecosystem benefits that sustain us (and all beings). When we plan activities, carry them out, and evaluate them, the first priority is responsibility for protection of nature and reciprocity for its benefits.

Professor Doug Tallamy sums up the challenge:

> It's not that we purposefully have nature in our sights. Rather, we simply refuse to share our spaces with the natural world. We have clung to the notion that humans and nature cannot coexist as if it were true (it's not) ... Fortunately,

there is a solution to this existential crisis. We can save nature by learning to live with it. We must now practice conservation not only within parks and preserves, but also outside of them, where we live, work, shop, farm, and play: that is in built, human dominated landscapes.[2]

Restoration proceeds through a process called *nature-directed stewardship* (NDS). The result in urban areas is what we call *nature-first cities*. To get there, we outline a process of restoration guided by new (and ancient) ways of relating to nature and to each other and by the knowledge that we are not removed from nature or from each other. This process requires more than changing planning techniques and development methodologies. It requires changing our ways of thinking and relating to nature (and to each other). It requires a new framing story.

Before we embark, clarification of some terms is in order.

Often nature's benefits are referred to as "ecosystem *services*." Although useful in certain contexts, this term can relegate nature to just another utility in service to humans, like an internet service. Considering ecosystem services in this way catches us in the framing story that gives monetary value precedence over intrinsic ecosystem benefits. This does not lead to restoration. Instead of taking that approach, we embrace ecosystem *benefits* as freely given.

"Urban nature" means fragments of natural ecosystem *character* (that is, natural ecosystem composition, structure, and function). The emphasis here is on "fragments" as opposed to intact ecosystems large enough to carry on the self-organizing and self-regulating processes characteristic of healthy ecosystems. Urban nature consists of small areas of natural or near-natural ecosystems isolated in a sea of urban development. These fragments are linked together into protected networks of nature, which as they regain natural ecological integrity, evolve into networks of "ecological reserves."

"Green spaces" are fragments of ecological integrity that need to undergo restoration. Think of them as *green* for living vegetation, *brown* for soil and decayed vegetation, and *blue* for the water movement network. Water courses through the soil to provide life to vegetation and animals and rises up through the vegetation to store carbon and form the basis of life.

With these terms in mind, we hope that you find the process outlined in the pages that follow interesting, informative, and inspirational.

With few exceptions, nowhere on Earth have ecological landscapes been more transformed and degraded than in cities and towns. Thus, nowhere on Earth is restoration more necessary than in urban areas. The process of restoration requires all hands on deck: residents, activists, students, academics, planners, elected officials, entrepreneurs, and developers. Regardless of who you are, we invite you to join us in putting nature first in cities.

Acknowledgments

Our first acknowledgement is to nature. With her guidance, we walked the path of putting nature first in cities. The path was a long one. It started with the recognition that we are not separate from nature. It led to the demand that prioritizing nature in cities must benefit cities, address threats to ecosystems, and improve equity. Along the way we listened to those who travelled the path before us. We embraced scientific inquiry and Indigenous knowledge, learned from community collaborations, and developed plans that tested theory and practice.

Many people sparked ideas and helped us develop the concepts set out in these pages. They include Julia Berry, David Boyd, Chloe Boyle, Brenda Brewer, Marina Brinkhurst, Claire Buchanan, Cherise Burda, Majora Carter, Emily Chan, Christian Charles, Fin Donnelly, Andréanne Doyon, Emily Doyle-Yamaguchi, Paul Friedland, Kaitlyn Fung, Susan Gordon, Deborah Harford, Cheeying Ho, Henry Lau, Tom Laviolette, Ken Lertzman, Derek Martin, Michael M'Gonigle, Bea Miller, Michelle Molnar, Catherine Parsons, Chris Pavsek, Bob Ransford, Anwen Rees, Jay Ritchlin, Carmen Rosen, Alison Shaw, Sabrina Spencer, Kacia Tolsma, and Anna Yamaoka-Enkerlin.

We are grateful to David Suzuki, Faisal Moola, and Tom Bradley, who generously shared their experience, passion, and insights.

The book would not have come together without the tenacity of those at UBC Press including Megan Brand, James MacNevin, Michelle van der Merwe, and Randy Schmidt. We extend our thanks to the funders who supported this work, including the Scholarly Book Awards (formerly, the Aid to Scholarly Publications Program [ASPP]), Furthermore, North Foundation, Simon Fraser University Publication Fund, School of Resource and Environmental Management (REM), SFU Faculty of Environment, Vancity Community Foundation, and the Vancouver Foundation.

Patience, love, and support from Isabel Brewer, Susie Hammond, Mel Markey, Grace Markey, and Lisa Yamaoka were, of course, indispensable.

Thank you all for helping to invite nature home.

Nature-First Cities

Introduction

Each age and society re-creates its "Others."
— Edward W. Said

Robert Moses had a problem. The New York City parks commissioner was trying to find space for nature. But the city was full. It was "filled with people, people with their endlessly intertwined, hopelessly snarled tangles of aspirations and antagonisms, hopes and fears, dreams and dreads."[1] The only option that Moses saw was to move the people. They had to be "evicted, dispossessed, thrown out, relocated"[2] to make room for nature. That was the only choice he saw, because he assumed that parks are where people are not. The map is either green or not green.

Yet the people make a city great. It is the "lack of space" and the diversity of people that sets cities abuzz. Colliding aspirations drive innovation. Creative scaffolding supports artistic dreams. Exploding antagonisms mark the front lines of social justice. And the snarled dreams and dreads expressed on front stoops, subway platforms, after-work patios, and opening-night galas are what speed the blood and stir brilliance.

And still, people need nature. People without nature in their daily lives suffer from depression and disease, reduced productivity, and shorter lives. Children face the cognitive and behavioural consequences of living apart from natural surroundings. Without ecosystems to disperse, store, and clean water, cities are saddled with crumbling pipes and sewers that municipal governments cannot afford to repair. Urbanites unable to hear the distress signals of nature are slow to notice a planet in crisis.

So how does one invite nature into a city without pushing people out of the way? Our answer starts with the premise that both nature and people belong in cities, intertwined as co-creators of the urban landscape. Nature belongs where we are, and we belong in nature. From that premise flows an invitation that enhances cities, restores our relationship with nature, and rebuilds our relationships with each other.

3

FIGURE O.I   Nature woven into the built environment of cities helps to restore our critical relationships with each other and with the ecosystems that support us.

For too long we have clung to the Western conception of nature as something outside cities; far away and disconnected from our daily lives. Nature too often has been understood as what Edward Said called the "other."[3] It has been seen as something separate, the other side of a false duality invented and used to justify exploitation. That is, people and nature are distinct from each other: "The place where we are is the place where nature is not."[4]

Damaging conceptions of the other have been exposed in other contexts. On a global scale, Andre Gunder Frank called out the "dual-society" view in which "developed metropolitan countries" extract resources from "satellite underdeveloped" countries.[5] On multiple scales, Black Lives Matter, #MeToo, environmental justice, and demands for Indigenous reconciliation lay bare unequal treatment on the basis of false dualities. We say that the time has come to set aside the false notion of nature as the other.

Evidence of harm from our delusion that we are divorced from nature abounds. Thousands of zoonotic viruses similar to COVID-19 wait for us to damage nature further so that they have an opportunity to jump to humans.[6] Carbon dioxide in the atmosphere has reached levels not seen for 4 million years (when the Earth was from two to four degrees Celsius warmer and sea levels were from ten to twenty-five metres higher).[7] Half the coral reefs are gone, 85 percent of wetlands have been lost, and at least 70 percent of land surfaces have been directly altered by humans.[8] Over a million species are threatened with extinction,[9] while animals in service to us are thriving: 70 percent of the birds on Earth are chickens and turkeys, and 60 percent of nonhuman mammals are pigs and cows.[10]

To correct course, we look to cities; the concrete expressions of a myth that humans are separate from nature. Cities reflect "the highs and lows of human civilization."[11] They manifest our values, priorities, and assumptions through a built environment that accommodates opulent luxury as readily as homelessness, global capitalism as easily as community theatre, parades of diversity as often as segregated tenements. Now home to the majority of people on Earth, cities embody in steel and asphalt the ghosts of decisions past while clustering the creativity and passion necessary to change course. In other words, cities are beautiful and flawed, just like the humans who built them. They suffer from what is missing because the people who designed and constructed urban landscapes failed to see what they were excluding.

We come to the task of writing about cities after decades of seeking to "save" the nature that exists out there somewhere, beyond the boundaries of cities. We redirected our efforts to cities because our environmental work "out there" remained disconnected from the day-to-day lives of most people. We realized that something more fundamental must be addressed – our relationship with nature itself. And that starts with putting nature first in cities.

Inviting Nature Home

This book calls for action based on the science and practice of nature-directed stewardship (NDS) developed by one of the authors, Herb Hammond, and the Silva Forest Foundation.

NDS was developed and refined through decades of experience in the context of protecting forest ecosystems from logging, mining, and other forms of exploitive development. NDS starts by focusing on what to leave (and restore), not on what to use (or take). What to leave and restore are the healthy ecosystems (communities of interacting species together with the physical environments that support them) that exhibit a full range of *composition* (the number and type of biophysical parts in the ecosystem), *structure* (the way in which the parts are arranged), and *function* (the cooperative processes that occur within the ecosystem and among ecosystems). In particular, NDS seeks to protect the *ecological integrity* or *natural character* of ecosystems: the composition, structure, and function that would occur naturally in a particular place. Character includes precolonial Indigenous stewardship of ecosystems. NDS establishes networks of ecological reserves at multiple spatial scales, from large landscapes down to small sites. Each protected network includes natural composition, structure, and function and provides for restoration as necessary.

In this book, we apply the concepts and methods of NDS to cities. The result is to put nature first in cities, creating what we refer to as nature-first cities. The challenge in cities is that little or no natural ecosystem character remains. Restoration is the focus. Specifically, urban NDS puts nature first in cities through plans and activities that

- identify the target watershed and describe its natural character;
- protect any remaining fragments of natural character;
- restore new fragments of natural character; and
- restore the *water movement network* (the natural timing and flow of water linking ecosystems through vegetated layers, permeable soils, surface water bodies, and the atmosphere).

Once these elements are identified and restoration work is under way, *restoration networks* can be designated at multiple spatial scales which, with effort and sufficient time, will mature into protected networks of healthy ecosystems. The process is illustrated in Figure o.2.

Recognizing that cities are full of people – arranged in a matrix of small properties, public and private, with multiple overlapping uses – we propose a *three-part process* for establishing an urban restoration network:

FIGURE O.2 **Nature-directed stewardship in cities**

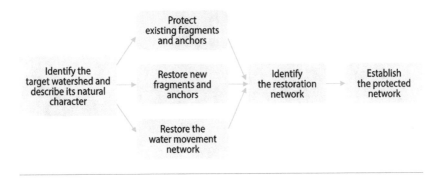

1 Local governments work with scientists, Indigenous knowledge holders, and long-time residents to identify and describe natural ecosystem character with enough detail to allow anyone in the city to engage in appropriate restoration.

2 Residents and their neighbours undertake voluntary restoration actions at the scale of individual properties, blocks, and neighbourhoods, guided by the information about natural character developed at the first stage and provided by the local government.

3 Government restoration actions leverage the voluntary actions of residents into larger-scale restoration on public lands, parks, streets, alleys, municipal buildings, and new developments. Government efforts at these larger scales are intended to inspire further small-scale voluntary action through an iterative process.

Over time, these restoration efforts at multiple spatial scales will reveal the contours of a restoration network. Enshrined in law by local governments, the restoration network will mature into a protected network of healthy ecosystems – a network of ecological reserves.

When we speak of *nature,* we mean ecological integrity, wild biodiversity, and ecosystems driven by natural processes, not the manicured green spaces of lawns and generic suburbia. By inviting this wild kind of nature back into cities, we will feed our biophilia ("the innate tendency to focus on life and lifelike processes"), ease our stress, clean our air and water, moderate the climate, and improve our health.[12]

Nature will save us money, improve our productivity, and inspire creativity and cooperation (especially in children). Restoring ecosystems in our cities will

FIGURE O.3   Untamed nature feeds the biophilia in each of us, strengthening physical and mental health, inspiring creativity, and connecting us to the biodiversity on which we depend. Why not bring those benefits to where most of us now live – in cities?

inspire us to care about the plight of ecosystems everywhere and reconnect us to Earth's systems at a time when our survival might depend on doing so.

We love cities. And we love nature. The goal of this contribution is to reconcile the two by dispelling the myth that humans are separate from nature. The practical outcome is restoration of an urban environment that reinforces our place in nature. Our thesis is that nature belongs in cities. By realizing this thesis, we hope to see a *physical* change in which cities are replete with biodiversity and intact ecosystems. We also hope to see a *conceptual* change that leads people to recognize that they are part of nature. By correcting our misconception of nature as a distant other to be treated with reckless exploitation, we take a step toward correcting cancerous misconceptions about each other.

This book began as a straightforward inquiry into whether nature-directed stewardship can be applied in cities. What emerged for us is an appreciation that this inquiry is fundamentally about restoration of our relationships with both nature and each other. This broad project of restoration demands that we develop a new relationship with nature, based on respect, responsibility, gratitude, and reciprocity. It demands what David Korten calls a new "framing story" that frees us from the limitations of our current misconceptions.[13]

Misconceptions of our relationships with nature, and of our relationships with each other, have led to the biodiversity crisis, the climate emergency, and massive social inequality. A new framing story recognizes that when "we restore the land, the land restores us."[14] And a new story demands that righting inequalities is at the core of righting our relationships with nature.

As Carolyn Merchant suggests, a "new story can be re-written only through action."[15] The plan of action presented in this book is based on the understanding that the essential ecosystem processes on which we depend – including climate moderation, carbon sequestration and storage, air and water purification, biological diversity, flood and drought regulation – benefit us all. Accordingly, we resist commodifying or diminishing these elements of life and instead insist on nature as a fundamental human right. As Dr. David Boyd, the UN special rapporteur on human rights and the environment, emphasizes,

> the right to a clean, healthy and sustainable environment is a compelling reminder that all humans share DNA with every other form of life on Earth. We are not separate from or superior to nature, but rather part of the incredible tapestry of life. We all breathe the same air and depend on healthy ecosystems and a livable climate for our health, wellbeing, and even our survival.[16]

The remainder of this book unfolds as follows. Chapter 1 examines the cost of expelling nature from our cities. The false premise that nature does not belong in cities has extracted an astounding human, ecological, and economic toll that we can no longer afford. Chapter 2 canvasses the role of urban planning in evicting nature and traces the evolution of ideas that inspire a more environmentally responsible approach to urban development. These are stepping stones to inviting nature home. Chapter 3 highlights some innovative examples of taking this further to create urban homes for nature. We conclude the chapter with a summary of what is still missing. Chapter 4 outlines our vision for nature-first cities. This vision rests on three core, interconnected principles: nature, equity, and density. We offer a glimpse of how this vision will unfold in healthy urban ecosystems, communities, and economies. Chapter 5 explains how the principles of nature and NDS in particular can be applied in urban areas. Chapter 6 recounts our experiences in applying NDS in the urban area of East Vancouver, including a brief contrast with an NDS plan for new urban development in an urban-forest landscape. Chapter 7 concludes with a three-part process for applying NDS in urban areas. This process moves upward to join individuals, neighbours, and community groups and downward from local governments to support the efforts of communities.

1 Nature Expelled

Nature waits for us to bring her home ... We have expelled it needlessly from our daily lives.

– Edward O. Wilson

The Western project of urbanization has proceeded (mostly) by removing nature from where the majority of us live. The replacement of nature with a "concrete jungle" created what Lewis Mumford described as a "polluted, bulldozed, machine-dominated, dehumanized" civilization.[1] It not only razed ecosystems but also severed people from ecological feedback, knowledge, and wisdom.

Manicured green space cannot replace functioning ecosystems. Such green spaces in cities merely capture and sentimentalize nature. As Jane Jacobs observed crisply, "nature, sentimentalized and considered as the antithesis of cities, is apparently assumed to consist of grass, fresh air and little else, and this ludicrous disrespect results in the devastation of nature even formally and publicly preserved in the form of a pet."[2] Or "preserve[d] ... as if it were a jar of pickles," as George Monbiot puts it.[3]

What has been expelled from our cities is something more than a pet; it is something wild and untamed. What is gone is *ecological integrity,* "the abundance and diversity of organisms at all levels, and the ecological patterns, processes, and structural attributes responsible for that biological diversity."[4] Dismissed from our cities is nature capable of offering spiritual, psychological, and physiological benefits to urban residents. Absent is nature that fosters empathy for and connectivity to other species and that might inspire ecosystem protection and ecological restoration around the planet.

In his seminal *Design with Nature,* Ian McHarg instructed that

> clearly the problem of man and nature is not one of providing a decorative background for the human play, or even ameliorating the grim city: it is the necessity of sustaining nature as a source of life, milieu, teacher, sanctum, challenge and, most of all, of rediscovering nature's corollary of the unknown in the self, the source of meaning.[5]

FIGURE I.I   Urban areas are often the products of excluding nature in favour of human-made elements – concrete, glass, and steel – arranged as if entirely detached from the surrounding ecosystems.

Witnessing the overwhelming expulsion of nature from our cities makes one wonder why. Why did we create an urban habitat – one that now holds the majority of humans – that is so bereft of nature?[6]

The answer starts with recognizing that it has been our choice to do so, and therefore we need to look to ourselves. Our conception of cities cannot be untangled from our conception of civilization or the aspirations of our culture. The Latin word *civis,* meaning "citizen," is the root of both the word *city* and the word *civilization.* The separation of cities from nature is tied to the separation of our civilization, our culture, and ourselves from nature.

Environmental historian William Cronon emphasizes that Western culture fabricated a human-nature duality. This duality is manifest in the development of cities where engineers have gone to great lengths to make urban existence as seemingly independent as possible from local ecosystems: the reliance on energy inputs from elsewhere, the homogenization of development irrespective of location or climate, the removal of vegetation and paving over of soil, the fabrication of infrastructure to replace ecosystem services, and the shielding of daily life from hydrological cycles, seasons, and weather. That shielding creates cities that are "ecologically impoverished and imperiled, constantly requiring a techno-logical fix to right the catastrophe prompted by a previous technological fix."[7]

Landscape architect Anne Whiston Spirn writes that "the belief that the city is an entity apart from nature and even antithetical to it has dominated the way in which the city is perceived and continues to affect how it is built."[8] Nature is perceived as existing only somewhere else, beyond the urban fringe. Nature is comprehended as the subject of documentaries and the location of weekend adventures – but daily urban living is led in purported isolation from it.

Sigmund Freud wrote that "the principal task of civilization, its actual raison d'être, is to defend us against nature."[9] His assertion reveals another layer of the human-nature duality expressed by urbanization. It is not just that nature is separate; it is also that Western civilization actively attempts to suppress, contain, and destroy nature. There has long been a perceived struggle through which cities overcome nature and keep it out so that they do not become "ruined," "overgrown," or fall into neglect.[10] Cities have been designed to suc-ceed by making nature succumb by "reclaiming" land from wetland ecosystems, by channelling rivers and levelling the earth, and by driving out most species and taming what nature is left. As University of California at Berkeley's Carolyn Merchant observes, "civilization is the final end, the telos, toward which 'wild' nature is destined."[11] In this epic battle, cities represent civilization's victory over nature.

Of course, the fabrication of a human-nature duality remains just that: a concoction, a myth. Our cities, our civilization, and our selves remain fully connected to, and dependent on, nature. In the words of the late Harvard University professor Edward O. Wilson, "the truth is that we never conquered the world, never understood it; we only think we have control ... The prevailing myths concerning our predatory actions toward each other and the environ-ment are obsolete, unreliable, and destructive."[12]

This mythical "victory" over nature, cemented in place as the DNA of our modern human settlements, comes at a price that we could never afford. In the decades since Bill McKibben's *The End of Nature* first grieved the loss of a planet untouched by humans, we have been collectively experiencing what Richard Louv calls *nature deficit disorder*, "the human cost of alienation from nature."[13]

Expelling nature from where we live robs us of our full human potential. Our children are growing up severed from Earth's systems at the very time that those systems are sending out dire warnings (from climate disruptions to pan-demics). We rely on manufactured and decaying grey infrastructure systems that mimic (fleetingly and expensively) the benefits that nature would otherwise provide in perpetuity and for free (e.g., purifying air, cleaning and transporting water, and regulating temperatures). A there-is-no-alternative mindset leaves us unable to envision solutions beyond further reliance on expensive manufactured systems. Entirely omitted from the calculus of our built environments are the ecological costs, paid at multiple scales across cities, including the fragmentation and isolation of ecosystems and habitats, the substitution of manicured yards for nature, and the concomitant degradation of ecosystems adjacent to urban areas.

HUMAN COSTS

> *We shall solve the city problem by leaving the city.*
> – Henry Ford[14]

Edward O. Wilson developed the concept of "biophilia" – "the innate tendency to focus on life and lifelike processes" – and concluded that "the degree to which we come to understand other organisms" will determine the degree to which "we will place a greater value on them, and on ourselves."[15] It is this "innately emotional affiliation of human beings to other living organisms" that allows us to be fully human and to reach our intellectual, emotional, and creative best.[16] The full development of this connection with nature depends, in the words of Yale University's Stephen Kellert, "on sufficient experience, learning, and cultural support."[17]

Yet our urban areas are too frequently devoid of nature, tormenting our biophilia. Stephen Kaplan points out, for example, that "directed-attention fatigue" comes from the exhaustion associated with continually blocking out competing stimuli – a ubiquitous challenge in urban life – and leads to irritability, reduced inhibitions, less ability to solve problems effectively, lower capacity for understanding the "bigger picture," impeded follow-through on plans, and reduced inclination to assist others.[18] The antidote, according to Kaplan, is exposure to natural environments that "turn out to be particularly rich in the characteristics necessary for restorative experiences."[19] Such natural experiences are capable of both reducing and preventing stress.

In his influential book *Last Child in the Woods,* Louv argues that Western alienation from nature manifests in a wide range of maladies affecting children and adults, families, and entire communities.[20] In short, our desire for engagement with nature is at odds with the reality of our daily urban experiences. The average North American spends 95 percent of his or her time indoors.[21] When we do venture outside, it is frequently into an urban landscape dominated by pavement, buildings, and fabricated green spaces with highly managed lawns, gardens, and playing fields. This combination of features taunts our need for real connections with nature.

FIGURE 1.2 Nature in cities, such as the Ramble in Central Park, offers an antidote to stress, a muse to creators, and a reminder of what matters.

Although the causal relationships between spending time in nature and improved mental and physical health are complex, recent literature underscores that "a wealth of human health benefits come[s] from experiencing nature and biodiversity."[22] These psychological and physiological benefits are forgone by people whose lives lack regular contact with nature. The positive effects of exposure to nature are also predicated on the safety of the experience (which is not adequately addressed in the literature or in practice, especially regarding racialized communities).[23]

Exposure to nature has been "consistently linked to lower levels of depression, anxiety, and stress."[24] Even "green space" (less than the full complement of nature) is positively correlated with restoration from stress and mental fatigue as well as improved mood and self-confidence.[25] People living within three kilometres of parks have been shown to be less affected by a stressful life event, and exposure to nature has been correlated with fewer depressive symptoms in pregnant women.[26] Time in nature has been linked to improved concentration and self-discipline and better cognitive function.[27] Compared with an urban walk, a walk through natural shrubs and trees has been shown to decrease anxiety.[28] Even exposure to indoor plants has been linked to lower indicators of stress.[29]

Clinical therapists recognize that "to no small degree, the origins of clients' problems involved the human dissociation from the natural world."[30] People's perceived general health is positively affected where there is green space nearby, and urban dwellers have been found to have lower mental distress if living near green spaces.[31] A study of 22,000 Germans found a positive relationship between green urban areas and life satisfaction rates.[32] In Canada, a study found an increase in perceived health for every ten extra trees on a city block – equivalent to one's perceived benefit from earning an extra $10,000 a year or being seven years younger.[33] In fact, connections to nature have been shown to predict happiness to an extent similar to one's level of education, marital status, and physical attractiveness.[34] After reviewing the evidence in his groundbreaking analysis of the connections between human health and a healthy environment, environmental lawyer David Boyd concluded that the psychological benefits of "ensuring everyone has access to green space" are of "fundamental importance for human health."[35]

There is also an association between exposure to nature and mortality, much of which can be explained through "mental health pathways of depression and social engagement, which subsequently affected mortality."[36] As a result, proximity to green areas has been shown to increase life expectancy.[37] In fact, a study of over 120,000 American women found that higher amounts of greenness around a participant's home were associated with lower rates of all-cause, non-accidental mortality, regardless of age or socio-economic status.[38]

Direct physiological health benefits from exposure to nature have also been revealed, including faster recovery from ill health, improved addiction recovery, and decreased obesity rates.[39] Cardiovascular disease in the elderly has been shown to be affected positively by living near green areas.[40] Reduced heart rates have been observed.[41] Emerging research on the ways in which visually-impaired individuals benefit from time in nature reveals our "diverse interactions with nature" and its fulfillment of a broader range of "sensory worlds."[42]

"Far from desiring intensively managed and manicured landscapes which is often assumed by engineers ... the public have shown a strong preference for: natural river banks and channels; trees and vegetational diversity."[43] A survey of American suburban and exurban residents found that – when asked to rank conventional subdivisions, conventional agriculture, and ecologically beneficial subdivisions in terms of perceived attractiveness – the ecologically beneficial features were found to be most attractive.[44] University of Michigan psychologists

Rachel Kaplan and Stephen Kaplan have extensively studied the effect of nature on people's health and assert that humans' "preferred environments" are natural settings with complexity and diversity.[45]

The expulsion of nature from our daily lives might be taking its greatest toll on children. The *Globe and Mail* reported that from 7 to 10 percent of Canadian children have been diagnosed with attention deficit hyperactivity disorder and that the condition is increasingly viewed as chronic, with the expectation that 60 percent of those afflicted will never outgrow it.[46] Yet contact with nature can improve attention in children.[47] Time spent in nature has been shown to decrease behavioural problems and result in fewer emotional symptoms and peer-related problems.[48] Nature also seems to improve the working memory of children, alleviate mental problems, and reduce the frequency of drug use.[49]

A significant body of research points to the developmental and socialization benefits of exposing children to nature, including "cognitive functioning and self-control, psychological wellbeing, self-care and spiritual development."[50] At a time when children are shaping their lifelong understanding of group decision making and interactions with others, playing in nature builds confidence, creativity, and cooperation. Children engage in open-ended activities when playing in nature. They value creativity and social skills over the singular quality of physical prowess prized in manufactured playground settings.[51] Playing in nature boosts self-esteem, stimulates imagination, encourages peacefulness, and builds the "cognitive constructs necessary for sustained intellectual develop-ment."[52] Sadly, access to nature has become a luxury, either because green space is inequitably distributed across cities or because of the expense of leaving cities. As a result, the "children in nature" movement has been criticized as idealistic, stemming from a "white, middle class, male, heterosexual cultural past that obscures race, class and gender politics."[53]

Although a complex set of factors contributes to obesity, the dramatic increase of childhood obesity in the United States has led to predictions that today's children might be the first generation since the Second World War whose mem-bers die at an earlier age on average than their parents.[54] Less than 10 percent of Canadian children and youth meet the current guidelines for moderate to vigorous physical activity – instead, they spend an average of more than seven hours of their waking day engaged in sedentary activities.[55] Paradoxically, while obesity has increased dramatically among children, the United States has seen "the greatest increase in organized children's sports in history."[56] Clearly,

▶ FIGURE 1.3   Natural settings, such as this portion of Central Park (top), offer children lessons in creativity, imagination, and cooperation not easily learned from the structured activities of this manufactured playground elsewhere in Manhattan (bottom).

organized sports are not a panacea, and highly structured play at a young age does not provide the physical and psychological benefits available from un-structured play in nature.

We are gambling with the consequences of generations more severed from Earth's systems than at any point in human history, and at a time when those systems are more stressed than ever before. Families, communities, and colleagues are burdened with the emotional, psychological, spiritual, and physiological wounds of an unfulfilled biophilia. Collectively, we have handicapped our health, creativity, and resilience by driving nature out of our neighbourhoods.

Economic Costs

Not only is the expulsion of nature bad for our health, but it is expensive. The economic costs of expelling nature are incurred in at least two ways. First, we lose the *ecosystem benefits* provided by nature. Second, we limit ourselves to costly manufactured replacements for those lost benefits. As we will see, this exchange of ecosystem benefits for manufactured services is neither effective nor affordable.

Humans are dependent on nature for survival. We benefit directly, consist-ently, and in innumerable ways from healthy ecosystems. The cornucopia of benefits, often termed "ecosystem services" (but what we refer to as ecosystem *benefits*) includes supporting services (e.g., nutrient cycling and soil formation), provisioning services (e.g., air, water, food, fibre, genetic resources, and pharma-ceuticals), regulating services (e.g., regulation of climate, stabilization of water flows, and protection from soil erosion, pests, and disease), cultural services (e.g., aesthetic aspects, spiritual and religious values, and recreational opportunities), and scientific and educational insights (e.g., the discovery of new medicines).[57]

Some efforts have been made to quantify the value of ecosystem services. For example, Canada's first urban national park, Greater Toronto's Rouge National Park, is estimated to provide over $10 million worth of ecosystem services every year (and the larger watersheds within which the Rouge is located provide over $115 million of such benefits).[58] Similar studies found that Toronto's Greenbelt furnishes approximately $2.6 billion of ecosystem services annually and that British Columbia's Lower Mainland dispenses about $5.4 billion.[59] The total global value of ecosystem services is some $33 trillion each year, and the cost of global biodiversity decline (under a business-as-usual scenario) is predicted to reach 7 percent of GDP by 2050.[60]

We pause to recognize that the term "ecosystem services" commodifies nature for its utility value to humans, like electricity or internet service. Consideration of the monetary value of the benefits provided by nature is interesting and somewhat enticing. However, we encourage readers to embrace these *benefits* as critical to human survival and thus beyond what can be valued by financial markets. In short, achieving the new relationship with nature and with each other that is necessary for our survival demands a different way of looking at value; a different framing story. David Korten refers to the "sacred life, living Earth" story[61] (which understands nature's priceless value) instead of the "sacred money and markets" story (which might assign a financial value to nature's benefits, thereby allowing them to be sold or discounted).

Korten's framing story is reflected in Indigenous knowledge. Glen Coulthard, for example, warns of the extent to which the capitalization of nature can exist as simply another form of the colonial enterprise, seeking to subject Indigenous cultures and lands further to the "cold rationality of market principles."[62] Similarly, Leanne Betasamosake Simpson explains that from an Indigenous perspective, "we have no such thing as capital. We have relatives. We have clans. We have treaty partners. We do not have resources or capital. Resources and capital, in fact, are fundamental mistakes."[63]

As our relationship with nature and its inherent value opens up, we recognize how even a small amount of *green infrastructure* (also known as nature-based solutions or blue-green infrastructure) – the "interconnected network of natural and engineered green elements" such as trees, bioswales, and green roofs, designed to mimic ecological functions and reduce the demand on them – can provide local ecosystem benefits.[64] For example, urban riparian wetlands provide "water quality maintenance, flood storage, carbon storage and sequestration, maintenance of biodiversity and wildlife habitat ... streambank stabilization, flood water storage ... and the provision of recreational and aesthetic resources."[65]

Too often these benefits are literally paved over. What was previously available for free is purchased through a Byzantine infrastructure of water filtration plants, stormwater management systems (which often pour raw sewage into waterways), stream channel diversion projects, flood protection structures, and stream bank stabilization and channelization measures.

Although paving makes ecosystems disappear, the demand for ecosystem benefits does not vanish. In fact, the aggregate demand for ecosystem benefits from cities is enormous, as has been shown through the ecological footprint analysis.[66] That demand is satisfied primarily by ecosystems outside urban areas, often located at great distances from those areas. These "metropolis-satellite relations" (using the term of Andre Gunder Frank) between the demanding city and the supplying hinterland tend to mask the ecological costs associated with consumption.[67]

And what of the pavement, metal, and cement – the grey (human-built) infrastructure? First, it is expensive. The global value of manufactured infrastructure represents approximately 70 percent of global gross domestic product (GDP).[68] That costly infrastructure has deteriorated extensively since it was installed. In Canada, for example, urban infrastructure – mostly built between the 1950s and the 1970s – is straining under increasing demands and decades of underinvestment. McGill University's Saeed Mirza concludes that much of Canada's core municipal infrastructure has reached the end of its useful life, and more than a trillion dollars are needed for restoration over the next fifteen to twenty years.[69]

This "municipal infrastructure deficit" represents the "total additional investment needed to repair and prevent deterioration in existing, municipally owned infrastructure assets."[70] It has risen markedly over the past decade as all levels of government have deferred maintenance and repairs.[71] In short, the level of reinvestment "has not met the annual rehabilitation needs of existing capital stock, or alleviated the backlog of maintenance and rehabilitation that accumulated."[72]

In Vancouver, for example, replacing the combined sewer and stormwater system, which continues to pollute beaches and rivers, would cost over $7 billion (or $11,000 for every person living in the city).[73] In 2017, the American Society of Civil Engineers gave the overall American infrastructure system a grade of "C-" and estimated that some $1.5 trillion is needed to make repairs.[74] Compounding the problem, the failing infrastructure is undermining the shift to green infrastructure. For example, methane from leaking natural gas lines in cities has been associated with elevated gas concentrations in soils and subsequent tree mortality.[75]

Clearly, a shift from the "design, build, and forget" paradigm is necessary.[76] The economic rationale alone is patent. Rather than spending vast sums of money on manufactured infrastructure that immediately begins to deteriorate, an investment in green infrastructure grows and improves over time.

Technical solutions exist, but "addressing our infrastructure deficit in a sustainable manner is not so much a technical issue as it is a challenge of awareness."[77] Activist and author Vandana Shiva points to what she terms "monocultures of the mind" – a habit of thinking that excludes alternatives, discounts a diversity of approaches in favour of a single approach, and manifests itself in controlled technology instead of uncontrolled nature. As she writes, "monocultures first inhabit the mind, and are then transferred to the ground."[78] By relying on a monoculture of manufactured systems and built infrastructure to support our cities, we have excluded the diversity of solutions available in nature while being trapped simultaneously in the expensive maintenance of our built infrastructure.

Since our urban environment consists primarily of human-made elements, one is tempted to see answers only in terms of more, expensive, human-made elements: more roads to alleviate traffic, more medical facilities to help the ill, and more sewers and treatment plants to manage waste and water. With little connection to the natural world, we become stuck in a cycle of unsustainable

FIGURE I.4   Natural features of a bioswale in East Vancouver allow rainwater to nourish plants, filter through the soil, and recharge the natural water movement network instead of overwhelming the manufactured (and expensive) rainwater drainage system.

and costly temporary fixes that make our long-term problems more acute and our cities less sustainable. As Darko Radovic argues, "if our actions are based on values that respect the environment, then our cities will be sustainable: if our guiding social values are not sustainable, then our cities become unsustainable, too."[79]

The urgency to replace grey infrastructure and recognize the value of ecosystem benefits is only part of the story. A full illumination of what is at stake comes from spotlighting climate disruption. The relentless and tragic news about climate disasters has focused the urgency to design with nature, rather than in opposition to it.

Every one-degree Celsius rise in temperature brings an expected trillion dollars in additional storm damage each year.[80] Municipalities are on the front lines of shouldering these costs. The Urban Climate Change Research Network, for example, estimates that by 2050 over 800 million people living in coastal cities will be at risk from sea level rise and coastal flooding, costing $1 trillion annually.[81]

The chances of a storm the magnitude of Hurricane Harvey – a storm that cost over $100 billion in damages in 2017 – are already six times higher than they were in the 1980s[82] and are predicted to be eighteen times more likely by the end of this century.[83] Indeed, the Intergovernmental Panel on Climate Change cautions that "local sea levels that historically occurred once per century ... are projected to become at least annual events at most locations during the 21st century."[84] In another example, Manhattan's power stations were built to withstand the highest known storm surge at the time of construction, a storm recorded back in 1956. But in 2012, Hurricane Sandy caused ocean surges that breached those barriers, knocked out power, and flooded the subway system. The subway faced recovery from Sandy's destruction while simultaneously trying to catch up from decades of delayed maintenance.[85]

The "atmospheric river" that flooded greater Vancouver and coastal British Columbia in November 2021 caused landslides, wiped out bridges, and closed all highways, pipelines, and railways connecting Vancouver to the rest of Canada for several days.[86] It was the costliest natural disaster in the province's history, and foreshadows Vancouver's future. The climate crisis has increased the probability of such an atmospheric river inundating Vancouver again by 60 percent and makes comparable peak stream flows in the region up to 330 percent more likely.[87]

Of course, floods are not the only climate disruption-induced threat to municipalities. Even after spending $10 billion on fighting fires in 2017, the United States saw fires consume 70 percent more acreage each year than in the 1990s.[88] Roughly 3,000 homes are lost to wildfires annually in the United States, such as those consumed in California's infamous fires in 2018 that destroyed Paradise.[89] The fires in 2016 that dislocated 80,000 people from Fort McMurray, Alberta, took over a year to extinguish.[90] The New South Wales bush fires in 2019–20 burned for 240 days, torching over 130,000 square kilometres of Australia's most populous state and more than 23 percent of the temperate forests in southeast Australia.[91] In 2020, 1.7 million hectares of California were ablaze, including a quarter of the largest fires in California's history in a single year.[92] And in 2023, more than 18 million hectares of Canada's forests went up in flames; enough to eclipse the previous record roughly three times over, and to prompt an expert at the University of British Columbia to caution: "These are the types of fires that I think will be ecosystem changing. It will take decades to centuries for those ecosystems to recover, if they recover, given the confounding influence of climate change."[93]

The frequency and power of climate disruption–induced storms leave communities with little time or resources to recover from one catastrophe before facing the next. It is foolish to assume that a "normally" infrequent storm pattern in the past should guide our response to the climate crisis of today. The phrase that we hear frequently from politicians that we have experienced a "once in a lifetime" storm or wildfire now rings hollow as we can expect catastrophic weather events to be habitual.

In 2016, the Canadian insurance industry paid $4.9 billion for property damage associated with weather-related events, including wildfire, flooding, and severe wind.[94] Yet that is only part of the story. Many victims of climate disasters are not insured, and for every dollar of insured loss borne by insurers there are three to four dollars borne by governments, homeowners, or businesses.[95]

Our response to the climate emergency must not be determined by political shell games designed to avoid paying the piper. Ownership of public infrastructure in Canada, for example, has been significantly downloaded to municipalities that struggle with maintenance costs and cannot afford new grey infrastructure investments to address climate change. Nor can our response be denial. For example, although most of southern Florida is only a few feet above sea level, and ultimately most of the population will have to move, "countless condos are going up in Miami-Dade County alone, and new beachside hotels are popping up all along the southern coast."[96] Why? One study concluded that the coastal Florida real estate system "has been set up to succeed for the benefit of local capital interests, even while its assets face long term devaluation."[97] In a "game of chicken," the coastal properties offer short-term returns on quick sales and even twenty- to thirty-year returns on the assumption that climate change will take a few decades longer to gut all the value.[98] But someone will end up holding the bag, and that kind of denial only makes the inevitable changes more difficult.

Rather than running from the threat of crumbling municipal infrastructure in a climate-changing world, we need to stop expelling nature from cities. Thankfully, there is enormous potential in adapting physical infrastructure and significant savings available from investing in green rather than grey infrastructure.[99] Investing the savings from a green infrastructure program into public transit reduces the need for roads, which in turn creates options for repurposing roads into components of restored urban nature. New York's subway system, for example, which has fewer kilometres of track today than in the 1940s and is chronically underfunded, could benefit from the dollars saved by forgoing grey infrastructure in favour of green infrastructure – as outlined in New York's Green Infrastructure Plan.[100]

ECOLOGICAL COSTS

The history of urban development has consisted predominantly of dislodging nature with such force that ecosystems are annihilated. Many cities have a legacy of planning and development which, in the words of Ian McHarg, is "the expression of the inalienable right to create ugliness and disorder for private greed" and has left "countless city slums and scabrous towns, pathetic subdivisions, derelict industries ... decimated land, befouled rivers and filthy air."[101]

That brutal history wrests obvious and direct ecological costs at a local level, and undermines our ability to deal with ecological challenges at regional, national, and international scales. Although the specific ecological effects vary by location, the development of cities generally has a detrimental effect on water dispersion and quality, the hydrological cycle, the local climate, the distribution and diversity of ecosystems, the composition and structure of ecosystems that remain, the diversity of species, and the health of terrestrial and aquatic ecosystems in and around cities.

Water

The hydrological cycle – the cycle of water through the atmosphere, the land, and the ocean – is essential for life on our planet. In cities, this cycle is mostly invisible. Water is diverted into pipes, culverts, and buried channels. Rainwater simply disappears down storm drains, unnoticed (unless it disappears too slowly). The technological advances in sanitation (piped water and sewer systems) helped to combat disease but led to the out-of-sight, out-of-mind attitude that plagues us today: "The benefits of sanitation and well drained streets are paid for by the costs of eroded and polluted rivers and a deteriorated larger environment."[102]

Diversions of water into culverts, pipes, and channels have profound effects on ecosystems. Complex vegetation cover and pervious soils are replaced with impervious surfaces. Longer-term water flows that balance seasonal fluctuations of moisture are swapped for rapid cycles of drought and flood. Dispersed water is replaced with concentrated water. In short, the extent to which water leaves land as surface water runoff is the extent to which soil will be short of moisture and the extent to which areas downstream will be oversaturated.[103]

Impervious surfaces – surfaces through which water cannot penetrate, such as asphalt roofs, paved roads, and concrete sidewalks – force water to run across the surface, where it picks up pollutants. The polluted water is concentrated into drains, pipes, and culverts, essentially biological deserts covered from sunlight and oxygen and unable to provide treatment or cleaning of the water.[104] When it is eventually released into streams, the concentrated (and polluted) water scours the bottom of streambeds, erodes banks, and raises peak flow levels.[105]

The relationship between the area of surface cover and the volume of runoff is not linear. Where impervious surfaces cover from 10 percent to 20 percent of a watershed area, surface runoff is double that of an area with no impervious surfaces.[106] This surface runoff alters the hydrology and geomorphology (physical form) of streams.

Surface runoff severely reduces water quality. Even catchments with only 2 percent impervious surfaces have noticeable changes in their water quality.[107] Impervious surfaces increase the loading of nutrients, metals, pesticides, and other contaminants in streams. Nearly all urban streams have elevated levels of chemical contaminants, including heavy metals (especially cadmium, chromium, copper, lead, manganese, nickel, and zinc), pesticides, petroleum products, and pharmaceuticals.[108] In the United States, "urban runoff [is] the primary source of [pollution] impairment for 13% of rivers, 18% of lakes, 32% of estuaries, and 55% of ocean shorelines."[109]

Impervious surfaces also raise the risk of flooding, contribute to the heat-island effect, and limit the areas that can be dedicated to green spaces.[110] Combined-sewer overflows further affect receiving water bodies with elevated temperatures, high velocities, bacteria and floatable material, and toxic organic compounds. The Pew Ocean Commission concluded that "by virtually every measure of ecosystem health, the streams, creeks, marshes, and rivers surrounded by hardened watersheds are less diverse, less stable, and less productive than those in natural watersheds."[111]

Marine habitats are polluted by the runoff of nutrients, heavy metals, and other toxins from adjacent lands.[112] Studies have shown that marine animals are exposed to a continual discharge of pharmaceuticals from sewage treatment plants.[113] Estuaries – among the most ecologically productive ecosystem types on Earth – are generally littered with large amounts of unnatural material.[114] Most of the oil pollution in the ocean comes from land-based sources, and 80 percent of pollution in the marine environment originated on the land.

Every year, between 1.1 and 2.4 million tonnes of plastic waste flow from rivers into oceans.[115] The million plastic bottles purchased each minute remain briefly in the hands of consumers.[116] After disposal, that plastic can break into small pieces that join the trillions of other pieces of plastic forming oceanic garbage patches larger than most countries.[117] By 2050, there will be more plastic in the ocean than fish.[118]

Urban soils, even where they are not covered with impervious surfaces, are mostly compacted and less able to absorb water, further increasing runoff and erosion.[119] The removal of multi-layered vegetation – such as the composite of overstory trees, understory trees, shrubs, herbs, mosses, and lichens – reduces rainwater interception and increases the amount of precipitation, both rain and snow, that reaches the ground.[120] Thus, the absence of multi-layered vegetation heightens the erosive capacity of a given amount of precipitation. Deforestation of riparian banks reduces the food availability in the aquatic habitat, raises stream temperature, increases storm drain runoff into the stream, and heightens the volume of sediments, harmful nutrients, and metals.[121] Erosion boosts turbidity (cloudiness) in the water column, thereby "increasing fish gill clogging and the burial of bottom-dwelling flora and fauna."[122] These changes result in urban streams that experience a decline in the richness of invertebrate and fish communities.[123]

Not surprisingly, urban streams are generally characterized by reduced diversity in channel morphology and the destruction of adjacent habitats.[124] Urban streams typically have "homogenized fish assemblages, with high richness and abundance of tolerant, cosmopolitan, and non-native species and relatively low richness and abundance of sensitive, endemic species."[125] Urban riparian communities are frequently more extensively invaded by exotic plants than nonurban riparian communities. For example, significant riparian and salmonoid habitat has been lost or damaged in British Columbia, and the most devastating impacts have been in rapidly urbanizing areas.[126]

Habitat

The radically human habitat that we call cities poses two interconnected problems for other species: loss of habitat and fragmentation of what remains.

Roads contribute to both problems. They splinter the city into segregated blocks, forcing a pattern of extreme habitat fragmentation that isolates populations of species. Approximately 25 percent of the urban landscape in North America is committed to roads, parking lots, garages, driveways, and gas stations. The ecological effects of a road can extend for more than hundreds of metres from the road itself and include "the loss and fragmentation of habitat; input of pollutants (e.g., noise, chemicals and dust) into adjacent air, soil, vegetation and water; direct mortality; and the creation of barriers to wildlife movement."[127] Roads also act as vectors for predators and for transporting weeds and pathogens.[128] Roads already directly affect roughly 20 percent of the entire American landscape, and the global length of roads is expected to increase by 60 percent between 2010 and 2050.[129]

The effect of roads as barriers to movement is species-specific. Highly adaptable species might find roads less of a barrier than more sensitive species. For example, the highest density of woodchucks ever recorded was in the middle of a suburban highway interchange in Ottawa, possibly because of abundant food, adequate burrow drainage, the lack of predators, and the ability of the woodchucks to cross two-lane roads.[130] In spite of such exceptions, roads remain the greatest cause of mortality for many urban mammals, especially for juveniles. The continual mortality of dispersing juveniles from habitat patches can decrease the vitality of local populations.[131] The rate of loss does not need to be high for there to be a demonstrable impact. Experiments have shown that roads as narrow as 2.5 metres create an impassable barrier for smaller species such as carabid beetles and wolf spiders, and the application of salt to roads is a significant deterrent to crossing for amphibians.[132]

Because of the high density of roads and other manufactured elements in the urban landscape, habitat patches tend to be small and isolated, which reduces biodiversity and threatens the survival of species in the patches. The isolated patches that remain are correctly classified ecologically as "islands" – disconnected ecosystems surrounded by an inhospitable terrain of pavement, concrete, and other barriers.

Robert MacArthur and Edward O. Wilson developed the theory of "island biogeography" to explain what happens to ecosystems that can be described as islands. Their first observation was that there is "an orderly relation between the size of a sample area and the number of species found in that area."[133] This relationship holds both for natural islands surrounded by water and for urban ecosystem islands surrounded by pavement. The smaller the island, the fewer the species. As acclaimed ecologist Reed Noss explains, "island biogeographic theory predicts that small, isolated islands (or patches of habitat that resemble islands) will experience higher extinction rates and lower immigration rates of species than large islands."[134] The theory of island biogeography explains species decline and extinction resulting from fragmentation and isolation.[135]

MacArthur and Wilson suggest that the two most significant consequences of island biogeography are habitat loss and habitat isolation.[136] Small islands of habitat mean that there is less habitat than in larger areas (i.e., habitat loss). Interior habitat areas – those parts of the habitat not directly affected by what is adjacent to it – are especially rare in fragmented landscapes.[137] Isolation occurs because the area between patches acts as a barrier, and the habitat that exists is influenced by adjacent areas.

Isolation affects more species than is initially obvious. For example, many birds have relatively poor dispersal abilities in spite of being able to fly and thus cannot easily overcome isolation.[138] The interactions between pollinator-friendly plant species and species that provide pollinator services are constrained by the built environment since it results in isolated patches of plants.[139]

Even if suitable habitat remains, isolated populations with a shrinking gene pool lead to the domination of recessive genes, resulting in "congenital defects (both physical and reproductive), rising infertility, and weakening of each animal's immune defence system."[140] Isolated populations are susceptible to two detrimental genetic effects: inbreeding and random genetic drift.[141]

In addition to the direct removal of habitat and the fragmentation of habitat patches, urban areas tend to provide very little connectivity between patches. And the *matrix* (the unprotected area between and among protected patches) is generally not conducive to dispersal. Even if urban habitat patches were enlarged and further protected, connectivity across the urban matrix remains necessary since "protecting green areas in isolation will not sustain the capacity of ecosystems to generate services" if the surrounding habitat continues to be fragmented and degraded.[142]

That matrix often includes manicured parks and yards with simplified ecological composition and structure designed to fit a narrowly conceived aesthetic: "Presupposed aesthetics of harmony and natural beauty" suppress "the wilder and more uncontrollable aspects of nature's performance."[143] Simplified parks and open spaces depend on high-energy inputs and maintenance to create a manicured, generic landscape (nature as a "pet" that Jane Jacobs derided) that fails to provide significant ecosystem benefits or habitat. More ecologically complex areas remain mostly on the edge of cities, accessible primarily by vehicle.[144]

Urban trees face numerous challenges. Trees planted along streets are stressed by poor drainage and compacted soil, are exposed to air pollution and direct sunlight, and typically have only 15 percent of the space for their roots than would be available in a forest setting.[145] Often planted in spaces insufficient for canopy and root system development, trees are stunted. Where there is space for trees to grow, such as in public parks, there is often high foot traffic, which leads to compacted soil that causes "reduced soil porosity, increased resistance to root growth, [and] reduced transmission of air and water."[146]

Forests are built on dead trees (which create the soil for new trees). Urban trees, in contrast, endure an interrupted nutrient cycle that leaves them dependent on imported nutrients in the form of fertilizers (instead of relying on nutrients from dead trees, branches, and leaves). A survey of urban tree trimming and landscape residue in the United States found that only 15 percent of wood residue is left or used on site.[147] This means that 85 percent is removed from the site's nutrient cycle that would otherwise be available to build soil for future tree and other vegetative growth and health. Mature trees are often felled and removed entirely (including, for example, an average of five large trees that are cut down daily in Vancouver).[148]

Urban habitats are often shackled in an early successional stage, limiting the diversity of species, reducing the variety of habitats, increasing homogeneity, and decreasing overall resilience. Urban mammal species are more susceptible to disease outbreaks and parasites because of their relatively concentrated resources and higher population densities. Raccoons in nonurban areas, for example, are typically found in densities of fewer than 20 per square kilometre, whereas urban raccoons live in densities of over 300 per square kilometre.[149]

Urban development occurred where it did partly because of biogeographical factors such as healthy soils, access to water, and protection from extreme weather. The ecological factors that make such locations attractive to humans for settlement are often the same factors that made those locations attractive to other species. It should not be surprising that the places where humans settled were also once the homes for many other species. Indeed, over a billion people now live in the top twenty-five biological hotspots on Earth.[150] For example, Ontario's Greenbelt, which surrounds the Greater Toronto Area (and was recently under threat of politically motivated development pressure), is home to 78 of Ontario's over 200 listed species at risk.[151]

As cities take over some of the most ecologically productive lands on the planet, the land that surrounds them is what remains of these invaluable ecosystems. The importance of limiting urban incursion into these adjacent areas (i.e., halting urban sprawl), minimizing the ecological contrast between urban and nonurban areas (i.e., providing ecological connectivity and habitat diversity to improve biological diversity throughout urban areas), and reducing activities within the urban area that are detrimental to surrounding ecosystems, cannot be overstated.

Unfortunately, our cities have not been particularly successful at any of those tasks. Between 1971 and 2001, Canadian urban areas encroached on 15,200 square kilometres of land adjacent to existing urban areas.[152] Since 2001, another 1,700 square kilometres have been added to the country's nine biggest metropolitan areas (an increase three and a half times the size of the Island of Montreal). And since urban sprawl (up 34 percent since 2001) has progressed on average faster than population growth (up 26 percent since 2001), each Canadian occupies, on average, more space, and that space is farther away from a city centre. In 2001, residents of the nine largest centres occupied an average of 317 square metres of urbanized territory; by 2021, that figure had risen by 19 square metres (6 percent increase), an area equivalent to one to two additional parking spaces for each inhabitant.[153]

At the same time, pressure on urban containment boundaries has been merciless, resulting in intense development along (and spilling across) the urban fringe. That development imposes a barrier to species in adjacent ecosystems and severs functional linkages (i.e., suitable habitat connections for species moving into or out of an urban area).

Moreover, urban activities have detrimental effects on surrounding landscapes and ecosystems. This burden includes an interrupted hydrological cycle, a persistently bright night sky, blocked species movement corridors, elevated ambient noise levels, transformed local climate, a polluted regional air shed, and a fragmented regional landscape.

One of these afflictions, the urban heat island effect (caused by the use of dark, nonreflective surfaces on roads and buildings), jacks up urban temperatures more than five degrees Celsius above surrounding exurban areas.[154] Within the city, roof and pavement temperatures on a hot day can be over twenty-five degrees Celsius hotter than the surrounding air, whereas shaded or moist surfaces remain closer to air temperatures.[155] These surfaces hold the heat well after sunset, making night temperatures in cities startlingly hotter than surrounding areas. For example, during the scorching summer of 2023 that saw Phoenix hit 110 degrees Fahrenheit (43.3 degrees Celsius) for 54 days in a row, NASA satellites detected that "built surfaces – roads, buildings, airport runways, and the like – retain heat, sometimes hovering around 100 degrees Fahrenheit (38 degrees Celsius) for hours after sunset."[156] These foreign temperatures, noxious to native habitats and species, affect wildlife migration corridors, increase the demand for energy and urban infrastructure,[157] and spill over to disturb the adjacent microclimate, species, and ecosystems.[158]

Species

Habitat loss, fragmentation, isolation, and modification in urban areas muster a landscape suitable only for a small number of species. With limited habitat, many native species are unable to exist in urban areas, and even fewer are able to thrive. In some cases, the species best suited to the urban landscape are non-native ones, able to out-compete and sometimes to dominate the urban environment.

Such invasive species are abundant in cities.[159] As hubs for transportation, tourism, and trade, cities hasten the introduction and dissemination of non-native species. If the habitat is favourable or similar to their original habitat – for example, because of the heat island effect, fragmented habitats, degraded sites, or altered disturbance regimes – the newly introduced species can thrive.[160] But these invasions threaten endemic species and habitats. They disrupt ecosystem services and reduce biodiversity.[161] As Edward O. Wilson emphatically states, "I cannot stress enough the menace of invasive species."[162] In monetary terms, it has been estimated that the economic costs of invasive species, in the United States alone, is over $130 billion annually.[163]

Terms introduced to describe birds and butterflies along the rural-urban gradient categorize species in cities as the following: "exploiter," "adapter," and "avoider."[164] The exploiters are "generally commensals that are almost entirely dependent on human subsidies" (meaning that they rely on humans for food). The adapters not only utilize human subsidies but also make significant use of "wild-growing" nourishment. And the avoiders "tend to rely only on natural resources."[165]

Urbanization allows for the flourishing of exploiter species such as the European starling, introduced as part of a misguided scheme to populate North America with all the birds mentioned in the works of Shakespeare (the first flock of starlings, let loose in Central Park in 1890, ironically found shelter under the eaves of the American Museum of Natural History before breeding and spreading).[166] But cities severely stress or extirpate populations of more sensitive avoider species, such as predator species and late-succession plants.[167] The result is a significant reduction in biodiversity with a bias toward a smaller number of human-dependent species.

The exploiter and adapter species sometimes modify their behaviour to survive. For example, birds use vocalization to warn of danger, defend a territory, and attract a mate, but in cities this vocalization must compete with elevated noise from traffic and busy humans.[168] House finches have altered the tone and length of their vocalization in order to compensate.[169] Other species have modified their reproductive patterns in response to the challenges of urban living, for example by having larger litters or reaching sexual maturity earlier.[170] Urban fox squirrels, for example, have more than one litter each year compared with nonurban fox squirrels, which have just one litter.[171]

Peregrine falcons in New York City have famously learned to thrive. In place of natural cliff ledges, they perch on skyscrapers and bridges. The updrafts created by tall buildings support their soaring as they search for prey, and the open water around Manhattan offers space for chasing their victims. These scorchingly fast attackers have even adapted to the city lights by hunting at night and preying on migrating birds disoriented by towers and bright lights.[172] Such advantages, coupled with its location on a major migratory flight path, have given New York City the highest concentration of peregrine falcons of any place in the world.[173]

Almost every North American city has a considerable population of coyotes. The most long-lived urban coyotes rely on rodents, fruit, deer, and rabbits for food – but avoid humans, garbage, and pets. Such successful urban animals tend to live longer than their wild cousins because they have plenty to eat, fewer predators, and ample resources during the winter.[174]

In some cases, urban green spaces are important refuges for native biodiversity. Urban parks in San Francisco support a higher mean abundance of bumblebees than parks outside the city, and the common frog has experienced increased populations in urban areas but declines elsewhere.[175]

Although these examples illustrate that some species have a remarkable capacity to adapt and even thrive in our cities, this good news must be understood in the proper context. That context is a global crisis of biodiversity. It is a context in which a million species are already threatened with extinction, and less than one-quarter of all species on Earth are likely to be around to see the end of this century.[176] It is a context in which the sixth great extinction, this time caused by humans, is taking place.[177] As Wilson put it, the global conservation movement has temporarily mitigated but hardly stopped the ongoing extinction of species. The rate of loss is instead accelerating. If biodiversity is to be returned to the baseline level of extinction that existed before the spread of humanity, and thus saved for future generations, the conservation effort must be raised to a new level. The only solution to this sixth extinction is to increase the area of inviolable natural reserves to half the surface of the earth or greater.[178]

Against this backdrop, cities must offer homes to more than just a few adaptable species. The range of nature's composition needs to be put first in cities.

Ecosystems Everywhere

How many of us can describe the annual cycles of local ecosystems? Or mark seasons by the acts of nonhuman species? Naomi Klein observes that "between the wrenching disasters, climate [change] is about an early blooming of a particular flower, an unusually thin layer of ice on a lake, the late arrival of a migratory bird – noticing these small changes requires the kind of communion that comes from knowing a place deeply."[179] But she asks, rhetorically, "how many of us still live like that?"[180]

Most of us live like foreigners in a strange land, smugly presuming that all is in order while we miss the signals and stumble into danger. Although most of us cannot read the signs, we do have interpreters (scientists, naturalists and Indigenous knowledge holders). But our disconnection from nature assumes that the scientists' stories are optional reading (or that their pleadings about our home are fictional yarns about some other place). Since we do not feel that we are part of nature, we (mistakenly) see the attacks on nature as having little impact on our lives. We do not notice from one generation to the next the increasingly degraded landscapes and ecosystems that we pass along to future generations, who, unaware of the past, think that their inheritance is natural. This phenomenon is known as the "shifting baseline syndrome."

Too many people are unable to see for themselves the evidence of an ecological crisis, and they are unwilling to listen when our interpreters describe it. Sure, we might accept that climate change is real. We might recite facts about the size of the oceans' garbage patches. We might understand the warning manifest in disappearing frogs. But our emotional reaction is kept in check by the psychological distance between ourselves and nature. That distance is caused, and locked in place, by the removal of nature from where we live. The ecological crisis is perceived as happening to the other, not to ourselves. If urban dwellers see the biodiversity problem at all, they likely see it as occurring in another country or at least outside their cities.[181] This distance from environmental

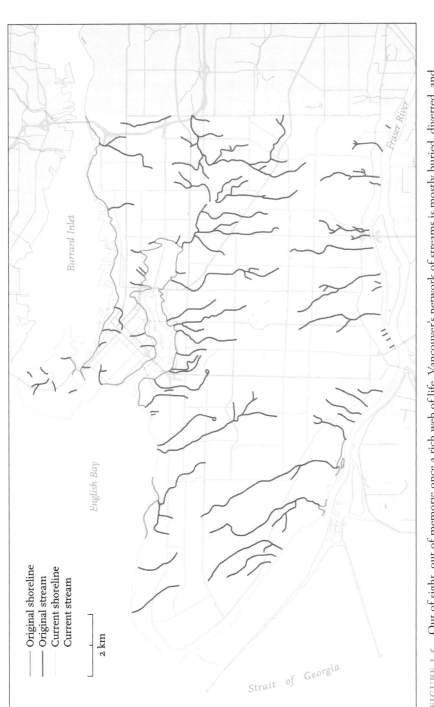

FIGURE 1.5   Out of sight, out of memory: once a rich web of life, Vancouver's network of streams is mostly buried, diverted, and culverted. | *Source:* Vancouver Aquarium. Adapted by Eric Leinberger.

problems further reduces motivation to take action in response at a time when action is critical.

In particular, a dearth of experiences in nature as a child undermines empathy for the natural world. Childhood experiences in nature positively influence environmental attitudes later in life and are predictive of stronger views about the seriousness of ecological problems.[182] Canada's Green Party co-leader, Elizabeth May, recognizes this: "I often think it was the closeness to nature I experienced as a child that made me an environmentalist."[183]

Professor Karen Malone argues that urban green spaces are essential to children's environmental learning.[184] Her research supports the conclusion that people's eventual ability to "contribute to environmental sustainable development will be largely dependent on the quality of their childhood environmental experiences" and that "there is a strong connection between a child's likelihood to develop a sense of empathy, belonging and responsibility to their environment and their direct experiences in it."[185] Other studies have concluded that "regular visits [to nature] during preschool were associated with a higher sense of responsibility for nature, suggesting that offering children regular nature experiences in preschool age could be beneficial for the development of responsibility toward nature."[186]

When we expel nature from cities, we also forgo a "sense of place" in the biophysical environment.[187] Along with childhood experiences in nature, a sense of place is a powerful catalyst for local environmental stewardship and is associated with pro-environmental attitudes in general.[188] A sense of place inspires people to care about where they live, which galvanizes demands for a healthy environment and animates participation in restoration (or conservation).[189] Pride in place and identity rooted in a particular location offer "motivation for enhancing ecosystem resilience and human well-being of the region they frequent" and "increase the likelihood of prioritizing long-term solutions over short-term benefits."[190]

This sense of place further encourages protection of local ecosystems and engenders a preference for the locally specific and ecologically valuable over the generic and disposable. In short, "an investment in place, an emotional commitment that surpasses real estate and financial imperatives," is key to a local environmental ethic, which translates into widespread environmental engagement.[191]

Sadly, this sense of place has been often expelled along with nature (and the homogenization of urban landscapes). German poet Rainer Maria Rilke observed over 100 years ago that "the movements of most of the people who live in cities have lost their connexion with the earth; they hang, as it were, in the air, hover in all directions, and find no place where they can settle."[192]

In contrast, Indigenous cultures have a strong sense of place rooted in framing stories that direct their ways of being, including their close relationship with nature. For example, the English meaning of the Innu word *Nitassinan* is "our land." Similarly, the Haida refer to "Islands of the People" as *Haida Gwaii.* This strong sense of place inherent in Indigenous cultures led naturally to a focus on protecting nature since the people understood that natural processes (i.e., nature) provide for their needs. In return for furnishing their needs, Indigenous cultures carry out a reciprocal relationship of respect with nature to ensure that its needs are also met. In no small way, a sense of place has been a major factor in the resilience of Indigenous cultures.[193] Putting nature first is a cornerstone of Indigenous ways of being.

When COVID-19 tore through communities around the world, taking lives and buckling the economy, many felt blindsided. Where did it come from? But as the co-chairs of the UN biodiversity assessments pointed out, "there is a single species that is responsible for the COVID-19 pandemic – us."[194]

The "story of COVID-19 is, at its core, a story of humanity's ever-encroaching relationship with all other living things on this planet."[195] More than 70 percent of emerging diseases already affecting people originated in wildlife and were transmitted to people because of activities such as "rampant deforestation, uncontrolled expansion of agriculture, intensive farming, mining and infrastructure development, as well as the exploitation of wild species."[196] As a Royal Society study concluded, "exploitation, as well as anthropogenic activities that have caused losses in wildlife habitat quality, have increased opportunities for animal-human interactions and facilitated zoonotic disease transmission."[197]

More than just COVID-19 awaits if our relationship with nature does not change. Roughly 250 zoonotic viruses have made the leap from animals to humans so far, but as many as 800,000 may be lurking in mammals and birds, awaiting the chance to cause the next pandemic.[198] "Any one of these could be the next 'Disease X – potentially even more disruptive and lethal than COVID-19."[199] If there was ever an urgent call to repair our relationship with nature, this is it.

Without a connection to the Earth, without a sense of place, we are left emotionally numb to the plight of other species, intellectually blocked from deciphering the cautions from nature, and ultimately distracted as citizens of this planet at a time when we can least afford to be.

2 Trajectories of Green Planning

The reason I worked very hard to get out of the city ... is because I get energy from the earth itself. I get optimism from the earth itself. I feel that as long as the earth can make a spring every year, I can. As long as the earth can flower and produce nurturing fruit, I can, because I'm the earth.

– Alice Walker

The worldview that compelled us to expel nature from cities found expression in the practice of urban planning – the collection of theories, processes, and techniques employed to shape our built environments. Its core theories and trends that shaped small towns and large cities alike were often well intended and perceived as necessary for the realization of broader social or economic goals (e.g., the eradication of disease or the provision of sanitation services). Yet the result was to banish nature and to embed structural inequalities throughout our cities.

The planning profession, however, should not be asked to shoulder more than its fair share of responsibility. As we explored in the previous chapter, there is a deeply rooted cultural explanation for why nature was kicked out of cities (our false perception that humans are separate from nature). Planning simply expressed this cultural (mis)perception.

Moreover, planning theorists and practitioners have a long history of attempts to overcome that misperception and to incorporate nature into cities. As we look forward to planning and restoring nature-first cities, the history of these urban planning innovations offers clues as to how to prepare and where to look for opportunities.

What do we mean by urban planning? Definitions of planning span the technical to the ideological. On the technical side, planning has been described as an exercise of "foresight in formulating and implementing programs and policies."[1] Similarly, the substantive issues associated with planning have been identified as the allocation and distribution of resources.[2] On the ideological side, planning has been described as "the guidance of future action. In a world of intensely conflicting interests and great inequalities of status and resources, planning in the face of power is at once a daily necessity and a constant ethical challenge."[3] From a generalist perspective, planning "is that profession that specifically seeks to connect forms of knowledge with forms of action in the public domain."[4]

As these various definitions suggest, planning theory has no central canon but tends to borrow from other fields.[5] We view this as a sign of interdisciplinary strength and flexibility. For example, the planning approaches described in the pages that follow – and in fact this book's entire enterprise of arguing for the potential of nature-directed stewardship – are heavily dependent on the field of ecology. Planning can embrace this interdisciplinary approach. Planning is a highly dynamic field that we view as advantageous in seeking to introduce new forms of practice and new rationales for pursuing NDS approaches.

In this chapter, we build a connection between planning theory, planning practice, and our relationship with nature. We start by illustrating the role that planning has played in our expulsion of nature. Then, on a more hopeful track, we trace the evolution of planning ideas and practices that inspire both a more environmental approach to planning and the integrative potential of sustainable development. The last two sections of the chapter support arguments for incorporating NDS principles in urban planning. These arguments offer evidence and a planning narrative to help convince skeptical politicians and cost-conscious citizens of the benefits of inviting nature home – of putting nature first in cities. We outline the dimensions of "co-benefits" in planning, the many additional benefits and value-added dimensions of nature-directed stewardship, to health, the economy, and society. We conclude the chapter with a reflection on a core purpose of planning: that is, to protect the public interest.

FORCES OF EXPULSION

The shapes of communities today, and the methods that we use to plan them, are legacies of the past. Cities' "form and functioning are the result of countless decisions made over the generations of their life, decisions that have embodied the needs, experience, values, and aspirations of their builders."[6] Once a freeway is built, for example, one must wait decades before even considering tearing it down. Once a stream is paved over, it is destined to flow in the dark for generations. We, and the natural world, must live with our built environments for long time scales. (Of course, a long *human* time scale is brief from the perspective of ecosystems.)

The legacy that we see in cities today is mostly an expression of planning perspectives embraced decades ago. Past planning decisions cannot be separated from the broader political-economic contexts of their times. The beliefs, practices, and ideologies of specific times influence the nature of planning contexts and stimulate responses. For example, the emergence of participatory planning arose to counter the hegemonic and distanced methods associated with more technocratic and top-down planning.

The macro setting also influences and determines the nature of the political landscape within which planning operates, and different viewpoints or ideologies frame planning decisions.[7] For example, governments might be more or less interventionist in terms of setting policies and establishing regulations to guide development.

A helpful way to understand twentieth-century planning traditions is to track the transition from a Keynesian-inspired interventionist model of planning after the Second World War to the post-1980s impact of neoliberal/neoconservative ideology in governance. The interventionist period was coupled with an intense belief in the power of science and technocratic system models to solve problems. Thus, while resources were being allocated in Western industrialized nations to create national standards in health, education, civic design, and infrastructure, the planning world was utilizing a relatively context-free scientific, positivistic approach to building neighbourhoods. This tremendous period of intervention and planning growth also proceeded with very little knowledge, or acknowledgment, of ecological principles or care for environmental assets and their links to social equity and health.

As researchers and members of the public began to rally against the exclusionary and top-down nature of technocratic planning (often referred to as the "rational comprehensive approach"), important changes were also taking place within the political and economic realms. In particular, the economic doctrine of neoliberalism took hold – free-market, laissez-faire economics, championed by Milton Friedman and the Chicago School of Economics, advocating "the elimination of the public sphere, total liberation for corporations and skeletal social spending."[8]

Emerging in the 1970s, and reaching full-scale implementation in the 1980s, neoliberalism radically altered the nature of governance in the Western world in favour of a noninterventionist, market-led approach to development and planning. With this approach, planning was to serve as an instrument for the reproduction of capital, primarily in the city. Urban planning served the interests of the wealthy and the market (which explains why we are currently struggling with many urban challenges that lie outside the market, such as homelessness, affordable housing, air quality, and loss of urban biodiversity).[9] Economic growth, as the dominant mantra of neoliberalism, largely ignores other dimensions of development, such as social justice, environmental health, and cultural diversity.

Planning within a neoliberal yoke shuns nature from our cities. Yet the planning discipline has a richer and longer history than the neoliberal phase, and, to understand fully how planning orchestrated the dance between nature and cities, we need to consider four fundamental forces in planning.

First, many of the urban challenges that we face today (sprawl, environmental degradation, social inequality, and isolation) are by-products of earlier efforts to solve pressing problems of the times. For example, the expansion of cities in the nineteenth century, spurred by processes of industrialization and mechanization, took place in the relative absence of coordinated planning or intentional form and process.[10] The speed of industrialization vastly outpaced the social policy and planning response to deal with it. The result was the catastrophic movement of large populations into confined, unplanned spaces characterized by disease and the lack of adequate sewer infrastructure, the constant threat of fire (again accompanied by a lack of water infrastructure), and a proliferation of slums.

In response, early social, health, and environmental reform movements emerged. Dating back to the 1800s, these movements form an important lineage in the progression of planning as a discipline and in the recognition that urban governance is necessary. The City Beautiful Movement, for example, sought to address the shabby appearance of cities. The Garden Cities Movement set its sights on the deterioration of living conditions. The Parks Movement was concerned about the loss of the natural environment, and efforts to install water and sewage infrastructure aimed to reduce inefficiency and waste.

The advancement of urban infrastructure in particular resulted in massive improvements in the quality of life for urban residents. The public health benefits alone were staggering. The problem from an ecological (and, as we will see later, social) perspective is that the transformation of the urban form was conducted according to a worldview that separates humans from nature.

Second, nature was treated crudely by the philosophical foundations of the Western worldview, in particular by Enlightenment thinking. As society wrestled with the Enlightenment goals of emancipation and self-realization, our systems of production were guided by a Cartesian "dualism between rational human subjects and the non-thinking world of objects."[11] This dualism, as we articulated in the previous chapter, extended to the separation of culture and nature. Nature was viewed solely in terms of capital assets (resources available for human exploitation). For example, "animals were no longer viewed as living assistants as they were in the Middle Ages and construed instead as machines."[12]

Unsurprisingly, the domination-of-nature approach is riddled with contradictions:

> The thesis of domination never deliberately embraced the destruction and despoliation of the natural world. Prudence would require the protection and enhancement of natural assets as a form of capital except under conditions of such abundance that free and unchecked depletion made rational sense. If destruction and depletion could be found, then it was a sign of such immense abundance that it did not matter. When it mattered the price system would adjust to indicate a condition of scarcity that required attention.[13]

Third, planning became a highly technocratic field. Planners were the "experts" who knew the rules and could apply scientific principles to frame city problems and propose planning solutions. Under the guise of rational planning, cities and communities were seen as systems that operated according to certain rules. Comprehensive, intentional community planning emerged after the Second World War, bent on subduing nature and buttressed by an intense belief in science and the scientific method. Sadly, "little attention has been paid to understanding the natural processes that have shaped the city's physical form and which in turn have been altered by it."[14]

As influential landscape architect Michael Hough (a former student of Ian McHarg) observed,

> humanity and nature have long been understood to be separate matters ... In the unique cultures from which the disciplines of intervention spring – civil engineering, building, planning and design – this perceived separation has also profoundly influenced the desire to control, not only nature, but also human behaviour. Thus, the nature of pedigreed design has had little time or understanding for the natural and cultural processes that shape human environments, or the particular needs of multicultural communities that are the norm in most cities today.[15]

The marginalization of ecological systems became standard practice in cities and neighbourhoods. Western cities prioritized growth, the interests of capital, and the pursuit of profit. The technocratic, distanced approach to planning made this narrow agenda more feasible because, after all, catering to the interests of capital is more easily facilitated when one can simply ignore ecological values and the preferences of citizens (or at least the disenfranchised). Wealthy interests have more direct access to decision makers, and the lack of engagement with lower-income people marginalizes their concerns about quality of life and how their communities are planned and transformed. Diverse perspectives are lost from the planning process.

Fourth, little financial value was assigned to nature. The dominant interests of capital in forming and shaping cities largely eradicated any substantive consideration of values beyond growth and profit. The problem, from a development perspective, is that if nature is not valued then it simply does not exist. It is not a matter of alienation from nature as much as annihilation of nature; there is simply nothing from which to be alienated. As Professor David Harvey explains,

> from their inception, cities have arisen through geographical and social concentrations of a surplus product. Urbanization has always been, therefore, a class phenomenon, since surpluses are extracted from somewhere and from

somebody, while the control over their disbursement typically lies in a few hands. This general situation persists under capitalism, of course; but since urbanization depends on the mobilization of a surplus product, an intimate connection emerges between the development of capitalism and urbanization. Capitalists have to produce a surplus product in order to produce surplus value; this in turn must be reinvested in order to generate more surplus value. The result of continued reinvestment is the expansion of surplus production at a compound rate – hence the logistic curves (money, output and population) attached to the history of capital accumulation, paralleled by the growth path of urbanization under capitalism.[16]

In the Canadian setting, it is not simply ignorance of ecological processes that has shaped our cities (and economies) but also the colonial lens through which the vast landscape has been seen. Deeply rooted in the Canadian psyche is an understanding that nature exists "out there" and contains virtually limitless and unclaimed resources to extract for our benefit. The enormous territory of the country is entrenched as a bountiful surplus of unpopulated nature. This means that there is always another place to go, that we are not limited to the resources that surround us, and that we can thus use resources in unsustainable ways to expand our urban landscapes and economies.

That myth led to the uncoordinated and unplanned conditions of our early settlements. From an economic perspective, natural (resource) abundance has facilitated the rash exploitation of nature, both in "resource-rich" hinterlands and in expanding urban environments. The perception of natural abundance, combined with the narrow profit-motivated interests and values of capital, has ravaged nature (with the exception of postage stamp greenery), marginalized Indigenous cultures that have stewarded natural landscapes for millennia, and purged essential ecosystem benefits from our built environments.

The confluence of all these planning forces left nature with little hope for an urban future. Yes, there are green spaces, parks, remnants of original stream systems, select intact areas, and habitats for certain nonhuman species. As the previous chapter made clear, however, we have mostly squandered the ecological integrity necessary to say that urban nature is a functioning ecosystem.

Perhaps the greatest danger from these planning forces is that they yield slow, incremental change. Small adjustments to the urban landscape unfold bulldozer by bulldozer, culvert by culvert, and suburb by suburb. Yet we fail to see the full continuum of what we have lost and are losing. The shifting baseline syndrome tells us that each successive generation views its surroundings, including the state of ecosystem health, as normal and "natural." There is no sense of what it used to be like, let alone an appreciation of what has disappeared and the consequences of cumulative losses.

Urbanization is associated with tremendous benefits to society; at a population level in terms of health, and at an individual (or class) level in terms of profit. These benefits create inertia. The reality is that we are very reluctant agents of change unless we have a clear sense of costs and benefits of any action and a clear picture of the alternative. In the following section, and in the following chapter, we begin to address these two preconditions for change. As Jeanne Wolf states, "planning is about change, and the common belief of all planners, no matter their specialty, expertise, skill or area of endeavour, is that change can be managed for the betterment of the community."[17]

The Evolution of Green City Planning

> *Ecological planning, or incorporating planning for the*
> *natural environment into our physical planning, is still a worthy*
> *if elusive goal after a hundred years and needs to become an*
> *integral part of the design of communities henceforth.*
>
> – Gerald Hodge and David Gordon[18]

There are various terms that capture our efforts to incorporate the environment and ecological principles into our planning processes: "green planning," "environmental planning," "nature-based solutions," "designing with nature," and so on. We add "nature-directed stewardship" to this list. But first we want to illustrate how these planning approaches are part of a long lineage of insights into and innovations on how we reconcile the built environment with nature and natural processes. This contextualizes NDS within a trajectory of continuous insight, learning, and action, and it presents NDS as something entirely possible.

To start, "green urbanism" and "green planning" are used as umbrella terms to capture more environmentally focused approaches to planning. Green urbanism is "the ability of an urban system to exist, grow, or shrink without negatively impacting the ecosystem in which it resides, thus maintaining a healthy balance between the urban environment concerned and its surrounding hinterlands."[19] Timothy Beatly provides a series of principles for cities that have adopted green city planning, including living within ecological limits, reducing ecological footprints, functioning in ways analogous to nature, thinking of the city as a circular rather than a linear metabolism, enhancing local and regional self-sufficiency, and creating livable neighbourhoods and communities.[20]

Green planning is linked with the concept of sustainable development, put forth by the Brundtland Commission in 1987. Its critical articulation of sustainable development, repeated in virtually every book related to the principles and practices of sustainability, is "development that meets the needs of the present without compromising the ability of future generations to meet their own needs."[21] Although "probably no other regional planning concept has been embraced so universally and so quickly as has that of sustainable development," some context is required.[22]

When sustainable development was enthusiastically adopted, its core ideas were found in Indigenous worldviews dating back millennia, but its application to professional practice was limited. Merging sustainable development with the larger enterprise of greening our cities took place when the concept of sustainable development was still in its infancy.[23] The Western circle of writers, researchers, and planners wrestling with the concept, and looking for ways to translate its principles into practice, was limited. Since that time, the concept of sustainability has expanded in sophistication and grown exponentially in terms of research attention and sectoral and disciplinary reach. Sustainability and sustainable development have become mobile discourses with tremendous impacts.

However, expansion of the concept has also raised concerns that the idea has been co-opted, that the emphasis has been placed on development rather than sustainability, and that the core principles of geographical and intergenerational equity have been lost. These critiques are accurate, particularly in specific contexts, but the concept of sustainable development retains value for two reasons. First, the idea is known, and it allows for dialogue on the process of integrating and valuing ecological, social, and economic considerations as part of our decision making (even if the political processes themselves value those elements unequally). Second, it remains a core tenet for planners (the endurance of sustainability "reflects the power and adaptability of the concept: sustainability is a resilient, sustainable idea") that provides a foundation for making the leap to NDS.[24]

Green Planning Trajectories

Predating, and eventually overlapping with green planning and sustainable development, are more specific planning traditions that sought to incorporate environmental considerations. These movements were driven by planners and urban visionaries who devised alternatives that consider the natural world (as well as social well-being and equity).

The squalor and declining conditions of the nineteenth-century industrial city prompted many efforts at reform from landscape architects and planners to change the conditions of the city and re-establish nature-society relationships. The public health movement, and social concerns to make cities more enjoyable and accessible for all socio-economic classes, culminated in the urban Parks Movement in the mid- to late nineteenth century.[25] Although the orientation of the movement was more concerned with health and recreation, it neverthe-less represents an important benchmark in terms of understanding the nature-society relationship and viewing green spaces as fundamental, interconnected parts of human settlements.

As we will see below, the role of parks in cities has also served as a barrier to understanding a more fundamental interconnection between nature and the built environment. The presence of parks has created in many ways a false sense of naturalness (recall Jacobs's notion of nature as a "pet"), leading to develop-ment entirely devoid of natural systems (see Figure 2.1). Some semblance of nature exists in the green postage stamp park space "over there," leaving de-velopers free to ignore natural processes in the landscapes of our built environ-ments. Park spaces also reflect broader discriminatory beliefs and practices, perpetuating inequalities in terms of access to, and experience of, space across the urbanized landscape.

In 1898, Ebenezer Howard published the landmark *Garden Cities of Tomorrow.* Howard believed that the cities of Europe and North America had become too densely populated, thus contributing to their deterioration as living environ-ments. His vision for garden cities sought to create new, self-contained cities of about 32,000 people who would be linked by train, road, and canal with

FIGURE 2.1   A flat expanse of grass prioritizes a narrow range of specific activities. Protection and restoration of nature in urban parks provide opportunities for a variety of activities and a sense of place amid natural biodiversity.

other garden cities and with a central, metropolitan city. His map of a garden city divides land into two different uses (representing one of the earliest Western forms of zoning), with plans to locate residential areas away from industrial areas. He also incorporated spaces for farms to supply the city.

In addition, his plan created buffer zones between each of the distinct land uses, again representing one of the earliest articulations of the greenbelt, a practice that became widely adopted in many cities in North America and Europe. There are examples of garden cities in England and more than a dozen in the United States, and the practice was adopted by Thomas Adams in Canada.[26] Its success, however, ended up being co-opted:

> While the early garden city projects represent some of the best aspects of the modern town planning movement and today remain beautiful settlements, as the idea was more broadly disseminated, it became increasingly diluted. By the late 20th century, garden city ideas had degenerated into premises that seem to support suburban sprawl. Vast swaths of housing surrounded by spacious gardens linked together with well-planned road networks have become a recipe for a new set of urban problems.[27]

In 1909, the Commission on Conservation was established by Clifford Sifton, then Canada's minister of the interior. Although the mandate of the commission was to investigate the "squandering of the Dominion's natural resources," it drew early connections to the significance and environmental impacts of urbanization.[28] It stated that "each generation is entitled to the interest on the natural capital, but the principal should be handed on unimpaired." Such language predates the Brundtland Commission by over seventy years: think of the possibilities if this had more fully penetrated the Canadian planning psyche. Nevertheless, the commission was important since it traced early thinking about and concern for the environment, and influenced subsequent planning practices, acts, and regulations.

Regional planning in Canada was not undertaken seriously until the middle of the twentieth century. Following the Second World War, federal governments undertook regional interventions in an attempt to counter spatial disparities in economic conditions and performance (mirroring policies undertaken in other jurisdictions). Our particular interest in the roots of regional planning reaches further back to the influence of Patrick Geddes, a pioneering Scottish town planner. Geddes recognized the need for large-area planning. One of the critical features of this approach is to connect human populations and their settlements with surrounding resource bases. Geddes promoted a trinity of factors to be taken into account when planning: folk (the people of the region), work (the economy of the region), and place (the geographical and natural environmental dimensions of the region).[29] Such thinking and practice was influential in the Garden Cities Movement and has appeared in some of the more recent ideas of New Urbanism as greenbelts and an understanding of the connection between the urban core and the rural fringe. (The ongoing relevance of the work of Geddes was confirmed and celebrated in a special issue of *Landscape and Urban Planning*.[30])

The year 1969 brought not only the "giant leap for mankind" taken by Neil Armstrong but also a giant leap for connecting nature with cities taken by Ian McHarg in his book *Design with Nature*. McHarg encouraged the employment of ecology in landscape and urban planning and sought to balance settlements with ecological principles. No longer was nature limited to a feeble green space; rather, the full ecology of nature was honoured. The principles of *Design with Nature* are: compact and complete communities; increased transportation options; reduced loads on water, waste, and energy systems; protected and restored urban green spaces; a lighter hydrological footprint; and protected streams.[31]

McHarg was a pioneer. He "drew transects through natural regions to analyze how ecological processes might interact with human activity. More importantly, he prepared maps of ecological, physiographic, and socioeconomic features that were overlaid to identify the areas of least environmental impact for urban expansion and highway projects."[32] Frederick Steiner and Billy Fleming note that "the basic idea that we should design *with,* rather than in opposition [to] or in control of, nature remains especially vital in the Anthropocene" (the current geological epoch in which humans are the most powerful force shaping the planet).[33] The *Design with Nature* approach is very relevant to NDS in terms of both method and terminology.

In response to the spreading problems of urban sprawl (legitimized in part by a distorted interpretation of the Garden Cities Movement), smart growth emerged as an alternative. Smart growth emphasizes high-density development and does so by focusing on existing developments in order to utilize current infrastructure and to preserve green space as open, natural space and farmland. One of its central tenets is to resist the constant expansion of development on greenfield sites at city edges. Smart growth planning principles include mixed land use; compact building design; a range of housing opportunities; walkable neighbourhoods; a strong sense of place; open spaces, farmlands, and critical environmental areas; strengthened existing communities; transportation choices; and community and stakeholder collaboration in development decisions.[34] The emphasis on preserving critical environmental areas provides a stepping stone to NDS, and greater density is important for preserving and protecting natural systems (see Figure 2.2). Smart growth does not, however, articulate the more complete integration between development and nature that is central to NDS.

FIGURE 2.2   High-density, complete communities provide affordable, low-impact urban living for all ages and an essential response to the climate emergency. Incorporating nature makes them truly home. | *Credit:* Melinda Markey.

Indigenous Planning

The resurgence of Indigenous planning, with its core appreciation of the importance of place and the inherent value of nature, is driving change in planning. There are two simultaneous directions of this change. First, Indigenous Nations and communities are increasingly exerting control of and sovereignty over community and regional planning in acts of self-determination (inclusive of Indigenous community planning and planning within traditional territories). Second, there are now processes of reconciliation and decolonization of Western planning practices in which local and senior governments (and private developers) consult with, plan with, and seek redress for the impacts of structural racism.

As Hirini Matunga, director of the Centre for Maori and Indigenous Planning and Development at Lincoln University, observes, "as an activity, 'planning' isn't owned by the West, its theorists, or practitioners. It just happens to be an English language descriptor for a universal human function with an abiding and justifiable concern for the future."[35] Indigenous Peoples have always engaged in planning activities. Their protection of ecological integrity, dedication to equity, and consideration of long timelines are conducive to multigenerational planning work. These aspects of Indigenous planning are mirrored in nature-directed stewardship.

The wisdom of what is often called traditional ecological knowledge, or more simply Indigenous knowledge, is being revived within Indigenous communities and now influences Western planning.[36] Duane Smith defines Indigenous knowledge as "a cumulative body of knowledge, know-how, practices and presentations maintained and developed by peoples over a long period of time. This encompasses spiritual relationships, historical and present relationships with the natural environment, and the use of natural resources. It is generally expressed in oral form, and passed on from generation to generation by storytelling and practical teaching."[37]

Scholars such as Leanne Betasamosake Simpson provide insights into how Indigenous knowledge can be employed in the practice of cultural revitalization and self-determination:

> Recovering and retaining Indigenous worldviews, philosophies, and ways of knowing and applying those teachings in a contemporary context represents a web of liberation strategies Indigenous peoples can employ to disentangle themselves from the oppressive colonizing control of state governments. Combined with the political drive toward self-determination, these strategies mark resistance to cultural genocide, vitalize an agenda to build strong and sustainable Indigenous national territories, and promote a just relationship with neighboring states based on the notions of peace and just coexistence embodied in Indigenous knowledge.[38]

Simpson also critiques, however, practices that seek to integrate Indigenous knowledge with Western colonial approaches. She cautions that settler uses of Indigenous knowledge can simply repeat "the mistakes of the past," even when the enterprise is reconciliation. Indigenous knowledge, separated from its life context – and absent self-determination and recovery of Indigenous national territories – can simply perpetuate Western capitalist land uses.

More recently, the planning profession has been addressing the depths and impacts of systemic racism within its practice. Professor Leonie Sandercock articulates that "the dominant settler culture's land-based interests were represented by the emerging planning practices of the colonial era, practices which asserted non-indigenous control over Aboriginal domains and concepts of space and place."[39] Planning was and remains a tool of colonialism. The work of mapping and erasure of Indigenous place names, Western conceptualization and application of private property to unceded Indigenous lands, overt environmental racism associated with the displacement and location of Indigenous reserve lands (i.e., often on marginally productive lands or proximate to toxic industrial sites), and application of racist policies in education and land use sought the cultural and abject genocide of Indigenous Peoples.

Initial steps toward reconciliation are being taken in the planning profession. For example, the Canadian Institute of Planning launched the *Policy on Planning Practice and Reconciliation* to serve as a "call to action for planning to engage in meaningful and sustained relationship building with Indigenous Peoples of Canada." The process of reconciliation is described as "the commitment to establish and maintain a mutually respectful relationship between Indigenous and non-Indigenous peoples. It is a long-term relationship-building, learning, and healing process, as opposed to a specific outcome to be achieved."[40] The policy seeks to understand Indigenous planning approaches, define the role of planners in reconciliation work, and embed reconciliation within the body of planning practice in order to build mutual capacity.

Ecological Planning and Beyond

The long lineage of theory, practice, and worldview summarized above seeks to address the false gap which separates nature (as our dominant culture perceives it) from society. These theories and methodologies help bring us closer to an approach to ecological planning that fundamentally values nature and Indigenous knowledge. But more is needed.

The next step is to integrate fully natural processes with urban planning. Michael Hough was a Canadian innovator who sought to unite urban ecology with community design in a variety of areas: climate, energy, water, wildlife, plants, and urban agriculture. Recognizing the lineage above, Hough reflected that

> Patrick Geddes, Ian McHarg, Philip Lewis and other eloquent voices concerned with bringing together nature and human habitat have shown that the processes which shape the land, and the limitless complexity of life forms that have been created over evolutionary time, provide the indispensable basis for shaping human settlements. The dependence of one life process on another, the interconnected development of living and physical processes of earth, climate, water, plants and animals, the continuous transformation and recycling of living and nonliving materials, these are the elements of the self-perpetuating biosphere that sustain life on earth and which give rise to the physical landscape. They are the central determinants that might shape all human activities on the land.[41]

Green planning must become ecological planning – the ecological restoration of human settlements and the conservation and protection of ecological systems. This is the potential of NDS to transform our cities and built environments and to renew the field of planning as a whole.

The thought leaders and pioneers in green city planning, to say nothing of planners and landscape architects in every town and city office seeking to implement green planning ideas, have been laying a foundation of understanding for an integrated approach to planning and development. Perhaps originally some of the roots of green city planning had more singular objectives, such as creating parks, improving public health, or increasing density. Even when there is a sole motivation for engaging in green city planning (and NDS), the benefits immediately start to show up (often for free) in other areas of society, such as the economy, social well-being, equity, or personal health.

In the planning lexicon, the multiple-benefits of green planning are known as co-benefits (or the "no regrets" approach to planning). This means that if one pursues green planning strategies and the adoption of green infrastructure (i.e., networks of natural, enhanced, and engineered assets that make use of natural processes to deliver multiple economic benefits), it will create tangible benefits in other areas of society, such as better air quality, reduced flood risk, improved water quality, and greater biodiversity.[42]

For example, an emphasis on co-benefits is an important pillar of the low carbon resilience (LCR) planning strategy advocated by the Action on Climate Team (ACT) at Simon Fraser University. LCR is an approach to climate change planning that seeks to integrate and coordinate options for adaptation (i.e., changes made to respond to the impacts of climate change) and mitigation (emissions reduction) (see Figure 2.3). ACT notes that "[adopting an LCR approach] in local government contexts could streamline resources and capacity, mainstream climate action in a way that prevents contradiction, and identify strategic co-benefits for health, infrastructure, equity and other municipal priorities. The multiplier benefits of climate action, or co-benefits, relate to pollution reduction, enhancing human health, and ecosystem-based adaptations that enhance biodiversity."[43]

Planning has a core commitment to serving the public interest. Reflecting the public interest is how planners seek social legitimacy for their plans, yet doing so is a complex matter.[44] At the built level, our communities are a mixture of different property types and purposes. At a collective level, in any given community there are "multiple publics." Each of these interests, or groups of people, might have entirely different views of what is, and what best serves, the public good (and indeed different levels of access to participate in its determination). Despite these complexities, if we consider the ecological, social, and economic costs associated with how our cities and built environments have developed, it is clear that the broader public interest is not well served.

Many of our current problems are by-products of steps taken to serve the public interest from certain perspectives at certain times. As a society, our cultural and ecological literacy is evolving. In a Canadian context, only now are we coming to terms with the meaning of an authentic reconciliation with Indigenous Peoples by building an awareness of the past, acknowledging the

FIGURE 2.3   **Low carbon resilience embodies climate action that coordinates and mainstreams adaptation, mitigation, and co-benefits in municipal planning and decision-making processes.**

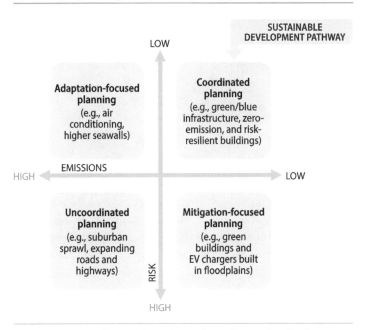

Source: Action on Climate Change Team, https://www.sfu.ca/act/low -carbon-resilience.html.

harms done, atoning for the causes of those harms, and taking action to change behaviour, as directed by the Truth and Reconciliation Commission.[45] The severing of Indigenous relationships with, and title to, the land under the auspices of colonial planning is a significant component of the harm done to Indigenous Peoples.

NDS offers a pathway to redefine how we approach the public interest in our planning and development decisions. Adopting its practices will require change. The good news is that the historical arc of planning has curved toward more active and engaged involvement with the diverse communities that it serves. This does not ignore the managerial and bureaucratic realities of the planning process (in which the control and power available to planners vary significantly). However, the pursuit of ecological, social, and economic justice through planning is a strong driver that motivates the interests and passions of the planning community. NDS is a way to channel those interests into practical steps to put nature first in cities.

3 From Green Planning to Ecosystem Approaches

Past green planning approaches and strategies are valuable stepping stones to planning and restoring nature-first cities. But we have a long way to go.

Isolated "green" initiatives – while delivering improved livability, important health outcomes, and enhanced green spaces – might do little to improve overall ecological integrity and ecosystem functioning. As Professor Ingrid Stefanovic warns,

> as important as these [green] initiatives are, however, there is a risk that something essential is missing. Is the building of a "natural city" simply a matter of integrating more parks into urban spaces? Of reducing the ecological footprint? Of encouraging local food production? Of mixed-use zoning? Moving forward will require more than assembling a compendium of such discrete initiatives. Most important will be to consider a repositioning of fundamental values, paradigms, and worldviews that sustain these efforts in the long-term.[1]

In this chapter, we identify some of the research challenges on the path to NDS and highlight some innovative international examples of urban areas that have sent initial invitations to nature. These exciting initiatives are moving from theory to application and creating urban homes for nature in spite of the messy (politicized) reality of doing so. As such, they serve as inspiration for other cities and have informed our work with Still Creek (which we detail in Chapter 6). Nevertheless, the examples in this chapter shine a light on what still must be done to implement NDS fully to create nature-first cities, and we demonstrate how these cases are different from our vision of NDS.

CHALLENGES

Growing recognition of the cumulative and transformative impacts of urban settlements on nature has precipitated a proliferation of planning strategies to mitigate the negative repercussions of urbanization. This proliferation brings at least four challenges that hinder the adoption of NDS.

First, the advancement of urban sustainability planning has attracted increased attention among researchers, each forwarding different concepts, frameworks, and tools. This marks an exciting period of emergent ecocentric planning, yet it has also produced confusing and often overlapping terms. For example, our research identified a variety of competing terms and frameworks, including "human ecosystem planning," "urban resilience planning," "sustainable landscape planning," "urban socio-ecological systems planning," "ecosystem management planning," "nature-based solutions," and others.

This is a natural, evolutionary process within any research discourse (especially one traversing multiple disciplines). However, it can be confusing and frustrating for practitioners. For planners who want to pursue greener, more sustainable approaches to planning, the list of terms, competing frameworks, and references can be overwhelming. Clearly, integrative efforts must be made to identify common principles and advance a synthesis.

The ecosystem-based management literature provides some help. Ray Tomalty identifies a conceptual divide between a focus on "ecology *in* cities" and "ecology *of* cities."[2] The former refers to situations in which specific sites, components of urban ecosystems, are studied and managed, typically by ecologists or environmental managers alone. The latter takes a broader, more integrative ecosystem approach (of the type that we advocate for in this book) that considers urban centres as ecosystems in themselves. The ecological character and limits of a city need to inform human behaviour. Similar to our proposal for NDS, the ecology of cities approach asks that we prioritize ecosystem integrity (and protection of remaining intact areas) as a foundation for making development decisions in our built environments.

Second, a barrier to the adoption of NDS is the lack of applied case studies demonstrating ecosystem-based approaches to urban planning. Not only is this a pure research gap, but it is also cited as a reason for municipalities not to pursue green urbanism.[3] Municipal officials and politicians have a tendency to be risk averse when engaging in planning. This is not meant as a criticism since their motivations for relying on tried and true (i.e., past) techniques are based on the fact that planning investments are often expensive and designed to last for a long time, and they can be the foci of heated political debates. If unproven techniques are approved, then there is a risk that systems might fail or not be durable in real-life applications, thus risking taxpayer, developer, or resident dollars (and, more importantly, depending on the type of infrastructure, human health). This barrier also affects the ability of city engineers to consider and sign off on projects that might apply new technologies or ecosystem approaches. If they are untested, or there is a significant knowledge gap regarding the efficacy of the design, then engineers might be unwilling to risk their professional reputations (let alone risk breaching the public safety obligations that underlie their professional codes of practice).

The lack of detailed case studies also means a lack of monitoring and evaluation of ecosystem planning projects. We simply do not know whether initiatives are having the desired effects on ecosystems and societies. Overcoming this barrier requires clear goals and a framework for nature-directed stewardship within which to evaluate success.

Case studies and rigorous analyses of green and NDS approaches help to reduce the risk associated with trying new things. Yet, in the face of the climate emergency, following the same old development path is likely *riskier,* especially in communities that are highly vulnerable to extreme weather events. And, as we mentioned in the previous chapter, effective alternatives can come with long lists of additional co-benefits to cities and their residents. Initiatives such as the Municipal Natural Assets Initiative,[4] which works with local governments in Canada, or the Long Term Ecological Research network in the United States,[5] help to build the confidence of cities to consider embracing green infrastructure solutions. (We pause to caution, however, as noted in the previous chapter, that commodifying components of nature as financial assets invites a narrow perspective that can overlook important ecosystem relationships that transcend particular financial assessments of green versus grey infrastructure choices.)

Third, it is a challenge to integrate work in the natural sciences with work in the social sciences. Disciplinary silos within each field add to further fragmentation. Simply put, natural scientists focus on ecological systems, and social scientists focus on administrative and institutional processes. Furthermore, complex theory and language specificity in each area diminish prospects for cross-pollination. NDS approaches demand that we reduce these barriers and work to integrate the natural and social sciences in order to understand ecological issues and to avoid (or, if necessary, mitigate) negative impacts on nature and society in our planning and management processes. We turn again to Ian McHarg in his support for human ecology in works such as *A Quest for Life* and *To Heal the Earth* for inspiration to bridge social and ecological disciplines. We welcome evidence of disciplinary integration and multidisciplinary research teams. Urban ecology, in particular, has become increasingly transdisciplinary.[6] This also includes the need to work collaboratively across different ways of knowing. Anne Salomon and her coauthors speak of the need to "democratize conservation science" from a top-down approach toward making science and participation accessible to everyone. They note that "whether intended or not, Western scientific imperialism marginalizes other knowledge sources and systems, creating strong power imbalances between those who are deemed able to define truth and those who are not."[7]

Fourth, there is relatively limited ecological research on cities. Ecologists, until very recently, have tended to view cities as unworthy sites for ecological research.[8] Thankfully, this gap is being addressed in part by our increasing understanding of the environmental impacts of cities, the logic of planning and developing at the scale of urban watersheds, the climate emergency, and the importance of benefiting from nature-based solutions.

Despite the long-standing obsession with expelling nature from cities, the scarcity of experiments with green planning, and the research barriers outlined above, some visionary municipalities and dedicated planners, landscape architects, ecologists, researchers, and community organizers are trail-blazing the path to nature-first cities. The response has been enthusiastic.

As indicated above, one of the best strategies for advancing our collective understanding of NDS is to share case stories and examples from multiple jurisdictions and contexts working to implement various dimensions of the approach. This comparison allows for a more integrated perspective on how different methods and approaches can complement each other – and, perhaps most importantly, raise the level of confidence in decision makers that employing NDS strategies can work – providing quality infrastructure and planning solutions while delivering all of the other co-benefits (health, economic, and social) to society.

NATURE-DIRECTED STEWARDSHIP: CASE STUDIES

In this section, we profile four examples of how some elements of NDS are being implemented. These examples, from different parts of the world (Melbourne, Portland, Wellington, and Durban), include two that focus on water and aquatic ecosystems and two that focus on terrestrial ecosystems. They all include elements that align with NDS since they adopt elements of an ecosystem-based approach. For each, we ask: what is the scale of the planning? What part of nature is protected or restored? Who participates? And who benefits? As we will see, these questions fit with our vision of NDS, presented in the next chapter. For now, the answers from these case examples not only provide hope and inspiration (and join a host of similar initiatives from around the world) but also send a clear message that further work remains to implement the full spectrum and potential of NDS.

Melbourne: Vegetation Communities to Manage Water

The first example focuses on water. Melbourne, home to over 5 million people, sought to enhance ecological integrity by restoring natural hydrological processes (water cycles).

Melbourne embarked on a series of collaborative research projects to test whether stormwater control technologies can improve in-stream ecological conditions.[9] Specifically, the primary ecological objectives of the project include reducing the frequency and magnitude of polluted peak (maximum) flows of water from impervious surfaces (e.g., roads) and restoring the quantity and quality of base (minimum) flows that had disappeared because of the impervious surfaces.

The project took place at multiple scales over a period of six years, including site-level implementation of stormwater infiltration systems (green infrastructure) and neighbourhood-wide structures throughout a watershed to improve the functioning of the creek. Although the stormwater infiltration systems are composed of vegetation, native species were not prioritized because community engagement indicated that public acceptance would be greater if vegetation complemented residents' existing garden spaces.[10]

The responsibility for stormwater management in Melbourne is divided among regional water authorities, municipalities, and private landowners.[11] The experiment therefore involved collaboration with the state government's urban development organization, Melbourne Water, the Cooperative Research Centre for Catchment Hydrology, and the University of Melbourne. Within each agency, the experiment further required collaboration among different departments. For example, within the municipality, councillors, senior management, engineering, and construction personnel interacted on implementing stormwater systems on public land.

The project leveraged local community actions, government practices, and planning regulations. Interestingly, sharing the risk of new plans and policies led to greater multi-organization and -jurisdictional commitment and willingness to invest – a lesson for wider-scale initiatives that demand regional governance across municipal or sub-territorial levels.

Melbourne residents were continually consulted throughout the experiment to incorporate local knowledge and build awareness throughout the community. Community feedback was incorporated into the policy incentives and the design of stormwater infiltration structures. The plans and systems developed were tailored to the sociocultural context of the community, and rainwater harvesting for household use was framed as a way to reduce household water bills.

Established as a pilot to inform potential action at larger scales, the initiative led to social and institutional changes within the catchment area.[12] It offers an example of the ecology-in-cities approach similar to the case study of Vancouver's Still Creek explored in Chapter 6. *Plan Melbourne 2017–2050* continues to build on Melbourne's progress in integrating an NDS approach into city planning. The plan seeks to enhance Melbourne's ecological integrity by creating a "network of green spaces" throughout the city, using water-sensitive urban design principles to protect urban waterways, and balancing ecological and social values in coastal use to ensure the sustainability of coastlines.[13]

Portland: Cooperative Watershed Management

Portland, the most populous city in Oregon (650,000 residents), also focused their planning efforts on water and aquatic ecosystems. The city adopted the *Portland Watershed Management Plan (PWMP)* and the *Framework for Integrated Management of Watershed Health* (the *Framework*), both of which focus on aquatic ecosystem integrity.[14] Portland's *Terrestrial Ecology and Enhancement Strategy (TEES)* complements those policies with a strategy for terrestrial ecological health.[15] Over the ten years since those watershed plans were approved, their implementation has catalyzed other city-wide strategies and programs, including the 2035 Comprehensive Plan.[16]

The *PWMP* and *Framework* provide a comprehensive approach to improving Portland's watershed conditions (i.e., the scale of implementation is watershed-wide). The *Framework* describes how the city will achieve and maintain healthy watershed conditions, which include natural hydrology, physical aquatic and terrestrial habitat, diverse biological communities, and distributions of native fish and wildlife populations.[17] The *Framework* is also designed to improve overall watershed health.

The primary causes of ecosystem degradation identified by the city include climate change, fragmentation, pollution, and invasive species, and the plans include actions to address those causes. The watershed plan responds with the primary objective to reduce and reverse degradation caused by human behaviours and land use changes, recognizing that restoration is much more difficult than prevention.[18] Accordingly, a land acquisition program aims to acquire high-quality terrestrial and aquatic habitat for conservation and restoration.[19] *TEES* explicitly prioritizes the protection and restoration of ecosystem integrity, and the plans direct that building takes place away from rare and high-quality habitat.[20]

The *Framework* and *TEES* recognize ecosystem connectivity through the hydrological processes across the watershed and through terrestrial connectivity throughout the city. Connectivity is enhanced by reducing impervious surface areas, removing barriers in stream channels, and creating terrestrial habitat corridors, anchor parks, and reserves. Various land use planning policies and regulations are aimed at reducing habitat fragmentation and degradation of existing habitat patches.[21] The full range of ecosystem composition, structure, and function, plant communities, and animal habitats and ranges are recognized explicitly in the *TEES,* in which landscape features are identified along with the wildlife that they support. At a broader scale, parklands within the city are being restored through revegetation initiatives, and programs are supporting the conservation of wildlife species at regional and national scales.[22]

With these strategies, Portland rejects the assumptions that urban watersheds are degraded beyond restoration and that restoration conflicts with growth and economic development. Instead, the plans recognize the need for sustained conservation and restoration.

The city also recognizes that the *Framework* and *PWMP* operate not only within the boundaries of city services, technically limited to Portland, but also within the regional ecosystem context. Portland recognizes the importance of coordinating with other jurisdictions to manage within ecological boundaries. It has both formal and informal partnerships with different city bureaus, higher-level government agencies, educational institutions, not for profits, and community groups. The city also works with state agencies (e.g., Department of Environmental Quality and Department of Fish and Wildlife) and conservation and restoration organizations (e.g., Columbia Land Trust, Audubon Society, and Society for Ecological Restoration) in programs aimed at wildlife conservation and restoration in regionally significant parks and rivers.[23]

PWMP and *TEES* contain scientific data that characterize the existing conditions of watersheds and terrestrial habitats. Portland developed the Portland Watershed Health Index, a comprehensive monitoring framework that collects data on important environmental health indicators and allows information to be communicated to other city departments and the public in a simple way. The city internally monitors public project implementation and policy effectiveness, helping it to implement individual projects and pilot approaches on public lands and to develop comprehensive watershed restoration and sustainable stormwater management projects.[24]

Portland incorporates local values and interests into the watershed and terrestrial ecology plans. The 2012–17 implementation plan for the watershed plan, for example, embraces equity in access to a healthy and safe environment as an explicit goal without diminishing its broader goal of supporting watershed ecological integrity.[25] The city works with neighbourhood-level watershed councils and environmental organizations when developing and implementing plans, thereby incorporating local values and interests and ensuring that the projects are place based. The city supports programs for outdoor schooling, year-round conservation education, and playing in nature to ensure that every student is exposed to a natural environment and has an opportunity to learn what individuals can do to improve local ecological health.[26] Portland provides resources for communities (targeted to individuals, organizations, businesses, and developers) to undertake local conservation and restoration initiatives, in the form of grants, technical support, reduced fees for permits, and rebates.

In its *Comprehensive Plan 2035,* the city builds on the *PWMP* and *TEES* to integrate goals for watershed health and restoration with the city's Urban Forest Management Plan, Climate Action Plan, Climate Change Preparation Strategy, Parks Plan, Natural Hazard Mitigation Plan, and plans addressing environmental equity. In the *Comprehensive Plan,* the city outlines goals for climate mitigation, watershed health, resilience, environmental equity, and community stewardship, and it provides specific policies for each of the five watersheds within the city's catchment.[27]

Wellington: Biodiversity Restoration

Wellington, New Zealand's capital and second most populous city (half a million people), took an innovative approach to enhancing terrestrial biodiversity. The city adopted *Our Natural Capital: Wellington's Biodiversity Strategy and Action Plan.* The plan aims to conserve and restore indigenous biodiversity throughout the city, including the natural plant communities and wildlife present prior to urban development.[28] In 2018, the plan won the Local Government New Zealand EXCELLENCE Award for Environmental Impact. The strategy follows urban revegetation initiatives undertaken since the 1990s – including the work of over 100 community groups that planted more than 35,000 plants annually – and continues with plans to preserve and enhance ecologically significant areas on both private and public land.[29]

The plan recognizes that habitat loss from development at any one site might not be significant, but the cumulative habitat loss of development on many sites will result in degradation at a city-wide scale.[30] Actions are therefore focused at the site level through private property residential incentives, development requirements, and council-implemented projects. Larger portions of the landscape, which provide connectivity, are considered at the city-wide scale and include larger parks, stream banks, and greenways. Connectivity to existing regional parks, and through regional conservation planning, thus establishes a network of indigenous biodiversity (key to NDS).

Wellington's plan also has strong ecosystem integrity features. It seeks to create integrated catchment management plans for the urban streams within city boundaries and to establish ecological links between regional parks and local islands for the preservation of larger wildlife and birds. Habitat size requirements are taken into consideration for planning conservation and restoration patch sizes.[31] Ecosystem structures with multilayer vegetation, ecosystem complexity, and a full range of organisms (primary producers, consumers, and decomposers) are recognized as critical for indigenous biodiversity.

Since the plan focuses on restoration of indigenous biodiversity, it includes Indigenous communities in the process. Iwi and other Maori groups are involved in planning and monitoring, and local Mana Whenua have opportunities to be involved in conservation initiatives.[32] The plan outlines the processes for adaptive management through data collection, monitoring, and joint decision making with community members, the Iwi, and various agencies. Local Maori groups will assist in determining sites of high biodiversity and cultural significance.

These partnerships play a role in educating the public about the importance of indigenous biodiversity.

The plan has a strong focus on equity. As opposed to conservation areas separated from human use, the plan encourages opportunities for people to exist in and interact with nature through recreational activities, restoration projects, and citizen science. All community members are invited to be actively involved. The involvement of children and youth is prioritized for projects, and more outdoor opportunities for children and youth will be created by encouraging schools to "adopt" portions of ecologically significant areas. City council aims to identify opportunities for increased business involvement to encourage sustainable business practices.

Although focused on protection and restoration of indigenous biodiversity, the plan does not seek to reframe fundamentally the development paradigm. However, the plan is comprehensive. And the City aims to reference nature, native species, and cultural forms in urban design and landscape architecture, which advances an ecology-of-cities approach while remaining grounded by an in-cities restoration model.[33]

Following the release of *Our Natural Capital,* Wellington released the *Wellington Resilience Strategy.*[34] It outlines three goals to improve the socio-ecological resilience of Wellington during social shifts, seismic events, and climate change. The strategy includes a program for "water and [the] natural environment."[35] That program aligns with *Our Natural Capital* to reiterate Wellington's commitment to restoring local ecosystems to improve the resilience of the city's water.

Durban: Biodiversity Network
Our final example, from Durban, South Africa, home to a regional population of 3.4 million, also focuses on terrestrial biodiversity. Over the past three decades, Durban (Thekwini Municipality) has been developing the Durban Metropolitan Open Space System (D'MOSS), which consists of a network of areas with high biodiversity value.[36]

D'MOSS seeks to operate at considerable scale. It is a system of threatened ecosystems and species, including grasslands, birds, and amphibians. D'MOSS is designed to maintain "as many functional ecosystems as possible, [the] widest range of open space types, link significant sources of biodiversity, and connect river catchments to marine sources of biodiversity."[37]

It consists primarily of publicly owned land throughout the municipality. The sites are located near, or nested within, the larger ecosystem area protected through D'MOSS.[38] Environmental conservation reserves are regionally protected on state and local government-owned lands. The boundaries of D'MOSS are delineated by the composition of habitats; however, the boundaries some-times change (increase or decrease) because of changes in land ownership. Development and regulation associated with D'MOSS protected ecosystems aim to connect valuable ecosystems to regional conservation areas.

The D'MOSS plan has a strong focus on ecosystem integrity. It focuses on what to leave (not on what to use) by seeking to conserve large-scale diverse ecosystems. However, the boundary can change given development pressures. The influence of the environmental planning department occurs primarily on developments adjacent to the D'MOSS, or other ecologically significant sites, and the department lacks the ability to regulate development throughout the entire municipal area.[39]

To enhance capacity, the municipality established the Durban Research Action Partnership (DRAP), a formal partnership between the municipal department of environmental planning and the University of KwaZulu-Natal. DRAP generates knowledge that assists managers in making planning-related decisions and provides an opportunity for researchers to apply their research directly to the municipality.[40] DRAP is funded by the municipality, the university, and other research grants.[41] The municipality also has a memorandum of understanding with the provincial conservation authority such that provincial conservation planning includes D'MOSS lands.

The research developed by DRAP considers community values, perceptions, and area uses that can be incorporated into conservation planning and decision making. A Biodiversity Forum was established to enhance communication be-tween civil society and government. Although the municipality recognizes that local communities need to be involved in the management of conservation areas, residents who participate in community-based conservation programs are still disconnected from the larger planning and decision-making process.[42] However, neighbourhood committees were struck to monitor and maintain sites jointly where endangered species occur. Other initiatives aim to establish formal partnerships with traditional authorities on tribal lands. The municipality has initiated large-scale reforestation and invasive species removal projects under the umbrella of public works. In these projects, skills development and employ-ment opportunities are offered to unemployed members of disadvantaged communities. These programs often lead community members to find employ-ment elsewhere or to work with the municipality.[43]

Although D'MOSS is generally protected from development, Indigenous and non-Indigenous communities engage and interact with the ecosystems on a regular basis. Tribal lands, governed by traditional leaders with traditional governance systems, are incorporated into the city's boundaries. Reforestation initiatives enable more vulnerable communities to have access to traditional sources of food and shelter. Part of the green-roofs project, for example, uses indigenous plants and aims to incorporate plant food sources into the green roofs to strengthen food security.

Durban has South Africa's highest percentage of people living in poverty and extreme levels of inequality.[44] The city recognizes that certain vulnerable populations would use these ecosystems for purposes different from those for which they have been protected (e.g., food or timber for building shelters). Rather than attempting to prevent these activities, Durban works with these vulnerable communities to ensure that the affected ecosystems can provide desired ecological benefits sustainably and without diminishing the other goals of D'MOSS.

The *Durban Climate Action Plan 2019* expands on the goals of D'MOSS and integrates climate change mitigation and adaptation goals. The plan establishes an intention to assess carbon sequestration by D'MOSS. Results from this assessment will aid Durban in achieving its goal of carbon neutrality by 2050.[45] The plan aims to safeguard biodiversity by increasing conserved land area, prioritize sites for restoration and protection from flooding and sea level rise through natural infrastructure, update spatial planning tools, purchase additional land for conservation, and continue to invest in community stewardship.

LESSONS LEARNED

The examples above illustrate different approaches to planning and restoration. Each brings us closer to applying nature-directed stewardship and creating nature-first cities. Although the cases are highly contextualized to their specific sociopolitical systems and ecosystems, a few general observations are possible.

First, things are happening. After the long trajectory of green planning that came before, ecosystem-based/nature-directed stewardship initiatives are emerging. The seeds of ecosystem-centric urban planning planted decades ago (e.g., Ian McHarg's concept of *Design with Nature* and Anne Whiston Spirn's *The Granite Garden*) are finally germinating and sprouting. The cases discussed here are by no means exhaustive. Other projects are taking place in small communities, such as the natural asset infrastructure project in Gibsons, British Columbia, and sprawling megacities, such as the "sponge city" approach being implemented in Beijing and Shanghai (which seeks to absorb rainwater through the widespread use of natural infrastructure such as wetlands, green rooftops, rain gardens, and permeable surfaces). Our landscape-level knowledge – the needed data for nature-directed planning – is also advancing.

Second, threats prompt actions. Echoing the history of reactive planning that characterizes many of the challenges faced in our built environments (e.g., affordability, poverty, health), planning to protect and restore nature is often motivated by the threat (or occurrence) of catastrophic flooding, the dawning realization of the costs of hard infrastructure solutions to climate change adaptation, or the loss of indigenous biodiversity. This is not necessarily a problem (those motivations are real), but we need to think holistically and proactively, from a truly nature-centric perspective, in order to ensure that one solution does not lead to new problems.

Third, indigenous ecosystems (including Indigenous management of those ecosystems) provide the starting point. That is, natural ecosystem *character* – the composition, structure, and function of the ecosystems that existed before the city did – provides a target of growing importance in the face of the climate emergency. Wellington's focus on indigenous biodiversity involves Maori groups in planning and identifying sites of high biodiversity, and Durban recognizes that multiple ecosystem uses can co-exist with broader biodiversity objectives. In fact, vertebrate biodiversity on Indigenous-managed land is greater than in parks and protected areas, and overall biodiversity is declining less on Indigenous-managed land than elsewhere, illustrating that nature succeeds when managed by Indigenous Peoples.[46]

To protect and restore indigenous ecosystems (natural ecosystem character) successfully, we must start by protecting the ecosystem patches that still exist and ensuring that they degrade no further. Even if the existing patches are small, they must be protected because, as Wellington recognizes, the cumulative effect of many site-scale losses is city-scale loss. Conversely, by protecting multiple site-scale patches, we have the beginnings of something grand. The full range of ecosystem composition, structure, and function must be protected and restored. This work is assisted by obtaining scientific data on what exists (as Portland does) and prioritizing habitat protection and restoration (as Wellington does).

Fourth, connectivity is key. Linkages, such as those identified in Wellington, and networks, such as those developing in Durban (and other greenbelt initiatives around the world), can grow from what already exists to a more robust network following restoration. Network boundaries need to be defined by ecological considerations rather than by the scraps ignored by developers. And aquatic as well as terrestrial networks are needed, as Portland has shown. Ultimately, these networks among protected areas need to be as large as possible, operating at multiple spatial scales.

Fifth, collaboration among residents (Indigenous and non-Indigenous alike), private landowners, local governments, higher-level governments, and Indigenous leaders is a prerequisite for success. No one actor is in charge, and no one authority can compel the full suite of necessary actions. Referencing Anne Salomon's work is again useful. Salomon uses the term "polycentric governance" (linking to Ostrom's 2005 work), which refers to "nested, quasi-autonomous decision-making units operating at multiple scales," to describe how we can share information and capacity among actors involved in conservation work.[47]

We learn from the cases presented here (and elsewhere) that engagement, collaboration, education, and inspiration are as indispensable as regulatory measures. Citizen participation, collaborative monitoring, multijurisdictional action, creative incentives, and adaptive management all have roles – and co-benefits can help to inspire action in unexpected ways. As the Inter-governmental Science-Policy Platform on Biodiversity and Ecosystem Services (IPBES) lays out, "managing landscapes sustainably can be better achieved through multifunctional, multi-use, multi-stakeholder and community-based approaches, using a combination of measures and practices, including well managed and connected protected areas and other effective area-based conservation measures."[48]

Initiatives must be considered in terms of their contextual applications in different settings. Although certain techniques can be easily transferable across different urban systems, other practices will require considerable reflection and research on their transferability, ecologically, culturally, and politically. There is a danger that if we all rush to adopt "best practices," then we risk homogeneity in our NDS practice and implementation.

As our cities confront the climate emergency and our urban citizens feel increasingly disconnected from the natural world, we need to move beyond "pilots" and case studies. The time has come for full-scale implementation of NDS. More research to understand better the efficacy, costs, and performance of different techniques will help, but we certainly know enough now to act.

NDS has moved beyond ideology – it is simply what "good planning" now looks like. It is time to fill in the details and take action. In the next chapter, we will sketch a vision for doing so.

4 The Vision for Nature-First Cities

*Our tragedy lies in the richness of the available alternatives, and
in the fact that so few of them are ever seriously explored ... [O]ur
age seems not merely tragic but tragic in the classical sense, that
despite all possibility, we seem trapped in just that remorseless
"working of things" that the Greeks saw as the core of tragedy.*

– Tom Athanasiou

Despite our ghastly record of expelling nature from cities, nature awaits. Ultimately patient and undiminished in potential, it is eager to be invited home to where we live, work, and play.

The invitation starts with rejecting the notion that civilization, manifested in cities, should suppress nature. Instead, as Jane Jacobs instructed, we need to adopt a view of "mankind and nature as partners, with nature as the senior partner and humans being the apprentices."[1] We need to break radically from the deeply held conviction that we are in charge of nature and instead allow nature to show us how to solve the problems that we created.

Lewis Mumford pointed out that this (Western) vision dates back over 2,000 years to "Hippocrates' famous medical work on Airs, Waters and Places[,] the first public recognition that man's life, in sickness and in health, is bound up with the forces of nature, and that nature, so far from being opposed and conquered, must rather be treated as an ally and a friend, whose ways must be understood, and whose counsel must be respected."[2]

As discussed in Chapter 2, a minority voice in defence of nature began to speak with the emergence of urban planning as a profession. From Frederick Law Olmsted to Ebenezer Howard, early visionaries saw the benefits of nature in cities: "All the advantages of the most energetic and active town life, with all the beauty and delight of the country, may be secured in perfect combination."[3] Contemporaneous with these early "green" planners were environmental efforts that included Ralph Waldo Emerson's 1836 essay "Nature," Henry David Thoreau's 1854 book *Walden,* and John Muir's 1892 founding of the Sierra Club. The influence of environmentalism on urban planning has strengthened significantly since that time, notably after the flowering of the environmental movement that began after Aldo Leopold's 1949 book *Sand County Almanac* and Rachel Carson's 1962 book *Silent Spring* with its explicit connection between environmental degradation and human health.

As environmentalism mushroomed in the early 1970s, it catalyzed "eco-city" activism. The various attempts to "green" cities have been influenced by a plethora of movements and paradigms, including "healthy communities, appropriate technology, community economic development, social ecology, the green movement, bioregionalism, [Indigenous] world views, and sustainable development."[4] Ecologically focused urban thinkers understand that "a built environment that mimics and complements rather than conflicts with nature is emerging as the Holy Grail of this movement."[5]

The call for inviting nature home to our cities has grown louder with the uncertainty associated with climate change and the recognition that our unpredictable future calls for a new approach to planning.[6]

In this chapter, we paint a hopeful picture of cities in which nature has accepted our invitation: nature-first cities. This picture is in fact a collage of existing images – of innovations already taking place in various cities, of insights from research across various disciplines, and of lessons from nature itself. As our apprenticeship with nature unfolds, the destination will sharpen. In the chapters that follow, we will outline a process to get there.

PRINCIPLES

Humanity's erroneous perception that nature is separate from (and less valuable than) human society has invited a reckless ruin of ecosystems, the climate emergency, and the biodiversity crisis. We nevertheless have faith that our species is wise enough to correct this misconception – and to do so before a sixth extinction, repeated pandemics, and wholesale climate collapse.

Ecologists are taking the value of urban ecosystems seriously. New species have been discovered in major metropolitan areas such as New York.[7] The green building community is moving beyond the building scale to embrace whole communities. Urban planners are seeking to understand how nature's composition, structure, and function can be restored through a respectful, reciprocal relationship that relieves aging infrastructure, protects against storm threats, and builds urban resilience.

Psychologists are trumpeting the myriad health benefits from nature next door, and physicians are recognizing the direct health-care savings that accrue from investments in green spaces. Economists see the path around our urban infrastructure deficit as green rather than paved. Environmentalists, perplexed by public apathy in the face of a worsening ecological crisis, recognize the precondition of a connection to nature for catalyzing action. Climate change pragmatists are embracing the efficacy of increased population density to slash carbon pollution, and environmental justice activists are insisting that urban green spaces must be more than playgrounds for the wealthy.

FIGURE 4.1   Inviting nature into cities means integrating it into day-to-day urban life. It means restoring the nature that existed before the city did and allowing it to flourish over and among the buildings and to grow into the forefront of urban life.

We offer a vision of humans as we truly are: part of nature, dependent on its bounty, and poised to benefit from our inherent, original relationship with the ecosystems that support us. In this chapter, we outline our vision for re-establishing our relationship with nature in a particular place – cities. Nature-first cities. We start by examining the three principles that guide us: nature, equity, and density.

The first guiding principle, nature, refers to the ecosystems that existed in a particular place before the city did and the extent to which those systems can be restored. Honouring this principle entails restoring, as much as possible, the full range of ecosystem *composition* (the parts of the system), *structure* (the way that the parts are arranged), and *function* (what the parts do individually and cooperatively). It means restoring ecosystem integrity and biological diversity through a network of ecological reserves at multiple spatial scales across the city. And, as we will explain, it means that nature needs to occupy at least half of the area within a city.

To right our relationship with nature, we suggest that our relationships with each other must also be righted. And vice-versa. By reducing inequality within human society, by no longer seeing less affluent people as less valuable others, we take a step toward correcting our distorted view of nature as the other. By repairing our relationship with nature, we open our minds to correcting our relationships with each other. In cities, at least two steps must be taken.

First, all residents of a city must be given an opportunity to discover and express their biophilia; to have direct experiences with nature. This correction requires that nature be distributed equally across the city regardless of the wealth of residents – a distribution also essential for maintaining and restoring ecosystem connectivity, biodiversity, and ecological integrity. In other words, by restoring ecosystem connectivity, biodiversity, and ecological integrity at all scales across the city, we can ensure opportunities for everyone in the city to connect with nature. Access needs to be available to all instead of only a privileged few.[8]

Second, people in wealthy communities must halt their disproportionate demands on nature. As we are reminded by George Monbiot, "it is not the needs of the poor that threaten the biosphere, but the demands of the rich."[9] Whereas the demands of the wealthy are chiefly responsible for global warming, species extinction, and ecosystem fragmentation, the burdens of these problems are carried predominantly by those least culpable. Nonhuman species, Indigenous cultures, and low-income people everywhere can afford neither excess consumption nor privatized protection from countless ecological injustices.

In cities, an equitable reduction of demands on nature starts by increasing density. The benefits of density are far reaching. As we will see, dense urban structures represent an effective way for cities to reduce their carbon pollution by using less energy and enabling accessible transportation choices other than the private automobile. By increasing density while simultaneously inviting nature home to our cities, we reduce the demands on nature, ease burdens on the less affluent, and reconnect everyone in the city with nature.

The goal of increasing density while simultaneously inviting nature home might seem to be paradoxical, but further attention to this enigma reveals its enormous potential and its inescapable necessity. In fact, it is nature (and other amenities) that make density work. We are not called to make nature available only in "sustainable" greenfield developments that ultimately serve to extend the urban boundary. Rather, we are summoned to something greater: to protect and restore nature in urban areas in conjunction with increasing density. With some vision and creativity, it is possible to do both.

Nature

Nature belongs in cities. We are part of nature, and where we live should not shun what is part of us. Accordingly, our first guiding principle is to accept this

FIGURE 4.2   Before there was a city, there was a natural ecosystem, such as this old-growth forest. The character of that ecosystem describes its parts (the composition), how those parts are arranged (the structure), and how they work cooperatively (the functions) to maintain nature.

reality and seize the strengths that come from inviting nature home. What do we mean by nature? As articulated above, we mean the ecosystems that existed in a particular place before the city did, the natural character of those systems, and the extent to which they can be restored. This requires some explanation.

Ecosystems

To start, an *ecosystem* is a community of interacting species together with the physical environment within which it exists. Healthy ecosystems exhibit a full range of naturally occurring composition, structure, and function. *Composition* refers to the parts of an ecosystem, the types and numbers of species (plants, animals, and micro-organisms) that occur in that system. An ecosystem's *structure* is how the parts of that system are arranged, such as the patterns of vegetation and topography across a landscape or the frequency and distribution of living and dead trees. *Function* refers to the cooperative processes that occur within an ecosystem and among ecosystems – processes that depend on the ecosystem parts and how they are arranged.

Ecosystems are thus webs of interactions and interdependencies among the parts. The parts are synergistic, meaning that the behaviour of a whole ecosystem cannot be predicted by the behaviour of any of the individual parts. Yet the result of the interactions is stability. Stability does not mean a lack of change, but rather change within a range of natural variability, analogous to the balanced movement of one riding a bicycle.

In a natural ecosystem, *natural disturbance regimes* (the types of natural disturbances) can range from landscape-level disturbances such as floods and windstorms to small-scale disturbances such as the activities of insects and fungi. Floods and windstorms are dramatic events, but they are far less frequent than small-scale disturbances.[10] For example, in a natural forest ecosystem, one of the most frequent disturbances (or agents of change) is the death of an individual tree or a small group of trees. Death can be from a wide range of causes, including bark beetles, root-decaying fungi, small wind events, patch fires, heavy snow accumulations, soil erosion, or combinations of these and other factors.[11]

Natural disturbances change composition, structure, and function. In the time interval between successive disturbances, the composition, structure, and function change through a process referred to as succession. Unlike once thought, succession does not necessarily lead to a stable "climax" character. Succession is highly variable, stochastic, and complex.[12] The variability in ecosystem composition, structure, and function that occurs through the dynamic process of succession is often referred to as the *range of natural variability.*[13]

Ecosystems can be tiny or enormous. In fact, each ecosystem has diffuse boundaries, meaning that it is hard to tell when one ecosystem ends and the next begins. Local ecosystems are connected to others in a network of larger and larger ecosystems that comprise watersheds, landscapes, regions, and eventually the entire Earth.[14] Ecosystems are interdependent, interconnected living systems. Links between the parts and processes of ecosystems are seldom obvious. They occur at many scales. Recognizing the interconnected, seamless links from large ecosystems to small ecosystems, and vice versa, stimulates humility about just how deep and far the impacts of our actions extend when we modify natural ecosystems.

The settlement and expansion of any particular city necessarily entailed modification of the ecosystems that existed before the city did. The ecological character of an area is a description of what it was and how it worked before modification by industrialized human societies (but not before modification by Indigenous management systems). The character of ecosystems at all spatial scales is described in terms of composition, structure, and function.[15]

The character of an ecosystem is a continuum in time and space. In other words, over time, an ecosystem is not static and unchanging. Natural disturbances constantly modify ecosystems as time passes. However, unlike disturbances from industrial activities and urbanization, natural disturbances serve to maintain ecosystem function and provide biological legacies that connect one

FIGURE 4.3   Paved, buried, removed, and replaced, urban nature is often reduced to no more than a hint of the past (and sometimes an alien past). Where the current condition offers little guidance, the natural character provides the compass bearing for restoring nature in cities.

successional phase to another. Natural disturbances maintain diversity, whereas urbanization and industrial resource extraction activities tend to decrease diversity. Urban and industrial developments simplify, homogenize, degrade, and often extirpate natural ecosystems.[16]

Ecosystem character can be contrasted with the current ecosystem *condition:* that is, the modification of natural composition, structure, and function by industrialized human societies. That modification includes development of the city, resource exploitation, settlement, urbanization, tourism, and other human activities but excludes preindustrial Indigenous management systems.[17] What remains in the current city of the pre-existing ecosystems – the residual composition, structure, and function after urban development – is often simplified, fragmented, and nonindigenous.

The climate emergency presents a challenge for defining and restoring natural character. In the face of climate disruption, natural character offers buffers such as water conservation, storm abatement, temperature moderation, and carbon sequestration and storage. As the restoration of nature proceeds toward natural character, the diversity inherent in the ecosystems that comprise natural character will provide for climate adaptation and resilience. Where appropriate, restoration can also incorporate climate change–resistant species and processes in restoration activities.

Nature-Based Planning

How do we protect, maintain, and (significantly) restore nature in urban areas? The answer is through the process of nature-directed stewardship (NDS), which puts nature first in cities.

NDS incorporates the concepts outlined above (nature, ecosystems, composition, structure, function, natural disturbance regimes, range of natural variability, character, and condition) into a process designed to protect, maintain, and restore the nature indigenous to the location of a particular city.

NDS starts with the recognition that we are part of nature. Nature functions fully and flawlessly without intervention from industrialized human societies, but the converse is not true. Consequently, our societies, cultures, and economies must be understood as *requiring* nature across scales of time and space as a precondition for their existence. Our economies are part of human cultures, and human cultures are part of ecosystems. Therefore, the protection of nature is a prerequisite both for healthy human cultures and for the economies that are part of these cultures.

Unlike industrialized colonial societies, Indigenous societies understand their place in nature. Their modifications of nature works cooperatively to maintain the healthy function of natural ecosystems.

Whereas human economies are open systems, the Earth is a closed system. This means that the Earth receives solar energy and reradiates energy to outer

FIGURE 4.4   **Nature-directed stewardship is based on a hierarchical relationship**

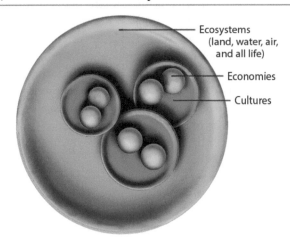

Ecosystems
(land, water, air,
and all life)

Economies

Cultures

Note: Economies are part of cultures, and cultures depend on the ecosystems that support them. Understood properly, there is not a single zone of overlap among these concepts; rather, human cultures and economies exist and flourish as part of nature.

space, but only insignificant amounts of material enter or leave the Earth.[18] Living organisms, including human beings, are born, grow and develop, and then decline and die. When living organisms die, their energy and material are recycled, in a process essential to ecosystem functioning. Since the Earth is a closed system, there are clear biological limits to growth for humans and all other organisms. Limits to growth ensure that we do not overtax the Earth's finite materials or over-encumber the Earth with waste.

Recognizing that we are part of nature leads one to take stock. Hence, the first step in NDS is analyzing ecosystem character and current condition. As explained above, character refers to natural ecological composition, structure, and function, whereas condition refers to how the character has been modified by the activities of industrial society. Assessing the condition of an ecosystem, and comparing that condition with its character, serves to identify areas in need of restoration, including the type and extent of restoration needed, areas appropriate for networks of ecological reserves, and ecological limits for human development activities.[19]

The character and condition of ecosystems are initially determined through analysis of *indirect* data sources including maps, aerial photos, satellite images, open-source geospatial data, and other imaging data. Determination of character involves researching historical sources including ecological descriptions and photographic images. Condition can be described through current data sources that show the locations and characteristics of various activities or disturbances from human activities, excluding traditional Indigenous management systems.

These indirect data are augmented by *direct* data in the form of field assessments. Character can be described from field assessments of benchmark undisturbed natural ecosystems such as those that once occupied the city and by reconstructing the composition, structure, and function of natural ecosystems by observing and describing remnant natural ecosystems within the city. Condition uses field assessments to describe impacts to and restoration needs of sites, watersheds, and landscapes.

Describing and comparing the character and condition – composition, structure, and function – of ecosystems at multiple spatial scales form the foundational process of NDS (see Figure 4.5). The process is guided by the principle of focusing first on what to protect and then on what to use.

Part of describing character and condition is identifying *ecological limits.* They are thresholds beyond which human activities cause changes to ecosystem composition, structure, and function outside the *range of natural variability.* Human activities beyond ecological limits initiate fundamental and detrimental changes to ecosystems and undermine *ecological integrity* (defined as a "system's wholeness, including presence of all appropriate elements and occurrences of

FIGURE 4.5   The nature-directed stewardship planning process

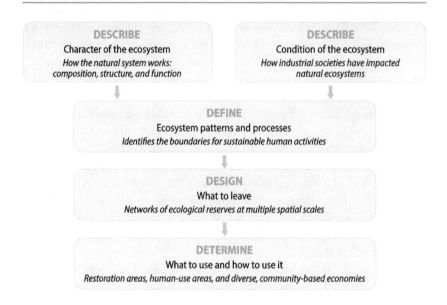

Note: Nature-directed stewardship starts with contrasting the natural character of an ecosystem with its current condition. Decisions about how to protect and restore the missing character aim to ensure ecosystem function by placing limits on human activities.
Source: Herb Hammond, *Maintaining Whole Systems on Earth's Crown: Ecosystem-Based Conservation Planning for the Boreal Forest* (Slocan Park, BC: Silva Forest Foundation, 2009), 38.

all processes at appropriate rates").[20] Such unwanted changes are fundamental changes to ecosystems, not merely fluctuations within them, such as those caused by natural disturbances.[21]

NDS is based on the premises that ecological limits will be respected and that human uses will be designed to prevent, as opposed to mitigate (or allow), damage to ecosystem functioning. Thus, identifying ecological limits is an important starting point for the development of nature-directed stewardship at all spatial scales.

Defining ecological limits is primarily a process of using Indigenous knowledge and scientific data in combination with sociopolitical information.[22] The *precautionary principle* is applied in all decisions: "When an activity raises threats of harm to human health or the environment, precautionary measures should be taken even if some cause and effect relationships are not fully established scientifically."[23] Ecological limits constrain or prohibit development to ensure that it errs on the side of protecting ecological integrity and biological diversity. As the results of adaptive management in NDS accumulate over time, ecological limits can be refined as required to protect ecological integrity.

Examples of major factors that define the ecological limits to human use of ecosystems include habitat and reproductive needs of species, shape of the terrain, slope gradient, soil depth, soil texture, amount of moisture available (both wet and dry conditions impose ecological limits), and local climatic conditions. When ecosystem processes (e.g., water cycles or carbon sequestration) become degraded, it generally means that ecological limits have been transgressed. Thus, healthy ecosystem processes are a good indicator that ecological limits are being respected.

When ecosystems lose composition and/or structure from human modifications, they lose or significantly decline in their ability to function in natural ways. Hence, whether or not we are aware of the purpose(s) of particular arrangements of composition and structure, NDS requires that the natural range of composition and structure be maintained across all spatial scales through time in order to ensure the maintenance of ecological integrity. Hopefully, by maintaining the visible composition and structure, we also maintain the composition and structure that we cannot see, particularly those beneath the surface of the soil and in the atmosphere.

Nature-directed stewardship sets cautious ecological limits and entails low-risk management. By respecting ecological limits, NDS strives to maintain, protect, and restore *ecological integrity:* "The abundance and diversity of organisms at all levels, and the ecological patterns, processes, and structural attributes responsible for that biological diversity and for ecosystem resilience."[24]

The probability of securing ecological integrity is increased by certain key actions: maintaining viable populations of all native species; protecting representatives of all native ecosystem types across their ranges of variation; maintaining evolutionary and ecological processes (i.e., disturbance regimes, hydrological processes, and nutrient cycles); managing over periods of time long enough to maintain the evolutionary potential of species and ecosystems; and accommodating human use and settlement within these constraints.[25]

These actions are brought together through nested plans at multiple spatial scales. This characteristic of NDS is rooted in the sciences of landscape ecology, hydrology, and conservation biology, which explain that landscapes, large and small, consist of interdependent, interconnected clusters of ecosystems. Such clusters are found in repeated patterns across regions, subregions, landscapes, and watersheds.[26] The repeating pattern of interconnected clusters of ecosystems found in areas of varying sizes, from large landscapes to small sites tells us that *nested networks of ecological reserves at multiple spatial scales* are needed to maintain ecological integrity.[27] Hence, NDS plans are prepared, and restoration activities are carried out at multiple spatial scales.

Nested ecological reserves are most effective if they are designed by first considering large areas and landscapes. Large reserves protect the ecological integrity of large areas, such as large or multiple watersheds. Once the large reserves are identified, we can establish interconnected networks of ecological reserves that protect the ecological integrity of areas outside those large reserves.[28] We then proceed by designing and connecting ecological reserves for progressively smaller areas, from small landscapes, to small watersheds, to sites.[29]

The general planning scales used in nature-directed stewardship are depicted in Figure 4.6. The networks of ecological reserves capture ecologically sensitive, unique, and representative areas across the planning area. Finer and finer composition and structure make up the protected networks as planning moves from large territories and landscapes to small landscapes, watersheds, and sites. Like "zooming in" with a telephoto lens, increasing detail and understanding of ecosystem composition, structure, and function are obtained as planning moves from large areas to small areas.

At the large landscape or watershed scale, the networks are referred to as *protected area networks,* which secure whole watersheds and landscapes as benchmark or reference ecosystems and provide the full range of habitat for the species of a particular region. Ecological reserve networks at the medium and small watershed levels are referred to as *protected landscape networks,* and ecological reserve networks at the patch or site scale are referred to as *protected ecosystem networks.* All three scales of ecological reserve networks are connected by linkages or corridors that contain a diverse array of ecosystems that provide satisfactory movement paths for animals, plants, and energy.

Watersheds can be tiny or all of the Earth. In fact, every crease on the face of the Earth is a small drainage basin that connects to adjacent creases to form slightly larger watersheds. Those ranging in size from approximately 100 to 100,000 hectares are commonly mapped for use in defining NDS areas. The larger the planning area, the larger the watershed stratification that is appropriate. Small watershed units can be easily aggregated into large watershed units. Thus, stratifying a planning area by smaller watershed areas at the start of an NDS plan both ensures that unique aspects of small watersheds are captured in reserve design and provides an efficient way to define watersheds for a variety of scales.

Nature-directed stewardship is carried out across multiple scales, not only for ecological reasons, but also in light of cultural, social, and economic factors. For example, NDS recognizes and supports the interconnected, interdependent nature of various portions of a watershed to Indigenous cultures as well as to the societies of urban and rural communities. This approach recognizes that

FIGURE 4.6　Multiple spatial scales of nature-directed stewardship

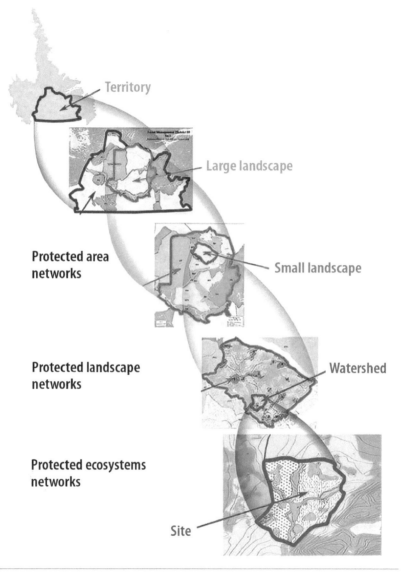

Note: Nature-directed stewardship applies at multiple spatial scales, from large territories and landscapes down to specific sites, with networks of protection and restoration at each level. Within larger-scale networks of protection and restoration are smaller-scale pockets of human use; within larger-scale zones for human use are smaller-scale pockets of protection and restoration. NDS thus respects ecosystem functions, large and small, playing out simultaneously across entire landscapes.

Source: Silva Forest Foundation, *EBCP Multiple Spatial Scales of Ecological Reserve Design* (Slocan Park, BC: Silva Forest Foundation, 2018).

FIGURE 4.7   Nature does not operate according to four-year election cycles or ten-year business plans. Indeed, ecosystem functions take place over both very short cycles (e.g., daily) and much longer cycles (e.g., thousands of years). Nature-directed stewardship considers a full range of temporal cycles even though the benefits might not be realized for generations to come.

healthy regional economies are dependent on the development and maintenance of healthy community economies. Like ecosystems, the interdependence of and interconnections between regional economies and community economies go in both directions.

Timelines relevant to ecosystems differ from timelines typically relevant to humans. Nature's timelines encompass full ecosystem cycles, such as the time that it takes for trees to germinate, live, and die; for the development of the ecological composition, structure, and processes that provide for water conservation; or for the creation of productive soils. Such timelines encompass hundreds and thousands of years and stand in stark contrast to most human endeavours, such as urban development plans, election cycles, or annual budgets.

Accordingly, NDS encompasses the longest reasonable ecological timeline in order to maintain ecological integrity from the smallest site to the largest landscape. This means planning horizons of 250–500 years and beyond. Generations of people live through the duration, modifying the plan as information and understanding change, while always erring on the side of protecting ecological integrity.

Inviting Nature Home

People in cities want nature nearby. In fact, as we saw in Chapter 2, people *need* nature nearby. But when developers and city planners seek to incorporate nature, they often settle for the wrong nature (homogenized green space), in the wrong location (isolated patches determined by economic considerations), and in the wrong amount (not enough).

NDS shows us how to do better. It guides us to the right nature (the natural character of ecosystems that existed before the city did), in the right places (interconnected networks of ecosystems at multiple spatial scales), and in the right amount (sufficient to provide ecological integrity). NDS rests on the applied theory of ecosystem-based conservation planning, developed by the Silva Forest Foundation; informed by the disciplines of landscape ecology, hydrology, and conservation biology; and refined over decades of practical experience. However, it has not yet been fully applied to urban areas. We suggest how this can be done.

How much nature should be restored in urban areas? How far should we go? The sobering calculation of Edward O. Wilson is that half of the Earth must be devoted to nature if we are to avoid losing most of the species on this planet.[30] We see no reason why the goal to protect 50 percent of nature should not apply to cities. To achieve this goal in cities will require a very large and ongoing commitment to ecosystem restoration. But, half the areas of cities consist of roads and rooftops. By repurposing many roads; rewilding alleys, yards, and buried streams; constructing bioswales, rain gardens, and green walls and roofs; and restoring and expanding natural character to the existing network of parkland, sharing half the area of a city with nature is not unrealistic.

Equity

> *In an awful turn, the climate crisis' path is first impacting those who have not only contributed to our emissions the least, but have already suffered greatly in the global history of inequality, colonialism and imperialism – stacking one injustice upon another.*
>
> – Alexandria Ocasio-Cortez[31]

In 2019, more than 11,000 scientists declared "clearly and unequivocally that planet Earth is facing a climate emergency."[32] The consensus document does not mince words: "The climate crisis has arrived and is accelerating faster than most scientists expected. It is more severe than anticipated, threatening natural ecosystems and the fate of humanity."[33]

Equally blunt is the scientists' assessment of responsibility for our global emergency: "The climate crisis is closely linked to excessive consumption of the wealthy lifestyle. The most affluent countries are mainly responsible for the historical GHG emissions and generally have the greatest per capita emissions."[34] The same unequal pattern of responsibilities and consequences applies to biodiversity, "declining faster than at any time in human history" as human actions now threaten a million species with extinction, driven by expanding consumption and economic activity.[35]

The primary responsibility of the few, coupled with the unjust impacts on the many, underscores the tragic inequity of the climate emergency. Although greenhouse gas emissions from anywhere contribute to climate change everywhere, different States and societies have starkly different historical and ongoing culpabilities for climate pollution.[36] Amplifying the inequity further, those with the least responsibility for the climate emergency not only face some of the greatest consequences but also have the fewest resources available to address them. In fact, human vulnerability and capacity to adapt to the climate emergency are generally inversely proportionate to historical responsibility for greenhouse gas pollution.[37]

Even within affluent countries, low-income communities have fewer resources to respond to climate disasters. For example, the Rockaways in Queens was one of the last pockets where home ownership was possible for middle-class families in New York City. But Hurricane Sandy changed the affordability equation after flooding 90,000 buildings, leaving almost 2 million people without power, and causing $19 billion in damage. The mostly Black, working-class families who owned homes in the Rockaways were pushed out when faced with skyrocketing flood insurance rates.[38]

Wealthier communities too are starting to realize that they are not immune from the damage done to nature. Commenting on yet another season of California wildfires, *New York Times* columnist Farhad Manjoo reflected that "our whole way of life is built on a series of myths – the myth of endless space, endless fuel, endless water, endless optimism, endless outward reach and endless free parking." He pointed the finger at the right target, our unsustainable lifestyle: "The fires and the blackouts aren't like the earthquakes, a natural threat we've all chosen to ignore. They are more like California's other problems, like housing affordability and homelessness and traffic – human-made catastrophes we've all chosen to ignore, connected to the larger dysfunction at the heart of our state's rot: a failure to live sustainably."[39]

In response to the inequalities of climate change, biodiversity loss, and myriad other symptoms of our failure to live sustainably, the project of inviting nature home to cities suggests two important steps. First, at a local scale, nature must be distributed equitably across the city so that the benefits of accessible nature

FIGURE 4.8   Hunts Point Riverside Park provides a waterfront oasis and passage through an industrial landscape to the Bronx River.

are available to all. Restoration of urban nature based on the needs of ecosystems will necessarily spread nature across the urban landscape, and it is critical that every community is given the tools to make that happen. Second, at a global scale, we must reduce our burden on nature. This imperative is particularly essential for communities with larger ecological footprints, and cities are well positioned to lead the way.

Local Equity: Nature Distributed across the City

From the perspective of nature, ecosystem integrity and connectivity across a community housing development are just as valuable as ecosystem integrity and connectivity across a billionaire's estate. As we have seen, the overall strength of urban nature depends on its coverage across the entire city. The benefits of doing so extend beyond strengthening ecosystems to reach the core of why our ecosystems are in peril in the first place: because we treat nature and each other as separate. To recalibrate our relationship with nature (and with each other), nature must be accessible and abundant to all. Thankfully, pioneers in doing so provide inspiring examples.

Hunts Point, in New York's South Bronx, is bounded by rivers on three sides. Yet, by the 1990s, its residents could not get to the water. Blocking their way was a toxic industrial landscape that contained two sewage treatment plants, four power plants, the world's largest food distribution centre, and waste

FIGURE 4.9   New York's High Line Park ushered in a new vision for urban parks: the conversion of decaying infrastructure (a rail line) into tentacles of accessible nature. Although inviting nature into a few neighbourhoods can spark gentrification, disparity is lessened if nature is restored in every neighbourhood.

handling facilities that accepted all of the Bronx's waste and more than 40 percent of New York's commercial waste. If that was not enough, another waste treatment plant was proposed. But lifelong resident Majora Carter had had enough. She stood up in the neighbourhood that she calls home, organized the community to successfully block new toxic facilities, and restored the polluted riverfront as a green oasis. She bravely led a grassroots effort that leveraged a $10,000 seed grant into a $3 million waterfront park – the Hunts Point Riverside Park – that became the first new park in the South Bronx in sixty years.

In a different part of New York, members of Manhattan's Chelsea community banded together in 1999 and successfully proposed saving a dormant elevated rail line snaking through their neighbourhood. Instead of tearing it down, they said that the rail line should be made into a park. The resulting High Line Park has become a celebrated Manhattan landmark that includes trees, native plant gardens, ecological information, art installations, and public events. It draws millions of visitors each year, offers fascinating views of the city, and supports over 500 species of plants.[40]

If imitation is the highest form of compliment, then the High Line Park must be flattered. Communities across the globe are trying to replicate its success. The High-Line Network consists of similar projects, including the Bentway in Toronto, the 606 in Chicago, and the Waterfront in Seattle. Frank Gehry is working with Los Angeles on its LA River project aimed at transforming the

Los Angeles "river of concrete" into infrastructure that "brings people and nature together."[41]

Not everyone was happy in Chelsea, however. Critics called the High Line Park a "tourist-clogged catwalk" and "another chapter in ... New York City's transformation into Disney World."[42] It has been criticized as a catalyst for gentrification as evidenced by luxury apartments designed by star architect Zaha Hadid and tourist development that pushed out traditional working-class establishments. Prior to its construction in 2003, adjacent residential land values were 8 percent below the Manhattan median, but by 2011 they had appreciated beyond borough-wide values.[43] Chicago's 606 project – also an elevated rail line turned into a park – similarly witnessed a 50 percent rise in the value of adjacent residential real estate during the first four years after the project began.[44]

The experiences of these projects are not surprising. A New York City study found that "land values of residential properties increase the closer they are to a park."[45] Urban forestry literature consistently finds lower levels of vegetation in low-income neighbourhoods.[46] Tree cover in five UK cities, for example, was found to be positively correlated with the social status of residents.[47] The most deprived 10 percent of English wards (local electoral districts) have five times less green space than the most affluent 20 percent of wards. In the United States, higher urban canopy cover is positively correlated with higher educational levels, older houses, larger house lots, and denser stream networks.[48] Other researchers have found that wealth, institutional investment, and social capital are the factors with strong positive correlations to protected forest lands in urban and suburban communities, and wealthier towns are more likely to have long-standing and active land trusts that effectively protect forest lands.[49]

These statistics reveal an underlying problem: "Nature has been seen as a superficial embellishment, as a luxury, rather than as an essential force that permeates the city."[50] In contrast to this misguided understanding of nature's place in cities, healthy urban nature must be distributed equitably. Nature is an urban necessity for all, not an indulgence for a few.

What about the threat of gentrification? Won't inviting nature into the city increase property values and lead to gentrification such that less advantaged people are forced to move? For example, across seven American cities studied, researchers found a positive and significant relationship between urban tree cover and median household income.[51] That is, the greater the tree cover, the higher the income – a trend also observed in Canada.[52] Greening low-income neighbourhoods can lead to higher housing prices.[53] The relationship can be the result of a feedback loop in which an abundance of tree cover increases property values and further attracts households with high incomes; those with higher incomes are then better able to afford the maintenance and enhancement of tree cover.

Conversely, the same study found that areas with low tree cover have lower property values, and residents might have less access to resources or less incentive to increase property values because they are renters or are on fixed incomes. It is not surprising, therefore, when residents in low-income neighbourhoods resist increases in tree cover to avoid gentrification and rising rents.[54]

Our response to these concerns about gentrification is threefold. First, as Majora Carter told us, ecosystem connectivity provides social connectivity.[55] This can be critical. She explained that the Hunts Point Riverside Park sparked eight additional miles of parkland along the Bronx riverbank. These parks link previously separated communities. Majora recalled that "most of us had never even talked to each other before and didn't know that we were connected by a river – because we couldn't even get to the river."[56] Thus, by connecting communities ecologically, social connectivity can follow. If nature is distributed evenly throughout the urban landscape, based on ecological boundaries, and in service of ecological integrity and connectivity, then it will not be skewed toward wealthier neighbourhoods. People from all neighbourhoods will be part of a network that binds together every corner of the city and offers access to all. However, that can only happen if nature is publicly accessible. If nature-directed stewardship solutions are integrated only into private developments, then this can lead "to a privatization of urban green space governed and managed outside the public realm, leading to a new process of spatial exclusion and control through 'green stealth.'"[57] Thus, ecological connectivity, as much as possible, must be public connectivity.

Second, everyone likes nature. Our concern should not be about what happens if nature is restored in low-income neighbourhoods; our concern should be about what will happen if it is not.[58] There is no basis for shying away from "greening the ghetto" simply because doing so shatters our damaging stereotype of low-income urban neighbourhoods. Improving the physical quality of neighbourhoods boosts the pride of residents. By increasing their self-esteem, residents can improve their lives and benefit from, rather than be displaced by, a revitalized community. Majora Carter explained it thus: "I'm not afraid that people in my community will get used to quality – I'm counting on it!"[59]

Moreover, if *all* communities have nature, then *no* community will be unique for having it. If nature is distributed equitably across the city, then its presence will no longer be something special that drives land values. Treating access to nature like other basic municipal services means that it will be available in every part of the city, and thus it will not increase relative property values. Just as garbage collection does not increase land values because it is available everywhere, so too will ubiquitous nature not drive high rent or damaging gentrification.

Third, municipal governments have a responsibility to ensure that safeguards are in place to guard against land speculation in the face of rapidly increasing property values. As Robert Hammond, a founder of the High Line Park learned, the local government "can't just build these [parks] and hope for increased property taxes." Rather, steps must be taken to keep the city accountable to the people who live there. The 11th Street Bridge Park project in Washington, DC, for example, foresaw this problem and took steps to put a local non-profit in charge of overseeing the project, including its social mission. Its plan mandates a "home buyers' club" to assist renters in buying property and a community land trust to ensure ongoing affordability.[60]

Global Equity: Reduced Burden on Nature

Cities are uniquely situated to reduce our burden on nature. To understand why, consider what green legal theorists Michael M'Gonigle and Louise Takeda posit as the "problematic" of environmental law.[61] They argue that industrialized liberal democratic state governments have a "contradictory mandate"[62] both to protect the environment and to be dependent on exploitation of the environment for economic growth. On the one hand, the state "has long been, and continues to be, the biggest developer around."[63] On the other hand, environmental law turns to the state to restrict development. Environmental law thus asks the liberal industrial state to "regulate against its own long history of economic expansion and notions of self-interest."[64] The result is "self-regulation" in which the state provides environmental protection "only to the extent that ... it does not seriously interfere with its economic priorities."[65]

Cities are uniquely motivated to take effective climate action because fossil fuel dependence costs municipalities. Auto-dependent suburban sprawl is expensive. It requires municipalities to provide new infrastructure and to assume ongoing maintenance and renewal costs. Although some up-front expenses are covered by developers, the net effect of suburban development is a significant financial cost to cities.[66] A survey of development scenarios in the United States found that dense, urban development costs one-third less in up-front infrastructure than suburban sprawl, costs less to maintain, and generates ten times as much tax revenue per acre.[67] A study of Toronto development patterns found that a "more compact and efficient development pattern" would save the city $500 million per year in capital and maintenance expenses.[68] The costs of sprawl are important to Canadian cities already facing a municipal infrastructure deficit of $388 billion.[69] A recent study indicates "that nearly 35% of municipal roads, municipal buildings, sport and recreation facilities, and public transit assets are in urgent need of attention and at risk of rapid deterioration, thereby increasing the risk of service disruption."[70]

Cities are also motivated to address the climate emergency because of their vulnerability and the high costs of adaptation. Most of the world's cities are built along rivers and coastlines, making them especially vulnerable to climate change. The global value of urban assets exposed to sea level rise and storm surge is estimated at $3 trillion or 5 percent of global GDP.[71] These high potential costs helped to motivate New York City to take legal action against oil companies for its climate change adaptation costs.[72] Cities such as New York and Vancouver now have elaborate climate change adaptation plans in place.[73]

When considered in the context of our current spending on the status quo, the financial investments required to invite nature home are a bargain. The International Monetary Fund estimates, for example, that the global fossil fuel industry received subsidies of $7 trillion (about 7 percent of total GDP) in 2022 alone – 78 percent of which consisted of undercharging for environmental costs and forgone consumption taxes.[74] In another example, by 2030 global spending on infrastructure will exceed $25 trillion each year.[75] We need to redirect some of these unsustainable investments into green infrastructure and a dense urban nature with carbon-free transportation alternatives.

Creative options abound. For example, an investment in a green space can be made without paying the full cost of acquiring land. Toronto's Rail Deck Park project – a proposal to cover the rail corridor between Bathurst Street and Blue Jays Way with a new twenty-acre urban park – is projected to cost far less than the real estate value of twenty acres of land in downtown Toronto.[76]

High income cities, in aggregate, have a massive ecological footprint and are enormous emitters of carbon pollution. Cities account for 71 to 76 percent of global carbon dioxide emissions associated with end uses of energy.[77] Urban GHG emissions (of which energy use is only a part) have been estimated to represent 37 to 49 percent of total emissions in one study and up to 70 percent or more in other studies.[78] On a per-capita basis, however, urbanites have significantly lower emissions than rural residents.[79] As one moves along the rural to urban gradient, and from less dense to more dense parts of a city, per-capita emissions drop markedly.[80]

In addition to already being leaps and bounds ahead in terms of lower per-capita emissions, cities have a wide range of effective strategies to reduce carbon pollution further. The key drivers behind emissions from cities are "density, land-use mix, connectivity, and accessibility," factors almost exclusively controlled by local governments.[81] Measures such as urban containment boundaries, mixed-use development zoning, infill and density incentives, transit-oriented communities, green building requirements, and community energy initiatives all contribute to an "enormous opportunity for cost-effective action [on climate change]."[82]

For these reasons, cities are on the front lines of adapting to and mitigating the climate emergency.[83] Waves of municipal climate action over the past two decades have included cities in the Global North and Global South, cities of all sizes, both pioneers and followers. Urban climate change innovation is taking place in all parts of the world, not just in North America and Europe, and city networks are taking action through shared technical support, voluntary commitments, and performance registries.[84] For example, the Compact of Mayors is "a cooperative effort among mayors and city officials to pledge to reduce greenhouse gas emissions, track progress and prepare for the impacts of climate change."[85] The Compact provides for cities what the Secretariat of the UN Framework Convention on Climate Change provides for sovereign states: a platform for making public commitments to reduce greenhouse gas pollution.

Cities have a number of advantages. Local responses can be initiated faster, draw from a wide range of potential actions, and be combined with complementary policies that have climate benefits.[86] Local governments can serve as laboratories for experimentation on climate emergency policies, and their initiatives can provide focal points for linkages and coalitions.[87] Cities have become the natural sites for sustainable development and the best hope for its achievement.[88] Linking climate action to sustainable development in cities can democratize efforts by engaging people directly in choices about competing policies and thus allow for engagement with social justice, development, and equity rather than simply offering climate-myopic responses that consider only GHG reductions.

Minimizing our demand on ecosystem processes is essential. As UBC Professor Emeritus William Rees challenges us, "if your 'solution' does not result in an absolute reduction in energy and material consumption and waste production, then it is part of the problem."[89] This is so partly because of the "rebound effect" (or Khazzoom-Brookes postulate), which predicts that gains from making products more energy efficient can be overwhelmed by increased use of the same products as they are embraced. For example, an energy-efficient car might be driven faster or more frequently for the same price as driving a gas-guzzling car slower and less often, resulting in no energy or pollution reduction benefits. In the words of J. Daniel Khazzoom, "increasing the fuel economy of new vehicles leaves the emission rate of the regulated pollutants unchanged."[90]

It is essential to remember this dynamic. As we restore nature in urban areas, and the benefits of healthy ecosystems emerge (including cleaning air and water, supporting pollination, providing habitat to increase biodiversity, and sequestering and storing carbon), we must not squander those benefits by enlarging the ecological footprints of our cities. As we improve the health of nature in urban areas, we need to secure these gains by asking less of nature.

In 1978, we crossed the threshold at which overall human demands for eco-system benefits became greater than what the biosphere can provide over the long term. Our current demands are 50 percent higher than this threshold (and still rising). Providing more ecosystems with natural character in the form of healthy nature in urban areas contributes to the need for more ecosystem benefits, but is only half of the equation. We need to simultaneously reduce our demands on the very nature that we are restoring. As Professor Robert Gibson suggests, we need to ask whether a particular strategy is "helping us move closer to a desirable and resilient future, or is it just *slowing* our descent into ever deepening unsustainability?"[91]

Unfortunately, many urban strategies aimed at sustainability assume that we can continue to pursue our unlimited material desires as long as we do so in a "green" fashion. New Urbanist pioneer Andrés Duany, for example, asserts that an approach to urban sustainability should avoid "the imposition of austerities and inconveniences" because "Americans will not voluntarily tolerate suffering."[92] What qualifies as "suffering," however, is relative to one's expectations and is tempered in the face of climate disasters and pandemics. In our view, meaningful suffering does not arise from forgoing sprawling greenfield development, reducing fossil fuel consumption, or taking responsibility for our own ecological debt.

Restoration efforts will be more successful if we first reduce demands on ecosystems. Researchers have pointed out, for example, that stream restoration efforts need to include "controls on fertilizers and toxicants, septic and sewer management policies, dam management policies, water use regulations, and road and utility crossing regulations" rather than just the riparian and in-stream restoration activities themselves.[93] As one stream restoration researcher explains, "the first and most critical step in ecological restoration is passive restoration, the cessation of those anthropogenic activities that are causing degradation or preventing recovery ... Unfortunately, structural additions and active manipulations are frequently undertaken without halting degrading land use activities or allowing sufficient time for natural recovery to occur."[94]

Green building innovations can help reduce our demand on healthy ecosystem processes. For example, green roofs reduce carbon emissions by lowering the demand for air-conditioning equipment and sequester carbon through the photosynthetic activity of the plants.[95] Rain barrels and rooftop collection systems, greywater on-site recycling, and low-flow fixtures all reduce the demand for potable water from off-site. Sewage treatment at the building scale makes effluent available for on-site uses, such as irrigation and toilet flushing, and avoids the nutrient-rich discharges associated with centralized systems.[96] Building and landscape strategies to reduce light pollution help birds and nocturnal wildlife survive in the urban environment.

Bringing nature into our cities also helps to reduce demand by offering urban dwellers local experiences with nature without requiring automobile use. Connecting greenbelts and other large patches of urban nature can transform them from greenbelts into "green cloak[s]" that provide direct contact with the very nature that our sustainability efforts are trying to restore.[97] The resulting fabric of nature in urban areas can be used to support local activities and food production and strengthen a local community economy as an alternative to increased energy-dependent consumption.[98]

Density

Increasing human density is the most effective action that cities can take to address climate change. High density has been called "the most important factor influencing fuel consumption and CO_2 emissions" and "a sustainability silver bullet."[99] Significant research has shown that "density remains the core strategy for achieving emission reduction targets" and that "higher densities provide a foundation for urban form characteristics that together reduce a community's GHG emissions."[100] In short, centralized cities are generally associated with lower carbon emissions, whereas decentralized cities have higher carbon emissions.[101]

FIGURE 4.10 Nature makes density work next to the Promenade Plantée in Paris. Rather than competing for space, nature joins other amenities to enrich the urban bargain that justifies density, blurs the line between public and private, and connects people across the city.

FIGURE 4.11   Density in Manhattan is softened by nature woven into narrow streets, drawing people out to shared spaces and invigorating the built environment.

Greater New York City, for example, accounts for the largest share of driving-related carbon dioxide of any urban area in the United States. But on a per-capita basis, New York City has the lowest rate of driving-related carbon dioxide in the country.[102] Doubling the density of the 125 largest urbanized areas in the United States would cause a 48 percent reduction in carbon dioxide emissions from travel and a 35 percent reduction in emissions from residential energy consumption.[103] These reductions are particularly compelling because household travel and residential energy use account for 42 percent of carbon dioxide emissions.[104] A similar study of Quebec City found that "land use diversity and residential density significantly lower GHG emissions."[105]

Density leads to lower carbon pollution in at least two ways. First, dense urban forms have lower energy consumption and therefore lower carbon emissions. Detached housing types, typical of low-density communities, use more energy than attached housing types.[106] One study found that comparable families living in single-family homes require 54 percent more energy for heating, and 26 percent more energy for cooling, than those living in multi-family buildings (and the increases in energy use are only partly explained by the larger homes).[107] Thus, dense communities consist of the types of residences that use less energy and therefore produce less carbon pollution.

Moreover, dense urban communities – consisting of a variety of urban forms and mixed land uses – are celebrated as beautiful, rewarding, and healthy places to live. Vancouver, with a mix of single-family homes and more dense townhouses and condominiums, is the densest city in Canada.[108] Yet New York, with more apartments and other attached residential structures, is twice as dense as Vancouver.[109] And Paris is twice as dense as New York.[110] But as Majora Carter pointed out, "nobody goes to Paris and says 'this is an ugly, horrible city.'"[111] Rather, density can create a wonderful place to live, one with a distinctly urban form.

Second, density allows for transportation choices other than the automobile. High rates of automobile use in the United States are largely the result of urban development: "Americans drive so much because we have given ourselves little alternative."[112] More precisely, municipalities have allowed developers to build in a way that gives us few alternatives to driving. Studies have shown that a lack of land-use regulation is strongly associated with higher rates of carbon pollution.[113] But with a dense urban form, public transit, walking, biking, and mode-sharing become viable. People drive 20 to 40 percent less in areas with compact development.[114] At the risk of pointing out the obvious, cities such as New York and Paris have extensive public transportation networks because they have sufficient population density. One estimate is that rapid transit requires roughly 150 people per hectare to be viable.[115]

Green space does not conflict with density. Rather, as Majora Carter explained to us, it makes density work.[116] It ameliorates the negative aspects of density.[117] Like all urban amenities – from coffee shops, art galleries, and restaurants to public pianos, daycares, and park benches – ecological amenities make the city a better place to live. When shared spaces are attractive, people want to be close to them. When the city outside one's front door offers so much, there is less emphasis on expansive real estate inside one's private residence. A compelling "third space," the space between home and work, makes smaller private spaces acceptable.

FIGURE 4.12   Patrick Blanc's L'Oasis d'Aboukir green wall in Paris showcases the potential for incorporating nature into the built environment. Combined with green roofs, repurposed laneways, and wildlife corridors, green walls are key to restoration networks in dense urban environments.

Increasing density is not as challenging as some assert. In most cities, more people can fit within the existing urban boundaries. Densification can be achieved by infilling (constructing new buildings in areas not previously built up), by building up former industrial sites, and by replacing low-density residential development with high-density buildings.[118] For example, Metro Vancouver's Residential Development Capacity Study found that the existing development capacity in the city is 42 percent more than the expected demand over the next thirty years.[119] A study in Toronto found that converting just 1 percent of the city's single-family homes into multi-family buildings would create approximately 44,000 new housing units.[120] Believing that there is no longer a justification for low-density housing in cities, Oregon in 2019 became the first US state to ban zoning for exclusively single-family homes in municipalities of more than 10,000 people.[121] In 2023, Vancouver opened up low-density residential zones to multiplex development.[122]

Rather than relying on towers for density, Cherise Burda, Executive Director of City Building Institute at TMU, calls for "distributed density," which means "distributing low, medium and higher residential densities throughout urbanized areas."[123] The urban form includes mid-rise buildings along main streets and transit corridors, walk-up apartment buildings and townhouses, redevelopment of plazas and underutilized spaces at arterial nodes into mixed-use communities, and conversion of single-family homes into multi-family buildings, laneways, and backyard suites. Doing so allows for the benefits of density to be spread through the city: "Distributed density can make our communities and region more healthy, livable and affordable for residents, while saving energy, protecting our natural environment and agricultural land, and helping to mitigate climate change."[124] Burda explained to us that "it's not about how dense we make our neighbourhoods; it's about how we make them dense. On the ground analysis shows that we can accommodate needed housing within

FIGURE 4.13 Vancouver's Olympic Village blends waterfront, high-density, mixed-used living with nature at multiple scales, from pedestrian-free groundcover to a restored shoreline around a new island. | *Credit:* Melinda Markey.

our already urbanized footprint without having to rely on 'tall and sprawl' development."[125]

As we fit more people into urban boundaries (increase density), it is possible to design a built environment that actually creates green space.[126] A study of five UK cities found that "at any given density, there is a substantial scope for maximizing ecological performance."[127] Vancouver's high-rise neighbourhoods, for example, have more space for urban forest than its neighbourhoods with large detached houses. The large mature trees planted decades ago in Vancouver's West End have matured to form thick canopies over roads and around multi-unit homes.[128] Skyscrapers built in the 1960s, 1970s, and 1980s had smaller footprints that allowed for more green spaces.[129] Retrofitting these buildings with green roofs and walls, some of which can provide food and all of which will purify water and cool the local climate, will result in even more room for nature.

Studies have confirmed that density and increased green space are not at odds. Per-capita parkland is less in New York City (nineteen square metres) than in Toronto (twenty-eight square metres), but the overall portion of parkland is much greater.[130] Over 21 percent of New York City is parkland, compared with only 12.7 percent in Toronto.[131]

COVID-19 caused a knee-jerk reaction against density – a reaction that the *New York Times* called "dangerously misguided" since "density remains the best way to limit the impact of humans on the environment" and because our dense cities "best enable us to care for each other."[132] Put differently, pandemics are no justification for abandoning density because

> density makes mass transit possible. It allows for more affordable housing. It creates environments where people can walk and where children can find playgrounds. It enables us to pool risk. It supports big public hospitals and stronger safety nets. It allows us to curb climate emissions, which present public health problems of an entirely different kind. Crucially, it enables the kind of redundancies that make communities more resilient during disasters.[133]

As has been pointed out frequently, "urbanites live longer and healthier lives than their counterparts in rural areas," and urban density "supports faster emergency-response times, better hospital staffing, and a greater concentration of intensive-care beds and other health-care resources."[134] In any case, the spread of COVID-19 cannot be explained by density alone. In New York City, for example, the highest rates of infection were in "suburban-like" areas such as Staten Island and the far edges of Brooklyn and Queens; Manhattan, in contrast, had the lowest infection rate, mirroring trends in other countries.[135]

The City experienced a 360 percent increase in mortality during the initial COVID-19 outbreak, whereas Bergamo province in Italy saw a 500 percent increase in mortality even though its density is only one-fifth of New York's.[136]

Yet concerns about social distancing in dense urban areas catalyzed conversations about returning urban spaces dominated by cars to people. Some cities, such as Seattle, permanently banned cars from certain streets, and others have gone further in reimagining what car-free streets might look like. UBC professor Patrick Condon, for example, proposes revitalizing plans for a network of blue-green arteries in Vancouver that would replace some streets with green infrastructure corridors to allow space for social distancing. As Condon asks, "wouldn't this be nice now? A capacious walkway down the middle of what used to be pavement prowled by cars, bordered by grassy swales, plenty of room for kids on bikes, dog walkers, ambling seniors, everyone cruising at their own pace and a safe social distance without feeling like they have to dodge each other."[137] As Farhad Manjoo has pointed out, we would be wise to "enshrine in our urban code a truth that has too long been ignored: Cities should be built for people, not cars."[138]

In short, we are called by a moral imperative to increase the density of our urban areas (as the most effective way for cities to reduce per-capita carbon emissions) while simultaneously increasing the green spaces that make density livable. This contribution to reducing the burden on nature is not only effective and necessary but also achievable as witnessed by the cities doing exactly that.

HEALTHY CITIES

> *The future of humanity lies in cities.*
>
> – Kofi Annan[139]

What will it look like if we invite nature home while ensuring equity and density? In the rest of this chapter, we offer a vision of some of the outcomes – some of the features – that appear on the ground after the process of inviting nature home. It is a glimpse of nature-first cities, those with healthy nature, communities, and economies.

Techniques for Healthy Urban Ecosystems

For those who have looked at their hometowns on Google Earth, it is probably no surprise to learn that building roofs cover 20 to 25 percent of cities.[140] Clearly, significant opportunities are available if these surfaces can become green roofs that provide ecological connectivity. Thankfully, green roofs are widely recognized for their significant ecological and economic benefits, including wildlife habitat, precipitation management, reduced energy use, urban cooling, and mitigation of noise and air pollution.[141]

It has been shown that "over time, substantial biodiversity can take hold on green rooftops, and in some cities ecological roofs can even help in re-establishing populations of endangered and threatened species."[142] Green roofs have been shown to maintain high functional diversity of arthropod communities, to be used by nesting birds and native avian communities, and to offer opportunities for native plants.[143] They reduce runoff into storm sewers by absorbing and filtering rainfall, significant portions of which evaporate or transpire back into the atmosphere by plants. And, in the process, the plants clean the air and sequester carbon dioxide.

Green roofs contribute to returning the local climate and air quality to pre-urbanization conditions, in turn assisting in the restoration of native plants and ecological communities. They have been shown to improve the microclimate, minimize the heat island effect, lower the building envelope temperature, reduce energy consumption and peak cooling load of the building, control sound pollution, absorb gaseous pollutants, and remove particulates from the air.[144]

The potential to reduce roof surface temperature is dramatic: up to fourteen degrees Celsius in Cairo and seven degrees Celsius in Paris.[145] This cooling effect can spread across the entire urban area. This has important health implications since excessive heat exposure contributes to 8,000 premature deaths annually in the United States, a figure that exceeds the number of mortalities resulting from hurricanes, lightning strikes, tornadoes, floods, and earthquakes combined.[146] Canada has also recorded increasing levels of mortality linked to heat, with 595 deaths in British Columbia alone in 2021.[147]

England's Green Infrastructure Partnership, established to help communities adopt green infrastructure projects, is seen as a strategy that will attract new business, increase property value, promote sustainable development, and create new employment opportunities.[148] The Toronto Green Roof Infrastructure Research and Demonstration Project, a three-year study of green roof potential, found that putting green roofs on only 6 percent of the roofs in Toronto would reduce its overall heat island effect by one degree Celsius, reduce greenhouse gas emissions by over two megatons annually, reduce smog alerts by up to 10 percent, improve air quality, and retain over 3.5 million cubic metres of stormwater each year. Building a storage tank for that volume of water would cost $60 million and provide no additional benefits.[149]

At the building level, green infrastructure and nature are broadly understood to provide long-term financial benefits for the owners. For example, William McDonough + Partners calculated that the green roof that they designed for GAP Corporation's headquarters in California, compared with a conventional

FIGURE 4.14   A rooftop farm on the Boston Medical Center yields thousands of pounds of fresh produce from twenty-five crops, helps to feed patients, and reminds us of our dependence on nature. | *Source:* Boston Medical Center.

roofing system, would pay for itself in eleven years through annual energy and operational savings.[150] The Village Homes project in Davis, California, utilized a series of "green fingers" to collect stormwater and provide community green spaces, along with fruit trees and landscaping with edible plants. The natural stormwater system saved the project approximately $600 per home.[151] The shading of buildings by trees has been shown to reduce cooling energy costs, and empirical evidence from the United States reveals an approximate 20 percent increase in property values from adjacency to a passive park.[152] Productivity returns to the workplace are also evident since studies of office workers have found that those with views of nature experienced less frustration and showed more work enthusiasm than those without such views.[153]

In Basel, Switzerland, which has greened over 15 percent of its roofs and has over a million square metres of rooftop greenery, green roofs are mandatory on all new flat-roofed buildings, and wildlife habitat needs to be considered in their design.[154] It seems to be working: a study of green roofs in six Swiss cities found ninety-one species of beetle, which inspired the authors to conclude that the roofs provide "ecological conditions of high conservation interest."[155] Copenhagen has similarly adopted a policy requiring green roofs for all new buildings with roof slopes of less than thirty degrees, and Toronto's Green Roof Bylaw requires green roofs on new buildings of 2,000 square metres or more.[156] Germany adds over 13 million square metres of green roof coverage each year, and 10 percent of its buildings now have green roofs.[157] The largest green roof in Canada covers 2.4 hectares on top of Vancouver's Convention Centre, features 400,000 indigenous plants, and supports an apiary that produces fifty-five kilograms of honey each year.[158] Boston Medical Center's organic rooftop vegetable garden (p. 97), pollinated by two onsite beehives that also furnish honey, produces between 5,000 and 7,000 pounds of organic food per year fed to patients, staff, and low-income people.[159]

Why stop with the roof? Green walls are vertical gardens retrofitted onto existing walls and increasingly designed as integrated components of building envelopes. In some cases, the plants grow without soil in hydroponic systems that drip nutrient-enriched water down the wall, and the excess water not used by plants is pumped up and recirculated.[160] Some walls even incorporate a pool at the base that includes fish or amphibians. Urban designers are quickly embracing these vertical landscapes as "representing a conceptual shift toward a synthesis between landscape and architecture" and offer the chance to embed building facades "within emergent, active, and responsive skins."[161]

Green walls have been shown to provide habitat for invertebrates as well as nesting, food, and shelter for birds.[162] The vertical gardens of Patrick Blanc (see Figure 4.12) are visually captivating, structurally diverse, and able to fill voids of all sizes in the urban landscape. At the extreme end of the vertical scale, Blanc's One Central Park residential tower project in Sydney is a 135-metre vertical garden designed with plant species that can withstand high winds at the top of the tower.[163] Europe's largest living wall, on London's Mint Hotel Tower, covers 350 square metres (3,767 square feet) and contains 184,000 plants.[164]

What can be used to connect isolated green walls and green roofs? Answers are plentiful. For example, an "officeduct" is a building designed with an urban wildlife overpass on the roof such that all the necessary functions of infrastructure, building, and ecology are able to coexist.[165] Other approaches rest on designing buildings that invite wildlife into them as opposed to treating wildlife as a nuisance and blurring the lines between indoors and outdoors so that people can live and work in both.[166]

Some designers have attempted to merge the built environment with the living vegetative environment. One such conceptual innovation, entitled "Launch," is "a combination of living and nonliving systems: a progression of vegetal growth and its correspondent structural scaffolding that is required to guide the plant's form and trajectory until it reaches stability."[167] The "scaffold" can be a transitional structure (i.e., biodegradable), it can be permanent, or it can be designed to evolve symbiotically. In some cases, the plants will either graft eventually with the inorganic structure in a process of "allofusion" or, "over the course of many years, the architecture and living materials are envisioned to swap structural roles: the architecture recedes, while conceding structural support to the living materials it originally supported."[168]

The visionary "StairScraper" is a vertical stack of cantilevered single garden houses, spiralling up around a central column so that each level has substantial sunlight exposure in support of extensive and stepped gardens reaching skyward. The designers explain that it "represents the idea of understanding a wider habitat, a system of complex social relationships with the environment in search of enjoyment of life, mixing different ambits, different uses."[169] A StairScraper would offer significant density as well as far more green space than would be possible were the entire building lot made into a grade-level park.

Singapore requires developers to replace any green space lost during development with vegetated elements such as green roofs, green walls, sky terraces, communal gardens, and urban farmland.[170] A landscape replacement area is calculated. The total softscape must be at least 30 percent to 40 percent of the landscape replacement area, and the total leaf area must be three to four times the size of the development site area.[171] The latter requirement is determined using a green plot ratio formula, and the municipality provides values for various plant species.

Roads offer significant opportunities for the restoration of nature.[172] Many cities are experimenting with strategies for integrating nature into the one-quarter of the urban landscape otherwise given to vehicles. These strategies include providing tree canopy over streets, repurposing sections of roads and alleys, and making road surfaces permeable.

Given the ubiquitous impacts that they have on nature, streets must become "places that harbor native plants and biodiversity, that collect and treat stormwater, and where pedestrians can experience intimate contact with nature as part of their daily routine."[173] Tree corridors can connect urban patches and peri-urban and suburban areas.[174]

Trees along streets have been shown to provide connectivity for a variety of species, including small mammals, birds, and insects.[175] These trees help manage stormwater, diminish noise, sequester and store carbon, and capture airborne pollutants.[176] The trees also mitigate the heat island effect – the fact that cities are generally warmer than the areas around them – by significantly reducing urban temperatures.[177] In fact, "nothing ameliorates the heat island effect as well as plants."[178] This cooling effect occurs because plants intercept the sun's energy, some of which is reflected but most of which is used in photosynthesis.[179] Through evapotranspiration, water is drawn up from the soil and released into the atmosphere through the stomata in leaves – a process that cools both the leaves and the surrounding climate.[180]

FIGURE 4.15   Permeable pavement on this trail in East Vancouver allows rainfall to disperse and enter the soil below rather than concentrating runoff, yet it still provides a stable pathway for people of all mobility levels.

Many cities recognize the benefits of tree-lined streets and have set goals for canopy cover or aggregate tree population on both public and private lands. Vancouver, for example, has embraced a range of canopy cover goals (9 percent for industrial lots, 15 percent for commercial areas, and 33 percent for single-family residential lots) in order to achieve its overall goal of 28 percent canopy cover.[181] New York City met its goal of planting an additional million trees within a decade.[182] Singapore's "City in a Garden" strategy has led to 2.9 million trees along its 6,000 kilometres of roads.[183]

Reducing the space dedicated to roads can happen through a dual strategy of increasing alternative transit options (so that the demand for road space is reduced) and narrowing or repurposing streets and alleys. In a well-established approach to sharing road space with nature, for centuries the German city of Freiburg has had a network of exposed narrow streams, collectively named the

FIGURE 4.16   Stepping from the heat of Manhattan's 1st Avenue to the cover of these mature trees that screen Peter Cooper Village, the temperature drops, a cool breeze fills the lungs with verdant air, and the sound of birds replaces that of traffic.

Bächle, that run through channels along urban streets. With such outcomes in mind, the Global Designing Cities Initiative provides guidance for replacing portions of street surfaces in cities with water features and stormwater management features.

Set at lower elevations than the remaining road surfaces, "rain gardens" and "bioswales" employ permeable soils and vegetation to hold and treat stormwater runoff. They are usually located close to the source of the stormwater runoff, and the biomass is used to retain nutrients and pollutants. Sunken rain gardens allow runoff to pool and then infiltrate deep into constructed and native soils below.[184] When linked together into tiered and open channels, the rain gardens become bioswales designed to attenuate and treat defined volumes of water. These features can reduce nitrate levels in the water by up to 33 percent, phosphorus by up to 60 percent, and fecal coliform by up to 100 percent.[185]

Multi-layered vegetation is critical. When precipitation falls on these natural layers (such as in old-growth forests), the rain or snow is first intercepted by large, tall, old trees with millions of leaves and collections of small plants, mosses, and lichens on their branches and trunks. The water gently drips through the upper forest canopy, filters down through the intermediate and shorter trees, and eventually reaches the shrubs, herbs, mosses, and lichens, which catch the water and slowly release it to the forest floor, where it percolates into the soil through another layer of organic matter. Filtered by the soil, the water eventually emerges in streams, ponds, and wetlands.

During this process, approximately 30 to 50 percent of the precipitation sublimates or evaporates back into the atmosphere, allowing for the broad distribution of water across local, regional, and continental landscapes. As the filtration of precipitation is slowed by multi-layered vegetation, soils have time to drain partially, ultimately allowing them to absorb more moisture. Large fallen trees decaying on the forest floor are the natural water storage and filtration system in old-growth forests. Decayed wood holds many times more water than the same volume of most mineral soils, acting as hydrological reservoirs and water purification plants for hundreds of years. The overall result is regulation of the energy, volume, and timing of water released from the atmosphere to terrestrial and aquatic ecosystems, providing a constant source of moisture – not too much during wet periods, not too little during dry periods – and avoiding surface runoff. By restoring (and mimicking) much of this multi-layered vegetation in urban areas, green infrastructure can recreate some of these vital hydrological processes.

Multi-layered vegetation also creates a cool environment that moderates the climate across the landscape. As they grow older and larger, trees continue to grow at significant rates.[186] The larger the tree, the more photosynthesis is carried out, and the greater the sequestration of carbon, stored in leaves, branches, trunks, roots, snags, fallen trees, and soil organic matter. For example, a 450-year-old Douglas-fir forest stores more than double the amount of carbon stored in a 60-year-old Douglas-fir forest.[187]

Where roads remain, "varied wildlife passages (tunnels, pipes, underpasses, and overpasses) operating for animal movement" can ameliorate their impacts.[188] The Compton Road vegetated overpass in Brisbane, Australia, for example, spans a four-lane road and provides connectivity for mammals, birds, reptiles, and amphibians between two urban green space patches.[189] Edmonton, Alberta, provides guidelines aimed at maintaining connectivity and reducing genetic isolation while reducing conflict between humans and wildlife.[190] In support of the guidelines, Edmonton provides information about the diets, habitats, and home ranges of certain species.[191]

FIGURE 4.17   Multi-layered vegetation interrupts rainfall; allows water to drip through levels of trees, shrubs, and groundcover; and provides soil with time to absorb, hold, and disperse the stormwater into the natural water movement network. Each layer of vegetation offers distinct habitats, increased biodiversity, and linkages for species' travel.

The hidden cousins of roads are urban alleys, waiting to be reborn as connectivity corridors and other forms of urban nature. Montreal's Ruelles Vertes program has converted more than 360 of the city's alleys into verdant corridors, gardens, and community gathering grounds.[192] Chicago, the "alley capital of America," with over 3,500 acres of paved alleys, launched a "green alley program" complete with a handbook to involve citizens and adjacent landowners.[193] The focus is on addressing precipitation (i.e., stormwater) management through the use of permeable pavement, rain barrels, detention ponds, bioswales, trees, and other vegetation.[194]

The roots of green infrastructure in cities date back to the late nineteenth century in Boston, where Frederick Law Olmsted created an "emerald necklace" system of "linear parks and flood management features such as wetlands, ponds and river channel enhancements that formed an extensive, contiguous greenway right through the heart of Boston."[195] Today green infrastructure is understood to include "components such as hydrologically functional landscapes, bioretention, infiltration, bioswales, greenways, rainwater harvesting,

FIGURE 4.18 With roughly 25 percent of cities dedicated to vehicles, individual laneways offer starting places to reclaim spaces for nature and people. Montreal's Ruelles Vertes program illustrates the potential to create a sense of place, incorporate green infrastructure, and facilitate density. | *Source:* Valérian Mazataud.

pervious pavement, and neighbourhood-scale constructed wetlands, storm-water detention, retention, and infiltration systems."[196] These approaches mimic natural processes and employ a variety of techniques to retain, detain, percolate, and evaporate stormwater.

Studies in Guelph, Ontario, suggest that "landscape integrity could be increased, urban wildlife habitat enhanced, and opportunities for residential non-consumptive wildlife recreation improved" by designing and incorporating urban stormwater management facilities into a network of greenways. The ecosystem benefits provided by green infrastructure are sweeping: "shade and cooling, water cleansing and management, noise abatement, light diffusion, wind protection, air filtering, soil conditioning and habitat for wildlife."[197] In a climate-changing world, nature's infrastructure offers shelter from warmer temperatures, stronger winds, increased flooding, and altered rainfall.[198]

Green infrastructure can improve aquatic habitat by providing cleaner water to ponds, streams, rivers, and lakes in our cities. These NDS solutions filter water by removing heavy metals, petroleum products, and fecal coliforms. The quality of the water flowing into aquatic habitats is determined not only by the size and composition of natural buffers but also by the extent of adjacent impervious surfaces. Studies have concluded that riparian cover only acts effectively as a buffer zone in urban areas with less than 45 percent imperviousness.[199] An evaluation of the impact of urbanization on stream habitat found that the amount of connected impervious surfaces in an urban watershed is the best measure for predicting the diversity and density of fish populations in urban aquatic habitat and concluded that fish require the watershed to have no more than 12 percent impervious surfaces as well as an undeveloped riparian buffer.[200] Other studies have pegged the threshold at 10 percent impervious surfaces.[201] But the overall conclusion is that reducing impervious surfaces is essential.

With abundant evidence that precipitation/stormwater management and water filtration are best handled by nature, municipalities large and small have embraced green infrastructure. New York City's Green Infrastructure Plan, for example, calls for capturing "the first inch of rainfall on 10% of the impervious areas" – a plan projected to save the city $1.5 billion over twenty years.[202] Since Philadelphia launched its Green City, Clean Waters program in 2011, a combination of public investments, incentive programs, design manuals, and regulations has resulted in a green infrastructure network that keeps over 1.5 billion gallons of polluted water out of rivers and creeks.[203] The project has an ultimate goal of reducing stormwater pollution by 85 percent. The SW 12th Avenue Green Street project in Portland includes a "networked sidewalk stormwater system" that connects a series of embedded planters designed so that water flows into one planter and, when it is full, out to the street, along the curb, and into the next planter, allowing for the use of smaller rain gardens collectively able to handle significant volumes of stormwater.[204] Seattle ran a "street edge alternatives" pilot "designed to provide drainage that more closely mimics the natural landscape prior to development than traditional piped systems."[205] The project was an unmitigated success: stormwater leaving the street was reduced by 99 percent.[206]

Many cities are revisiting the concept of a park in order to establish more natural ecosystem composition, structure, and function. "Ecology parks" seek to apply ecological landscape design principles to urban open spaces. In a pioneering demonstration project, Pollution Probe developed Toronto's ecology park in 1987. London's Olympic parkland, the largest new park development in the city since Victorian times, is designed to promote sustainable living through a focus on growing food (orchards and urban farming) and creating wildlife habitats, including wetlands, wooded valleys, and other areas.[207]

The search for new urban patches and corridors of nature has led some cities to their abandoned industrial lands. For example, Seattle's Gas Works Park folded the remnants of an old factory into an iconic urban park.[208] New York's

FIGURE 4.19   Sprouting above wood piles near the final destination of the *Titanic*'s rescued passengers, New York's Little Island at Pier 55 transforms a former commercial and industrial site into an innovative pocket of nature.

commercial piers made way for an elevated park, Little Island, floating above the Hudson River.

In other cases, inoperative infrastructure has been repurposed to support creative new elements of urban nature. The Promenade Plantée in Paris, the world's first elevated park (and inspiration for New York's High Line Park), opened in 1989 after the repurposing of the former Bastille Railway Line and offers over four kilometres of pedestrian walkway surrounded by trees, plants, and pools of water.[209]

Urban green spaces are important refuges for native biodiversity. Prevalent and natural systems, well connected across the city, create wildlife corridors so that species can move around safely.[210] Urban woodland patches are particularly important for supporting a diversity of bird species.[211] Within the woodlands, bird species richness is associated with spatial heterogeneity of vegetation, complex vertical structure, and diverse species of vegetation.[212]

Urban riparian areas are also particularly important for biodiversity. Studies have found that urban protected networks that rely significantly on riparian habitat are better for providing habitat continuity and quality for a variety of organisms.[213] Parks in San Francisco, for example, support a higher abundance of bumblebees than parks outside the city, and populations of the common frog have increased in urban areas in spite of declines elsewhere.[214] Of the sixty-nine known species of mammal in Sweden, forty-three reproduce in or near Stockholm.[215] Fourteen percent of the British fox population (some 33,000 foxes) live in cities.[216]

A number of species have modified their behaviour in order to succeed in urban areas. Successful urban coyotes have switched from a diurnal to a nocturnal lifestyle.[217] Birds, such as the great tit (*Parus major*), have modified their song in urban areas in order to communicate in noisy locations, and some plants in fragmented urban landscapes have switched to local seed dispersal strategies.[218] Overall, successful urban animals tend to live longer than their wild cousins because they have plenty to eat, face fewer predators, and are better able to survive winter.[219]

Yet it has been observed that cities currently contain "high proportions of exotic species, distinctive disturbance regimes, few top predators, and elevated levels of nutrients and pollutants."[220] These characteristics do not replicate natural ecosystem character but instead favour exploiter and adapter species. Cities are notorious for having significant rat populations, often at densities of more than 3,000 per square kilometre.[221] New York City alone has some 28 million rats. Three bird species – the house sparrow, the European starling, and the rock dove – have adapted exceptionally well to living in cities worldwide, and urban areas tend to have higher bird abundances than adjacent exurban or rural areas, although only a few species contribute to the majority of this abundance.[222]

FIGURE 4.20 Promenade Plantée (or Coulée verte René-Dumont), a converted nineteenth-century viaduct that has matured into a lush sanctuary swooping above Parisian streets, inspired New York's High Line Park and other innovative urban parks.

FIGURE 4.21 Several nesting bald eagles find habitat and prey in Vancouver's Stanley Park. Large anchors of nature in cities serve to support species that venture widely and play key roles in urban biodiversity. | *Source:* Scott Yamaoka.

Our vision is that cities will support endemic rather than exotic species through connectivity and restoration of the natural ecosystem composition and structure that existed before the city did.

Healthy Communities

As we explained in Chapter 2, cities without nature are cities with elevated health risks:

> When the city evokes a sense of disorientation, confusion, stress, or apprehension; when building indiscriminately gorges on resources; when social inequalities feed discrimination; when cultural prejudice breeds hatred; when inappropriate technologies are wasteful and heavy-handed; and economics are short-sighted, and when a sense of place is at risk, we implicitly know that this "unnatural" place is not one to which we belong.[223]

Richard Louv calls nature the "antidote."[224] Studies have proven him right. There is an overwhelming body of evidence connecting the health and vibrancy of urban nature with human health and well-being.

Nature is literally the best medicine for many of our physiological and psychological ailments. Increased exposure to nature is linked to lower levels of depression, anxiety, and stress.[225] Proximity to nature has been shown to increase life expectancy, to lead to faster recovery from illness, and to decrease obesity.[226] Take air pollution, for example. Transportation, heat for buildings, and industrial activities are significant contributors to air pollution in urban areas. Common air pollutants include particulate matter (PM), sulphur dioxide (SO_2), ground-level ozone (O_3), nitrogen dioxide (NO_2), and carbon monoxide (CO). Nature helps to ameliorate the health impacts of these pollutants. Green areas in London, for example, are reported to remove 852 tons of PM10 annually. Similarly, an analysis of ten American cities indicated that up to 64.5 tons of fine particles (PM2.5) are removed annually by urban trees.[227] Nature in urban areas cleans the air, which is critical in the face of the 7 million deaths annually attributed to air pollution.[228] Although it is widely reported that urban vegetation helps to reduce air pollution, the reduction varies according to the particular species, temporal fluctuations, and spatial distribution.[229]

The COVID-19 pandemic underscored the importance of air quality. Not only does air pollution increase the odds of catching a virus such as COVID-19, but it can also cause or exacerbate respiratory illnesses, making one more susceptible to the most dangerous symptoms of lung infections.[230] The small airborne particles of pollution can carry viruses farther and wider than in areas with better air quality.[231]

Nature offers terrific mental health benefits. Time spent in nature has been shown to decrease behavioural problems in children and to result in fewer emotional symptoms and peer-related problems.[232] Nature also improves the working memory of a child,[233] and playing in nature boosts self-esteem, stimulates imagination, and encourages peacefulness and cooperation.[234] With adults, there is a strong connection between the "need for restoration (to reduce worries and stress), the use of environmental self-regulation strategies (favourite places), and restorative outcomes."[235] Exposure to nature and green space can decrease the symptoms of stress, offer a reprieve from noise pollution, and soften the chaos of urban life.

As nature in urban areas becomes healthier, so do urban communities and their residents. Planning visionary Ebenezer Howard recognized this:

> The key to the problem [of] how to restore the people to the land ... that beautiful land of ours, with its canopy of sky, the air that blows up on it, the sun that warms it, the rain and dew that moisten it ... is the key to a portal through which, even when scarce ajar, will be seen to pour a flood of light on the problems of intemperance, of excessive toil, of restless anxiety, of grinding poverty.[236]

Howard's insight has been reiterated by other urbanists. Berkeley's Professor Emeritus of Urban Design Randolph Hester argues that "nature make us more civil ... [E]xperiencing nature more increases our ability to listen to others, to empathize, and to be concerned about their needs as well as our own ... Exposure to nature reduces our aggression and makes us less violent."[237] MIT's Anne Whiston Spirn argues that "the social value of nature must be recognized and its power harnessed, rather than resisted."[238] Professor of Urban Design Darko Radovic asserts that "environmental and cultural sustainability cannot be separated."[239] Hester sums it up: "Naturalness nurtures good health and heals us when we are sick, fatigued, and stressed. Naturalness spurs us to play with reckless abandon, frees us from artificial affectations and inhibitions, instils in us divergent ways of thinking, and reawakens our naiveté. Naturalness helps us discover our fundamental character ... Naturalness touches our hearts."[240]

Enhanced green space also provides opportunities for recreation. It can include organized sports or informal activities such as playing, walking, and using green space as an active transportation corridor – recreational opportunities that offer perhaps the highest valued ecosystem services in cities.[241] For example, rehabilitated dike systems can become integrated with active transportation networks. British Columbia's Cowichan Valley Regional District expanded and rehabilitated a dike system to increase safety and mitigate flood events. The new system provides multiple benefits to the community, including an active transportation trail and habitat for species at risk.[242]

Nature provides a calming sense of place rooted in the unique ecology and history of a particular location. Singapore's vast Gardens by the Bay, for example, were inspired by the orchid – a plant emblematic of Singapore.[243] When Minneapolis called for design proposals to transform an eighteen-kilometre stretch of urban waterfront, the design requirement was simply to "put the river first."[244] The history of Minneapolis has been tied to the river, and the winning proposal intends to "forge a harmonious and symbiotic relationship between the city's people, river, wildlife and landscape."[245]

Calgary's RiverWalk park centres on the Bow and Elbow Rivers and attempts to connect people with their riverfront history and identity.[246] A similar approach taken by the City of Prince George, British Columbia, embraced plans to reintroduce river access to the core of the city as a way to recognize and celebrate the long history of Indigenous and colonial settlement at the confluence of the Nechako and Fraser Rivers. The restoration experiences of Kakamigahara City, on the fringes of Nagoya, Japan, which received the 2005 Prime Minister's Award for Greening Cities, showed that "reuniting nature and the man-made environment based on the ecological context in each locality was the fundamental method for regenerating the city for future generations."[247]

FIGURE 4.22   Urban areas located in biologically rich locations, such as the confluence of the Fraser and Nechako Rivers in Prince George, British Columbia, warrant expansive urban parks and the restoration of nature at large scales.

Indigenous Peoples understand the meaning of a reciprocal relationship with nature, grounded in a sense of place. That relationship flows from accepting responsibility for multiple generations that will rely on the same ecosystems, and it has enabled Indigenous Peoples and their cultures to thrive for millennia. Carrying that understanding into contemporary urban settings prioritizes the protection of nature and fosters a respectful sense of gratitude.

In an urban setting, the elements of nature that provide a sense of place can be large or small. Grand public parks such as New York's Central Park, Vancouver's Stanley Park, and Cape Town's Table Mountain provide an enduring and "monumental" sense of place "woven into the identity, practices, and rituals of city dwellers."[248] At the smaller end of the scale, "there is something in every neighbourhood that people value and which provides the starting point for developing a clear and compelling vision."[249] Finding such a starting point can support an ecological restoration effort that has significant momentum. Even a single large tree can "provide a sense of permanence and stability."[250] As more of these places are restored, additional momentum is built that leads to further enhancement of nature in urban areas.

FIGURE 4.23   The foresight (and protests) that protected Stanley Park's oceanfront forest from twentieth-century development gave Vancouver a priceless endowment of nature. Large urban patches of relatively intact nature serve as anchors and inspiration for restoration networks. | *Credit:* Scott Yamaoka.

The sense of place attachment specific to nature is the key to predicting pro-environmental behaviour.[251] However, both a sense of place and an appreciation of the need for the restoration of nature in urban areas are necessary. If the members of a community are generally satisfied with the status quo of their environment, they are less likely to be motivated to engage in ecosystem stewardship, even if they have a strong sense of place. Yet people are more willing to fight for a place central to their identity if they believe that it is in a "less-than-optimal condition" that might be improved.[252]

Majora Carter learned that telling people what she saw as threatening to her South Bronx community was not sufficient to catalyze action – she had to show them what could be done. By showing people the beauty of a tree, river, or park, she opened up space for and interest in a conversation about cleaning air, reducing asthma, and making life better.[253] As residents of the South Bronx took ownership of their new park, community esteem rose, and people were ready to fight for the nature to which they now felt connected.

FIGURE 4.24   New York City is inconceivable without its historic investment in Central Park. Its planned biodiversity thrives among millions of people for whom it delivers identity, respite, and inspiration.

Researchers agree with Carter that ecosystem connectivity creates social connectivity.[254] The social functions of urban nature include "attractors of recreational use and conduits for the movement of people ... link[ing] together diverse populations ... influenc[ing] patterns of *social interaction* within and between neighbourhoods ... [and] build[ing] *social capital* – the networks of social ties and interactions that provide a crucial basis for trust, cooperation, and successful social, economic, and political activity."[255] Professor Paul Milbourne has seen how community garden projects – started to provide inexpensive quality food, to build community pride and confidence, and to foster new spaces for public participation – initiate broader forms of social change.[256] Children in particular display "absolute enjoyment and enthusiasm ... when they are experiencing the touch, smell and fun to be had during all stages of the growing cycle."[257]

We have all heard the slogan "think globally, act locally," but it is often hard to translate that message into action. The restoration of nature in urban areas catapults local action into global benefits. Healthy nature in urban areas supports ecosystems across the planet because nature in cities encourages a strong and lasting Earth-based ethic among residents. It has been shown that direct and frequent experience with nature as a child "is necessary for concern for the environment in later life"[258] and that one's sensitivity to environmental issues is determined significantly by one's personal exposure to nature.[259] Direct experiences with nature during the formative years of childhood appear to be particularly critical for the development of an environmental or Earth-based ethic.

Access to nature also shows adults how to read environmental signals and how to look to nature for inspiration in addressing the many challenges ahead. This sort of "ecological literacy" is necessary to design our cities better, connects us directly to the natural ecosystems that we seek to restore, and builds support for action to address our many global ecological challenges.[260] Nature in urban areas thus takes urban citizens on a journey to restore ecosystems elsewhere.[261] Green design pioneer William McDonough suggests that "we can begin to see the city not only as an elegant self-sustaining place, but as a revitalizing force in its region."[262] Timothy Beatley lists various ways that cities can catalyze an environmental ethic: celebrations of locally unique nature and biodiversity spectacles (e.g., the running of salmon, the return of migratory birds), environmental education programs for adults, citizen science and community-based monitoring programs, nature "rangers or coaches" who provide local ecological interpretation, gardening, bird-watching programs, and swimming locations in natural waterways.[263]

Healthy Economies

We benefit directly, consistently, and vitally from nature. Nature sequesters carbon, forms soil, treats waste, and pollinates plants. Food, air, water, raw materials, medicines, and genetic resources all come from nature. And nature inspires artists, enlightens our spirits, and patiently teaches those willing to listen.[264]

Yet too often those benefits are ignored. Consider, for example, urban areas built on floodplains (New York City has over $100 billion in property located on its 100-year floodplain), in forests, and on top of filled wetlands.[265] The natural buffers and processes that existed predevelopment are easily lost, leaving built areas more vulnerable to damages, especially in the face of the climate emergency. Impermeable surfaces in urban areas result in 60 percent more runoff than vegetated areas, exacerbating storm surges into the expensive and crumbling grey infrastructure system already under mounting pressure from a disrupted climate.

Nature can help. Studies have shown that well-placed green infrastructure with high infiltration capacity can reduce 100 percent of stormwater runoff during normal precipitation years and from 77 percent to 88 percent during high precipitation years.[266] Green roofs and bioretention cells are capable of reducing peak flows of stormwater runoff in urban areas. For small to medium storm events, bioretention cells have shown a 96.5 percent reduction of peak flows. Moreover, nature-directed stewardship provides green infrastructure better equipped to adapt to changing conditions in the future than technical infrastructure solutions, making the investment in green infrastructure safer over the long term.[267]

An investment in green infrastructure to restore nature is compelling when contrasted with the staggering (and overdue) bill of repairing cities' deteriorating built infrastructure. As we saw in Chapter 2, that bill in Canadian cities alone will be more than a trillion dollars over the next fifteen to twenty years.[268]

Since we are not keeping up with the maintenance costs associated with our existing built infrastructure, why are we spending money on new infrastructure while failing to appreciate what nature is able to provide for less or even for free? Optimistically, some cities have recognized that nature provides most infrastructure needs for free and with limited upfront capital costs. For example, New York City compared a green infrastructure plan with a grey infrastructure plan to meet its stormwater management objectives and found that the former plan would cost US $1.5 billion less (US $5.3 billion for the green infrastructure plan compared with US $6.8 billion for the grey infrastructure plan) over twenty years and provide "significant sustainability benefits ... not available through the grey strategy."[269] In attempting to quantify some of these benefits, New York's Department of Environmental Protection concluded that "New Yorkers would receive between $139 million and $418 million in additional benefits through reduced energy bills, increased property values, and improved health."[270]

New York City has also recognized that protecting an urban watershed is less expensive than building water treatment plants. It has contributed US $1.5 billion to protect the quality of its source waters, and by doing so has avoided the need for a water filtration plant that would have cost at least US $10 billion.

Detroit cancelled plans for $1.3 billion in traditional grey infrastructure projects and replaced those plans with $814 million in combined green and grey projects to meet the same needs.[271] Philadelphia's twenty-five-year Green City, Clean Waters plan, at $2 billion, aims to reduce waterway pollution by 85 percent.[272] Over its forty-five-year planning horizon, the city anticipates that the value of benefits will exceed the money spent.[273] The Biden administration's $1.2 trillion infrastructure package includes green infrastructure and nature-based solutions.[274] In addition, certification systems, such as the Sustainable SITES initiative, help to incorporate and better account for ecosystem services in the built environment.

To safeguard the gains made by inviting nature home, we would be wise to reduce simultaneously the systemic pressures that erode nature. This includes

FIGURE 4.25 Rainwater in cities often falls unimpeded to the pavement or other hard surfaces, where it collects pollutants such as oil, pharmaceuticals, and plastics, concentrates them in a drainage system, and discharges the mix into local water-bodies. Replacing pavement with green infrastructure offers the compound benefits of dispersed and filtered water, low maintenance costs, and increased capacity over time. The green infrastructure in this North Vancouver parking lot keeps water out of drains, even during a downpour. | *Source:* Chloe Hartley.

our economic system. In particular, the economic system predicated on perpetual economic growth on a finite planet that stresses the ecosystems on which we depend. This is clear to the more than 11,000 scientists referred to earlier who conclude that "excessive extraction of materials and overexploitation of ecosystems, driven by economic growth, must be quickly curtailed" and that "our goals need to shift from GDP growth and the pursuit of affluence toward sustaining ecosystems and improving human well-being by prioritizing needs and reducing inequality."[275]

Our dominant economic system is predicated on perpetual growth.[276] There are two primary problems with perpetual physical economic growth: depletion of the Earth's finite materials and conversion of these materials to waste. Depletion is encouraged by classifying the Earth's materials as "resources" and believing the illusion that the Earth's materials belong to us, offering little value until they are turned into products important to us. Waste results because all materials and energy used in economic activities, even with some of them recycled, are degraded by those activities and eventually end up as environmental waste.[277] Thus, the modern economic imperative of perpetual growth depletes finite materials and increases environmental waste, thereby increasing the degradation of ecosystems and their essential processes on which life depends.

By inviting nature home, cities can shift priorities toward a more just and restorative economy. We suggest that this can happen in two important ways.

First, by inviting nature home, we see nature as the commons in which we all have a stake rather than as an externality for which nobody takes responsibility. As we will explain later in greater detail, creating a healthy nature in urban areas is a collective effort that results in shared benefits. Everyone in the city can join in the process and share in the outcome, whether the restoration is carried out on individual properties, through collaborations along a block or across a neighbourhood, or with city-wide green connections.

By understanding ecosystems as the commons, we share responsibility for the protection and careful use of ecological processes that provide for our well-being. Water storage and filtration, carbon sequestration and storage, air purification, climate moderation, and spiritual and mental renewal – all the gifts of healthy ecosystems – are common property resources and not "owned" under fee-simple property rights. Nor are they "services" from a provider, akin to services from an electrical utility. These common properties are essential realities for the well-being of all life forms. And the process of inviting nature home entails a collective effort to restore these common properties.

Green spaces become the commons when decision-making about their stewardship is shared by local governments and residents and is guided by ecological and social objectives. In other words, if they are governed as the commons, then they become the commons, regardless of the actual ownership structure.[278] What are sometimes termed "nature-based solutions" – living, natural features designed to address ecological challenges while simultaneously providing multiple economic, social, and ecological benefits – are important urban common areas, particularly in low-income neighbourhoods.[279] For example, green linear parks can create both social and ecological connections, as Majora Carter found with the Hunts Point Riverside Park.[280] Thus, seeing watersheds and their ecosystems as the commons, where their protection is the first priority, is a good starting point for reorienting our economic activities toward the restoration and protection of nature.

Second, restorative economic activities support the process of inviting nature home. Such activities prioritize protection of the health and overall integrity of nature, communities, and equality rather than economic growth.

There are fundamental differences between a diverse, community-based economy and a growth-driven corporate economy. Community-based economies see meaningful, life-sustaining jobs as profits, whereas corporate-based economies see jobs as costs. In other words, community-based economies strive to maximize the number of meaningful jobs that they provide, whereas corporate-based economies create the minimum number of jobs to meet their needs. Community-based economies recognize that the economy is wholly dependent on healthy, intact nature, protected and conserved by a healthy society. In contrast, corporate economies are based on financial appraisals in which nature has no inherent value.

These differences support the move from a corporate-based economy to a community-based economy as part of inviting nature home through the restoration of ecological integrity and the affirmation of equity within our cities, indeed across the Earth.

The "doughnut" model of social and planetary boundaries offers an economic guide for community-based economies. As Kate Raworth explains,

> the hole in the middle reveals the extent to which people worldwide are falling short on life's essentials, such as food and water, healthcare and housing, gender equality and political voice – the 12 social priorities set out in the United Nations Sustainable Development Goals. Beyond the Doughnut's outer ring, however, humanity risks putting so much pressure on Earth's critical life-supporting systems, known as planetary boundaries, that we kick them out of kilter, such as by causing climate breakdown, ocean acidification and extreme biodiversity loss. Between these two sets of boundaries lies a possible future for humanity in which it is feasible to meet the needs of all within the means of the planet.[281]

Amsterdam has envisioned a set of objectives based on the doughnut model, including targets for housing availability, social equity, political involvement, diversity, jobs, income, education, and connectivity. It seeks a city that will "thrive within its natural habitat," meaning that its "buildings, greenways, and infrastructure aimed to clean as much air, filter as much water, store as much carbon, and house as much biodiversity as their host habitat does."[282]

Another approach is a "steady-state economy" that respects ecological limits.[283] A steady-state economy calls for a stabilized GDP, an equitable distribution of wealth, and an efficient allocation of resources.[284] By giving priority to the restoration of natural ecological integrity, the process of inviting nature home facilitates the development of steady-state economies that exist within the closed system of the Earth. Waste is reduced to manageable levels so that ecosystem processes (and the life dependent on those processes) can thrive.

Community-based economies such as these are regenerative, distributive, and ecologically responsible. As such, they support the process of inviting nature home. Economic development in cities (as distinguished from merely economic growth) involves more local work and a more complex division of labour. Jane Jacobs said that this kind of urban economic development entails import product replacement: that is, demand is satisfied by locally produced items. The result is "urban vibrancy without excessive consumption."[285]

5 Nature-Directed Stewardship in Cities

It's not the deer that is crossing the road; rather, it's the road that is crossing the forest.

– Author unknown

Nature-directed stewardship, formerly known as ecosystem-based conservation planning, was developed in the context of forest protection and logging. NDS cut its teeth by addressing the decidedly nonurban challenge of protecting ecosystems and the rural communities that depend on them in the face of relentless resource extraction. As an alternative to clear-cut logging, NDS focuses on what to protect – ecological integrity, biological diversity, healthy watershed ecosystems, community employment, and diverse, stable communities – not on what to use (the commercially valuable timber). NDS shows that by giving priority to the protection of ecosystems, long-term economic and natural stability follows.

NDS has not been fully applied to urban areas. Although the examples in Chapter 3 offer glimpses, application of the complete suite of philosophies, principles, and processes of NDS in cities described in Chapter 4 remains elusive.

Can it be done? Does the concept of "focus on what to protect, not on what to use," have a place in urban development? How can a protected network of ecological reserves be established and maintained in a dense landscape of roads and buildings? What kind of nature goes into urban ecological reserves? Where are the boundaries of planning areas where jurisdiction rests with countless private and public landowners? What will a nature-first city look like when nature is restored in an ecologically meaningful way? Will the city still function? These questions were the catalyst for this book, and after years of uncovering answers we are more hopeful than when we began. In short, yes, NDS can be applied to cities.

Of course, the more ubiquitous the urban development, the fewer the options for straightforward ecological restoration. In newer cities, there might be more options for ecological restoration, whereas older, established cities have more thoroughly degraded ecological conditions. Yet, in either case, we remain hopeful. NDS can be applied in all urban settings.

Before we explain the details of applying NDS in cities, we want to emphasize that restoration is neither a quick fix nor primarily a human endeavour. Restoration of a reasonable level of ecological integrity to degraded ecosystems in urban areas, or for that matter anywhere, is a slow process that requires decades or more. Restoration depends primarily on assisting nature to reactivate natural processes. Thus, restoration is nature's endeavour in which we can be a helpful assistant and sometimes a catalyst for positive change.

Accompanying the commitment to restoration is a commitment to stop doing the things that created the need for restoration to begin with. To achieve this obvious but often ignored goal requires that all new designs and developments protect ecological integrity, occur within ecological limits, and fit people into ecosystems.

In this chapter, we outline how to apply NDS in cities, and in the next chapter we detail the efforts to do so in a specific urban watershed in East Vancouver.

NDS in cities starts by understanding the natural *character* of the ecosystems that existed in a particular place before the city did. This natural character is contrasted with the existing *condition,* and the gap in ecological integrity between the two is the *restoration target.*

A primary objective of urban NDS is the re-establishment of ecological integrity (to varying levels). That is, NDS aims to re-establish natural ecosystem character (composition, structure, and function). And it aims to do so over an entire watershed.

Instead of creating a network of primarily *existing* ecological integrity (as one would usually encounter when applying NDS in forests, grasslands, and other natural landscapes), urban NDS aims to establish a *restoration network* in which restoration activities will lead eventually to *future* ecological integrity.

A restoration network is created through four steps:

1 Identify the target watershed and describe its natural character. As we will explain, NDS seeks to restore ecological integrity in a *focal watershed* – the largest watershed that is fully (or almost fully) contained within the urban boundary.
2 Protect existing fragments of natural ecosystem character. These fragments can become important *anchors* in a network of reserves (and provide a semblance of ecological integrity).
3 Restore new fragments and anchors of natural ecosystem character at all spatial scales. They include both common and rare ecosystem types, habitats for endemic species, hotspots of biological diversity, natural forests, riparian areas and stream channels, and natural topography. With restoration efforts

and the liberation of natural processes, these restoration features will develop natural composition, structure, and function as they become established ecological reserve areas.

4 Identify and restore the natural *water movement network.* This work includes daylighting streams and wetlands; installing green roofs and walls; establishing rain and greywater collection and dispersal systems; restoring multilayer vegetation (from tall trees, to intermediate trees and shrubs, down to lichens and fungi); installing bioswales, rain gardens, and food gardens; and ensuring that as much as possible of the urban landscape is permeable so that water can once again access the soil and re-establish natural water movement patterns.

As these components emerge – existing fragments and anchors of ecological integrity, newly restored fragments and anchors, and the water movement network – the shape of a *restoration network* appears. Linking the components together at multiple spatial scales will establish and strengthen a restoration network across the watershed. With enough time and effort, this restoration network will mature into a *protected network* of ecosystems with ecological integrity, from small sites to the focal watershed within which the city is located. The diagram below, Figure 5.1, illustrates the process, and the rest of this chapter explains how it works.

We have no illusion that this change will happen overnight. However, once initial barriers to implementing NDS are overcome, we anticipate that restoration will gather momentum. Enthusiasm and commitment will emerge at the community level from people who are healthier and happier with nature around them. City planners and administrators will witness the cost effectiveness and many co-benefits associated with NDS. And, in the big picture, ecologically focused restoration will fix our relationship with nature (and help to fix our relationships with each other).

FIGURE 5.1   **Nature-directed stewardship in cities**

Where: Watersheds

A watershed is the basic landscape unit for planning and restoration. Water is the connector. Water is life. Water acts as the veins and arteries of an ecosystem, from its component parts to the entire system.

The concept of a watershed, however, is a slippery one. A watershed is the area of land where all of the water that falls drains to a common outlet.[1] In other words, it is a drainage basin that functions like a kitchen sink. A watershed can be as small as a crease in the ground or as large as the portion of a continent that drains into a major river. Indeed, as mentioned earlier, the whole Earth is a watershed.

Every watershed, regardless of its scale, is multidimensional. Watersheds are longitudinal (from upstream to downstream), lateral (from floodplains to uplands), vertical (from below the water to riparian areas), and temporal (their dimensions change over time). A watershed is an interconnected, interdependent ecological feature that needs to be maintained and restored to protect ecological integrity.

Smaller watersheds are interconnected, interdependent subsets of larger watersheds. Since small watersheds are nested within larger watersheds, networks of ecological reserves for smaller areas need to be nested within ecological reserves for larger areas. In this way, NDS provides for the interdependent, interconnected properties of ecosystems across the multidimensional scales of a watershed. Thus, planning and managing on the basis of watersheds are logical ways to ensure that the interconnected, interdependent nature of ecosystems is protected and restored.

In an urban area, NDS seeks to protect and restore a focal watershed – the largest watershed fully (or almost fully) contained within the urban boundary. The larger the watershed chosen, the greater the number of landscape-scale ecological processes that can be restored and protected through the plan (e.g., biological diversity, climate moderation, and water protection). NDS starts with as large a landscape as possible and operates at multiple spatial scales, from large watersheds to small patches comprising a fraction of a hectare. It identifies and restores all of the tributary watersheds (many of which are buried or culverted in urban areas) and provides a common-sense approach to and clear vision of urban ecological restoration activities.

Watersheds provide logical planning boundaries because of their visibly interconnected and interdependent nature. This nature of watersheds at different scales is referred to as the water movement network. As we will see, a primary goal of NDS is to protect or restore the water movement network.

In the urban context, watersheds need to be redefined through identification of the natural water movement networks and reconstruction of the natural character of the riparian and upland portions of the watershed.[2] Identifying these networks will allow neighbourhoods to demarcate their watershed boundaries, and with appropriate government encouragement and assistance neighbourhood residents can become catalysts for ecological restoration and apply NDS in their neighbourhood watersheds.

WHAT: ECOLOGICAL INTEGRITY

Nature-directed stewardship starts by focusing on what to protect (and restore), not on what to use (or pave). What to protect (and restore) is *ecological integrity:* that is, "the abundance and diversity of organisms at all levels, and the ecological patterns, processes, and structural attributes responsible for that biological diversity and for ecosystem resilience."[3]

NDS in urban areas offers a way to reach a level of ecological integrity as close as reasonably feasible to natural ecological integrity. The higher the level of ecological integrity within an urban area and adjacent landscapes, the higher the level of *ecological resilience* to both human perturbations and natural disturbances. Resilience can be described as "the property that allows the fundamental functions of an ecosystem to persist in the face of extremes of disturbance."[4] Ecological resilience depends on maintaining or restoring natural ecological integrity, which provides the composition, structure, function, and necessary ecosystem processes.

Ecosystems vary in their capacity to tolerate disturbances. There are limits, and when these limits are exceeded the ecosystem degrades rapidly, often into a state that seldom if ever occurs naturally.[5] Most urban development practices eradicate ecological integrity and cause a near-total loss of ecological resilience.

Urbanization has turned a self-organizing, self-regulating complex system into a simple, homogeneous system that bears little resemblance to the natural ecosystems that once occupied the area.[6] With extreme simplification and/or eradication of natural composition, structure, and function comes the loss of free ecosystem benefits (e.g., nature's ability to manage water, moderate climate, purify air, and furnish the biological diversity that organizes and regulates ecosystem function).

Thus, with the absence or near absence of complex natural ecosystems in urban areas, *complicated* manufactured systems (i.e., urban grey or basic green infrastructure) must be developed, installed, and maintained frequently to provide a partial measure of the water management, climate moderation, and air purification once carried out by natural ecosystems. Although these complicated systems reflect a high degree of human ingenuity and engineering, they are neither self-regulating nor self-organizing. Thus, compared with natural, resilient ecosystems, complicated urban systems require continual maintenance and updating.[7]

For example, in the urban landscape, the natural storage and filtration of water and the regulation of water flows found in natural ecosystems have become severely diminished or ceased to exist altogether. As large trees and shrubs disappear from much of the urban landscape, so do their water management functions, air purification services, and climate regulation processes of sequestering and storing carbon. As landforms and soils are altered with development, the water purification functions of healthy soils are lost, and the movement patterns of groundwater are altered.

Ecological integrity allows for the dynamic, often unpredictable, natural processes of change that maintain biological diversity in a self-sustaining balancing act. Balance is the gift of diversity. However, without unpredictable change, diversity is not maintained. Without diversity, healthy ecosystems do not exist.[8]

Urban development tends to favour homogeneity over diversity and seeks to limit and control change. Both approaches erode diversity and balance. In applying NDS in urban landscapes, homogeneous patterns are replaced with diverse patterns. Regularity is replaced with irregularity. Change needs to be embraced in ways that maintain ecosystem stability and balance. Doing so has been referred to as the "renaturing of cities,"[9] a biodiversity-led approach that recognizes that urban green infrastructure needs to be designed as part of the ecological restoration plan to re-establish ecosystem benefits.[10]

Natural Character

The ecological integrity that must be protected and restored in an urban area is not untethered from the location of the city. Rather, the appropriate ecological integrity is that which existed in that specific place before the city did. In other words, determining the target for the restoration of ecological integrity is informed by an analysis of natural character and current condition. This is where the work begins.

We pause to recognize that climate change complicates the appropriateness of guiding restoration by the ecological integrity that existed before the city did. Given the degraded nature of ecosystems in cities, restoration activities will need to start with early successional plants (some of which are climate resilient) to mid- and late-successional species. The latter successional stage is where substituting some climate-resilient species will likely become more important, dependent of course on the climate change vulnerabilities of each particular location.

Natural character, as we have explained, refers to the composition, structure, and function of the pre-existing ecosystems (before the city arose). For example, the natural character of a city might be a temperate rainforest, the eastern broadleaf forest, or a semi-desert. The natural character provides the appropriate baseline or benchmark of ecosystem integrity that offered the full range of ecosystem processes prior to modification by industrial civilizations. Protection, maintenance, and/or restoration of natural character is necessary to receive the benefits of ecosystem processes that provide for human well-being. Guidance from anything less than natural character means accepting a degraded ecological condition from the start.

Consideration of natural character calls for an appreciation of the *range of natural variability.* Which composition and which structure fall within the range of natural variability? The answer will help identify the level of natural ecological integrity that remains in a particular urban area.

In contrast to natural character, the *current condition* describes how the composition, structure, and function of the natural character have been modified or affected as a result of human activities. The *integrity gap,* or loss of ecological integrity from the natural character to the current condition, represents the restoration target. In many cities, the lacuna between character and condition is formidable. Consider, for example, how little remains of the wetland that became the notorious Five Points area of southern Manhattan and is now entombed under the New York County Supreme Court. Or reflect on the northeast False Creek region of Vancouver that covers a marshland and tidal zone, which once connected to Burrard Inlet (effectively making what is now downtown Vancouver an island at high tide).[11]

NDS is challenged by the extensive time required for the implementation and maintenance of restoration treatments. We recognize that restoring the extensive loss of ecological integrity in urban areas will involve facilitating regenerative natural processes, many of which require long periods of time to reach a state of near-natural character. Natural processes, even when assisted by human-designed restoration treatments, take time. Our lack of knowledge about the composition and structure of natural character suggests that even more time may be required. Thus, a likely outcome of urban restoration in the medium term is substantially improved ecological integrity, in the form of a restoration network that ultimately, after generations, might become a protected network of ecological reserves.

This is not sidestepping the task of applying NDS in cities. Rather, it is a recognition that the restoration required in nature-first cities takes time. Significant changes to urban form are necessary to fully restore natural ecosystems, and each community will determine how far it wants to go. We will return to this topic in Chapter 7.

We pause here to underscore that achieving substantially improved ecological integrity is realistic, achievable, and complementary to all that makes cities great. The existing chasm between natural character and current condition is the result of choices made before there was full comprehension of what was being lost. The costs of expelling nature from cities were not understood when wetlands were filled in to make room for new arrivals, when the first strip of pavement invited automobiles into urban life, or when the idea of piping rainfall away with sewage was embraced as a tool for fighting disease. Today, however, we are planning from a different perspective – with a fuller appreciation of the toll of excluding nature. And we can modify the legacy of past decisions by charting a new direction. The gulf between natural character and current condition can be narrowed significantly and even fully closed in some parts of the city. Enormous strides can be made in a relatively short period of time to invite nature home.

Fragments and Anchors: Remnants of Ecological Integrity

Remaining *fragments* of natural ecosystem character, few and far between as they might be in an urban watershed, must be protected as critical toeholds for restoration. The more significant fragments are *anchors* or places from which restoration activities can radiate to assist natural processes to re-establish ecological integrity. Depending on the spatial scale at which NDS is being planned, these anchors can range in size from small patches of natural or semi-natural composition and structure that are a fraction of a hectare (e.g., a backyard or vacant lot) to large patches of several hundred hectares or more (e.g., a large park).

Once areas of remnant natural ecological integrity are identified, a subobjective is to identify and protect *linkages* or fragments of linkages between remnant natural ecosystems. They, too, are protected as a primary directive in NDS. Even if the linkages are not fully intact ecologically, they should be protected as areas for restoration.

The *range of natural variability* helps to identify the important remaining fragments and anchors. In particular, NDS seeks to re-establish the most longlasting natural successional phase that would have existed in the natural ecosystem condition. Protecting the composition and structure characteristic of the most long-lasting successional phase means that we are protecting the ecological phase with the highest level of biodiversity and the most specialist species. Thus, achieving this goal helps natural processes to re-establish the full range of essential elements of ecological integrity and biological diversity at multiple spatial scales and to rebuild resilience across the urban landscape.

The existing fragments and anchors of natural ecosystem character are critical. They must be identified and protected. But these fragments are generally isolated islands in an ecologically desolate expanse of pavement, concrete, steel, lowdensity residences, and automobiles. It would be silly at this point to map out a network of protected areas since most of the network would be devoid of nature. And, since the process of restoring nature in cities depends on the disparate actions of a multitude of residents, NGOs, local governments, businesses, churches, community groups, higher-level governments, schools, and nature itself, it would be futile to predict exactly where and when meaningful restoration will take place. Thus, even once the existing fragments and anchors of ecological integrity have been identified and protected, more must be done to develop the connectivity inherent in a network. This is where extensive restoration is brought to bear.

How: Connectivity through Networks

Once existing fragments and anchors of ecological integrity have been identified, we have laid the groundwork for NDS restoration activities. This restoration has two targets. First, additional fragments and anchors of natural ecosystem character at all spatial scales are to be identified and restored. Second, the natural water movement network must be restored. Only then will we be equipped to map out a restoration network (which, given enough time, will mature into a protected network of ecological reserves).

These two restoration efforts can occur simultaneously as mutually reinforcing strategies. That is, additional fragments and anchors can be identified and restored at the same time that the water movement network is restored. This is particularly wise in cities since the opportunities for restoration may be driven by political and economic considerations. Thus, when opportunities arise, we must seize them. In any case, there is significant overlap between these restoration objectives. In most cases, water movement networks cannot be restored without identifying ecological fragments and anchors.

Restoration Features: Additional Fragments and Anchors

In most established urban areas, remaining natural ecosystems are tiny, disconnected fragments. Habitats for all but a small number of generalist species have usually been eradicated. To re-establish networks of ecological reserves, restoration needs to re-establish a reasonable number of natural patches and linkages between them.

Building on existing pockets of ecological integrity, NDS uses spatial analysis to identify the missing natural composition and structure that would have existed before the city did. The missing composition and structure are the substance of *restoration features* – fragments and anchors that will be linked together as parts of a *restoration network*.

Restoration features include habitat for naturally rare and/or endangered species, rare ecosystem and habitat types, unique areas, old-growth and other primary forests, hotspots of biological diversity, and common, representative ecosystems typical of the particular climate and landforms. Areas that have ecological limits need to be targeted as restoration features. They include wetlands, stream channels, riparian areas, moisture-limited areas, steep slopes, unstable terrain, and sites with shallow soils. Rather than modify areas with ecological limits (as one might be prone to do with access to enough bulldozers), NDS focuses on protection and restoration of naturally occurring and ecologically limited ecosystems. These areas often play essential roles in facilitating the storage, filtration, and movement of water, among other ecological processes.

As restoration proceeds, and as natural processes take over, increased levels of ecological integrity will return. Natural composition, structure, and function will return. Nature will return.

Restoration of Water Movement Networks

Connectivity is more than meets the eye. It is not just the living components of ecosystems that need restoration but also something more elemental. Water must be restored. Specifically, the movement of water must be restored. The challenge is immediate in cities because the natural movement of water is generally buried under impervious surfaces and replaced with a fabricated water movement network consisting of pipes and culverts.

In natural, intact ecosystems and landscapes, water is dispersed. In contrast, cities tend to concentrate water along curbs and in ditches, pipes, and gutters by establishing compacted and impermeable surfaces (from roads to roofs, from laneways to sidewalks) and by removing multi-layered complex vegetation structures. As we discussed in Chapter 1, this interruption of the hydrological cycle has grave consequences for ecosystems above ground, below ground, and in water bodies. Once the hydrological cycle is broken, moderate, regular water flows that balance seasonal fluctuations are replaced with rapid cycles of drought and flood. Dispersed water is replaced with concentrated water. Clean water is replaced with polluted water.

In conjunction with the establishment of a restoration network, as described above, NDS calls for the restoration of the *water movement network* in cities. In natural, intact ecosystems – particularly forests, naturally permeable systems from the top of the tallest vegetation through to the soil and subsoil – water evaporates and sublimates to be moved elsewhere. It drips onto, soaks into, and is gathered up by natural ecosystem composition and structure. Multi-layered vegetation is the norm. Wetlands, small streams, bogs, rivers, and estuaries disperse water throughout a water movement network at the heart of a watershed. In cities, these critical veins of water are buried, blocked, polluted, removed, and forgotten. Without the support of water movement networks, the fragments and anchors of ecological integrity identified and established through NDS will be unable to thrive.

Thus, re-establishing natural water movement in urban areas is essential. Identifying locations and characteristics of natural water movement networks at multiple spatial scales is the logical starting point.[12] Restoration treatments start with the smallest watersheds that can be imagined and weave these small watersheds together into a water movement network that comprises the entire focal watershed. This approach leads to whole watershed restoration and provides for absorption and natural dispersal of water.

Thankfully, there are many proven strategies for restoring an urban water movement network that can serve as starting points for planning. At the site scale, bioswales can significantly restore water movement in small watersheds. Multi-layered natural vegetation in (and adjacent to) bioswales assists in the re-establishment of natural vegetation composition and structure while filtering and dispersing water. If designed with structural complexity and diverse composition, then bioswales can be established and serve as fine-scale tributaries to sub-watersheds and ultimately to the focal watershed. In this way, bioswales become part of a network of restoration features connecting other restoration features, contributing to the establishment of a network of restored ecological reserves.

Rain gardens (vegetated areas that collect runoff in small water bodies) can be designed to restore the water movement network and thereby improve connectivity. As important restoration focal points, rain gardens help to restore a diffuse pattern of water movement. The scale of rain gardens in ecological restoration will vary from backyards to extensive parts of the water movement network across the focal watershed. Natural composition and structure can be mimicked by rain gardens, which function like ephemeral streams in well-drained sites.

Green roofs store rainwater and delay its dispersal. Thus, green roofs moderate and regulate flow and contribute to the more natural movement of water. The temperature of water draining from a green roof is significantly lower than the temperature of water draining from a conventional roof. This improves aquatic habitat and diversity and supports connectivity from terrestrial ecosystems to aquatic ecosystems.

Green roofs, particularly intensive green roofs, support variations of natural composition and structure, including multi-layered vegetation. Unlike conventional roofs, this characteristic of green roofs enables them to sequester and store carbon. Where green roofs are able to support soil depths that will maintain multi-layered vegetation, they can sustain vegetable gardens.

Living walls similarly provide for the retention of water, particularly in storms, and can be designed to remove pollutants. Water vapour from living walls cools the environment and mitigates the heat generated by dark, impermeable surfaces. These functions assist in restoring a natural, healthy water movement network and moderating the urban climate. Where numerous living walls are installed, they assist in the restoration of interconnected habitats. Establishing connectivity through living walls will be improved by establishing natural, multi-layered vegetation between and among the living walls. For example, complex arrangements of trees, shrubs, and vegetated groundcover among a series of living walls can result in important connectivity.

Rainwater harvesting (from green roofs or conventional roofs) can also help to redirect water from piped infrastructure and back into the natural water movement network. If harvested rainwater is used to feed surface water sources (e.g., wetlands, creeks, rivers, ponds, and lakes), then it should first pass through intact, natural soil profiles or be purified with a treatment system (e.g., bioswales) to remove pollutants. Once free of contaminants, harvested rainwater can feed a significant portion of the water movement network. Intact natural soils, bioswales, rain gardens, and existing watershed tributaries all assist in introducing harvested water in dispersed, natural ways that mimic the functioning of an intact ecosystem.

Slowing down and dispersing rainwater improves connectivity in the soil and subsoil. If harvested rainwater drains directly into ecosystems where natural composition and structure have been restored, then water quality is improved, as is connectivity in the soil and subsoil. This is critical because the soil profiles and surficial geology in urban areas tend to be highly modified. In these instances, there might be the need to restore water movement networks both above and below ground in concert with restoring above-ground natural composition and structure.

Community gardens can be important components of a water movement network. Gardens that provide growing spaces for neighbourhoods are a local way not only to meet community food needs but also to build soil and vegetative cover, including multi-layered perennial cover – composition and structure that manage water naturally and contribute to a diversity of ecosystem processes. Gardens should not be limited to larger spaces developed for multiple gardens but need to be encouraged in every backyard, alley, and small space. Friable, permeable garden soils that support multi-layered vegetation create a much more water-permeable, water-filtering, and water-purifying biodiverse ecosystem than monocultural lawns and many types of formal plantings.

Trees play an essential role in the water movement network by intercepting precipitation. Unlike natural, intact forests, however, cities generally do not have continuous, multi-layered canopies with ladders or layers of vegetation. Cities are also short on decaying wood, such as large fallen trees (which store and filter water) and large areas of permeable soil. As a result, precipitation is not intercepted in the same way in cities as it is in natural, intact forests. For example, urban trees are often widely spaced compared with the variable distribution of trees in a natural forest. The single canopy layer of urban trees is in stark contrast to the multiple layers of vegetation in forests. Wind cannot easily penetrate dense forests but whistles freely among urban trees, affecting the patterns of interception and dispersal of precipitation. Higher wind speeds, warmer temperatures, and lower humidity levels in areas of urban trees result in water loss compared with water conservation in most natural forests, particularly older forests.

The volume of water dispersed through interception and absorption by trees and the ground beneath them is known as bioremediation. In coastal southern California, for example, research shows that one large deciduous tree can reduce rainwater runoff by over 4,000 US gallons per year.[13] And coniferous trees hold significantly more water because of the compact, dense layers of leaves that create many narrow spaces in conifers compared with more open, less dense layers of leaves in deciduous trees.[14]

Water interception and storage capacities of trees increase as trees grow and their crowns expand. Thus, rapidly growing young trees are useful for water interception and storage in areas without larger trees. However, with the passage of time, their growth might slow, and trees that grow more steadily can surpass them in developing large crowns with broad shapes that intercept and store more water. Thus, it is wise to establish an urban forest with a mixture of trees, some that grow more rapidly and some that grow more slowly while developing large crowns for greater water interception and storage over time. The species, growth characteristics, and crown structure of trees needs to be considered when establishing trees or deciding whether to protect existing trees in urban areas.[15]

When choosing whether to maintain or establish deciduous or coniferous trees to manage rainfall, one must consider when the rain falls. If most of the precipitation occurs in winter, then conifers are the best choice. If most precipitation occurs when foliage is present on deciduous trees, then a mixture of conifers and deciduous trees might be the best choice.[16]

Urban trees, particularly large, established trees, are vital in managing water. Their effectiveness is increased where these trees are associated with layers of vegetation, decayed plant matter on the ground, and permeable soils beneath the vegetation. Thus, the overall focus in restoring vegetation in urban areas needs to be on multi-layered vegetation. To be most effective, such vegetation needs to include a complete vegetation "ladder," including large (usually old), tall trees with full crowns, intermediate-height trees, sapling and seedling or shaded-height trees, shrubs, herbs, mosses, lichens, liverworts, and fungal fruiting bodies.

Establishing such a complex, multi-layered canopy of vegetation will generally require multiple restoration treatments, including restoring permeable soil and seeding and planting layers of vegetation. It will also require patience to wait for vegetation to grow and establish. Thus, re-establishment of natural vegetation ladders needs to be a priority in restoration, for this step will require an extended period of time in most urban areas. The challenge of restoring complex, multi-layered vegetation should not diminish the importance of protecting existing layers of vegetation, or discourage the development of new layers of vegetation, particularly as steps are taken toward developing more complete multi-layered vegetation.

Under the ladder of vegetation is the soil, home to incredible biodiversity and a key element of the water movement network. But urban soils too often are sealed under impervious surfaces. The natural infiltration-dominated system has been replaced by a surface-runoff-dominated system.[17] For example, the surface runoff in a natural, undeveloped watershed in the Pacific Northwest is less than 1 percent of the precipitation falling on the watershed, compared with approximately 30 percent surface runoff in an urbanized watershed.[18] NDS seeks to shift this back by significantly increasing permeable surfaces, and thus decreasing surface runoff and its concomitant concentration of water in urban areas. Achieving this goal results in the dispersal of water, and in water quality, quantity, and timing of flows similar to what would have occurred in the natural functioning watershed.

NDS recognizes the need to change impermeable surfaces to permeable vegetated ones. This means removing, narrowing, and repurposing roads (especially those dedicated to private automobiles). Where smooth surfaces continue to be needed, permeable pavement offers an alternative. Permeable pavement includes individual paving blocks, fibrous grid systems filled with plants, and specialty mixes of concrete or asphalt. A low-tech alternative is drain gravel or coarse gravel that maintains void spaces (pores) between the pieces of rock and does not pack such that it becomes impermeable or semi-impermeable. This type of permeable material is cost effective and easily installed as walkways around residences, laneways, and other locations where a smooth surface is not essential.

The most charismatic strategy for restoring a water movement network is daylighting streams: that is, "liberat[ing] waterways that were [once] buried in culverts or pipes" in order to expose "some or all of [their] flow."[19] As we will see with Vancouver's Still Creek, bringing a stream back into a community attracts enthusiasm, builds momentum, and can be leveraged into additional restoration gains.

The action of bringing a buried stream back to the surface, on its own, is a crucial component of a re-established water movement network that has been tried city wide (in Zurich) and even in arid locations (Riyadh).[20] Less sexy, but equally important for water movement and ecosystem restoration, is re-establishing wetlands for water storage, water purification, sediment buffers, and biological diversity.

Restoration Network

We started this chapter on a quest to establish a restoration network. As you will recall, the components that we have discussed thus far – existing fragments and anchors of ecological integrity, additional newly restored fragments and anchors, and the water movement network – will link together at multiple spatial scales to form the restoration network.

Once those components emerge, the location and shape of a restoration network can be plotted. Restoration networks are planned around watershed boundaries as opposed to political boundaries. In an urban setting, the largest watershed within the city is the *focal watershed*. This is the scale at which the largest-scale restoration network is designed. A landscape restoration network will be designed and established for the focal watershed, and smaller-scale ecosystem restoration networks will be designed and established for neighbourhoods, parks and recreational areas, school and institutional grounds, vacant lots, small parks, backyards, and laneways.

Designating a large-scale restoration network for the focal watershed aims ultimately to protect the ecological integrity of the large watershed. It is supported by finer-scale linked and interconnected networks of ecological reserves that protect and restore the ecological integrity of areas outside large-scale reserves and restoration features.[21] One proceeds by designing and connecting ecological reserves for progressively smaller areas.[22]

Starting with the focal watershed, large restoration areas will include the largest fragments and anchors of ecological integrity. At each successively smaller scale, another nested restoration network consisting of fragments and anchors of ecological integrity is established. In the process, all remaining intact remnants of natural ecosystems are protected. Given the extensive modification of natural ecosystems in urban areas, it is essential to protect unmodified and relatively unmodified ecosystems as anchors for networks of ecological reserves.

The *matrix* is the area of human activities embedded within restoration networks. The integrity and resilience of protected areas depend directly on maintaining ecological integrity within the matrix: "Practices that maintain or improve the suitability of the matrix are fundamental to the conservation of biodiversity."[23] Greening the matrix can be extremely challenging in a city. Yet even fine-scale and moderate-scale restoration networks woven throughout a matrix of intense human use are vital for restoring a reasonable degree of ecological integrity. As we will see, restoring a water movement network across the matrix helps to restore connectivity both above and below ground in an otherwise ecologically hostile environment.

Connectivity operates from microscopic scales to continental scales. Thus, nature-directed stewardship needs to maintain and restore connectivity across a wide range of scales. For example, when it comes to microscopic connectivity that occurs within soils, we assume that restoring natural above-ground composition and structure will restore, over time, below-ground composition and structure, including microscopic connectivity by organisms such as mycorrhizal fungi. Above-ground connectivity ranges from re-establishing fallen trees that link organisms and processes in small patches to restoring riparian corridors and cross-watershed or cross-valley linkages at the watershed and landscape levels. Establishing above-ground connectivity also supports re-establishing natural levels of biological diversity. In particular, restoring and linking the natural ranges of habitat types are essential for biodiversity.

The act of restoration can cause unintended harm, so it must be carried out cautiously. Restoration activities risk causing soil erosion, for example, which can lead to aquatic pollution and damage to freshwater biological diversity. Sediment in water can block sunlight, clog fish gills, and smother feeding sites and spawning areas.[24] In many jurisdictions, controlling erosion and sediment is required for any activity that could pollute runoff in order to protect fish and other aquatic species. Thus, developing an erosion control plan as part of ecological restoration is necessary and protects water quality, riparian ecosystems, and aquatic environments. Preventing soil erosion maintains natural soil profiles, including the organic matter in topsoil and the stability of subsoils, thus encouraging the development of diverse, healthy vegetative communities.

Once a restoration network has been established, its success can be secured by requiring that any development fits into natural ecosystem features, and by giving priority to the maintenance or restoration of ecological integrity. Achieving this development standard requires respecting ecological limits, protecting remnant natural ecosystems, and making precautionary decisions that err on the side of protecting ecological integrity. It also means dismantling inappropriate infrastructure and assisting natural processes to restore ecological integrity. Deciding to protect ecological integrity (and to not carry out development) might often be the best choice where the area in question constitutes a rare fragment of a natural ecosystem.

As natural ecosystem processes take over, ecological integrity strengthens, and biodiversity increases, the restoration efforts shift slowly to maintenance efforts. Given enough time, the restoration networks will mature into protected networks of ecological reserves.

We recognize that this will happen faster in some cities than in others. Some cities are older than others; some cities are established, and their urban boundaries are full, whereas other cities are newer with more undeveloped land (as we will show with our case studies in the following chapters). If one were to consider the range of cities on a continuum from new cities (more undeveloped land) to established cities (fully developed land), then NDS will unfold differently at the two extremes of that continuum.

New urban areas can move quickly from restoration to networks of ecological reserves. In such cases, NDS can be applied much like it is applied in unfettered, relatively undisturbed natural landscapes through the design and implementation of networks of protected ecosystems at multiple spatial scales. The extent of restoration required in new urban areas depends on the degree of ecological integrity existing within the new urban area and the surrounding landscape. Intact natural ecosystems and fragments of intact natural systems become anchors or starting points from which to develop networks of ecological reserves. As much as possible, development in new urban areas will be ecosystem-based, aimed to fit within networks of protected ecosystems at multiple spatial scales. An example is Shawnigan Lake, presented in the text boxes in the next chapter.

At the other end of the continuum, established urban areas will require extensive restoration efforts and a significant amount of time (and courageous decisions) for the restoration network to mature. A key aspect of restoring degraded landscapes in established urban areas is committing to the activities as ongoing, not just as short-term (or single-year) projects. Restoration treatments need to be regularly maintained and enriched by connecting restoration features to each other as the number and location of restoration features expand. The goal is to develop restoration networks packed with restoration treatments that continue over time until enough ecological integrity exists that the restoration networks become protected networks of ecosystems that possess natural or near-natural character across spatial scales. An example is Still Creek in East Vancouver, presented as the main example in the next chapter.

6 Nature-Directed Stewardship in East Vancouver

We can reduce the threat of climate disruption by restoring natural system function. From this we see that this is not the end of the world. It is just the beginning of another.

– Bob Sandford, UN University Institute for Water, Environment and Health

Our theoretical model of how nature-directed stewardship would unfold in urban areas in general prepared us to apply NDS to a specific urban setting: a watershed in East Vancouver, British Columbia. In this chapter, we summarize the results of a multiyear project that we carried out in collaboration with community partner Still Moon Arts Society, and others, to develop an NDS plan for Vancouver's Still Creek watershed.

In order to illustrate the extensive challenges encountered with applying NDS in the established urban area of East Vancouver, we contrast it with a new residential development in an urban-rural fringe forested location. Specifically, we contrast Vancouver's Still Creek watershed with an NDS plan developed for the Shawnigan Lake watershed, just north of Victoria, British Columbia, a rapidly urbanizing area. The contrasting experience of applying NDS in a predominantly forested residential development is discussed in text boxes throughout the discussion of applying NDS in East Vancouver. As you will see, NDS applies across the spectrum of urbanization.

THE STILL CREEK WATERSHED

The Still Creek watershed is found on unceded Indigenous land in the eastern portion of Vancouver and crosses municipal boundaries into the cities of Burnaby and New Westminster. For thousands of years, the Still Creek watershed was occupied and used by the Squamish, Musqueam, and Tsleil-Waututh Nations, none of whom ceded the land to colonial control. Indigenous Peoples actively protected, managed, and lived as part of the ecosystems that comprised the Still Creek watershed. Archaeological and anthropological evidence shows, for example, their cultivation of *wapato* (Indian potato) in wetlands, their pruning and transplanting of berry bushes, and their use of low brush fires to stimulate thicker bark production on Douglas-fir trees for fire fuel.[1]

FIGURE 6.1   Exposed reaches of Still Creek offer glimpses of the water movement network that was the backbone of ecological functioning in the natural character of Vancouver. The restoration network will link these remnants, daylight further stretches of the creek, and add connectivity across the watershed.

This human presence helped to shape the natural character of the landscape that George Vancouver, Richard Moody, James Douglas, Edward Lytton, and other European settlers inaccurately perceived to be an empty wilderness waiting for their agents to act as "pioneers in the work of civilization."[2] Early European accounts of the area mistakenly describe the Still Creek watershed as "a country without habitation."[3] In fact, nothing could have been further from the truth. Unlike present-day human activities on the watershed, however, Indigenous Peoples lived, and often still live, in ways "responsive to [rather than dominating of] the local ecology."[4]

The Still Creek watershed's transformation from an old-growth forest to the present-day cityscape began with the establishment of Fort Langley. This outpost of the Hudson's Bay Company attracted an influx of European fur traders to the area.[5] A short time later, the Fraser River gold rush began, attracting many more newcomers and prompting the establishment of the Crown Colony of British Columbia.[6] During this time of rapid population growth, the British Royal Engineers were dispatched to assist with maintaining law and order and to survey the landscape for settlement, resource extraction potential, and roads.[7]

The roads would serve to connect the newly established Hastings townsite on the shores of Burrard Inlet – now the site of the Pacific National Exhibition in East Vancouver – and the City of New Westminster on the Fraser River. The road system included an early transit corridor in the form of a regular stage-coach service between the new towns.[8] Lumber mills were established along Burrard Inlet and the first shipments sent abroad marked the start of British Columbia's export lumber trade.[9]

The ecological impacts of land-use decisions were already noticeable. A report on Musqueam land use and occupancy, for example, recalls the disappearance of game animals from hunting areas because of forest cover loss and habitat destruction from logging.[10] Decisions were made based on short-term goals and without an understanding of local ecological systems or their limits.

Late 1800s to Early 1900s

The next 100 years would see even more dramatic changes to the Still Creek watershed and surrounding area; changes that would begin to create both physical and psychological distance between people and the ecosystems that sustained them. With population growth and increased agricultural settlement, additional transportation infrastructure followed.[11]

A number of land use decisions made during the early nineteenth century had a lasting effect on the Still Creek watershed. The installation of dams along Still Creek (to enable the transportation of logs from nearby sawmills) altered the natural flow of water. Farming in the Still Creek watershed caused agricultural runoff to enter the creek.[12] Many tributaries of Still Creek were encased in concrete or metal culverts as part of the installation of the Vancouver, New Westminster and Yukon Railway line.[13] And the first land use plan for Vancouver and the surrounding region, the Bartholomew Plan of 1928, set in place priorities that remain entrenched today.

The Bartholomew Plan, completed by a Missouri-based consulting firm, recommended road design, public park layout, the appearance of residential

FIGURE 6.2   The ancient coastal western hemlock character of Vancouver (shown on the left in Stanley Park in the 1850s) was mostly eradicated, sometimes by dynamite (below), to chase a vision of cities without nature, Indigenous Peoples, or a sense of place. | *Source:* For "ancient coastal rainforest": Vancouver Archives, COV_StPkP264_AForestPathway StanleyPark.jpg; for "stump blasting": Vancouver Archives, COV_CVA99-83Blasting.jpg.

properties, and street tree planting guidelines, many of which are still visible today.[14] For example, the plan provided that "every lot should have one or two shade trees" in addition to "a smooth, weedless lawn" not "spot up" with trees and shrubs.[15] Almost 100 years later, a drive down almost any residential street in the Still Creek watershed will find lawns (which might or might not be entirely "weedless") with little to no other vegetation, except perhaps a "shade tree." With the exception of avoiding development in areas with steep slopes, very few of the recommendations appear to be based on ecological character or limits (understandable, perhaps, given the colonial thinking at the time).[16] In contrast, as you will recall, NDS recognizes that natural character is the baseline for plans and that ecological limits provide the boundaries for human activities.

By 1928, Still Creek along with its immediate shoreline was well on its way to becoming an industrial corridor. Residential and commercial development was progressing quickly in the upland areas, where conditions were drier. But population growth soon pushed development to expand into the lowlands of the watershed.[17] The overall effect was a loss of vegetation and an increase in impermeable surfaces throughout the watershed. Trees and other vegetation intercepted rain, tempered the volume and speed of precipitation as it fell to the ground, and offered shade that reduced evaporation and maintained moisture in the soil so that the ground was nearly always able to absorb rain. Without the trees, the watershed was unable to cope with rainfall, and a series of major floods occurred in the 1920s.

In an attempt to prevent future flooding, work was undertaken in the late 1920s to channelize and deepen Still Creek and to lower Burnaby Lake.[18] Although the politicians, planners, and engineers of the day were doing what they thought was best, Still Creek was being transformed into a conveyance channel, creating only a temporary solution that would lead to a growing problem.

Mid-1900s
In the wake of the Great Depression, the provincial government sought to bolster economic stability and assumed direct control of the City of Burnaby. New oil and automotive industries were encouraged to set up their businesses within city limits.[19] This economic activity, combined with the availability of undeveloped land close to Vancouver, led to a "Burna-boom" period in which Burnaby was an attractive location for postwar residential subdivisions, retail centres, and industrial parks.[20] That attractiveness was enhanced by earlier residential development and sewer infrastructure in Vancouver that pushed sprawl into the Burnaby side of the watershed.

With an ever-growing population on both sides of the political boundary, local governments saw the need to create the first regional and municipal planning bodies and the first Official Regional Plan. The plan described criteria for determining "suitable land utilization" and temporarily designated "areas of water, steep slope, [and] floodplain ... to be reserved in large parcels until such time as detailed studies document the need for more intensive use of these areas."[21] Preservation of such ecologically sensitive areas in the Still Creek watershed would have helped to retain a degree of ecological integrity. Alas, riparian areas were set aside for more "intensive use."

By 1955, a significant portion of land adjacent to Still Creek had become an industrial zone, possibly because low-lying riparian areas were more flood prone and less desirable for residential use and almost certainly as a result of the proximity of the New Westminster and Yukon Railway line built five decades earlier. The new policy to enclose Still Creek would allow industrial lands to expand to the very edge of, or even over the top of, Still Creek.

During the 1960s and 1970s, Still Creek became noticeably contaminated, eventually prompting the City of Vancouver to advise against human contact with the water.[22] Both Burnaby and Vancouver halted further enclosure of Still Creek by the 1980s, but significant damage had already been done, and more development was yet to come.[23] The 1986 Expo Line Skytrain brought two transit hubs to the Still Creek watershed (Brentwood Town Centre and Holdom Station), each adding new development pressure.

The 1990s Onward

The 1990s saw further disruption of the flow of water in the Still Creek watershed. Vancouver embarked on a city-wide program to pave its hundreds of kilometres of laneways, originally established to hide garbage and provide parking.[24] At the same time, an Integrated Stormwater Management Strategy (ISMS) was completed for a watershed adjacent to Still Creek (the Stoney Creek watershed). The ISMS acknowledged the negative impacts of impermeable surfaces on watershed hydrology and aquatic ecosystem health and thus considered ecosystem functioning as part of a stormwater management plan for the first time.[25] The ISMS cautioned, however, that "restoring the environment to pre-development condition ... [is] desirable but may be beyond the affordability threshold."[26]

The concept of integrated stormwater management planning was widely accepted by the early 2000s as a more comprehensive approach to land-use planning that enables local governments to be proactive in protecting property and aquatic habitat.[27] For example, the Still Creek Integrated Stormwater Management Plan not only presents strategies for accommodating and managing growth and development "in an integrated manner that takes into account the rainwater cycle, [and] environmental and recreational issues," but also aims to "protect and enhance streamside and aquatic habitats ... [and] maintain and increase native species biodiversity."[28] Conversely, the Metro Vancouver Regional Growth Strategy seeks to protect the supply of industrial land, including along the Still Creek riparian zones, making ecological restoration more challenging.[29]

Since 2010, significant steps have been taken to enhance ecosystems in Vancouver and Burnaby. For example, both municipalities have strengthened their tree-protection bylaws and adopted urban forest strategies. Burnaby has a sustainability strategy and street standards that encourage rain gardens, Metro Vancouver has an urban forest climate adaptation guide and green infrastructure resources, and Vancouver has an Integrated Rainwater Management Plan and a RainCity Strategy that aims to "capture (infiltrate, evapotranspire, and/or reuse) and clean (treat) a minimum of 90% of Vancouver's average annual rainfall volume" over the long term.[30]

ECOLOGICAL INTEGRITY OF THE STILL CREEK WATERSHED

You will recall that NDS begins by analyzing natural ecosystem character and current condition. Character refers to the natural ecological composition, structure, and function, and condition refers to how the character has been modified by industrial civilization's activities.[31] The integrity gap, or loss of ecological integrity from the natural character to the current condition, represents the restoration target.

Natural Character

The Still Creek watershed was once a sea of green with blue veins and arteries of water connecting the complex biological diversity of a temperate rainforest, as illustrated in Figure 6.3. Walking through that watershed was to bounce along a plush carpet of soil, mosses, and lichens. To breathe the air was to inhale a pungent scent of cedar vapour, hemlock mist, and grizzly odour. The wings of eagles mixed ocean mist with healing fragrances from the foliage and bark of a towering fir that germinated a millennium ago. Neither the summer sun nor winter storms could push the temperature from the moderate range that gave this temperate rainforest its name. Seasons marked by the cycle of salmon made life thrive. The rhizosphere, soil directly influenced by root secretions and micro-organisms, hid from sight the watershed's highest level of biological diversity. Channels in the soil purified water and moderated its flow. On its back was the visible plant and small animal diversity that provided a foundation for keystone species such as chum salmon, and umbrella species such as coastal grizzly bears.

The old-growth forests of the Still Creek watershed – in the Pacific Northwest's Coastal Western Hemlock Zone – consisted of diverse mixtures of trees, including western red cedar, western hemlock, Douglas-fir, Sitka spruce, Pacific yew,

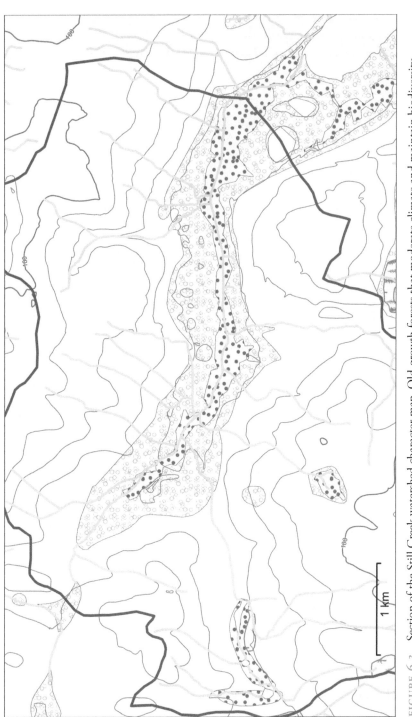

FIGURE 6.3 Section of the Still Creek watershed character map. Old-growth forests that moderate climate and maintain biodiversity are the natural character of the Still Creek watershed.

red alder, and big-leaf maple.[32] These forests were dominated by conifers, many of which approached or exceeded seventy metres in height and commonly were more than 500–600 years old, with individuals exceeding 1,000 or 2,000 years of age.

Massive trees in the Still Creek old-growth forest were part of multi-layered canopies that included shrubs, herbs, and groundcover. Standing dead trees (snags) and fallen dead trees (logs), in various states of decay, offered habitat for a wide variety of birds, amphibians, and mammals, while holding and purifying water as the trees' nutrients slowly returned to the soil. Dense canopies, moderately dense canopies, and openings were mixed across the watershed.

When rain falls on such a multi-layered, diverse, old-growth, temperate rainforest, a significant amount is intercepted. The tall, dense canopies of conifers and deciduous trees and shrubs that once occupied the Still Creek watershed caused 40 percent or more of the precipitation (rain and occasionally snow) falling in a storm to be evaporated or sublimated back into the atmosphere by wind and solar radiation and moved elsewhere. The remaining precipitation dripped, a drop at a time, to the absorbent forest floor of decayed wood and permeable deep soils. Thus, despite annual rainfall that could exceed two metres, the Still Creek watershed's old-growth forest managed the water such that the forest was wet in a storm, but not overwhelmed, and drier in the summer, but never parched. Significant overland flows and floods were infrequent.

The subtle, relatively low-lying topography of the Still Creek watershed, coupled with abundant annual precipitation, resulted in small year-round and ephemeral streams virtually everywhere in the landscape (see water movement network, Figure 6.14). In the lower part of the watershed, wetlands were interspersed with forests on moderately well-drained humps. In many locations, salmon literally swam between the roots of trees. Both the lower and the upland portions of the Still Creek watershed contained a dense water movement network. Much of that network was readily visible above ground, and soil and landform characteristics shaped the network below ground. The Still Creek water movement network played a major role in determining which plants, animals, and micro-organisms lived there (as well as the characteristics of the ecological processes).

The rich biological diversity supported vibrant Indigenous societies that fulfilled their needs from the watershed while maintaining its natural character. Most changes were brought about by natural disturbances, such as windstorms, heavy snow, and saturating rain. Diversity was maintained through activities by all beings, including humans, that occurred within ecological limits. Old-growth forests represent interconnectedness among everything – air, water, trees, other plants, soil, fungi, bacteria, and animals (including us). We owe our survival to such primary ecosystems with natural ecological integrity.

SHAWNIGAN LAKE NATURAL CHARACTER

The natural character of the Shawnigan Lake watershed is also that of an old-growth temperate rainforest, specifically of the Coastal Douglas-Fir Zone.[33] The tree species that cloaked this forest landscape were dominated by large, disturbance-resilient, old-growth Douglas-firs, many of which likely reached or exceeded 1,000 years of age. On moist to wet, nutrient-rich sites, western red cedar and western hemlock were partners with Douglas-fir and often dominated these areas. Western white pine accompanies those three tree species across the landscape, with the exception of very wet or very dry sites. Very dry, nutrient-poor sites often contained Garry oak and arbutus, with scattered Douglas-fir.

Old-growth forests are more than big, old trees. These forests contain an assemblage of species and processes that represent thousands of years of evolution. Old-growth forests have the greatest number of species overall, as well as the greatest number of specialist species, compared with any other forest phase. The rich biological diversity of old-growth forests provides for the well-being of the old forest, the well-being of adjacent landscapes and their ecosystems, and the biological legacies that will support future forests. Their biological diversity gives intact old-growth forests many options for adapting to climate change not found in ecosystems simplified by human development.

This character of the Still Creek watershed is an expression of its optimal design, which resulted in thousands of years of ecological integrity and the stable conditions in which humans have been able to develop and thrive. Understanding the character of the watershed provides a baseline condition against which the current condition needs to be contrasted and from which restoration targets can be identified.

Current Condition

The Still Creek watershed's sea of green with blue veins and arteries has been transformed into a biological desert. The watershed now blocks natural water flow. Water is concentrated rather than dispersed throughout the watershed. Soils are covered with impervious lanes, roads, freeways, parking lots, sidewalks, and buildings. In a word, the current condition of the Still Creek watershed can be described as impermeable. Figure 6.4 shows the dominance of residential areas (white), and streets and industrial-commercial complexes (grey). The current Still Creek watershed boundary is shown by a red line, and the estimated

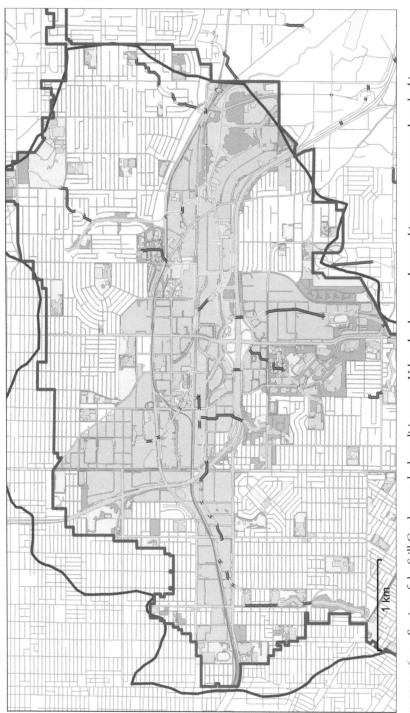

1 km

FIGURE 6.4 Section of the Still Creek watershed condition map. Urban development destroyed intact ecosystems and resulted in the current condition of the Still Creek watershed being highly vulnerable to the impacts of climate change.

natural watershed boundary is shown by a magenta line.[34] The dark blue lines indicate the location of buried and culverted streams, and the light blue lines represent surface streams.

More than 81 percent of the watershed is covered with impermeable surfaces: 35 percent consists of major transportation corridors such as roads and freeways; 46 percent consists of residential streets, roofs, driveways, sidewalks, alleys, paved yards, and other impermeable surfaces.[35] Levels of impervious or impermeable surfaces as high as those found in the Still Creek watershed stop

FIGURE 6.5
The natural water movement network is blocked by impermeable surfaces – pavement, concrete, asphalt roofs – that cover much of the Still Creek watershed.

water from infiltrating the soil. Instead, rainwater runs rapidly off hard surfaces, moving pollutants such as heavy metals, chemicals, and pesticides into creeks, ponds, or other exposed water bodies (or into groundwater, which eventually ends up in surface water bodies).[36] In conjunction with the lack of vegetation, impermeable surfaces are the primary causes of surface runoff and the loss of ecosystem processes.

The natural topography created a Still Creek watershed of approximately 3,100 hectares. That natural character was maintained within ecological limits by the Indigenous Peoples who occupied and used this area for millennia. However, commencing in the early 1800s, colonial culture altered the topography and largely erased the natural character, leaving a smaller watershed of approximately 2,800 hectares. In the process, streams, gullies, wetlands, and water-collecting depressions were filled in, drained, or captured in drainage structures and buried. Thus, "development" transformed a fully functioning watershed into an ecologically impoverished watershed through various forms of urbanization, industrialization, and other human activities.

The remaining green space is dominated by lawns and manicured parks utterly unrelated to the watershed's former grandeur. Approximately 5 percent of the Still Creek watershed is an urban forest (defined as a group of trees covering an area larger than fifteen metres by thirty metres, having a canopy cover of greater than 35 percent, and exhibiting some natural stochastic distribution rather than trees planted in a row). Depending on their size and complexity, urban forests can have many desirable qualities similar to the composition and structure of natural forests. However, urban forests are often isolated fragments of natural forest vegetation. Because of their small, isolated nature, urban forests play only a minimal role in managing water, moderating climate, sequestering and storing carbon, and providing biological diversity in the Still Creek watershed.

Slightly more than 11 percent of the Still Creek watershed is occupied by vegetation other than forests. The majority of this area consists of turf grass, which, though absorbent, does not allow effective interception and dispersal of water during storms like that provided by natural forest ecosystems. Some of this area can contain useful fragments of multi-layered vegetation, but most of it is ineffective at managing water, particularly during intense storms.

With the removal of natural vegetation and the loss of natural water quality, quantity, and timing of flow, many species – from Pacific salmon and grizzly bears to raptors and martens – have either been lost or are in severe decline. Their absence indicates a loss of ecological integrity and a deficit of biological diversity in the soil. Keystone species can occupy the soil (even if we are not yet aware of them), and without their presence the health and survival of above-ground ecosystems can be threatened, particularly given the stresses of climate disruption.

FIGURE 6.6 Open stretches of Still Creek and remnants of nature are isolated fragments, creating biological "islands" ripe for connection to a restoration network.

Our analysis of the current condition of the Still Creek watershed shows how much change has occurred in the roughly 200 years since the watershed was occupied by old-growth temperate rainforests. Those forests were an integral part of an interconnected, interdependent water movement network consisting of deep permeable soils, myriad small tributary streams, wetlands of various sizes, and the main stem of Still Creek. Virtually none of this remains.

Fragments and Anchors: Remnants of Ecological Integrity

Few remnants of ecological integrity remain in the Still Creek watershed to furnish *anchors* (or, more accurately, lifeboats) for restoring ecological integrity. Where these fragments exist, they tend to be isolated in a sea of urban infra-structure devoid of nature, further impeding the re-establishment of natural ecosystem composition and structure. Specifically, the only remaining fragments of natural character are in a small area in the watershed's bottomlands where relatively natural riparian ecosystems remain and a few small patches of native vegetation in the lower elevations.

As explained earlier, remnants of natural composition and structure are an-chors for ecological restoration in urban nature-directed stewardship planning. *Anchors* are fragments of ecological integrity that can be linked to other frag-ments (or areas of restoration) through a restoration network across the degraded landscape. Anchors, foundational places from which restoration activities

Shawnigan Lake basin is a watershed of approximately 7,165 hectares. Significant colonial development began with railway logging and home-steading in the late 1800s followed by clear-cut truck logging and larger-scale agriculture. More than 70 percent of the watershed still consists of second-growth forest (some of which has been recently logged), 10 percent is part of the provincial Agricultural Land Reserve, 4 percent is residential, 1 percent is industrial, and the remainder consists of parks and protected areas. Proximity to Victoria, coupled with comparatively lower real estate values and a relatively natural environment, has attracted increasing urban development.

Today, Shawnigan Lake is a landscape of urban development, village shops, industrial forestry (still characterized by clear-cutting), agriculture, small-scale farming, and a variety of industrial activities, from gravel pits to a former toxic soil remediation site that is now closed. Loss of natural ecological integrity, resulting from extensive human development activities, charac-terizes the current ecological condition throughout the Shawnigan Lake watershed.

Clear-cut logging with short-cycle tree plantations has caused the great-est harm to water quality and biological diversity. Since the early 2000s, this condition has been followed closely by the impacts of human settlement and urban development. Old-growth forests of the past in the Shawnigan Lake watershed left a legacy of decaying wood on top of and within the soil. However, with the ongoing prevalence of clear-cut forestry predicated on short-rotation (i.e., short-cycle) tree farms, and urban development in the watershed, the vital natural water management structures of natural old forests are disappearing.

Cooperation among diverse organizations and individuals will be es-sential to restore degraded areas and conserve the remaining natural eco-logical integrity, not only in the face of global heating but also because of the fragmented property ownership patterns. Slightly more than 70 percent of the Shawnigan Lake watershed is under private ownership, and only approxi-mately 12 percent is provincial crown land. The remainder of the watershed is found in public parks, private railway rights-of-way, public roads rights-of-way, and utilities.

FIGURE 6.7   Most of Shawnigan Lake's watershed has been logged at least once. In the background are second-growth forests that regenerated naturally. In the foreground is a third-growth tree plantation, the result of recent clear-cut logging.

FIGURE 6.8   Relatively large and intact patches of nature, including segments of Still Creek's bottomlands near the Fraser River, provide anchors of ecological integrity. | *Source:* Melinda Markey.

radiate, are incorporated into networks of ecological reserves as they emerge (after restoration) at multiple spatial scales.

Given the intense urbanization of the Still Creek watershed, we did not expect to identify an ecosystem reserve network with much ecological integrity. We were hopeful, however, that patches of vegetation and stream fragments would be found that could serve as anchors for an initial network and, in so doing, define priority areas for starting ecological restoration.

The Still Creek watershed retains some trees and small patches of forest. Established trees, especially the larger and older ones, multi-layered vegetation, and remnant natural areas need to be protected. Collectively, these portions of the watershed provide important ecological benefits that slow the effects of climate change and help ecosystems adapt to the climate emergency. As the areas of vegetation grow, they increasingly sequester and store carbon, moderate heat and storms, conserve water, and harbour biological diversity.

Many of the trees that comprise the residential and industrial areas of the Still Creek watershed are nonindigenous, broadleaf species. At first glance, one might think that replacing these deciduous trees with native coniferous trees would be the right course of action. However, if deciduous tree species can survive in the predicted future climate, then maintaining those trees offers important advantages. The existing large trees store enormous amounts of carbon, and the deciduous trees sequester carbon more rapidly than coniferous trees.[37] Replacing these trees with small, young seedlings or saplings will release greenhouse gases and impair climate moderation functions. Many decades would pass before the level of carbon sequestration and storage and climate moderation offered by the existing big trees are re-established. Thus, retaining both nonindigenous and indigenous established trees is an important part of the nature-directed stewardship plan for the Still Creek watershed.

Based on the existing patches of vegetation and exposed stream reaches, we plotted an initial network through the watershed's bottomlands at a scale of 1:12,500 (Figure 6.9). The (current condition) watershed boundary (at the top of the slope) is shown with a red line, streams are shown in blue (light blue for the surface reaches, dark blue for the buried sections), and the potential network is outlined in yellow along the valley bottom of the watershed. This potential network sought to connect the fragments of ecological integrity along natural riparian areas.

Zooming in to 1:5,000, significant challenges to the initial network design emerge (Figure 6.10). Specifically, streets and freeways, buried portions of streams, impermeable industrial and residential areas, and a virtual absence of natural riparian ecosystems have obliterated connectivity and ruined all but a few disconnected fragments of nature.

FIGURE 6.9 Potential ecosystem restoration network at 1:12,500

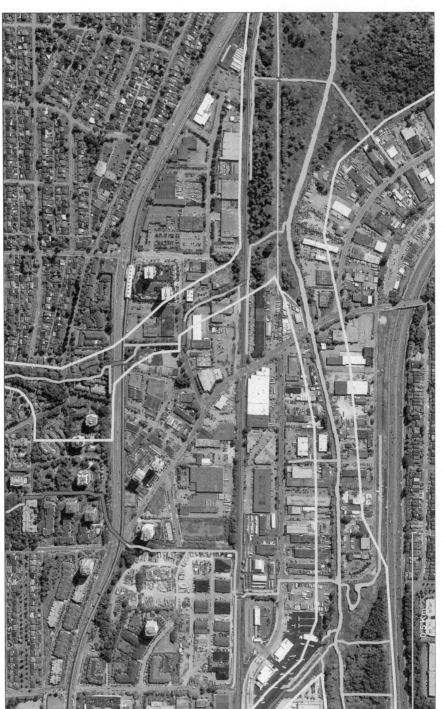

FIGURE 6.10 Potential ecosystem restoration network at 1:5,000

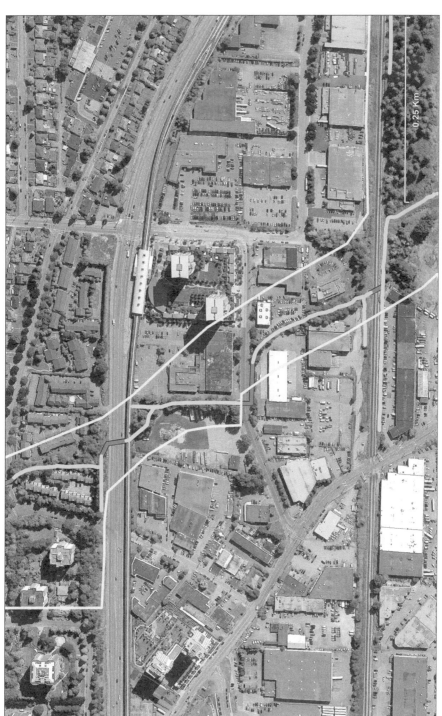

FIGURE 6.11   Potential ecosystem restoration network at 1:2,500

With some notable exceptions, such as the significant wetland found in the southeast corner of Figure 6.10, anchors are far from obvious, and there is little basis for selecting one fragment of vegetation, or one stream channel, over another.

Zooming in further to 1:2,500 (Figure 6.11) only highlights the challenges. The "very hard to modify" human infrastructure – including roads, highways, streets, buried streams, and large buildings – creates daunting restoration tasks. Since virtually no significant anchors of natural ecological integrity remain in the Still Creek watershed, linking the widely scattered fragments that do remain is onerous and arbitrary. All traces of ecological integrity have been erased from the matrix. The bits of nature are lonely green dots on a canvas of pavement, concrete, and tar-coated roofs. Until ecological restoration has been planned and carried out in representative portions of the Still Creek watershed, including riparian ecosystems, bottomlands, and uplands, there will be no clear ecological guidance to design, locate, and implement a restoration network.

Thus, imposing a restoration network is not yet feasible, logical, or defensible in the Still Creek watershed (or indeed in most cities). However, this conclusion simply underscores the need for NDS to direct all urban development planning, with particular priority given to areas with little modification by urbanization or other human activities. And it underscores the need for taking action through the three-part process outlined in the next chapter that mobilizes both bottom-up and top-down efforts.

Connectivity Networks in the Still Creek Watershed

In most cities, the absence of sufficient fragments of ecological integrity and anchors of natural character means that restoration is necessary. NDS must proceed in urban areas by starting with restoration wherever and whenever it is possible in order to build up new fragments and anchors and to restore a water movement network. Natural character and topography of the watershed determine where to start restoration.

As you will recall, these restored components of ecological integrity join forces with the existing fragments and anchors to create a restoration network. Eventually, that restoration network will mature into an urban protected ecosystem network (see Figure 6.12).

Restoration Features: New Fragments and Anchors

In established urban areas, such as Still Creek, restoration features should be enhanced to establish multi-layered vegetation that intercepts and disperses precipitation, purifies air, and sequesters and stores carbon. Where there are large established trees, layers of smaller trees can be added. Along with smaller

FIGURE 6.12   Nature-directed stewardship in cities

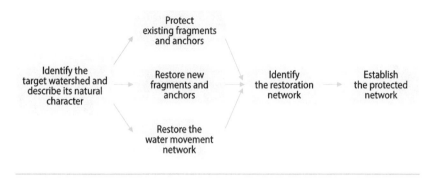

trees, shrubs, herbs, mosses, and lichens can be restored to enrich ecological processes. Piece-by-piece, restoration efforts add layers and complexity to the beginning of an urban forest.

Save for a few isolated patches, the Still Creek watershed is devoid of forests. Restoration of forests as part of a protected ecosystem network is an important long-term goal which, even with neighbourhood and government commitment to restoration, will take decades or longer. Long-term dedication needs to include ongoing commitment to maintain and improve restoration of previously restored areas. Restoration is neither a "one and done" activity nor a short-term fix.

The restoration journey starts with the re-establishment of natural composition and structure wherever possible – parks, residential yards, empty lots, alleys, rooftops, schoolyards, commercial spaces, sidewalks, bike lanes separators, and any place that a community of trees might take root. When deciding where to use deciduous or coniferous trees, water availability is an important consideration. Although deciduous trees are better at capturing carbon than coniferous trees, they demand copious volumes of water to maintain the large surface areas of their leaves.[38] Thus, where water availability is low, it is best to choose coniferous trees or deciduous trees with smaller leaves (e.g., trembling aspen). In many cases, a mixture of deciduous and coniferous trees is a good hedge against an uncertain future climate. In degraded landscapes, including all landscapes affected by development in industrialized societies, restoration features (new fragments and anchors) will include unique areas, ecologically sensitive areas, biologically rich sites, and areas representative of the matrix or the most common ecosystems. These features are likely to be degraded or eradicated by development. The restoration network will eventually provide linkages between restoration features that are being rebuilt by natural processes with our assistance.

FIGURE 6.13   Restoration in progress in Still Creek. Restoration in open segments of Still Creek led to reduced channelization, more riparian vegetation, and slowed water flow. | *Source:* Melinda Markey.

Restoration of the Water Movement Network

As we have seen, human infrastructure and activities in the Still Creek watershed have changed water movement from dispersed to concentrated. The pre-existing natural watershed surface was tightly packed with ephemeral streams, permanent streams, creeks, and wetlands; water oozed through the soils and fallen trees, pulsed into vegetation, and saturated the air. Today those interconnected networks are fragmented and disconnected (both above and below ground). The biologically rich soils, streams, lakes, and wetlands have been forced into channelized ditches, culverts, and buried streams. Rain that used to drip slowly through multi-layered canopies of trees, shrubs, herbs, mosses, and lichens now falls virtually unimpeded from storm clouds to impervious surfaces below.

We mapped the natural water movement network in the Still Creek watershed, reconstructed from historical topographical and vegetation maps, onto the current urban land use (see Figure 6.14). The coloured shading is a digital elevation model, with green showing the lowest elevations and orange the highest elevations. The original watershed boundary appears as a purple line, and the current watershed boundary is demarcated in red.

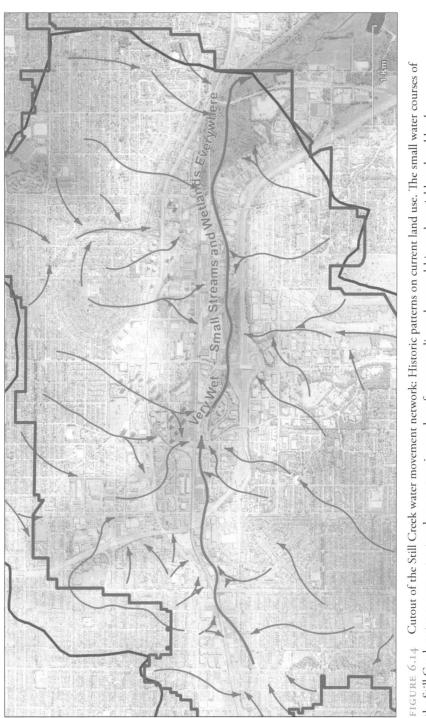

Very Wet — Small Streams and Wetlands Everywhere

FIGURE 6.14   Cutout of the Still Creek water movement network: Historic patterns on current land use. The small water courses of the Still Creek water movement network are restoration anchors for nature-directed stewardship at the neighbourhood level.

In order to establish a restoration network capable of eventually maturing (back) into its rich, natural character, the protected ecosystem network must contain ecological integrity and the full range of natural composition, structure, and function, and as much of the natural water movement network as possible. Without the natural flow and dispersal of water, ecosystem health will be compromised, and restoration to natural character will be thwarted.

We therefore focus on restoring the natural water movement network in the Still Creek watershed by designing linkages that connect vegetation fragments within existing and buried portions of the tributary or sub-watersheds of the Still Creek watershed. Restoration activities consist of converting impermeable surfaces to permeable surfaces. This top priority must happen at all scales, across all surfaces that concentrate water and block its natural flow across every type of land use and property tenure.

Along with permeable surfaces, multi-layered vegetation is critical to slow the rush of water from rainclouds to impermeable surfaces and into sewers. Additional vegetation in the smallest sub-watersheds (e.g., a yard or road edge) can be connected with bioswales and rain gardens that capture water, purify it, and direct it out of the grey infrastructure system. Bioswales and rain gardens serve as tributaries to reconstructed streams flowing into Still Creek.

The blanket of rooftops in the Still Creek watershed is interrupted only occasionally by vegetated roofs. This is nothing but opportunity. Green roofs connected to living walls, community gardens, adjacent multi-layered vegetation, and permeable surfaces would go a long way toward restoring natural water movement patterns.

The focal point of the watershed's water movement network, Still Creek itself, is one of the few streams in Metro Vancouver that is, at least partially, daylighted. Its restoration has been led by the Still Moon Arts Society, whose skill at community building through art incorporates significant ecological innovation. For example, Still Moon built "living structures" in Still Creek that hold and disperse water and thus restore natural water movement networks and ecological integrity.

Assisting nature to restore natural water movement networks and ecological integrity is not just a matter of technical planning and implementation of restoration treatments. Still Moon builds community energy, enthusiasm, and love for ecosystems through art in many forms. For example, studio space for art, environmental stewardship, a "Cracks in Creeks" performance, sonic installation, and visual eco-art presentation on the banks of Still Creek all connect the community to the creek. But there is more. Still Moon, alone and in partnerships with watershed schools, offers a natural dye garden to support pollinators, medicinal plant programs, and oyster mushroom and alder ephemeral sculptures that enrich the ecosystem.

FIGURE 6.15　Art installation in Still Creek. Nature can instill a compelling sense of place. Here biodegradable art reminds the Still Creek community of the essential role of beavers in shaping their watershed. | *Source:* Carmen Rosen.

　The rest of the community has opportunities to step up. To facilitate action, we developed conceptual approaches to three urban situations: industrial-commercial, schoolground, and single-family residential. These concepts were developed to stimulate thinking about site-specific ecological restoration actions focused on the water movement network. These approaches encompass a diversity of restoration treatments but do not include all types of restoration that will be necessary. We hope that these conceptual restoration diagrams catalyze further restoration ideas and actions.

Conceptual Restoration: Industrial Areas

In industrial-commercial areas, the focus is on changing impermeable surfaces to permeable surfaces through green roofs and water collection systems or water harvesting systems. Bioswales and rolling dips in streets made of readily permeable material disperse water into subsoil ecosystem processes (instead of into storm sewers). The bioswales and rolling dips provide links to vegetation features, including the riparian ecosystem of Still Creek. As mentioned earlier, the industrial-commercial areas in the watershed are significantly located along the banks of Still Creek. Restoration of the riparian ecosystems is initiated with multi-layered vegetation along those banks and progressively widening the area of vegetation to form riparian reserves. Shrub and tree vegetation is restored in areas of sparse or simple vegetation composition as the first step

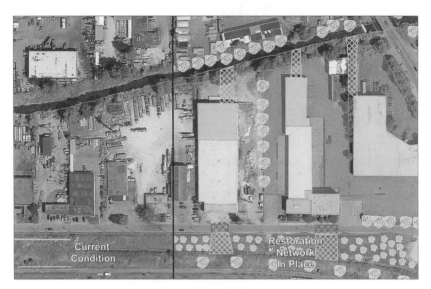

FIGURE 6.16   Conceptual restoration in Still Creek – industrial areas. The ecological restoration concepts shown here are examples of appropriate restoration treatments for industrial/commercial areas. Depending on the specific situation, a variety of ecological treatments may be necessary to rehabilitate ecosystems.

toward developing more complex, multi-layered vegetation. These riparian areas serve as important foci for biodiversity and enriching the aquatic eco-system. Natural changes will be encouraged along Still Creek's riparian areas (e.g., trees falling into streams and bank erosion and deposition to diversify stream channel composition and structure).

Conceptual Restoration: Schoolgrounds

On schoolgrounds, the mixture of ecological restoration treatments is suitable for student involvement in planning, implementation, and maintenance:

1 School buildings are retrofitted with green roofs and/or roof water collection systems that can be connected to water harvesting systems. Roof drains utilize water from green roofs and/or roof water collection systems to irrigate re-stored shrub vegetation and feed bioswales, where rainwater is dispersed into the soil and subsoil.
2 Streets leading to schools are converted from impermeable to permeable surfaces using various forms of permeable material, including permeable pavement. Rainwater is collected and dispersed into the soil and subsoil through rolling dips in the street that contain continuous water drains of readily permeable material.

FIGURE 6.17   Conceptual restoration in Still Creek – schoolgrounds. The diverse mixture of conceptual restoration treatments for schoolgrounds aims to re-establish many of the important aspects of natural ecosystem composition, structure, and function that once occurred. Implementation of these restoration treatments will provide students with a living laboratory of what is possible in re-establishing ecological integrity throughout the urban area.

3 Parking areas are converted to permeable surfaces, reduced in size, and broken up with restoration patches and linkages.
4 Shrub vegetation and multi-layered vegetation are restored wherever such restoration activities will not conflict with the use of schoolgrounds. The priority for ecological restoration is multi-layered vegetation patches and permeable surfaces around activity areas. Bioswales and rain gardens are nested among shrub vegetation and multi-layered vegetation to provide for improved storage and dispersal of rainwater, and natural playgrounds are designed and installed.

Conceptual Restoration: Single-Family Residential Areas

Single-family residential areas are predominantly located in the upland portion of the Still Creek watershed. Watershed restoration in these areas starts with green roofs and roof water collection systems that serve to reduce runoff and conserve water that can be used for household and landscape purposes. Locating bioswales and/or rain gardens in strategic places around houses would improve the functioning of green roofs and roof water collection systems. Driveways and walkways are converted to permeable surfaces using a variety of permeable materials from gravel and permeable pavement to gravel pavers and grass pavers. Laneways are converted to permeable surfaces using a similar variety of permeable materials and eventually liberated from automobiles and fully restored with multi-layered vegetation.

Residential streets are converted to permeable surfaces and fitted with rolling dips that collect and disburse rainwater into soil and subsoil. Multi-layered vegetation is established wherever possible around residences and along streets and sidewalks.

Leveraging actions at the site scale can build momentum for larger modifications of infrastructure. For example, the restoration work carried out by the Still Moon Arts Society and others contributed significantly to the return of chum salmon to spawn in Still Creek after an eighty-year absence. This monumental achievement sparked community pride and interest in the ecological history of the creek. Incredibly, in spite of the dramatically altered stream channel, the salmon found their way home to spawn again in this recovering urban stream.

▶ FIGURE 6.18 Conceptual restoration in Still Creek – residential areas. This conceptual plan shows an approach to restoration of ecological integrity in single-family residential areas. Because of the predominance of single-family houses in Still Creek and other urban areas, these restoration activities have wide application.

Restoration Network in Place

Current Condition

25 m

FIGURE 6.19   Initial restoration efforts yield amazing results. After an eighty-year absence, chum salmon returned to the heart of East Vancouver to spawn in Still Creek. | *Source: Burnaby Now*

Swimming farther with this success entails daylighting the rest of Still Creek and unearthing some of its tributaries. Patrick Condon suggests that Vancouver's Rain City Plan, which would introduce a network of green infrastructure in streets that run along the locations of former streams, needs to be expanded to improve ecological integrity.[39] Implementing blue-green networks in the Still Creek watershed would daylight water movement in stretches of lost streams while restoring surface vegetation and offering bike paths (which reduce the demand for expansive and impervious road surfaces for cars).

Restoration Network
As you will recall, the essence of NDS is the design and implementation of networks of ecological reserves at multiple spatial scales. In urban areas such as East Vancouver, there is currently very little nature to include in protected networks, so a restoration network must be established first. Over time, restoration networks are increasingly led by natural processes, which improve their integrity and allow them to evolve into mature protected networks with natural ecological integrity at multiple spatial scales.

This is a long-term project. For at least the short term, establishing restoration networks is the main objective in the Still Creek watershed. As the water movement network is restored, and as additional new fragments and anchors of ecological integrity are restored, they will be linked with the existing fragments and anchors of natural ecosystem character. The emerging restoration network will take shape, and the maps shown above (potential ecosystem reserve networks) can be redrawn. Restoration activities need to be distributed throughout the focal watershed. Distribution improves the full spectrum of ecological composition and structure by assisting natural processes and offers social inspiration to expand and maintain restoration toward natural character. As we have emphasized, equity also demands that nature is distributed across the watershed.

As the features of a restoration network are revealed, the local governments of Vancouver and Burnaby can strengthen the restoration network with larger-scale restoration of public spaces, repurposed roadways, and municipal buildings and properties that will then provide further components of the restoration network.

SHAWNIGAN LAKE: PROTECTED ECOSYSTEM NETWORKS

In contrast to East Vancouver, the Shawnigan Lake watershed has sufficient fragments and anchors of ecological integrity to jump straight into establishing a protected network with substantial ecological integrity. As such, its residential areas provide an example of what a protected network might look like after sufficient restoration in urban areas such as East Vancouver. However, a significant difference between the two locations is that East Vancouver has a higher density of residences than Shawnigan Lake. East Vancouver thus offers the opportunity to restore nature and embrace density as a verdant response to the climate emergency.

In the Shawnigan Lake watershed, the largest portions of the matrix are second- and third-growth forests managed for short-term timber crops. This approach to logging steadily degrades ecological integrity, exacerbates global heating, and degrades water and biological diversity. Under nature-directed stewardship, timber exploitation in the matrix needs to be replaced with forest protection and restoration. In large part, this is achieved through designing and implementing networks of protected ecosystems at multiple spatial scales.

Key features of these networks are the full-cycle trees that will be allowed to reach their maximum natural age and size, and to die, fall, and decompose in place. Over time, as full-cycle trees die and fall, replacement trees are identified so that the site maintains continuous large tree forest cover. The minimum number of full-cycle trees is usually 25 percent of the large, upper-canopy trees, well distributed spatially and by species. Under the constraints of the climate emergency, preference for replacement full-cycle trees needs to be given to species resilient to climate disruption.

Small protected areas and linkages in the network of ecological reserves include areas with valuable natural ecological structure and composition, high levels of biodiversity (e.g., large trees, multi-layered canopies, large fallen trees, unique species), ecologically sensitive areas (e.g., small and ephemeral riparian ecosystems, rocky hills, steep slopes, wet areas), and areas that will form linkages in the network of ecological reserves.

The nature-directed stewardship plan for the Shawnigan Lake watershed incorporates restoration anchors, other areas of natural or near-natural ecosystem composition and structure, and restoration areas at multiple spatial scales throughout the watershed. With the exception of a few parks, all of the young forests, particularly those with remnant old-growth trees, are scheduled for logging in the near future. Thus, implementation of the recommended changes to land use and application of ecological restoration techniques are urgent steps that must be taken before irreplaceable anchors for the maintenance and restoration of natural ecological integrity are lost.

In Figure 6.20, the yellow polygons and light green polygons (legislated protected areas) enclose a diversity of natural ecosystems within a large, landscape-scale protected areas network (PAN). The protected landscape network (PLN) designed at the watershed scale includes the blue polygons (riparian ecosystem reserves), the green polygons (nodes of high levels of biological diversity), and the orange polygons (linkages). The white areas on the maps represent the matrix in which human uses occur and ecological integrity will be protected and restored at a finer scale.

Protected ecosystem networks (PENs) establish even finer-scale protection across the matrix. The matrix surrounds the networks of protected ecosystems. Thus, what occurs in the matrix affects, either positively or negatively, the ecological composition, structure, and function of the entire watershed. Establishing PENs maintains and/or restores ecological integrity in the matrix as well as in the adjacent networks of protected ecosystems.

Zooming in reveals a PEN for a residential area along the shore of Shawnigan Lake and for the forest-urban transition sites. In Figure 6.21, the PEN has been superimposed onto a photo of the residential development showing ecological reserves at the site or patch level. Reserves are shown by small, green tree symbols bounded by magenta lines. The green polygons are areas with relatively high levels of biological diversity, and the orange polygons are linkages. The riparian reserve along the Shawnigan Lake shoreline contains numerous residences that fragment a biological diversity "hotspot" and contribute to pollution of the lake. These shoreline ecosystems are high priorities for restoration.

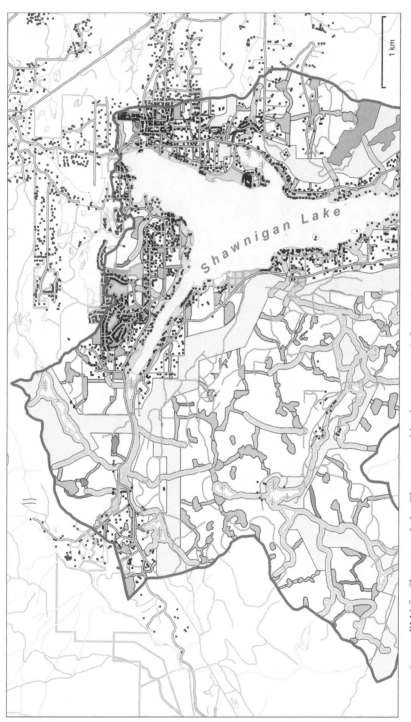

FIGURE 6.20 PLN for Shawnigan Lake. The protected landscape network for the Shawnigan Lake watershed maintains and/or restores natural ecological integrity, connectivity, biodiversity, and climate resilience.

FIGURE 6.21 PEN for residential areas. Protected ecosystem networks maintain and/or restore ecological integrity, connectivity, biodiversity, and climate resilience for areas in the matrix where human activities occur.

Vancouver and Burnaby can further strengthen the restoration network by requiring that new development fits into ecosystem features. The cities must prioritize the maintenance and restoration of ecological integrity. This means adherence to ecological limits and precautionary decisions in light of the emerging restoration network. It means high-density development designed around water movement networks, both above ground and below ground. And it means prioritizing space for people (density) over automobiles so that the excessive space currently occupied by streets and highways can be given over to green infrastructure in the restoration network.

For a variety of reasons, the community is the main catalyst for nature in the Still Creek watershed. First, community groups and individuals are key knowledge holders of local ecosystems. This can include historical data or current information about how the surrounding area is used. Second, NDS, particularly in urbanized settings such as East Vancouver, demands the active participation of citizens and landowners. Community organizations can help to facilitate these processes, and their knowledge of different neighbourhoods and residents is invaluable. Third, community leadership helps to foster a sense of ownership. NDS is a long-term process (with actionable steps that need to be taken throughout the process), and community groups can help to sustain attention to planning in the long term, even as different municipal or regional government actors come and go.

Consistent leadership in the Still Creek watershed continues to come from the Still Moon Arts Society. Since 2004, Still Moon, under the direction of Carmen Rosen, has manifested the "belief in the power of artistic experiences to move and engage people ... to bring together art, environment, and community in the ... neighbourhood and Still Creek watershed."[40]

Their long-standing work to restore Renfrew Ravine, a natural remnant of the riparian ecosystem of Still Creek, engaged us and led to the NDS plan described here.[41] Still Moon provided recommendations to the Vancouver Parks Board for the development of Renfrew Ravine Park so that it would be developed in ways consistent with the NDS plan, and consulted with the Vancouver Parks Board and Engineering Department for a process to implement the NDS plan in the park eventually.[42]

SHAWNIGAN BASIN SOCIETY

At Shawnigan Lake, a community organization also led the charge. The NDS plan was catalyzed and guided by the Shawnigan Basin Society (SBS), which has a mission to "protect and secure the long-term health and safety of the Shawnigan Lake Community Watershed and the drinking water it provides."[43] SBS participated in fieldwork associated with the plan, consulted with the community, held public presentations at various points in the planning, and reviewed the plan at several stages of its development. The Shawnigan Basin Society works closely with the local government, the Cowichan Valley Regional District.

Dr. Bruce Fraser, the former regional district director from Shawnigan Lake and one of the founders of the SBS, formulated an ecological governance policy, which identified the need for development of an ecologically based plan for the Shawnigan Basin to guide activities in the watershed.

Based on the NDS for Shawnigan Lake, the SBS developed an "Evaluation Framework for Watershed Land Use Applications" adopted by the Shawnigan Lake Advisory Planning Commission. This framework is not an official component of the Official Community Plan; however, applications for development are evaluated using the framework and the community leads in nature-directed stewardship.

7 A Process for Inviting Nature Home

Perhaps it will be the city that reawakens our understanding and appreciation of nature.

– Jane Jacobs

The previous chapters sketched a homecoming for nature in cities. We tallied the unaffordable cost of expelling nature from where we live, work, and play. We canvassed the significant efforts of urban planners, ecologists, and environmentalists to make our cities sustainable. We embraced nature-directed stewardship and its underlying disciplines of restoration ecology, conservation biology, hydrology, and landscape ecology. We acknowledged the creativity and innovation taking place in cities around the world. And we offered a vision for nature-first cities based on the principles of nature, equity, and density.

As we trust is now apparent, NDS applies to cities. Recall that the appropriate planning unit is a focal watershed – the largest watershed that fits within the boundaries of a city. Orientation within that watershed comes from the natural character of the ecosystems that existed in that watershed before the city did. Contrasting the natural character with the current condition exposes the gap in ecological integrity. Closing that gap is the task of restoration. Since most cities have little, if any, natural ecological integrity left, the restoration challenge appears to be Herculean. So we have broken it down into manageable steps.

Start by assembling bits of ecological integrity in three categories. First, protect existing fragments of natural or near-natural ecosystem character. Second, add new fragments and anchors of natural ecosystem character. Third, restore the natural water movement network.

As the components of natural character are reassembled, the shape of a restoration network will appear. With the passage of time, combined with regular effort, this restoration network will mature into a protected network of ecological reserves (see Figure 7.1).

Still, significant questions remain unanswered. Who does what (i.e., what are the roles for individuals, community groups, and governments)? What is the sequence of restoration steps? How is restoration coordinated across countless

FIGURE 7.1 Nature-directed stewardship in cities

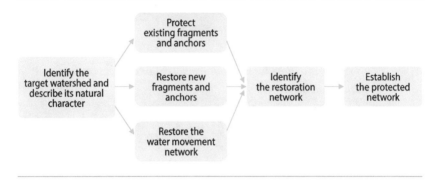

property, zoning, and jurisdictional boundaries? To answer these questions, we propose a three-part process for restoration (see Figure 7.2).

A THREE-PART PROCESS

It should come as no surprise that our three-part process for restoration starts with describing the natural ecosystem character of the largest watershed in the city. Natural character is the ecosystem composition, structure, and function that existed in the focal watershed before the city did. This is the guide for restoration at all spatial and temporal scales across the city. By identifying and describing ecosystem character, we obtain our bearings for restoration. We determine which nature to invite home.

Given the effort required to describe accurately and thoroughly the natural character of the city, we suggest that this task be undertaken by qualified scientists

FIGURE 7.2 A three-part process for restoration in cities

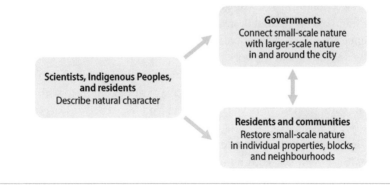

(ecologists, biologists, hydrologists, botanists, landscape ecologists), holders of traditional ecological knowledge (Indigenous Peoples), and long-time residents with memories of pre-existing character (in addition to historical records). The cost of assembling descriptions of natural character is borne by local and higher orders of government.

The second part is voluntary action at the scale of individual properties, blocks, and neighbourhoods. These "bottom-up" efforts, by definition, are small individually, but the aggregate of these actions provides the essential fragments, anchors, and components of the water movement network (without which a restoration network will not emerge). Restoration actions are guided by the information about natural character provided by scientists, Indigenous Peoples, and long-time residents, but they are driven by individual and collective choices made by residents and their neighbours. Community groups can encourage voluntary small-scale restoration. Each neighbourhood and its residents can determine where and when restoration initiatives take place rather than being subjected to decisions made outside their communities.

The third part is government action that builds on the voluntary steps taken in the second part. The government harnesses the city's resources to connect the small-scale fragments, anchors, and water movement network components established by residents and then adds larger-scale anchors and the water movement network on public lands, parks, streets, alleys, municipal buildings, and new developments. Government efforts at these larger scales are intended to inspire further small-scale voluntary action through an iterative process that reaches across all spatial and temporal scales in the city.

This three-part process seeks to address key challenges that have held back urban ecosystem restoration efforts in the past: heterogeneity of land use and multiple tenure holders, scale mismatches, and the need for both bottom-up and top-down approaches.[1] These challenges boil down to the fact that cities consist of multiple land uses and owners. Although ecosystems function at, and must be restored at multiple spatial scales, no single decision maker has authority over all of the spatial scales in a city. Individual decision makers, from landowners to city councils, focus on only some of the spatial scales. Hence, we need to engage all decision makers, and the three-part process is designed to do so. The inability to mobilize such a process is why so many urban greening and conservation plans remain just that: plans that sit on a shelf with limited to no implementation.

The oversimplification of urban land classification (into residential, industrial, commercial, and green spaces) also poses a hurdle to restoration. It shapes the perception of urban lands and "creates an unfortunate divide between urban areas for biodiversity conservation and areas used for other purposes."[2] A binary divide between green space and everything else makes it harder to accept that nature has a place in "everything else." Lost is a common understanding that nature belongs everywhere in cities. Our three-part process offers a way to encourage restoration of natural, connected ecological processes on all urban lands, including those dedicated primarily to other purposes.

Scale mismatches between management or political frameworks, on the one hand, and ecological patterns and processes, on the other, are particularly pronounced in urban landscapes.[3] The cross-scale interactions are often neglected by planners. In response, Environment Canada's Jean-Pierre Savard proposed a hierarchical approach to manage biodiversity across scales from backyards to local parks and vegetation corridors that provide multiscale connectivity across the city and to greenbelts surrounding cities.[4] Architect Peter Gisolfi proposes a spectrum of ecosystem reclamation project categories, ranging from "modest-scale landscape reclamation" to "reclamation of an entire ecosystem."[5] Several research studies suggest that applying ecosystem principles to urban areas might be most effective at sub-municipal scales and that an integrative approach that bridges multiple scales and tenures is necessary.[6] Vancouver's Cities Plus Project recommended a green web "that connects a hierarchy of green spaces, ranging from protected watersheds and agricultural land, right down to hedgerows and private gardens."[7] Others suggest linking government agencies and civil society, possibly through social networks.[8] Our three-part process picks up on these suggestions in an attempt to ensure that restoration actions have agents at all scales.

Our process also addresses the inevitable question of "how much is enough?" We follow the lead of Edward O. Wilson, who argued convincingly that half of the Earth needs to be dedicated to nature.[9] Since our cities are generally located in ecologically valuable areas (biodiversity hotspots), and since there are innumerable benefits of having nature in our cities, we see no reason to not embrace this goal of 50 percent. If this goal seems impossible, recall that half of cities is currently occupied by roads and rooftops. Reclaiming roads, planting roofs with native vegetation, and restoring ecosystems in the land among these features will go a long way toward covering 50 percent. Add to this green walls, manicured lawns restored to nature, and above-ground corridors connected to vast networks of green roofs, and suddenly this objective is within reach.

NDS adheres to the precautionary principle. In the context of urban areas, there is never an ecological justification for concluding that enough restoration has been achieved. As long as the urban landscape is dominated by people, there will always be an ecological rationale for further restoration. Given that urban areas are often located where unique and highly productive ecosystems once existed, there is an additional need to embrace the precautionary principle in an attempt to restore unique and threatened ecosystems.

Uncertainty supports adherence to the precautionary principle. The climate emergency thrusts cities into an uncharted future that demands mitigation and adaptation. Since the full range of composition, structure, and function that might be restored at any given spatial or temporal scale is indeterminate, there is a continual need to err on the side of caution and to strive for additional restoration. Moreover, change in natural systems can occur in abrupt and discontinuous ways, thus reinforcing the need for caution.[10] Even if change has occurred in a linear manner, observers in an urban environment often have trouble reading ecosystems' signals of distress. And "ecosystems themselves often 'fail to signal' the long-term consequences of loss of resilience, continuing to function in the short term even as resilience declines."[11] This lack of feedback – or at least the incapacity to recognize the feedback – again underscores the necessity of caution.

Consistent with the behaviour of ecosystems and the need for ecological resilience, restoration of 50 percent of the surface area of cities to nature is a prudent target in the face of the climate and biodiversity crises.

Part 1: Describe Natural Character

As we know, the starting place for NDS in a city is the natural character of the ecosystem that existed where the city now does: the natural composition, structure, and function of the ecosystem. The natural character compared with the current condition informs the task of restoration in every site, small water-shed, backyard, alley, neighbourhood, and the entire focal watershed. The character tells us what needs to be restored.

Ecosystem character is the compass bearing for the journey of restoration. Natural character is the direction to take with voluntary and government action. It points to seeking out Indigenous experts who can provide Indigenous knowledge and explain Indigenous ways of being with ecosystems. It points to native vegetation and native ecosystem functions. It points to buried streams, multi-layered vegetation, and migratory patterns. Rather than wandering aimlessly in a generic landscape of turf grass, hedges, and ornamental plants, ecosystem character points us home. It tells us where we live, how this place once functioned, and what makes it unique.

A city is not built on a *tabula rasa*. It entails modifications to a particular place with a unique combination of biotic communities, landforms, climate, and Indigenous cultures. Landscape architect Christina von Borcke explains that urban development is "built on land and landform that is unique to its location, with its own natural landscape and its intrinsic sense of place. Recognizing this simple fact brings a completely different approach to the roles of landscape in the city ... [It] suggests that the city is added to the natural setting and responds to it rather than the other way around."[12]

Natural ecosystem character provides a wealth of information about the restoration activities that are appropriate and most likely to be effective, offers a compelling sense of place, and establishes an unwavering benchmark against which the current condition can be compared. Although many urban areas share common features such as trees, gardens, parks, and lawns, each city is unique in its environmental and historical contexts.[13] Recognizing these contexts is essential for inviting nature home in a meaningful way.

Character provides "restoration insights unobtainable from current biological studies," and consequently restoration must "target the ecosystems' former structural diversity and the ecological and cultural processes that maintained it."[14] Before one even begins to plan for green space and green infrastructure, the "pre-urban landscape" must be understood.[15] Michael Rosenzweig, who conceived of "reconciliation ecology," holds that "to design effective new habitats, we must carefully study the old ones to find out what makes [them] so suitable."[16] A focus on character is "fundamentally different" than a focus on "sustainability as a policy goal, which, at worst, may serve only to sustain the present misery."[17] Targeting natural character also "counters the tendency to use as a baseline the state of things as they were at the start of our careers."[18]

The current condition – how the composition, structure, and function of the natural character have been modified or affected as a result of the activities of industrialized human societies – contrasts with the natural character and serves to identify the type and extent of restoration needed. The condition describes the existing highly fragmented and modified urban landscape. Together, an understanding of character and condition informs restoration activities.

The effort required to describe character and condition accurately and completely is beyond the capacity of individual urban residents. It calls for the involvement of scientists, Indigenous Peoples, and long-time residents, paid for and coordinated by governments and institutions. Dr. Nancy Olewiler of Simon Fraser University argues that governments have a role to play in providing "essential data on the physical quantities and attributes of natural capital and their changes over time."[19] This information must be made accessible and easily understandable by laypeople so that voluntary action is effective. "It is not enough that scientific information is known. It must be also available for all stakeholders and actors. This means that it must be easy to understand, and usually comprehensive."[20]

Information about ecosystem character needs to be fine grained enough to help individual residents determine the appropriate restoration efforts for their specific location and to have an informed conversation with their neighbours about doing the same. The information needs to describe the composition, structure, and function of ecosystems in ways that facilitate appropriate restoration (or at least create conditions for it to happen). The information about character needs to be presented in a compelling way that builds excitement, fosters wonder, and strengthens a sense of place.

Restoration is not simply landscaping.[21] Restoration proceeds from an ecological perspective, guided by descriptions of character. That guidance needs to be clear about appropriate vegetation for planting, and about which invasive plant species to avoid or remove. Local governments must produce maps, guides, and species lists and make them available for free to everyone. Governments and civil society organizations can help by providing hands-on guidance through workshops and individual instruction in appropriate restoration methods and content. Public education materials at varying levels of detail should include guided and self-guided walking tours through remnant natural ecosystems, restored fragments and anchors, and restored elements of a local water movement network.

Engaging people in "citizen science" can also gather knowledge about the remaining fragments of natural ecosystem character and document current condition. If supported by public outreach, training, education, and a scientific data collection methodology, then citizen science initiatives can collect a large body of data that is flexible enough to be applied at various temporal and spatial scales.[22] Collecting data and monitoring ecosystem health also help keep individuals engaged in the process of restoration after they have done some initial work.

A description of character is not just a description of the past. Character is a description of what is possible. It is a vision of a city deeply rooted in its ecological place. Knowing the character of one's home is like knowing one's self. It reveals the direction necessary for healing, it resists the generic in favour of the appropriate, and it fosters the pride and confidence that allows real transformation.

Part 2: Residents and Communities Restore Nature at Small Scales

Equipped with details about character and condition, residents and community organizations can take effective action toward restoration. This action is aimed at the restoration of new fragments and anchors of natural ecosystem character at whatever scale is available: a rooftop, exterior wall, yard, alley, traffic island, roadside strip, neighbourhood park, or residential common area. The aim is to restore the water movement network (at the available scale) with multi-layered vegetation, rain gardens, bioswales, rainwater collection systems, permeable surfaces, and green roofs. Residents can identify and protect existing fragments and anchors of ecological integrity. Ultimately, these elements combine to form a restoration network at smaller scales, nested within restoration networks at larger scales.

Small-scale voluntary action does not depend on a top-down planning process. However, governments can support and accelerate small-scale voluntary options. In addition to guidance on natural character, local governments can provide property tax relief and other tax incentives for industrial and residential property owners to increase permeable surfaces, provide for natural dispersed water movement, put in place living structures, and conduct other activities that generally restore water movement, ecological integrity, and biological diversity. These incentives are investments. Although such programs might result in lower taxes collected in the short term, the savings that result from natural ecosystems management of temperature and water, storage of carbon, and moderation of weather pay important dividends over the long term. Recall the trillions of dollars needed in coming decades to replace crumbling grey infrastructure? The aggregate contribution of multiple green infrastructure components installed at small scales across the city poses a welcome reprieve for local government budgets.

A municipality can offer small grants, such as Vancouver's Greenest City Neighbourhood Small Grants program, which provides funding for "small-scale neighbourhood-led community projects that meet greening goals."[23] Support can also take the form of development incentives (e.g., set-back leniencies, density bonuses, permit fee reductions, or permit fast-tracking) or amenities (e.g., the installation of vegetated traffic-calming devices).

Tools must be available for all types of land use: residential, commercial, and industrial. Tools must support initiatives at various scales, from site to neighbourhood. Land parcels located on sites whose natural ecosystem character is unique – such as coastline, riparian, or wetland areas – should be provided with additional restoration incentives. Areas with a comparative under-representation of nature, such as low-income neighbourhoods, the downtown core, and industrial land, would benefit from additional incentives. As restoration takes place, it must be locked in wherever possible through covenants, zoning changes, or land transfers to a public land trust or non-profit owner who puts in place legal covenants to protect the restored area.

Closely located projects need to be provided with options to leverage their individual initiatives into greater connectivity at the block or neighbourhood scale. For example, if sufficient homeowners on a block pursue restoration on their own properties, then they should be given the opportunity to transform shared community laneways into an anchor of natural ecosystem character that might include a daylighted stream reach, a pollinator garden, and other fragments of natural character, perhaps with a bike or pedestrian path. In another example, private yards and gardens can provide considerable biodiversity benefits. Collective restoration of multiple, adjacent yards and gardens in accordance with defined restoration characteristics can create "wildlife friendly"

FIGURE 7.3   A resident in Victoria, British Columbia, shared with us her surprise at how little effort it took to transform her yard, shown above, from grass to native habitat: "This is easier to do than one might think!"[26] Her yard, transformed from conventional turf grass to a restoration sanctuary with species indigenous to a Garry oak meadow ecosystem, offers habitat and refugia for local species. For example, birds feast all winter on seeds from the native ocean spray shrubs, whose decaying blossoms later line the birds' nests. | *Source:* Maleea Acker.

management across interconnected yards and gardens.[24] Since "no single land parcel may be large enough to contain a self-sustaining population," collaboration among multiple residents is necessary to restore sufficient habitat for targeted species.[25]

Voluntary action can come from individual residents, but community groups can also be especially effective, as we saw with East Vancouver's Still Moon Arts Society. Formal and informal groups, interest-based "clusters" of people such as gardening clubs, neighbourhood associations, school groups, or business-improvement associations, might lead restoration.[27] Experiences in places such as Cape Town, New Orleans, and Phoenix illustrate that community involvement in environmental stewardship encourages ecosystem protection and that "urban governance need[s] to harness social networks of urban innovation to sustain ecosystem services."[28] Research from Stockholm suggests that management by a diversity of local actor groups sustains rich levels of biodiversity and essential ecosystem processes.[29]

Chicago's Save Our Urban Lands project engaged at-risk youth to GIS map the ecological resources of neighbourhoods. Their data were combined with other data to create a plan of action for each neighbourhood that includes community gardens, aquaculture, and tree planting.[30] A block-scale volunteer initiative in the United Kingdom, dubbed "Full Frontal" by the woman who pioneered it, successfully encouraged homeowners to green the fronts of their row houses by instilling a sense of fun and community pride into the effort.[31] San Francisco's Nature in the City is a non-profit organization that supports individual-scale ecosystem restoration of the city's biodiversity and habitats.[32] And experience from stream restoration efforts in the Lower Mainland of British Columbia have shown that the most effective restoration efforts take an inclusive approach based on collaboration led by citizens and community groups.[33]

Citizen action aimed at creating and maintaining desirable environments, sometimes referred to as "civic environmentalism," flows from the "responsibility" that comes with being "embedded in place."[34] McGill University's Ray Tomalty points out that commitment to place can be fostered through urban ecosystem restoration and vice versa: "Collaborative efforts will be easier when people have retained or developed a sense of community, and a commitment to a place."[35] Not surprisingly, a sense of place encourages ecosystem restoration, and successful restoration strengthens a sense of place.[36]

Volunteer initiatives kick-start a process that is then handed off to municipal and regional governments, which in turn take actions that inspire further small-scale volunteer actions. This "cyclical and iterative" progression ratchets up the quality and quantity of fragments and anchors of ecological integrity and strengthens the water movement network.[37] Volunteer initiatives build momentum. Other residents, community groups, and businesses are likely to be inspired to follow suit. Local governments should see the political opportunity of creating incentives to support voluntary action, and be emboldened to embark on restoration projects at a broader scale. In the end, we achieve what Mohsen Mostafavi, of Harvard University's Graduate School of Design, says are "the necessary and emancipatory infrastructures for an alternative form of urbanism, one that brings together the benefits of both bottom-up and top-down approaches to urban planning."[38]

Part 3: Governments Restore Character at Larger Scales
Governments pick up where individual and community groups leave off. Through operations at larger scales, local and regional governments identify and protect remaining patches of ecological integrity, restore new patches of natural ecosystem character, and restore the water movement network. Government engagement is crucial for restoration of large-scale linkages across the focal watershed.

As noted, government action inspires further individual action in a cyclical and iterative dynamic: governments take steps at neighbourhood, city, and regional scales, in turn inspiring further voluntary action at smaller scales. The processes must operate at multiple spatial scales to overcome the challenge of many small land holdings across the urban landscape: "It is essential that homeowners realise that their own local actions can contribute to the larger collective effort that would culminate in the creation of a real biological corridor that facilitates the movements of several species throughout the city."[39]

Multiscale connectivity is possible if we halt the degradation of the remaining natural ecosystem components and protect the network of green spaces that is available for restoration. Large-scale public areas such as parks, greenways, greenbelts, nature reserves, and protected watersheds are generally in need of restoration but can provide important anchors in a restoration network. Very little if any human activity should be permitted in watersheds that contain drinking water reservoirs, highly productive ecosystems such as estuaries, and/or ecologically limited landscapes and their ecosystems. In other cases, human activity needs to be limited to specific locations (e.g., trails), and in some cases limited human activity can coexist with ecosystem restoration. Green spaces often have multiple objectives, including "habitat protection, flood hazard reduction, water quality, historic preservation, education, [and] interpretation," and "biodiversity is a most important greenway goal."[40] Accordingly, a myopic focus on human recreation is being abandoned. This change in the public mindset makes the redirection of existing green spaces toward the restoration of nature easier politically for governments.

The momentum of individual voluntary actions at smaller scales can be used by governments to provide new fragments and anchors of ecological integrity that augment existing fragments and anchors of ecological integrity. For example, significant voluntary action at block and neighbourhood levels can lead to enough support to restore an alley, repurpose a street, daylight a neighbourhood stream, or replace parking spots with habitat features, rain gardens, or bioswales.

Enshrining a Restoration Network

As the iterative approach described above unfolds, the existing fragments and anchors of natural character will be protected, new fragments and anchors will be restored, and the water movement network will flow again. All of this occurs at multiple spatial scales across the focal watershed and the city.

At this point, the contours of a restoration network will emerge. The local government, in a process with residents, community groups, and civil society, protects and enhances the restoration network. The network must be explicit at multiple spatial scales. Over time, with consistent, ongoing effort and patience,

FIGURE 7.4   After decades of industrial use, a segment of False Creek's shoreline reveals a glimpse of its natural estuary character. This ecological treasure, rooted in the heart of Vancouver, anchors the growth of a restoration network through the highest urban density in Canada. | *Source:* Melinda Markey.

this restoration network will mature into a protected network of ecological reserves at multiple spatial scales.

The restoration network needs to follow ecological rather than political boundaries as much as possible.[41] At small scales, individual voluntary initiatives connect with other initiatives on the block and in the neighbourhood to develop connectivity across property lines. At large scales, connectivity involves the restoration of public spaces, creation of new large-scale anchors, establishment of linkages, and cooperation with adjacent jurisdictions.[42]

Interjurisdictional cooperation among adjacent municipalities, regional governments, and higher-level state/provincial and federal governments can strengthen the resilience of the restoration network. Strong species-at-risk legislation, for example, helps support the establishment of new habitat patches and linkages with existing habitat. Research in the Netherlands and Brazil has shown how supportive national policies, such as riparian protection laws, can influence the creation of local green spaces.[43]

If local ecosystem values are significant, international recognition can help to secure greater local protection. For example, in Cape Town, South Africa, urban biosphere reserves are part of the UNESCO World Network of Biosphere Reserves.[44] The Cape Town biosphere reserves have social inclusion and poverty alleviation objectives as well as ecosystem restoration objectives. Such multiple objectives are becoming more common and can help to build the consensus necessary to establish a restoration network.[45] Inclusion of green infrastructure objectives related to stormwater management or water filtration can help to attract the funds necessary to provide bike or rapid-transit corridors that encourage the transformation of roads or alleys to green spaces.

CONCLUDING THOUGHTS

As we have tried to illustrate, the problem faced by Robert Moses – how to invite nature into a city filled with people – has a solution. There is ample space in the city for both if we recognize that nature and people belong together.

The premise of this book is that we are not separate from nature and not separate from each other. Nature in cities makes us healthier. It nourishes our biophilia. It makes our children calmer, our communities stronger, and our lives longer. Nature does for free and forever what trillions of dollars in urban infrastructure do only temporarily. Putting nature first in the planning, development, and restoration of cities opens up solutions and benefits far beyond anything that Moses envisioned.

As part of nature, we are part of something enduring. The natural ecosystem character of where we live tells us something about our own character; about our place on the Earth. We learn about ourselves through the nature connected from our backyards and blocks to grand parks and watersheds. Nature that we restore locally links with nature globally. When we see those links where we live, we start to care again about nature elsewhere.

Inviting nature into *everyone's* home means that nature is not just for *some* people. Nature is for us all. That chips away at what divides us. The demand for nature *and* density means that we take responsibility for the climate and biodiversity crises, give nature everywhere a fighting chance, and value equity. Inviting nature home means that cities will not look the same. Nature will be spread equally across a city. Density will increase among new green tentacles. Ecological integrity will return.

We have advanced ecological, social, and economic reasons to apply nature-directed stewardship in cities. NDS is a practical, proven system that allows people to meet their needs through a respectful, responsible, and reciprocal

FIGURE 7.5   Nature-first cities, abuzz with densely populated communities woven together by thriving ecosystem networks, restore our connections to nature and to each other.

relationship with nature. Nature-first cities will benefit from the full range of self-organizing, self-regulating, complex ecosystem processes and will reduce the need for expensive, complex, technological urban infrastructure services. The initial investment in nature might seem to be significant, but restoration costs will be recouped from myriad free ecosystem benefits. Water flows will be regulated without charge. Climate will be moderated. Our health will improve, and our communities will be more resilient.

We have proposed a three-part process that harnesses local-scale leadership supported by government resources. Meaningful collaboration among settler communities, Indigenous Peoples, and different levels of government is essential. So is having the right intention. Unless we do as David Korten suggests – "change the story" from a money-based ethic to a nature-based ethic – we will continue to face the crippling problems of climate change, biodiversity collapse, and extreme inequality.[46]

Even with collaboration supported by our three-part process, there will be those who claim that NDS cannot be applied to cities. To those who say that it is "too idealistic" and "not realistic," we ask what is wrong with striving? We seek perfection (or near perfection) in human endeavours such as art, music, athletics, and medicine. So why not strive for perfection where we live? Why not seek the ideal response to the self-imposed threats that we created with our imperfect relationships with nature and with each other?

To those who say that nature-first cities are not politically achievable, we point to the promise of democracy and activism. We have the power, indeed the responsibility, to pursue cities that provide ecologically healthy urban environments and lasting equity for all residents. Shirking that responsibility only perpetuates the ethic that brought us to the brink of crisis: the suicidal focus on the short-term monetary benefits that come from abusing nature rather than the expansive long-term vision of ecosystem benefits for all people and all nonhuman life.

We can do better.

We have proposed a robust, community-based vision and process that start when you put this book down. The process starts when you walk into your neighbourhood, join with others, and invite nature home.

Notes

Foreword

1 W. Neil Adger et al., "Urbanization, Migration, and Adaptation to Climate Change," *One Earth* 3, 4 (2020): 396–99, doi:10.1016/j.oneear.2020.09.016.
2 United Nations, Department of Economic and Social Affairs, Population Division, *World Urbanization Prospects: The 2018 Revision,* https://population.un.org/wup/.
3 United Nations, *World Urbanization Prospects.*
4 Faisal Moola et al., "Protecting Not-So-Wild Places Helps Biodiversity," The Conversation, September 28, 2022, https://theconversation.com/protecting-not-so-wild-places-helps-biodiversity-109168.
5 Moola, Lukawiecki, and Roth, "Protecting Not-So-Wild Places."
6 Faisal Moola, "EcoHealth and the Role of Urban Nature in Public Health," GEOG3210(DE01): Indigenous-Settler Relationships in Environmental Governance, University of Guelph, 2023.
7 Stephen Bede Scharper, "Want a Healthier, More Just City? Plant Trees," *Toronto Star,* July 27, 2015, https://www.thestar.com/opinion/commentary/2015/07/27/want-a-healthier-more-just-city-plant-trees.html.
8 Moola, "EcoHealth."
9 Nathaniel Rich, "When Parks Were Radical," *Atlantic,* August 12, 2016, https://www.theatlantic.com/magazine/archive/2016/09/better-than-nature/492716/.
10 *Frederick Law Olmsted (1872).*
11 Andrea J. Reid et al., "'Two-Eyed Seeing': An Indigenous Framework to Transform Fisheries Research and Management," *Fish and Fisheries* 22, 2 (2021): 243–61, doi:10.1111/faf.12516.
12 Paul Nadasdy, "The Politics of TEK: Power and the 'Integration' of Knowledge," *Arctic Anthropology* 36 (1999): 1–18.

Preface

1 On the notion of a framing story, see David Korten, *Change the Story, Change the Future: A Living Economy for a Living Earth* (Oakland, CA: Berrett-Koehler, 2015), 34, 35, 136, 137.
2 Doug Tallamy, "Designing the Future," *Ecological Restoration* 40, 2 (2022): 81–82, doi: 10.3368/er.40.2.81.

Introduction

Epigraph: Edward W. Said, *Orientalism* (New York: Vintage Books, 1979), 332.
1 Robert Caro, *The Power Broker* (New York: Vintage Books, 1974), 478.

2 Caro, *The Power Broker*, 478.

3 Said, *Orientalism*, 332.

4 William Cronon, "The Trouble with Wilderness," in *Uncommon Ground: Toward Reinventing Nature*, ed. William Cronon (New York: W.W. Norton, 1995), 69–81.

5 Andre Gunder Frank, "The Development of Underdevelopment," *Monthly Review* 18:4, September 1966, 17–31.

6 Josef Settele et al., "COVID-19 Stimulus Measures Must Save Lives, Protect Livelihoods, and Safeguard Nature to Reduce the Risk of Future Pandemics," April 27, 2020, https://www.ipbes.net/covid19stimulus.

7 Martin Siegert et al., "What Ancient Climates Tell Us about High Carbon Dioxide Concentrations in Earth's Atmosphere," Grantham Institute Briefing Note No. 13, Imperial College, London, May 2020.

8 Sandra Díaz et al., "Pervasive Human-Driven Decline of Life on Earth Points to the Need for Transformative Change," *Science* 386 (2019): https://www.science.org/doi/10.1126/science.aax3100.

9 Sandra Díaz et al., *Summary for Policymakers of the Global Assessment Report on Biodiversity and Ecosystem Services* (Bonn: Intergovernmental Science-Policy Platform on Biodiversity and Ecosystem Services, 2019), 3.

10 Yinon M. Bar-Ona, Rob Phillips, and Ron Milo, "The Biomass Distribution on Earth," *Proceedings of the National Academy of Science of the United States* 115, 25 (2018): 6506–11.

11 Darko Radovic, "Introduction: Towards a Theory of Eco-Urbanity," in *Eco-Urbanity: Towards Well-Mannered Built Environments*, ed. Darko Radovic (London: Routledge, 2009), 1.

12 Edward O. Wilson, *Biophilia* (Cambridge, MA: Harvard University Press, 1984).

13 David Korten, *Change the Story, Change the Future: A Living Economy for a Living Earth* (Oakland, CA: Berrett-Koehler, 2015).

14 Robin Wall Kimmerer, *Braiding Sweetgrass: Indigenous Wisdom, Scientific Knowledge, and the Teachings of Plants* (Minneapolis: Milkweed Editions, 2013), 336.

15 Carolyn Merchant, "Reinventing Eden," in *Uncommon Ground: Toward Reinventing Nature*, ed. William Cronon (New York: W.W. Norton, 1995), 132–59.

16 David Boyd, in discussion with Cam Brewer, April 22, 2022.

CHAPTER 1: NATURE EXPELLED

Epigraph: Edward O. Wilson, "Foreword," in *Biophilic Cities*, ed. Timothy Beatley (Washington, DC: Island Press, 2011), xv.

1 Lewis Mumford, "Introduction," in *Design with Nature*, ed. Ian L. McHarg (Garden City, NY: Natural History Press, 1969), viii.

2 Jane Jacobs, *The Death and Life of Great American Cities* (1961; reprinted, New York: Vintage Books, 1992), 446.

3 George Monbiot, *Feral: Rewilding the Land, the Sea and Human Life* (Toronto: Allen Lane, 2013), 9.

4 Coast Information Team – Compendium Team, *The Scientific Basis of Ecosystem-Base Management* (Victoria, BC: Cortex Consultants, 2004), 13.

5 Ian L. McHarg, ed., *Design with Nature* (Garden City, NY: Natural History Press, 1969), 19.

6 United Nations, *World Urbanization Prospects – The 2009 Revision: Highlights* (New York: UN Department of Economic and Social Affairs, Population Division, 2010).

7 Randolph T. Hester, *Design for Ecological Democracy* (Cambridge, MA: MIT Press, 2006), 9.

8 Anne Whiston Spirn, *The Granite Garden* (New York: Basic Books, 1984), 5.

9 Sigmund Freud, "The Future of an Illusion," in *The Standard Edition of the Complete Psychological Works of Sigmund Freud*, ed. James Strachey et al. (London: Hogarth Press, 1927), 15.

10 Daniel Mason, "City of Seeds," *Lapham's Quarterly* 3, 4 (2010): 186–91, 187.

11 Carolyn Merchant, "Reinventing Eden," in *Uncommon Ground: Toward Reinventing Nature,* ed. William Cronon (New York: W.W. Norton, 1995), 132–59, 147.

12 Edward O. Wilson, *Biophilia* (Cambridge, MA: Harvard University Press, 1984), 140.

13 Richard Louv, *Last Child in the Woods* (Chapel Hill, NC: Algonquin Books of Chapel Hill, 2008), 36.

14 Henry Ford, quoted in Paul Mees, *Transport for Suburbia: Beyond the Automobile Age* (London: Earthscan, 2010), 12.

15 Wilson, *Biophilia,* 1, 2.

16 Edward O. Wilson, "Biophilia and the Conservation Ethic," in *The Biophilia Hypothesis,* ed. Stephen Kellert and Edward O. Wilson (Washington, DC: Island Press, 1993), 31.

17 Stephen Kellert, *Building for Life: Designing and Understanding the Human-Nature Connection* (Washington, DC: Island Press, 2006), 4.

18 Stephen Kaplan, "The Restorative Benefits of Nature: Toward an Integrative Framework," *Journal of Environmental Psychology* 15, 3 (1995): 169–82.

19 Kaplan, "The Restorative Benefits of Nature," 169.

20 Louv, *Last Child in the Woods.*

21 David Nicholson-Lord, "Why We All Need to Get out More," *New Statesman,* January 24, 2005, https://www.newstatesman.com/long-reads/2005/01/why-we-all-need-to-get-out-more.

22 Patrick ten Brink et al., *The Health and Social Benefits of Nature and Biodiversity Protection* (London: Institute for European Environmental Policy, 2016), 73–74; Paul A. Sandifer, Ariana E. Sutton-Grier, and Bethney P. Ward, "Exploring Connections among Nature, Bio-diversity, Ecosystem Services, and Human Health and Well-Being: Opportunities to Enhance Health and Biodiversity Conservation," *Ecosystem Services* 12 (2015): 1–15.

23 Carlos Andres Gallegos-Riofrío et al., "Chronic Deficiency of Diversity and Pluralism in Research on Nature's Mental Health Effects: A Planetary Health Problem," *Current Research in Environmental Sustainability* 4 (2022): https://www.sciencedirect.com/science/article/pii/S2666049022000263.

24 Peter James et al., "Exposure to Greenness and Mortality in a Nationwide Prospective Cohort Study of Women," *Environmental Health Perspectives* 124, 9 (2016): 1350.

25 Jenny J. Roe et al., "Green Space and Stress: Evidence from Cortisol Measures in Deprived Urban Communities," *International Journal of Environmental Research and Public Health* 10, 9 (2013): 4086–4103; Katherine Drayson and Guy Newry, *Green Society: Policies to Improve the UK's Urban Green Spaces* (London: Policy Exchange, 2014).

26 Agnes E. van den Berg et al., "Green Space as a Buffer between Stressful Life Events and Health," *Social Science and Medicine* 70, 8 (2010): 1203–10; R.R.C. McEachan et al., "The Association between Green Space and Depressive Symptoms in Pregnant Women: Moder-ating Roles of Socioeconomic Status and Physical Activity," *Journal of Epidemiology and Community Health* 70, 3 (2015): 253–59.

27 Ten Brink et al., "The Health and Social Benefits of Nature and Biodiversity Protection," 86; J. McSweeney et al., "Indoor Nature Exposure (INE): A Health-Promotion Framework," *Health Promotion International* 30, 1 (2014): 126–39.

28 Gregory N. Bratman et al., "The Benefits of Nature Experience: Improved Affect and Cognition," *Landscape and Urban Planning* 138 (2015): 41–50.

29 McSweeney et al., "Indoor Nature Exposure."

30 Patricia H. Hasbach, "Ecotherapy," in *Ecotherapy: Science, Totems, and the Technological Spe-cies,* ed. P.H. Kahn Jr. and Patricia H. Hasbach (Cambridge, MA: MIT Press, 2012), 115–16.

31 Jolanda Maas et al., "Green Space, Urbanity, and Health: How Strong Is the Relation?," *Journal of Epidemiology and Community Health* 60, 7 (2006): 587–92; Matthew P. White et al., "Would You Be Happier Living in a Greener Urban Area? A Fixed-Effects Analysis of Panel Data," *Psychological Science* 224, 6 (2013): 920–28.

32 Christian Krekel, Jens Kolbe, and Henry Wüstemann, "The Greener, the Happier? The Effect of Urban Land Use on Residential Well-Being," *Ecological Economics* 121 (2016): 117–27.

33 Omid Karden et al., "Neighbourhood Greenspace and Health in a Large Urban Center," *Scientific Reports* 5, 1 (2015): 1610.

34 Colin A. Capaldi, Raelyne L. Dopko, and John M. Zelenski, "The Relationship between Nature Connectedness and Happiness: A Meta-Analysis," *Frontiers in Psychology* 11, 5 (2014): 976.

35 David R. Boyd, *Cleaner, Greener, Healthier: A Prescription for Stronger Canadian Environmental Laws and Policies* (Vancouver: UBC Press, 2015), 25.

36 James et al., "Exposure to Greenness," 1349.

37 T. Takano, K. Nakamura, and M. Watanabe, "Urban Residential Environments and Senior Citizens' Longevity in Megacity Areas: The Importance of Walkable Green Spaces," *Journal of Epidemiology and Community Health* 56, 12 (2002): 913–18; Richard Mitchell and Frank Popham, "Effect of Exposure to Natural Environment on Health Inequalities: An Observational Populations Study," *Lancet* 372, 9650 (2008): 1607–1706.

38 James et al., "Exposure to Greenness."

39 Ten Brink et al., "The Health and Social Benefits," 86; Larry W. Bennett et al., "Effects of a Therapeutic Camping Program on Addiction Recovery," *Journal of Substance Abuse Treatment* 15, 5 (1998): 469–74; Payam Dadvand et al., "Risks and Benefits of Green Spaces for Children: A Cross-Sectional Study of Associations with Sedentary Behavior, Obesity, Asthma, and Allergy," *Environmental Health Perspectives* 122, 12 (2014): 1329–35.

40 Abdonas Tamosiunas et al., "Accessibility and Use of Urban Green Spaces, and Cardiovascular Health: Findings from a Kaunas Cohort Study," *Environmental Health* 13, 1 (2014): 20.

41 Chorong Song et al., "Physiological and Psychological Responses of Young Males during Spring-Time Walks in Urban Parks," *Journal of Physiological Anthropology* 33, 1 (2014): 8.

42 Sensing Nature: Visual Impairment and the Natural Environment, https://sensing-nature.com.

43 M.A. House, J.B. Ellis, and R.B.E. Shutes, "Urban Rivers: Ecological Impact and Management," in *Urban Waterside Regeneration: Problems and Prospects,* ed. K.N. White et al. (West Sussex, UK: Ellis Horwood, 1993), 320.

44 Joan Iverson Nassauer et al., "Exurban Residential Subdivision Development: Effects on Water Quality and Public Perception," *Urban Ecosystems* 7 (2004): 267–81.

45 Stephen Kaplan and Rachel Kaplan, eds., *Humanscape: Environments for People* (Ann Arbor, MI: Ulrich's Books, 1982).

46 Carolyn Abraham, "Part 3: Are We Medicating a Disorder or Treating Boyhood as a Disease?," *Globe and Mail,* October 18, 2020, https://www.theglobeandmail.com/news/national/time-to-lead/part-3-are-we-medicating-a-disorder-or-treating-boyhood-as-a-disease/article4330080/.

47 Terry Hartig et al., "Nature and Health," *Annual Review of Public Health* 35 (2014): 207–28, 217.

48 Birute Balseviciene et al., "Impact of Residential Greenness on Preschool Children's Emotional and Behavioral Problems," *Journal of Environmental Research and Public Health* 11, 7 (2014): 6757–70.

49 Payam Dadvand et al., "Green Spaces and Cognitive Development in Primary Schoolchildren," *Proceedings of the National Academy of Sciences of the United States of America* 112, 26 (2015): 7937–42; Margarita Triguero-Mas et al., "Natural Outdoor Environments and Mental and Physical Health: Relationships and Mechanisms," *Environmental International* 77 (2015): 35–41.

50 Anna Roberts, Joe Hinds, and Paul M. Camic, "Nature Activities and Wellbeing in Children and Young People: A Systematic Literature Review," *Journal of Adventure Education Outdoor Learning* 20, 4 (2020): 300.

51 Karen Malone, "Holding Environments: Creating Spaces to Support Children's Environmental Learning in the 21st Century," *Australian Journal of Environmental Education* 20, 2 (2004): 53–66, 59–60.

52 Robin Moore, "The Need for Nature: A Childhood Right," *Social Justice* 24, 3 (1997): 203–20.

53 E. Dickinson, "The Misdiagnosis: Rethinking 'Nature-Deficit Disorder,'" *Environmental Communication* 7 (2013): 315–35.

54 Louv, *Last Child in the Woods,* 47.

55 "Kids Get Less Physical Activity than Parents Believe," CBC News, April 18, 2012, http://www.cbc.ca/news/health/story/2012/04/18/physical-activity.html.

56 Louv, *Last Child in the Woods,* 48.

57 United Nations Environment Program (UNEP), Millennium Ecosystem Assessment, *Ecosystems and Human Well-Being* (New York: UNEP, 2005).

58 Sara Wilson, *Canada's Wealth of Natural Capital: Rouge National Park* (Vancouver: David Suzuki Foundation, 2012).

59 Sara Wilson, *Natural Capital in BC's Lower Mainland* (Vancouver: David Suzuki Foundation and Pacific Parklands Foundation, 2010).

60 Robert Costanza et al., "The Value of the World's Ecosystem Services and Natural Capital," *Nature* 387 (1997): 253–60; L. Braat and P. ten Brink, *The Cost of Policy Inaction: The Case of not Meeting the 2010 Biodiversity Target* (London: Institute for European Environmental Policy, 2008).

61 David Korten, *Change the Story, Change the Future: A Living Economy for a Living Earth* (Oakland, CA: Berrett-Koehler, 2015).

62 Glen Coulthard, *Red Skin White Masks: Rejecting the Colonial Politics of Recognition* (Minneapolis: University of Minnesota Press, 2014).

63 Leanne Betasamosake Simpson, *As We Have Always Done: Indigenous Freedom through Radical Resistance* (Minneapolis: University of Minnesota Press, 2017).

64 K. Wilkie and C. Ascroft, "From Grey to Green: The Transformation of Canada's Infrastructure," *Plan Canada* 49, 1 (2009): 11–14, 13.

65 Emilie K. Stander and Joan G. Ehrenfeld, "Urban Riparian Function," in *Urban Ecosystem Ecology,* ed. Jacqueline Aitkenhead-Peterson and Astrid Volder, Agronomy Monograph 55 (Madison, WI: American Society of Agronomy, Crop Science Society of America, Soil Science Society of America, 2010), 254.

66 Mathis Wackernagel and William E. Rees, *Our Ecological Footprint: Reducing Human Impact on the Earth* (Gabriola Island, BC: New Society, 1996).

67 Andre Gunder Frank, "The Development of Underdevelopment," in *Development Studies: A Reader,* ed. Stuart Corbridge (London: Edward Arnold, 1995), 27.

68 Saeed Mirza and M. Shafqat Ali, "Infrastructure Crisis – A Proposed National Infrastructure Policy for Canada," *Canadian Journal of Civil Engineering* 44, 7 (2017): 539–48.

69 Mirza and Ali, "Infrastructure Crisis."

70 Saeed Mirza, *Danger Ahead: The Coming Collapse of Canada's Municipal Infrastructure* (Ottawa: Federation of Canadian Municipalities, 2007), 7.

71 Mirza, *Danger Ahead,* 7.

72 Mirza, *Danger Ahead,* 6.

73 Patrick Condon, "A Safe, More Enjoyable Street for Our New Times," *Tyee,* May 12, 2020, https://thetyee.ca/Analysis/2020/05/12/Vancouver-Could-Save-Money-On-Sewage-With-Swales/.

74 American Society of Civil Engineers, "America's Infrastructure Scores a 'C-,'" November 15, 2022, https://infrastructurereportcard.org/.

75 Claire Schollaert et al., "Natural Gas Leaks and Tree Death: A First-Look Case-Control Study of Urban Trees in Chelsea, MA, USA," *Environmental Pollution* 263 (2020): https://www.sciencedirect.com/science/article/pii/S0269749119376717.

76 Mirza and Ali, "Infrastructure Crisis," 544.

77 Sean Connelly, Sean Markey, and Mark Roseland, "Strategic Sustainability: Addressing the Community Infrastructure Deficit," *Canadian Journal of Urban Research* 18, 1 (2009): 2.

78 Vandana Shiva, *Monocultures of the Mind* (London: Zed Books, 1993), 7.

79 Darko Radovic, "Eco-Urbanity: The Framework of an Idea," in *Eco-Urbanity: Towards Well-Mannered Built Environments,* ed. Darko Radovic (London: Routledge, 2009), 9–18.

80 Anthony J. Webster and Richard H. Clarke, "Insurance Companies Should Collect a Carbon Levy," *Nature* 549 (2017): 152.

81 Urban Climate Change Research Network, *The Future We Don't Want: How Climate Change Could Impact the World's Greatest Cities* (New York: Urban Climate Change Research Network, 2018), 35, 38.

82 Webster and Clarke, "Insurance Companies," 152; Kerry Emanuel, "Assessing the Present and Future Probability of Hurricane Harvey's Rainfall," *Proceedings of the National Academy of Sciences of the United States of America* 114, 48 (2017): 12681–84.

83 Emanuel, "Assessing the Present and Future Probability."

84 Intergovernmental Panel on Climate Change, *Special Report on the Ocean and Cryosphere: Summary for Policymakers* (Cambridge, UK: Cambridge University Press, 2019), 28.

85 Brian M. Rosenthal, Emma G. Fitzsimmons, and Michael LaForgia, "The Making of a Meltdown," *New York Times,* 19 November 2017.

86 Nathan P. Gillet et al., "Human Influence on the 2021 British Columbia Floods," *Weather and Climate Extremes* 36 (2022): 1–13, https://www.sciencedirect.com/science/article/pii/S2212094722000287.

87 Gillet et al., "Human Influence."

88 Oliver Milman, "Why Are Ferocious Wildfires Plaguing Southern California?," *Guardian,* 7 December 2017, https://www.theguardian.com/us-news/2017/dec/07/why-are-ferocious-wildfires-plaguing-southern-california; William E. Mell et al. "The Wildland–Urban Interface Fire Problem – Current Approaches and Research Needs," *International Journal of Wildland Fire* 19 (2010): 238–51.

89 Jonathon Gatehouse, "Why Catastrophic Wildfires Are Razing So Many Communities," CBC News, December 7, 2017, http://www.cbc.ca/news/thenational/the-national-today-california-fires-al-franken-rogerio-157–1.4433830.

90 Canadian Press, "Devastating Fort McMurray Wildfire Declared out 15 Months Later," CBC News, September 1, 2017, http://www.cbc.ca/news/canada/edmonton/fort-mcmurray-fire-beast-extinguished-out-1.4271604.

91 Helen Sullivan, "Australia's Fire Season Ends, and Researchers Look to the Next One," *New York Times,* April 21, 2020, https://www.nytimes.com/2020/04/21/science/australia-wildfires-technology-drones.html; Gillet et al., "Human Influence."

92 Hugh D. Safford et al., "The 2020 California Fire Season: A Year Like No Other, a Return to the Past or a Harbinger of the Future?," *Global Ecology and Biogeography* 31, 10 (2022): 2005–25; "Scientists Want New Framework for Understanding California Wildfire Costs, Risks," *Insurance Journal,* October 29, 2020, https://www.insurancejournal.com/news/west/2020/10/29/588768.htm.

93 Benjamin Shingler and Graeme Bruce, "Five Charts to Help Understand Canada's Record-Breaking Wildfire Season," *CBC,* October 19, 2023, https://www.cbc.ca/news/climate/wildfire-season-2023-wrap-1.6999005.

94 Council of Canadian Academies, *Canada's Top Climate Change Risks: Expert Panel on Climate Change Risks and Adaptation Potential* (Ottawa: Council of Canadian Academies, 2019), 17.

95 Gillet et al., "Human Influence"; Council of Canadian Academies, *Canada's Top Climate Change Risks,* 16.

96 Omar Akkad, "Come Hell or High Water: The Disaster Scenario That is South Florida," *Globe and Mail,* July 18, 2015, https://www.theglobeandmail.com/news/world/come-hell-or-high-water-the-disaster-scenario-that-is-south-florida/article25552300/.

97   Andew Kirby, "The Right to Make Mistakes?," *Challenges* 13, 1 (2022): 25.
98   Kirby, "The Right to Make Mistakes?," 25.
99   Council of Canadian Academies, *Canada's Top Climate Change Risks,* 36.
100 Rosenthal, Fitzsimmons, and LaForgia, "The Making of a Meltdown"; New York City, *NYC Green Infrastructure Plan* (New York: New York City, Department of Environmental Protection, 2010).
101 McHarg, *Design with Nature,* 23.
102 Michael Hough, "Formed by Natural Processes – A Definition of the Green City," in *Green Cities,* ed. David Gordon (Montreal: Black Rose, 1990), 15–16.
103 Jim Patchett and Tom Price, "Stormwater Systems," in *Sustainable Urbanism: Urban Design with Nature,* ed. Douglas Farr (Hoboken, NJ: John Wiley and Sons, 2008), 175.
104 William B. Honachefsky, *Ecologically Based Municipal Land Use Planning* (Boca Raton, FL: Lewis, 1999), 99.
105 Honachefsky, *Ecologically Based Municipal Land Use Planning,* 101.
106 United States Environmental Protection Agency (hereafter USEPA), *Percent Impervious Area: Fact Sheet* (Research Triangle Park, NC: USEPA, 2020), 2.
107 Allison H. Roy, Michael J. Paul, and Seth J. Wenger, "Urban Stream Ecology," in *Urban Ecosystem Ecology,* ed. Jacqueline Aitkenhead-Peterson and Astrid Volder, Agronomy Monograph 55 (Madison, WI: American Society of Agronomy, Crop Science Society of America, Soil Science Society of America, 2010), 344.
108 Roy, Paul, and Wenger, "Urban Stream Ecology," 344.
109 J. Odefey et al., *Banking on Green: A Look at How Green Infrastructure Can Save Municipalities Money and Provide Economic Benefits Community-Wide* (Washington, DC: American Rivers, 2012), 28.
110 Maggie Baynham and Mark Stevens, "Are We Planning Effectively for Climate Change? An Evaluation of Official Community Plans in British Columbia," *Journal of Environmental Planning and Management* 57, 4 (2014): 557–87.
111 Dana Beach, *Coastal Sprawl: The Effects of Urban Design on Aquatic Ecosystems in the United States* (Washington, DC: Pew Ocean Commission, 2002), 677.
112 M.G. Chapman and A.J. Underwood, "Urbanisation in Marine and Terrestrial Habitats," in *Ecology of Cities and Towns: A Comparative Approach,* ed. Mark J. McDonnell, Amy K. Hahs, and Jürgen H. Breuste (Cambridge, UK: Cambridge University Press, 2009), 51–69.
113 F. Comeau et al., "The Occurrence of Acidic Drugs and Caffeine in Sewage Effluents and Receiving Waters from Three Coastal Watersheds in Atlantic Canada," *Science of the Total Environment* 396 (2008): 132–46.
114 M.G. Chapman et al., "Effect of Urban Structures on Diversity of Marine Species," in *Ecology of Cities and Towns: A Comparative Approach,* ed. Mark J. McDonnell, Amy K. Hahs, and Jürgen H. Breuste (Cambridge, UK: Cambridge University Press, 2009), 156–76.
115 Laurent C.M. Lebreton, "River of Plastic Emissions to the World's Oceans," *Nature Communications* 8 (2017): 15611.
116 Sandra Laville and Matthew Taylor, "A Million Bottles a Minute: World's Plastic Binge 'as Dangerous as Climate Change,'" *Guardian,* June 28, 2017, https://www.theguardian.com/environment/2017/jun/28/a-million-a-minute-worlds-plastic-bottle-binge-as-dangerous-as-climate-change.
117 Oliver Milman, "Great Pacific 'Garbage Patch' Sprawling with Far More Debris than Thought," *Guardian,* March 22, 2018, https://www.theguardian.com/environment/2018/mar/22/great-pacific-garbage-patch-sprawling-with-far-more-debris-than-thought.
118 United Nations, "UN's Mission to Keep Plastics out of Oceans and Marine Life," *United Nations News,* April 27, 2017, https://news.un.org/en/story/2017/04/556132-feature-uns-mission-keep-plastics-out-oceans-and-marine-life.

119 Steven J. Burian and Christine A. Pomeroy, "Urban Impacts on the Water Cycle and Potential Green Infrastructure Implications," in *Urban Ecosystem Ecology,* ed. Jacqueline Aitkenhead-Peterson and Astrid Volder, Agronomy Monograph 55 (Madison, WI: American Society of Agronomy, Crop Science Society of America, Soil Science Society of America, 2010), 285.
120 Burian and Pomeroy, "Urban Impacts," 285.
121 Michael J. Paul and Judy J. Meyer, "Streams in the Urban Landscape," *Annual Review of Ecology, Evolution, and Systematics* 32 (2001): 333–65.
122 Burian and Pomeroy, "Urban Impacts," 281.
123 Paul and Meyer, "Streams in the Urban Landscape."
124 House, Ellis, and Shutes, "Urban Rivers."
125 Roy, Paul, and Wenger, "Urban Stream Ecology," 325.
126 Marvin L. Rosenau and Mark Angelo, *The Role of Public Groups in Protecting and Restoring Habitats in British Columbia, with a Special Emphasis on Urban Streams* (Vancouver: Pacific Fisheries Resource Conservation Council, 2010).
127 Rodney van der Ree, "The Ecology of Roads in Urban and Urbanising Landscapes," in *Ecology of Cities and Towns: A Comparative Approach,* ed. Mark J. McDonnell, Amy K. Hahs, and Jürgen H. Breuste (Cambridge, UK: Cambridge University Press, 2009), 185.
128 W.M. Lonsdale and A.M. Lane, "Tourist Vehicles as Vectors of Weed Seeds in Kakadu National Park, Northern Australia," *Biological Conservation* 69 (1994): 277–83.
129 Richard T.T. Forman and Lauren E. Alexander, "Roads and Their Major Ecological Effects," *Annual Review of Ecology and Systematics* 29 (1998): 207–31; Pierre L. Isbisch et al., "A Global Map of Roadless Areas and Their Conservation Status," *Science* 54, 6318 (2016): 1423–27.
130 Van der Ree, "The Ecology of Roads," 185.
131 Van der Ree, "The Ecology of Roads," 185.
132 Forman and Alexander, "Roads and Their Major Ecological Effects."
133 Robert H. MacArthur and Edward O. Wilson, *The Theory of Island Biogeography* (Princeton, NJ: Princeton University Press, 1967), 8.
134 Reed F. Noss, "Wildlife Corridors," in *Ecology of Greenways,* ed. Daniel S. Smith and Paul Cawood Hellmund (Minneapolis: University of Minnesota Press, 1993), 44.
135 M.E. Soulé, "Land Use Planning and Wildlife Maintenance: Guidelines for Conserving Wildlife in an Urban Landscape," *Journal of American Planning Association* 3 (1991): 313–23.
136 MacArthur and Wilson, *The Theory of Island Biogeography.*
137 James F. Thorne, "Landscape Ecology: A Foundation for Greenway Design," in *Ecology of Greenways,* ed. Daniel S. Smith and Paul Cawood Hellmund (Minneapolis: University of Minnesota Press, 1993), 29.
138 Noss, "Wildlife Corridors," 53.
139 Ernest Ireneusz Hennig and Jaboury Ghazoul, "Plant-Pollinator Interactions within the Urban Environment," *Perspectives in Plant Ecology, Evolution and Systematics* 13 (2011): 137–50.
140 Honachefsky, *Ecologically Based Municipal Land Use Planning,* 84.
141 Noss, "Wildlife Corridors," 53.
142 Stephan Barthel, "Sustaining Urban Ecosystem Services with Local Stewards Participation in Stockholm," in *From Landscape Research to Landscape Planning: Aspects of Integration, Education and Application,* ed. Bärbell Tress et al. Wageningen UR Frontis Series, vol. 12 (Wageningen, Netherlands: Wageningen UR, 2006), 314.
143 Maria Hellström Reimer, "Unsettling Eco-Scapes: Aesthetic Performances for Sustainable Futures," *Journal of Landscape Architecture* 5, 1 (2010): 24–37, 28.
144 Joan Roelofs, "Building and Designing with Nature: Urban Design," in *The Earthscan Reader in Sustainable Cities,* ed. David Satterthwaite (London: Earthscan, 1999), 246.
145 Renata Cacik and Valentin Schaefer, *City of Surprises: Discovering Urban Wildlife Habitats* (Vancouver: Douglas College Centre for Environmental Studies and Urban Ecology, 1997), 83.

146 Astrid Volder and W. Todd Watson, "Urban Forestry," in *Urban Ecosystem Ecology*, ed. Jacqueline Aitkenhead-Peterson and Astrid Volder, Agronomy Monograph 55 (Madison, WI: American Society of Agronomy, Crop Science Society of America, Soil Science Society of America, 2010), 228.

147 Jack Whittier, Denise Rue, and Scott Haase, "Urban Tree Residues: Results of the First National Inventory," *Journal of Arboriculture* 21, 2 (1995): 57–62.

148 Kerry Gold, "Who Will Speak for Vancouver's Trees and Gardens?," *Globe and Mail*, May 10, 2014, https://www.theglobeandmail.com/real-estate/who-will-speak-for-vancouvers-trees-and-gardens/article18590224/.

149 Robert McCleery, "Urban Mammals," in *Urban Ecosystem Ecology*, ed. Jacqueline Aitkenhead-Peterson and Astrid Volder, Agronomy Monograph 55 (Madison, WI: American Society of Agronomy, Crop Science Society of America, Soil Science Society of America, 2010), 90.

150 Richard P. Cincotta, Jennifer Wisnewski, and Robert Engelman, "Human Populations in the Biodiversity Hotspots," *Nature* 404 (2000): 990–91.

151 Amber Cowie, *Biodiversity in Ontario's Greenbelt* (Vancouver: David Suzuki Foundation, 2011).

152 Canada Green Building Council, *LEED 2009 for Neighbourhood Development Rating System with Canadian Alternative Compliance Paths* (Ottawa: Canada Green Building Council, 2011).

153 N. Shiab and I. Bouchard, "We Used AI to Measure Canada's Urban Sprawl," Radio-Canada, March 7, 2022, https://ici.radio-canada.ca/info/2022/03/etalement-urbain-densite-population-villes-transport-commun-changements-climatiques/en.

154 USEPA, *Cooling Summertime Temperatures: Strategies to Reduce Urban Heat Islands* (Washington, DC: USEPA, 2003).

155 USEPA, *Heat Island Impacts* (Washington, DC: USEPA, 2020).

156 NASA Jet Propulsion Laboratory, "NASA Data Shows Fierce Surface Temperatures During Phoenix Heat Wave," April 8, 2023, https://www.jpl.nasa.gov/news/nasa-data-shows-fierce-surface-temperatures-during-phoenix-heat-wave.

157 Canada Green Building Council, *LEED Reference Package for New Construction and Major Renovations* (Ottawa: Canada Green Building Council, 2004).

158 USEPA, *Heat Island Impacts*.

159 Mirijam Gaertner et al., "Managing Invasive Species in Cities: A Framework from Cape Town, South Africa," *Landscape and Urban Planning* 151 (2016): 1.

160 Ingo Kowarik, "Novel Urban Ecosystems, Biodiversity, and Conservation," *Environmental Pollution* 159, 8–9 (2011): 174.

161 Giovanni Trentanovi et al., "Biotic Homogenization at the Community Scale: Disentangling the Roles of Urbanization and Plant Invasion," *Diversity and Distributions* 19, 7 (2013): 738.

162 Edward O. Wilson, *Half-Earth: Our Planet's Fight for Life* (London: W.W. Norton, 2016), 37.

163 Wilson, *Half-Earth*, 38.

164 Robert B. Blair, "Birds and Butterflies along Urban Gradients in Two Ecoregions of the United States," in *Biotic Homogenization*, ed. Julie L. Lockwood and Michael L. McKinney (New York: Plenum, 2001), 33–56.

165 Michael L. McKinney, "Urbanization, Biodiversity, and Conservation," *Bioscience* 52, 10 (2002): 883, 887.

166 Sarah Zielinski, "The Invasive Species We Can Blame on Shakespeare," *Smithsonian Magazine*, October 4, 2011, https://www.smithsonianmag.com/science-nature/the-invasive-species-we-can-blame-on-shakespeare-95506437/.

167 McKinney, "Urbanization," 883.

168 Eyal Shochat, Susannah Lerman, and Esteban Fernández-Juricic, "Birds in Urban Ecosystems: Population Dynamics, Community Structure, Biodiversity, and Conservation," in *Urban Ecosystem Ecology*, ed. Jacqueline Aitkenhead-Peterson and Astrid Volder, Agronomy

Monograph 55 (Madison, WI: American Society of Agronomy, Crop Science Society of America, Soil Science Society of America, 2010), 78.

169 Shochat, Lerman, and Fernández-Juricic, "Birds in Urban Ecosystems," 78.

170 Robert McCleery, "Urban Mammals," in *Urban Ecosystem Ecology*, ed. Jacqueline Aitkenhead-Peterson and Astrid Volder, Agronomy Monograph 55 (Madison, WI: American Society of Agronomy, Crop Science Society of America, Soil Science Society of America, 2010), 91.

171 McCleery, "Urban Mammals," 91.

172 Robert DeCandido and Deborah Allen, "Nocturnal Hunting by Peregrine Falcons at the Empire State Building, New York City," *Wilson Journal of Ornithology* 118, 1 (2006): 53, 56.

173 "Planet Earth II," BBC, http://www.bbc.co.uk/mediacentre/mediapacks/planet-earth-ii/cities.

174 Drew Nelles, "There Goes the Neighbourhood," *Walrus* 12, 6 (2015): 40–47, 44.

175 Mark A. Goddard, Andrew J. Dougill, and Tim G. Benton, "Scaling Up from Gardens: Biodiversity Conservation in Urban Environments," *Trends in Ecology and Evolution* 25, 2 (2010): 90–98, 90.

176 Sandra Díaz et al., *Summary for Policymakers of the Global Assessment Report on Biodiversity and Ecosystem Services* (Paris: Intergovernmental Science-Policy Panel on Biodiversity and Ecosystem Services, 2019), 2; Wilson, *Half-Earth*, 56.

177 Elizabeth Kolbert, *The Sixth Extinction: An Unnatural History* (New York: Henry Holt, 2014).

178 Wilson, *Half-Earth*, 167.

179 Naomi Klein, *This Changes Everything: Capitalism vs. the Climate* (New York: Simon and Schuster, 2014), 158–59.

180 Klein, *This Changes Everything*, 159.

181 Timothy Beatley, "Land Development and Endangered Species: Emerging Conflicts," in *The Sustainable Urban Development Reader*, ed. Stephen M. Wheeler and Timothy Beatley (London: Routledge, 2004), 116–20.

182 Terry Hartig et al., "Nature and Health," *Annual Review of Public Health* 35 (2014): 207–28; Elizabeth K. Nisbet et al., "The Nature Relatedness Scale: Linking Individuals' Connection with Nature to Environmental Concern and Behavior," *Environment and Behavior* 41, 5 (2009): 715–40.

183 Elizabeth May, *Who We Are* (Vancouver: Greystone Books, 2014), 12.

184 Malone, "Holding Environments."

185 Malone, "Holding Environments," 64.

186 Katri Savolainen, "More Time Children Spend in Nature during Preschool Is Associated with a Greater Sense of Responsibility for Nature: A Study in Finland," *Ecopsychology* 13, 4 (2021): 273.

187 Michael E. Patterson and Daniel R. Williams, "Maintaining Research Traditions on Place: Diversity of Thought and Scientific Progress," *Journal of Environmental Psychology* 25 (2005): 361–80.

188 F. Stuart Chapin et al., "Design Principles for Social-Ecological Transformation toward Sustainability: Lessons from New Zealand Sense of Place," *Ecosphere* 3, 5 (2012): 40; Capaldi, Dopko, and Zelenski, "The Relationship between Nature Connectedness and Happiness," 2.

189 S. Markey et al., "Evidence of Place: Becoming a Region in Rural Canada," *International Journal of Urban and Regional Research* 39, 5 (2015): 874–91.

190 Chapin et al., "Design Principles," 16.

191 Hough, "Formed by Natural Processes," 16.

192 Rainer Maria Rilke, *Selected Works: Volume I Prose* (New York: New Direction Books, 1960), 13.

193 L. Liebenberg et al., "Spaces and Places: Understanding Sense of Belonging and Cultural Engagement among Indigenous Youth," *International Journal of Qualitative Methods* 18 (2019): https://journals.sagepub.com/doi/10.1177/1609406919840547.

194 Settele et al., "COVID-19 Stimulus Measures."
195 Emma Gilchrist, "What the Coronavirus Pandemic Tells Us about Our Relationship with the Natural World," *Narwhal,* March 17, 2020, https://thenarwhal.ca/what-coronavirus -covid-19-pandemic-tells-us-about-relationship-natural-world/.
196 Settele et al., "COVID-19 Stimulus Measures."
197 Christine K. Johnson et al., "Global Shifts in Mammalian Population Trends Reveal Key Predictors of Virus Spillover Risk," *Royal Society Proceedings B* 287 (2020): 20192736.
198 Zoë L. Grange et al., "Ranking the Risk of Animal-to-Human Spillover for Newly Discovered Viruses," *Proceedings of the National Academy of Sciences* 118, 15 (2020): e2002324118; Inter-governmental Science-Policy Platform on Biodiversity and Ecosystem Services (IPBES), *IPBES Workshop on Biodiversity and Pandemics* (Bonn: IPBES, 2020).
199 Settele et al., "COVID-19 Stimulus Measures."

CHAPTER 2: TRAJECTORIES OF GREEN PLANNING

Epigraph: Alice Walker, *The World Has Changed: Conversations with Alice Walker,* ed. Rudolph P. Byrd (New York: New Press, 2010), 194.
1 Barclay Hudson et al., "Comparison of Current Planning Theories: Counterparts and Contradictions," *Journal of the American Planning Association* 25, 4 (1979): 387.
2 Ernest R. Alexander, *Approaches to Planning: Introducing Current Planning Theories, Concepts and Issues* (New York: Gordon and Breach, 1992).
3 John F. Forester, *Planning in the Face of Power* (Berkeley: University of California Press, 1989), 3.
4 John Friedman, "Toward a Non-Euclidian Mode of Planning," *Journal of the American Planning Association* 59, 4 (1993): 482.
5 Scott Campbell and Susan Fainstein, eds., *Readings in Planning Theory* (Malden, MA: Blackwell, 2003).
6 Gerald Hodge and David Gordon, *Planning Canadian Communities: An Introduction to the Principles, Practice, and Participants* (Toronto: Nelson, 2014), 3.
7 Jill Grant, ed., *A Reader in Canadian Planning: Linking Theory and Practice* (Scarborough, ON: Thomson Nelson Academic, 2008).
8 Naomi Klein, *The Shock Doctrine: The Rise of Disaster Capitalism* (Toronto: Vintage Canada, 2007), 17.
9 David Harvey, *Justice, Nature and the Geography of Difference* (Oxford: Blackwell, 1996).
10 Jeanne Wolfe, "Our Common Past: An Interpretation of Canadian Planning History," *Plan Canada* 26, special issue (1994): 12–34.
11 Ingrid Stefanovic and Stephen Bede Scharper, eds., *The Natural City: Re-Envisioning the Built Environment* (Toronto: University of Toronto Press, 2012), 21.
12 Harvey, *Justice,* 121.
13 Harvey, *Justice,* 125.
14 Michael Hough, *Cities and Natural Process a Basis for Sustainability* (New York: Routledge, 2004), 1.
15 Hough, *Cities and Natural Process,* 8.
16 David Harvey, "The Right to the City," *New Left Review* 53 (2008): 23–40.
17 Wolfe, "Our Common Past," 12–13, 16–19, 22–34, 26.
18 Hodge and Gordon, *Planning Canadian Communities,* 14.
19 Michael Steinberg Lindfield, *Florian Urban Development: Green Cities* (Mandalayong: Asian Development Bank, 2012), 5.
20 Timothy Beatley, *Green Urbanism: Learning from European Cities* (Washington, DC: Island Press, 2000), 6.

21 World Commission on Environment and Development (Brundtland Commission), *Our Common Future* (New York: Oxford University Press, 1987), 56.

22 Gerald Hodge and I. Robinson, *Planning Canadian Regions* (Vancouver: UBC Press, 2001), 394.

23 Scott Campbell, "The Planner's Triangle Revisited: Sustainability and the Evolution of a Planning Ideal That Can't Stand Still," *Journal of the American Planning Association* 82, 4 (2016): 388–97.

24 Campbell, "The Planner's Triangle Revisited," 392.

25 Lisa Benton-Short and John Short, *Cities and Nature* (New York: Routledge, 2008).

26 Benton-Short and Short, *Cities and Nature.*

27 Grant, *A Reader in Canadian Planning,* 6.

28 Wolfe, "Our Common Past," 12–13.

29 Hodge and Gordon, *Planning Canadian Communities,* 226.

30 Robert Young and Pierre Clavel, "Planning Living Cities: Patrick Geddes' Legacy in the New Millennium," *Landscape and Urban Planning* 5 (2017): 166.

31 Kim Stephens, *Design with Nature Philosophy Guides Water Sustainability Action Plan for British Columbia,* Water Bucket Online, November 2022, http://www.waterbucket.ca/cfa/sites/wbccfa/documents/media/372.pdf.

32 Hodge and Gordon, *Planning Canadian Communities,* 126.

33 Frederick Steiner and Billy Fleming, "Design with Nature at 50: Its Enduring Significance to Socio-Ecological Practice and Research in the Twenty-First Century," *Socio-Ecological Practice Research* 1 (2019): 173–77; P. Crutzen, "Geology of Mankind," *Nature* 415 (2002): 23.

34 Smart Growth Network, *This Is Smart Growth,* 2006, https://www.epa.gov/sites/default/files/2014-04/documents/this-is-smart-growth.pdf.

35 Hirini Matunga, "Theorizing Indigenous Planning," in *Reclaiming Indigenous Planning,* ed. Ryan Walker, Ted Jojola, and David Natcher (Montreal and Kingston: McGill-Queen's University Press, 2013), 3–32.

36 Leanne Betasamosake Simpson, *As We Have Always Done: Indigenous Freedom through Radical Resistance* (Minneapolis: University of Minnesota Press, 2017).

37 Peter Armitage and Stephen Kilburn, *Conduct of Traditional Knowledge Research – A Reference Guide* (Whitehorse: Wildlife Management Advisory Council, 2015).

38 Leanne Betasamosake Simpson, "Anticolonial Strategies for the Recovery and Maintenance of Indigenous Knowledge," *American Indian Quarterly* 28, 3–4 (2004): 373–84, 373.

39 Leonie Sandercock, "Commentary: Indigenous Planning and the Burden of Colonialism," *Planning Theory and Practice* 5, 1 (2004): 118–24.

40 Canadian Institute of Planning, *Policy on Planning Practice and Reconciliation* (Ottawa: CIP, 2019).

41 Hough, *Cities and Natural Process,* 6.

42 Carlos Bartesaghi Koc et al., "Towards a Comprehensive Green Infrastructure Typology: A Systematic Review of Approaches, Methods and Typologies," *Urban Ecosystems* 20 (2017): 15–35; José Puppim de Oliveria and Christopher Doll, "Climate Co-Benefits in Urban Areas," in *Urbanization and Climate Co-Benefits: Implementation of Win-Win Interventions in Cities,* ed. José Puppim de Oliveria and Christopher Doll (London: Routledge, 2017), 1–24.

43 Action on Climate Change Team, *Low Carbon Resilience Interventions* (Burnaby: Simon Fraser University, 2019), 7.

44 Hodge and Gordon, *Planning Canadian Communities.*

45 Truth and Reconciliation Commission of Canada, *Honouring the Truth, Reconciling for the Future* (Ottawa: Truth and Reconciliation Commission of Canada, 2015).

CHAPTER 3: FROM GREEN PLANNING TO ECOSYSTEM APPROACHES

1 Ingrid Stefanovic, "In Search of the Natural City," in *The Natural City: Re-Envisioning the Built Environment,* ed. Ingrid Stefanovic and Stephen Bede Scharper (Toronto: University of Toronto Press, 2012), 18.

2 Ray Tomalty, "The Ecology of Cities," *Alternatives Journal* 35, 4 (2009): 18–21.

3 Vivek Shandas and W. Barry Messer, "Fostering Green Communities through Civic Engagement: Community-Based Environmental Stewardship in the Portland Area," *Journal of the American Planning Association* 74, 4 (2008): 408.

4 See https://mnai.ca/.

5 See https://lternet.edu/.

6 Jianguo Wu, "Urban Ecology and Sustainability: The State-of-the-Science and Future Directions," *Landscape and Urban Planning* 125 (2014): 209–21, 218.

7 Anne K. Salomon et al., "Democratizing Conservation Science and Practice," *Ecology and Society* 23, 1 (2018): 44.

8 Wu, "Urban Ecology and Sustainability."

9 Christopher Walsh et al., "Restoring a Stream through Retention in Urban Stormwater Runoff: A Catchment-Scale Experiment in a Social-Ecological System," *Freshwater Science* 35, 1 (2015): 1161–69.

10 Darren Bos and Helen Brown, "Overcoming Barriers to Community Participation in a Catchment-Scale Experiment: Building Trust and Changing Behavior," *Freshwater Science* 34, 3 (2015): 1169–75.

11 Toby Prosser et al., "Integrating Stormwater Management to Restore a Stream: Perspectives from a Waterway Management Authority," *Freshwater Science* 34, 3 (2015): 1186–94.

12 Walsh et al., "Restoring a Stream through Retention."

13 Victoria State Government, *Plan Melbourne: 2017–2050* (Melbourne: Victoria State Government, 2017), 121.

14 Portland Bureau of Environmental Services, *Portland Watershed Management Plan* (Portland: Portland Bureau of Environmental Services, 2005).

15 City of Portland, *Terrestrial Ecology Enhancement Strategy* (Portland: City of Portland, 2011).

16 City of Portland, *Comprehensive Plan 2035* (Portland: City of Portland, 2020).

17 Portland Bureau of Environmental Services, *Summary of the Framework for Integrated Management of Watershed Health* (Portland: City of Portland, 2005).

18 Portland Bureau of Environmental Services, *Portland Watershed Management Plan.*

19 Portland Bureau of Environmental Services, *Portland Watershed Management Plan 5-Year Implementation Strategy 2012–2017* (Portland: City of Portland, 2012).

20 City of Portland, *Terrestrial Ecology Enhancement Strategy.*

21 City of Portland, *Stormwater Management Manual* (Portland: City of Portland, 2016).

22 City of Portland, *Citywide Invasive Plant Management and Natural Areas* (Portland: City of Portland, 2015).

23 Audubon Society of Portland, *Portland Resource Guide for Bird-Friendly Building Design* (Portland: Audubon Society, 2012).

24 Portland Bureau of Environmental Services, *Portland Watershed Management Plan.*

25 Portland Bureau of Environmental Services, *Portland Watershed Management Plan.*

26 Portland Bureau of Planning and Sustainability, *The Portland Plan Progress Report* (Portland: Portland Bureau of Planning and Sustainability, 2017).

27 City of Portland, *Comprehensive Plan 2035.*

28 Wellington City Council, *Our Natural Capital: Wellington's Biodiversity Strategy and Action Plan 2015* (Wellington: Wellington City Council, 2015).

29 Nicky Oliver Smith, "Biodiversity Outcomes of an Urban Revegetation Programme in Wellington, New Zealand: The Role of Patch Size, Isolation, Age and the Urban Matrix," MSc thesis (Victoria University of Wellington, 2015).

30 Wellington City Council, *Our Natural Capital.*

31 Wellington City Council, *Our Natural Capital.*

32 Wellington City Council, *Our Natural Capital.*

33 Wellington City Council, *Our Natural Capital.*

34 Wellington City Council, *Wellington Resilience Strategy* (Wellington: City of Wellington, 2017).

35 Wellington City Council, *Wellington Resilience Strategy,* 90.

36 Richard Boon et al., "Managing a Threatened Savanna Ecosystem (KwaZulu-Natal Sandstone Sourveld) in an Urban Biodiversity Hotspot: Durban, South Africa," *African Biodiversity and Conservation* 46, 2 (2016): 1–12.

37 eThekwini Municipality, *What Is the Durban Metropolitan Open Space System?* (Durban: eThekwini Municipality, 2016).

38 Boon et al., "Managing a Threatened Savanna Ecosystem."

39 Debra Roberts et al., "Exploring Ecosystem-Based Adaptation in Durban, South Africa: 'Learning-by-doing' at the Local Government Coal Face," *Environment and Urbanization* 24, 1 (2012): 167–95.

40 Mathieu Rouget et al., "Improving the Management of Threatened Ecosystems in an Urban Biodiversity Hotspot through the Durban Research Action Partnership," *Bothalia: African Biodiversity and Conservation* 46, 2 (2016): 1–3.

41 Jessica Cockburn et al., "How to Build Science-Action Partnerships for Local Land-Use Planning and Management: Lessons from Durban, South Africa," *Ecology and Society* 21, 1 (2016): 28.

42 Sizwe Nkambule et al., "Opportunities and Constraints for Community-Based Conservation: The Case of the KwaZulu-Natal Sandstone Sourveld Grassland, South Africa," *Bothalia: African Biodiversity and Conservation* 46, 2 (2016).

43 Roberts et al., "Exploring Ecosystem-Based Adaptation in Durban, South Africa."

44 Rouget et al., "Improving the Management of Threatened Ecosystems."

45 eThekwini Municipality, *Durban Climate Action Plan 2019* (Durban: eThekwini Municipality, 2019).

46 See, respectively, Richard Schuster et al., "Vertebrate Biodiversity on Indigenous-Managed Lands in Australia, Brazil, and Canada Equals that in Protected Areas," *Environmental Science and Policy* 101 (2019): 1; Sandra Díaz et al. "Pervasive Human-Driven Decline of Life on Earth Points to the Need for Transformative Change," *Science* 366 (2019): 1327; and Sandra Díaz et al., eds., *Summary for Policymakers of the Global Assessment Report on Biodiversity and Ecosystem Services* (Bonn: Intergovernmental Science-Policy Platform on Biodiversity and Ecosystem Services, 2019), 5.

47 Anne K. Salomon et al., "Democratizing Conservation Science and Practice," *Ecology and Society* 23, 1 (2018): 44.

48 Díaz et al., *Summary for Policymakers,* 31.

CHAPTER 4: THE VISION FOR NATURE-FIRST CITIES

Epigraph: Tom Athanasiou, *Divided Planet: The Ecology of Rich and Poor* (Boston: Little, Brown, 1996), 307.

1 Jane Jacobs, "The Greening of the City," *New York Times Magazine,* May 16, 2004, https://www.nytimes.com/2004/05/16/magazine/the-greening-of-the-city.html.

2   Lewis Mumford, "Introduction to Ian L. McHarg," in *Design with Nature,* by Ian L. McHarg (Garden City, NY: Natural History Press, 1969), vi–vii.

3   Ebenezer Howard, *Garden Cities of Tomorrow* (London: Faber and Faber, 1966), 15.

4   Mark Roseland, "Dimensions of the Future: An Eco-City Overview," in *Eco-City Dimensions: Healthy Communities, Healthy Planet,* ed. Mark Roseland (Gabriola Island, BC: New Society, 1997), 4.

5   Charles J. Kibert, "Preface," in *Reshaping the Built Environment: Ecology, Ethics, and Economics,* ed. Charles J. Kibert (Washington, DC: Island Press, 1999), xv–xvi, xv.

6   Henrik Ernstson, "Urban Transitions: On Urban Resilience and Human-Dominated Ecosystems," *AMBIO: A Journal of the Human Environment* 39, 8 (2010): 531.

7   "New Frog Species Discovered in NYC," *Toronto Sun,* March 14, 2012, https://torontosun.com/2012/03/14/new-frog-species-discovered-in-nyc.

8   Judy Bush and Andréanne Doyon, "Planning a Just Nature-Based City: Listening for the Voice of an Urban River," *Environmental Science & Policy* 143 (2023): 55–63. https://doi.org/10.1016/j.envsci.2023.02.023.

9   George Monbiot, "Is Protecting the Environment Incompatible with Social Justice?," *Guardian,* February 13, 2012, https://www.theguardian.com/environment/georgemonbiot/2012/feb/13/protecting-environment-social-justice.

10 David A. Perry, *Forest Ecosystems* (Baltimore: Johns Hopkins University Press, 1994).

11 Perry, *Forest Ecosystems.*

12 Norman Christensen Jr., "An Historical Perspective on Forest Succession and Its Relevance to Ecosystem Restoration and Conservation Practice in North America," *Forest Ecology and Management* 330 (2014): 312–22.

13 Peter B. Landres et al., "Overview of the Use of Natural Variability Concepts in Managing Ecological Systems," *Ecological Applications* 9, 4 (1999): 1179–88.

14 Perry, *Forest Ecosystems,* 1–2.

15 Herb Hammond, *Maintaining Whole Systems on Earth's Crown: Ecosystem-Based Conservation Planning for the Boreal Forest* (Slocan Park, BC: Silva Forest Foundation, 1994), 34.

16 David B. Lindenmayer and Jerry F. Franklin, *Conserving Forest Biodiversity: A Comprehensive Multiscaled Approach* (Washington, DC: Island Press, 2002), 55–60.

17 Lindenmayer and Franklin, *Conserving Forest Biodiversity,* 55–60.

18 Lindenmayer and Franklin, *Conserving Forest Biodiversity,* 55–60.

19 Dave Eagan and Evelyn Howell, *The Historical Ecology Handbook: A Restorationist's Guide to Reference Ecosystems* (Washington, DC: Island Press, 2001).

20 Jerry F. Franklin et al., *Simplified Forest Management to Achieve Watershed and Forest Health: A Critique* (Seattle: National Wildlife Federation, 2000), 1.

21 Rachel F. Holt and Glenn Sutherland, *Environmental Risk Assessment: Base Case: Coarse Filter Biodiversity* (Nelson, BC: Veridian Ecological Consulting, 2003), 4–13.

22 Edward Morgan, *Understanding the Role of Science in Defining Ecological Limits* (Brisbane: Wild Law Conference, 2015).

23 Nicholas Ashford et al. "Wingspread Statement on the Precautionary Principle" (1998) https://www.gdrc.org/u-gov/precaution-3.html.

24 Coast Information Team, *The Scientific Basis of Ecosystem-Based Management* (Victoria: Cortex Consultants, 2004), 13.

25 Coast Information Team, *CIT Compendium: A Science Compendium: Ecosystem-Based Management, Science and Its Application* (Victoria: CIT Integrated Land Management Bureau, 2003).

26 Richard T.T. Forman and Michael Godron, *Landscape Ecology* (New York: John Wiley and Sons, 1986), 8–11.

27 Richard T.T. Forman, *Land Mosaics: The Ecology of Landscapes and Regions* (Cambridge, UK: Cambridge University Press, 1995).

28 Michael E. Soule and John Terborgh, *Continental Conservation: Scientific Foundations of Regional Reserve Networks* (Washington, DC: Island Press, 1999).

29 Richard B. Primack, *A Primer of Conservation Biology* (Sunderland, MA: Sinauer Associates, 2012).

30 Edward O. Wilson, *Half-Earth* (New York: W.W. Norton, 2016).

31 Alexandria Ocasio-Cortez, speech given at G40 Mayors' Summit, Copenhagen, October 11, 2019.

32 William J. Ripple et al., "World Scientists' Warning of a Climate Emergency," *BioScience* 20 (2019): 8.

33 Ripple et al., "World Scientists' Warning," 9.

34 Ripple et al., "World Scientists' Warning," 8.

35 UN Intergovernmental Science-Policy Platform on Biodiversity and Ecosystem Services, *Summary for Policymakers,* May 6, 2019.

36 Daniel H. Cole, "The Problem of Shared Responsibility in International Climate Law," (2015) *Articles by Mauer Faculty* https://www.repository.law.indiana.edu/facpub/2408.

37 Jonathan A. Patz et al., "Climate Change and Global Health: Quantifying a Growing Ethical Crisis," *EcoHealth* 4, 4 (2007): 397.

38 Sophie Kasakove, "New York's Invisible Climate Migrants," *New Republic,* July 11, 2019, https://newrepublic.com/article/154044/new-york-superstorm-sandy-economic-climate -migrants.

39 Farhad Manjoo, "It's the End of California as We Know It," *New York Times,* October 30, 2019, https://www.nytimes.com/2019/10/30/opinion/sunday/california-fires.html.

40 Karrie Jacobs, "High-Line Network Tackles Gentrification," *Architect* 10 (2017): 111.

41 LA River, "Frank Gehry and the Los Angeles River" https://www.riverla.org/frank_ gehry_and_the_los_angeles_river.

42 Jeremiah Moss, "Disney World on the Hudson," *New York Times,* August 21, 2012, https:// www.nytimes.com/2012/08/22/opinion/in-the-shadows-of-the-high-line.html.

43 New York City, "Economic Snapshot," August 2011, https://www.nycedc.com/sites/default/ files/files/economic-snapshot/EconomicSnapshotAugust2011_0.pdf, 2.

44 Jacobs, "High-Line Network."

45 New York City, "Economic Snapshot," 2.

46 Tenley M. Conway and Lisa Urbani, "Variations in Municipal Urban Forestry Policies: A Case Study of Toronto, Canada," *Urban Forestry and Urban Greening* 6 (2007): 181–92.

47 Jamie Tratalos et al., "Urban Form, Biodiversity Potential and Ecosystem Services," *Landscape and Urban Planning* 83 (2007): 308–17.

48 Nikolas C. Heynen and Greg Lindsey, "Correlates of Urban Forest Canopy Cover: Implications for Local Public Works," *Public Works Management and Policy* 8, 1 (2003): 33–47.

49 Warren Paige et al., "Social and Institutional Factors Associated with Land Use and Forest Conservation along Two Urban Gradients in Massachusetts," *Landscape and Urban Planning* 102, 2 (2011): 82–92.

50 Anne Whiston Spirn, *The Granite Garden* (New York: Basic Books, 1984), 115.

51 The cities studied were Baltimore, Los Angeles, New York, Philadelphia, Raleigh, Sacramento, and Washington; Kirsten Schwartz et al., "Trees Grow on Money: Urban Tree Canopy Cover and Environmental Justice," *PLOS One,* 2015, https://journals.plos.org/plosone/article?id= 10.1371/journal.pone.0122051.

52 N. Hotte et al., *The Social and Economic Values of Canada's Urban Forests: A National Synthesis* (Ottawa: Canadian Forest Service, 2015).

53 Christine Haaland and Cecil Konijnendijk van den Bosch, "Challenges and Strategies for Urban Green-Space Planning in Cities Undergoing Densification: A Review," *Urban Forestry and Urban Greening* 14 (2015): 764.

54 Schwartz et al., "Trees Grow on Money."

55   Majora Carter (Majora Carter Group), in discussion with Cam Brewer, January 16, 2018.
56   Carter, in discussion with Brewer.
57   Mark Scott and Mick Lennon, "Nature-Based Solutions for the Contemporary City," *Planning Theory and Practice* 17, 2 (2016): 268.
58   Carter, in discussion with Brewer.
59   Carter, in discussion with Brewer.
60   The 11th Street Bridge Park Equitable Development Plan is available at http://bridgepark. org/sites/default/files/Resources/EDP%20Final%20-%20UPDATED.pdf.
61   Michael M'Gonigle and Louise Takeda, "The Liberal Limits of Environmental Law: A Green Legal Critique," *Pace Environmental Law Review* 30, 3 (2013): 1005–1115.
62   M'Gonigle and Takeda, "The Liberal Limits of Environmental Law," 1013.
63   M'Gonigle and Takeda, "The Liberal Limits of Environmental Law," 1054.
64   M'Gonigle and Takeda, "The Liberal Limits of Environmental Law," 1058.
65   M'Gonigle and Takeda, "The Liberal Limits of Environmental Law," 1054.
66   Sustainable Prosperity, "Suburban Sprawl: Exposing Hidden Costs, Identifying Innovations," 2013, http://thecostofsprawl.com/report/SP_SuburbanSprawl_Oct2013_opt.pdf.
67   Smart Growth America, "Building Better Budgets," 2013, http://www.smartgrowthamerica. org/documents/building-better-budgets.pdf.
68   C.D. Howe, "Municipal Finance and the Pattern of Urban Growth," 2002, http://www. urbancentre.utoronto.ca/pdfs/elibrary/Slack_Mun-Finance-Urb-Growt.pdf, 6.
69   Saeed Mirza and Shafqat Ali, "Infrastructure Crisis – A Proposed National Infrastructure Policy for Canada," *Canadian Journal of Civil Engineering* 44, 7 (2017): https://doi.org/10.1139/cjce-2016-0468.
70   Mirza and Shafqat, "Infrastructure Crisis."
71   Susan Hanson et al., "A Global Ranking of Port Cities with High Exposure to Climate Extremes," *Climatic Change* 104, 1 (2011): 89.
72   *The City of New York v BP PLC,* Docket #18–2188cv, SDNY.
73   City of New York, "A Stronger, More Resilient New York," 2013, http://www.nyc.gov/html/sirr/downloads/pdf/final_report/Ch19_Funding_FINAL_singles.pdf; City of Vancouver, "Climate Change Adaptation Strategy," 2012, http://vancouver.ca/files/cov/Vancouver -Climate-Change-Adaptation-Strategy-2012-11-07.pdf.
74   Simon Black et al., IMF Fossil Fuel Subsidies Data: 2023 Update, IMF Working Papers 2023, 169, https://doi.org/10.5089/9798400249006.001.
75   Karen C. Seto, Burak Güneralp, and Lucy R. Hutyra, "Global Forecasts of Urban Expansion to 2030 and Direct Impacts on Biodiversity and Carbon Pools" *Proceedings of the National Academy of Sciences of the United States of America* 109, 40 (2012): 16083–88.
76   Graham Haines and Claire Nelischer, "The Opportunity of Rail Deck Park," Ryerson City Building Institute, Toronto, 2017, 1, 7.
77   Shuaib Lwasa et al., "Urban Systems and Other Settlements" in IPCC, *Climate Change 2022: Mitigation of Climate Change. Contribution of Working Group III to the Sixth Assessment Report of the Intergovernmental Panel on Climate Change,* P.R. Shukla et al., eds. (Cambridge: Cambridge University Press, 2022), 866.
78   Peter John Marcotullio et al., "The Geography of Global Urban Greenhouse Gas Emissions: An Exploratory Analysis," *Climatic Change* 121, 4 (2013): 621; David Dodman, "Blaming Cities for Climate Change? An Analysis of Urban Greenhouse Gas Emissions Inventories," *Environment and Urbanization* 21 (2009): 185–201.
79   Dodman, "Blaming Cities for Climate Change?"
80   Elisa Campbell and Jackie Teed, "Getting to Minus 80: Urban Form Strategies for Measurably Achieving Greenhouse Gas Emission Reduction Targets," *Plan Canada* 50, 4 (2010): 18.

81 Lwasa et al., 897.
82 Jan Corfee-Morlot et al., "Cities, Climate Change and Multilevel Governance," OECD Working Papers No. 14, 2009, 8.
83 Cynthia Rosenzweig et al., "Cities Lead the Way in Climate-Change Action," *Nature* 467 (2010): 909–11.
84 Stepan Wood and Kevin Thompson, "Transnational Voluntary Climate Change Initiatives for Local Governments: Key Variables, Drivers and Likely Effects," in *Local Climate Change Law: Environmental Regulation in Cities and Other Localities,* ed. Benjamin J. Richardson (Cheltenham, UK: Edward Elgar, 2012), 29–66.
85 United Nations Climate Change, "The Compact of Mayors – Catalysing City Climate Actions across the Globe," 2015, https://unfccc.int/news/the-compact-of-mayors-catalysing -city-climate-actions-across-the-globe.
86 Benjamin J. Richardson, ed., *Local Climate Change Law: Environmental Regulation in Cities and Other Localities* (Cheltenham, UK: Edward Elgar, 2012).
87 Richardson, *Local Climate Change Law,* 14; Hari M. Osofsky and Janet Koven Levit, "The Scale of Networks? Local Climate Change Coalitions," *Chicago Journal of International Law* 8, 2 (2008): 409–37.
88 Ileana M. Porras, "The City and International Law: In Pursuit of Sustainable Development," *Fordham Urban Law Journal* 36 (2009): 537–601.
89 William E. Rees, "What if 'Can Do' Can't? The Vulnerability and Resilience of Cities," address given at Gaining Ground – Resilient Cities Conference, Vancouver, October 20, 2009.
90 J. Daniel Khazzoom, "An Economic Model of the Regulated Emissions for Fuel-Efficient New Vehicles," *Journal of Environmental Economics and Management* 28, 2 (1995): 190–204.
91 Robert Gibson, "Sustainability and the Greenbelt," *Plan Canada* 51, 3 (2011): 38.
92 Andrés Duany, "Foreword," in *Sustainable Urbanism: Urban Design with Nature,* ed. Douglas Farr (Hoboken, NJ: John Wiley and Sons, 2008), 9.
93 Allison H. Roy, Michael J. Paul, and Seth J. Wenger, "Urban Stream Ecology," in *Urban Ecosystem Ecology,* ed. Jacquelin Aitkenhead-Peterson and Astrid Volder, Agronomy Monograph 55 (Madison, WI: American Society of Agronomy, Crop Science Society of America, Soil Science Society of America, 2010), 347.
94 Boone J. Kauffman et al., "An Ecological Perspective of Riparian and Stream Restoration in the Western United States," *Fisheries* 22, 5 (1997): 12.
95 Bradley D. Rowe and Kristin L. Getter, "Green Roofs and Garden Roofs," in *Urban Ecosystem Ecology,* ed. Jacquelin Aitkenhead-Peterson and Astrid Volder, Agronomy Monograph 55 (Madison, WI: American Society of Agronomy, Crop Science Society of America, Soil Science Society of America, 2010), 55.
96 Liat Margolis and Alexander Robinson, *Living Systems: Innovative Materials and Technologies for Landscape Architecture* (Basel: Birkhäuser, 2007), 112.
97 Gibson, "Sustainability and the Greenbelt," 38–40.
98 Paul Hellmund and Daniel Somers Smith, *Designing Greenways: Sustainable Landscapes for Nature and People* (Washington, DC: Island Press, 2006).
99 François Des Rosiers et al., "Greenhouse Gas Emissions and Urban Form: Linking Households' Socio-Economic Status with Housing and Transportation Choices," *Environment and Planning B: Urban Analytics and City Science* 44, 5 (2017): 964–85; Douglas Farr, ed., *Sustainable Urbanism: Urban Design with Nature* (Hoboken, NJ: John Wiley and Sons, 2008), 103.
100 Campbell and Teed, "Getting to Minus 80," 21; Maged Senbel et al., *The Relationship between Urban Form and GHG Emissions: A Primer for Municipal Decision Makers* (Vancouver: Urban Design Lab, School of Community and Regional Planning, University of British Columbia, 2010), 6.

101 Edward L. Glaeser and Matthew E. Kahn, "The Greenness of Cities: Carbon Dioxide Emissions and Urban Development," Working Paper No. 14238, National Bureau of Economic Research, Boston, 2008.

102 Nadja Popovich and Denise Lu, "The Most Detailed Map of Auto Emissions in America," *New York Times,* October 10, 2019, https://www.nytimes.com/interactive/2019/10/10/climate/driving-emissions-map.html.

103 Sungwon Lee and Bumsoo Lee, "The Influence of Urban Form on GHG Emissions in the U.S. Household Sector," *Energy Policy* 69 (2014): 534–48, 546.

104 Lee and Lee, "The Influence of Urban Form."

105 Des Rosiers et al., "Greenhouse Gas Emissions and Urban Form."

106 Reid Ewing and Fang Rong, "The Impact of Urban Form on US Residential Energy Use," *Housing Policy Debate* 19, 1 (2008): 1–20.

107 Ewing and Rong, "The Impact of Urban Form."

108 "City of Vancouver in Middle of the Pack When It Comes to Density," CBC News, January 9, 2018, http://www.cbc.ca/news/canada/british-columbia/vancouver-density-report-jan-2018-1.4479501.

109 "City of Vancouver in Middle of the Pack."

110 "City of Vancouver in Middle of the Pack."

111 Carter, in discussion with Brewer.

112 Reid Ewing et al., *Growing Cooler: The Evidence on Urban Development and Climate Change* (Washington: Urban Land Institute, 2008), 2.

113 Glaeser and Kahn, "The Greenness of Cities."

114 Ewing et al., *Growing Cooler,* 4.

115 Cherise Burda, Alison Bailie, and Graham Haines, *Driving Down Carbon* (Toronto: Pembina Institute, 2010).

116 Carter, in discussion with Brewer.

117 Haaland and van den Bosch, "Challenges and Strategies," 760, 764.

118 Haaland and van den Bosch, "Challenges and Strategies," 760.

119 Metro Vancouver, *Regional Growth Strategy Backgrounder: Residential Development Capacity Study* (Burnaby: Metro Vancouver, 2009).

120 Cherise Burda et al., *Density Done Right* (Toronto: City Building Institute, 2020), 14.

121 Laura Bliss, "Oregon's Single Family Zoning Ban Was a Long Time Coming," July 19, 2019, CityLab.com https://www.bloomberg.com/news/articles/2019-07-02/upzoning-rising-oregon-bans-single-family-zoning.

122 City of Vancouver, "Vancouver Reforms Single Family Neighbourhoods" https://vancouver.ca/news-calendar/vancouver-reforms-sf-neighbourhoods.aspx.

123 Burda et al., *Density Done Right,* 9.

124 Burda et al., *Density Done Right,* 3.

125 Cherise Burda (executive director, City Building TMU, Toronto Metropolitan University), in discussion with Cam Brewer, September 2021.

126 Michael Richards, "Solving the Green Design Paradox," *Green Places* 72 (2011): 34–39.

127 Tratalos et al., "Urban Form."

128 Chad Pawson, "High-Density Neighbourhoods Leave Room for Trees, Says Metro Vancouver," CBC News, September 22, 2019, https://www.cbc.ca/news/canada/british-columbia/tree-canopy-metro-vancouver-dense-neighbourhoods-have-more-trees-1.5291636.

129 Pawson, "High-Density Neighbourhoods."

130 Haines and Nelischer, "The Opportunity of Rail Deck Park."

131 Haines and Nelischer, "The Opportunity of Rail Deck Park."

132 *New York Times* Editorial Board, "The Cities We Need," *New York Times,* May 11, 2020, https://www.nytimes.com/2020/05/11/opinion/sunday/coronavirus-us-cities-inequality.html.

133 Emily Badger, "Density Is Normally Good for Us. That Will Be True after Coronavirus, Too," *New York Times,* March 24, 2020, https://www.nytimes.com/2020/03/24/upshot/coronavirus-urban-density-risks.html.

134 Scott Wiener and Anthony Iton, "A Backlash against Cities Would Be Dangerous," *Atlantic,* May 17, 2020, https://www.theatlantic.com/ideas/archive/2020/05/urban-density-not-problem/611752/.

135 Jonathan Miller, "The Overstated COVID-19 Blame on Urban Density in Favor of Suburban Living," *Forbes,* May 14, 2020, https://www.forbes.com/sites/jonathanmiller1/2020/05/14/the-overstated-covid-19-blame-on-urban-density-in-favor-of-suburban-living/.

136 Adam Rogers, "How Does a Virus Spread in Cities? It's a Matter of Scale," *Wired,* May 28, 2020, https://www.wired.com/story/how-does-a-virus-spread-in-cities-its-a-problem-of-scale/; "Coronavirus Tracked: The Latest Figures as Countries Fight to Contain the Pandemic," *Financial Times,* May 17, 2020, https://www.ft.com/content/a26fbf7e-48f8-11ea-aeb3-955839e06441.

137 Patrick Condon, "A Safe, More Enjoyable Street for Our New Times," *Tyee,* May 12, 2020, https://thetyee.ca/Analysis/2020/05/12/Vancouver-Could-Save-Money-On-Sewage-With-Swales/.

138 Farhad Manjoo, "We've Got to Stop Requiring Parking Everywhere," *New York Times,* June 2, 2022, https://www.nytimes.com/2022/06/02/opinion/california-parking.html.

139 Kofi Annan, "Future of Humanity Lies in Cities," paper presented at the Conference on Urban Development, Moscow, June 5, 2002, https://press.un.org/en/2002/sgsm8261.doc.htm.

140 Ahmet B. Besir and Erdem Cuce, "Green Roofs and Facades: A Comprehensive Review," *Renewable and Sustainable Energy Reviews* 82 (2018): 915–17.

141 Rowe and Getter, "Green Roofs and Garden Roofs."

142 Timothy Beatley, *Biophilic Cities* (Washington, DC: Island Press, 2010), 121.

143 Sonja Braaker et al., "Habitat Connectivity and Local Conditions Shape Taxonomic and Functional Diversity of Arthropods on Green Roofs," *Journal of Animal Ecology* 86, 3 (2017): 521–31; Nathalie Baumann, "Ground-Nesting Birds on Green Roofs in Switzerland: Preliminary Observations," *Urban Habitats* 4, 1 (2006): 37–50.

144 Tobi Eniolu Morakinyo et al., "Temperature and Cooling Demand Reduction by Green-Roof Types in Different Climates and Urban Densities: A Co-Simulation Parametric Study," *Energy Buildings* 145 (2017): 226–27.

145 Morakinyo et al., "Temperature and Cooling Demand Reduction," 226–27.

146 USEPA, *Heat Island Impacts* (Washington, DC: USEPA, 2020).

147 R. Schmunk, "595 People Were Killed by Heat in BC This Summer, New Figures from Coroner Show," CBC News, November 1, 2021, https://www.cbc.ca/news/canada/british-columbia/bc-heat-dome-sudden-deaths-revised-2021-1.6232758.

148 "StairScraper Wins Abu Dhabi Housing Competition," *Green Places* 72 (2011): 20–21.

149 Earth Pledge, *Green Roofs: Ecological Design and Construction* (Atglen, PA: Schiffer), 128.

150 Earth Pledge, *Green Roofs,* 20.

151 Stephen M. Wheeler and Timothy Beatley, eds., *The Sustainable Urban Development Reader* (London: Routledge, 2004), 305.

152 Astrid Volder and W. Todd Watson, "Urban Forestry," in *Urban Ecosystem Ecology,* ed. Jacqueline Aitkenhead-Peterson and Astrid Volder, Agronomy Monograph 55 (Madison, WI: American Society of Agronomy, Crop Science Society of America, Soil Science Society of America, 2010), 55; John L. Crompton, "The Impact of Parks on Property Values: Empirical Evidence from the Past Two Decades in the United States," *Managing Leisure* 10, 4 (2005): 203–18.

153 Richard Louv, *Last Child in the Woods* (Chapel Hill, NC: Algonquin Books of Chapel Hill, 2004), 104.

154   K. Vijayaraghavan, "Green Roofs: A Critical Review on the Role of Components, Benefits, Limitations and Trends," *Renewable and Sustainable Energy Reviews* 57 (2016): 740–41; Living Architecture Monitor, "How This Swiss City Is Using Green Roofs to Combat Climate Change," 2022, https://livingarchitecturemonitor.com/news/how-this-swiss-city-is-using -green-roofs-to-combat-climate-change; Rowe and Getter, "Green Roofs and Garden Roofs."

155   Gaël Pétremand, "Ground Beetle (Coleoptera: Carabidae) Communities on Green Roofs in Switzerland: Synthesis and Perspectives," *Urban Ecosystems* 21, 1 (2017): 119–32.

156   Philip Proefrock, "Copenhagen Adopts a Mandatory Green Roof Policy," 2010, http:// inhabitat.com/copenhagen-adopts-a-mandatory-green-roof-policy/; City of Toronto, Bylaw C. Green Roofs, 492-2.

157   Erica Oberndorfer et al., "Green Roofs as Urban Ecosystems: Ecological Structures, Functions, and Services," *BioScience* 57, 10 (2016): 823–25; Vijayaraghavan, "Green Roofs."

158   "Canada's Largest Living Roof Is a Cut Above," *Green Places* 80 (2011): 42.

159   Boston Medical Center, *Rooftop Farm,* 2020, https://www.bmc.org/nourishing-our -community/rooftop-farm.

160   Capital Regional District, *Green Stormwater Infrastructure, Living Walls* (Victoria: Capital Regional District, 2020).

161   Margolis and Robinson, *Living Systems,* 15.

162   Robert A. Francis and Jamie Lorimer, "Urban Reconciliation Ecology: The Potential of Living Roofs and Walls," *Journal of Environmental Management* 92, 6 (2011): 1429; Caroline Chiquet, John W. Dover, and Paul Mitchell, "Birds and the Urban Environment: The Value of Green Walls," *Urban Ecosystems* 16 (2013): 453.

163   Oliver Giles, "Urban Jungles," *Prestige,* 2015, http://prestigeonline.com/hk/art-culture/ interviews/urban-jungles/.

164   "Living Wall Unveiled," *Green Places* 75 (2011): 17.

165   Robert Snep, Wim Timmermans, and Robert Kwak, "Applying Landscape Ecological Principles to a Fascinating Landscape: The City," in *Ecology of Cities and Towns: A Comparative Approach,* ed. Mark J. McDonnell, Amy K. Hahs, and Jürgen H. Breuste (Cambridge, UK: Cambridge University Press, 2009), 456–69.

166   Mike Archer and Bob Beale, *Going Native: Living in the Australian Environment* (Sydney: Hodder, 2004); Beatley, *Biophilic Cities,* 119.

167   Margolis and Robinson, *Living Systems,* 14.

168   Margolis and Robinson, *Living Systems,* 34.

169   "StairScraper Wins Abu Dhabi Housing Competition," 21.

170   Singapore Urban Redevelopment Authority, "Update to the Landscaping for Urban Spaces and High Rises (LUSH) Programme: LUSH 3.0," 2017, https://www.ura.gov.sg/uol/ circulars/2017/Nov/dc17–06.

171   Singapore Urban Redevelopment Authority, "Update."

172   Beatley, *Biophilic Cities,* 106.

173   Beatley, *Biophilic Cities,* 99.

174   Ina Säumel, Frauke Weber, and Ingo Kowarik, "Toward Livable and Healthy Urban Streets: Roadside Vegetation Provides Ecosystem Services Where People Live and Move," *Environmental Science and Policy* 62 (2016): 24–28.

175   Jennifer Mullaney, Terry Lucke, and Stephen J. Trueman, "A Review of Benefits and Challenges in Growing Street Trees in Paved Urban Environments," *Landscape Urban Plan* 134 (2015): 157–66.

176   Matthew Tallis et al., "Estimating the Removal of Atmospheric Pollution by the Urban Tree Canopy of London, under Current and Future Environments," *Landscape Urban Plan* 103, 2 (2011): 129.

177   Mullaney, Lucke, and Trueman, "A Review of Benefits and Challenges."

178 Sheryn D. Pitman, Christopher B. Daniels, and Martin E. Ely, "Green Infrastructure as Life Support: Urban Nature and Climate Change," *Transactions of the Royal Society of South Australia* 139, 1 (2015): 97–101.

179 Pitman, Daniels, and Ely, "Green Infrastructure as Life Support."

180 Pitman, Daniels, and Ely, "Green Infrastructure as Life Support."

181 City of Vancouver, "Tree Canopy Achievement Program," https://www.cityofvancouver.us/publicworks/page/tree-canopy-achievement-program-treecap.

182 New York City Parks, "NYC Parks Celebrates One Millionth Tree with Bronx Community Members," https://www.nycgovparks.org/parks/joyce-kilmer-park/dailyplant/23507.

183 Geoffrey Davidson, "Singapore's Life in the Trees," October 28, 2015, https://www.thenatureofcities.com/2015/10/28/life-in-the-trees/.

184 Capital Regional District, *Green Stormwater Infrastructure, Permeable Paving* (Victoria: Capital Regional District, Education and Environment, Green Stormwater Infrastructure, 2020).

185 M. Demuzere et al., "Mitigating and Adapting to Climate Change: Multi-Functional and Multi-Scale Assessment of Green Urban Infrastructure," *Journal of Environmental Management* 146 (2014): 107–15.

186 N.L. Stephenson et al., "Rate of Tree Carbon Accumulation Increases Continuously with Tree Size," *Nature* 507 (2014): 90–93.

187 Herb Hammond, *Seeing the Forest among the Trees: The Case for Wholistic Forest Use* (Vancouver: Polestar Press, 1992), 102.

188 Richard T.T. Forman and Lauren E. Alexander, "Roads and Their Major Ecological Effects," *Annual Review of Ecological Systems* 29, 207 (1998): 225.

189 Mel McGregor, Kelly Matthews, and Darryl Jones, "Vegetated Fauna Overpass Disguises Road Presence and Facilitates Permeability for Forest Microbats in Brisbane, Australia," *Frontiers Ecology and Evolution* 5 (2017): 5.

190 City of Edmonton, "Wildlife Passage Engineering Design Guidelines," 2010, https://www.edmonton.ca/city_government/documents/PDF/WPEDG_FINAL_Aug_2010.pdf.

191 City of Edmonton, "Wildlife Passage Engineering Design Guidelines."

192 "Ruelles Vertes," Eco-quartiers, https://www.eco-quartiers.org/ruelles-vertes.

193 City of Chicago, *The Chicago Green Alley Handbook* (Chicago: City of Chicago, 2010).

194 City of Chicago, *The Chicago Green Alley Handbook* (Chicago: City of Chicago, 2010).

195 Christopher McGuckin and Robert Brown, "A Landscape Ecological Model for Wildlife Enhancement of Stormwater Management Practices in Urban Greenways," *Landscape and Urban Planning* 33, 1–3 (1995): 227–46.

196 Steven J. Burian and Christine A. Pomeroy, "Urban Impacts on the Water Cycle and Potential Green Infrastructure Implications," in *Urban Ecosystem Ecology,* ed. Jacqueline Aitkenhead-Peterson and Astrid Volder, Agronomy Monograph 55 (Madison, WI: American Society of Agronomy, Crop Science Society of America, Soil Science Society of America, 2010), 280.

197 Pitman, Daniels, and Ely, "Green Infrastructure as Life Support," 97–98.

198 Pitman, Daniels, and Ely, "Green Infrastructure as Life Support," 97–98.

199 Michael J. Paul and Judy J. Meyer, "Streams in the Urban Landscape," *Annual Review of Ecology, Evolution, and Systematics* 32 (2001): 333–65.

200 Lizhu Wang et al., "Impacts of Urbanization on Stream Habitat and Fish across Multiple Spatial Scales," *Environmental Management* 28 (2001): 255–66.

201 Burian and Pomeroy, "Urban Impacts on the Water Cycle," 282.

202 New York City, *NYC Green Infrastructure Plan: A Sustainable Strategy for Clean Waterways* (New York: New York City, 2010), 30.

203 James Kenney, "As Green Infrastructure Pioneers, Philadelphia Is Primed for Workforce Development," Brookings, May 15, 2017, https://www.brookings.edu/blog/the-avenue/2017/05/15/as-green-infrastructure-pioneers-philadelphia-is-primed-for-workforce-development/.

204 Margolis and Robinson, *Living Systems,* 70.
205 City of Seattle, "Street Edge Alternatives," 2011, http://www.seattle.gov/util/About_SPU/
     Drainage_&_Sewer_System/GreenStormwaterInfrastructure/NaturalDrainageProjects/
     StreetEdgeAlternatives/.
206 City of Seattle, "Street Edge Alternatives."
207 Reimer, "Unsettling Eco-Scapes."
208 Peter Harnik and Ryan Donahue, "Turning Brownfields into Parks," *Planning* 77, 10 (2010):
     13–17.
209 Sol Hurwitz, "Promenade Plantée Is One of Paris' Best Kept Secrets," *Boston Globe,* February
     19, 2012, https://www.bostonglobe.com/lifestyle/travel/2012/02/19/promenade-plantee-one
     -paris-best-kept-secrets/FFg6nyYnEUmcc5e8HVx39J/story.html.
210 Hillary Rudd et al., "Importance of Backyard Habitat in a Comprehensive Biodiversity
     Conservation Strategy: A Connectivity Analysis of Urban Green Spaces," *Restoration Ecology*
     10 (2002): 368–75.
211 Jean-Pierre Savard, Philippe Clergeau, and Gwenaelle Mannechez, "Biodiversity Concepts
     and Urban Ecosystems," *Landscape and Urban Planning* 48 (2000): 131–42.
212 Savard, Clergeau, and Mannechez, "Biodiversity Concepts and Urban Ecosystems."
213 Joan G. Ehrenfeld and Emilie K. Stander, "Habitat Function in Urban Riparian Zones," in
     Urban Ecosystem Ecology, ed. Jacqueline Aitkenhead-Peterson and Astrid Volder, Agronomy
     Monograph 55 (Madison, WI: American Society of Agronomy, Crop Science Society of
     America, Soil Science Society of America, 2010), 114.
214 Mark A. Goddard, Andrew J. Dougill, and Tim G. Benton, "Scaling Up from Gardens:
     Biodiversity Conservation in Urban Environments," *Trends in Ecology and Evolution* 25, 2
     (2010): 90–98.
215 Dagmar Haase, "Reflections on Urban Landscape, Ecosystem Services and Nature-Based
     Solutions in Cities," *Planning Theory and Practice* 17, 2 (2016): 276–77.
216 Elizabeth Renzetti, "Urban Menace? More Like an Urban Myth," *Globe and Mail,* April 7,
     2012, https://www.theglobeandmail.com/arts/are-foxes-an-urban-menace-more-like-urban
     -myth/article4098397/.
217 Renzetti, "Urban Menace?"
218 Mark J. McDonnell and Ian MacGregor-Fors, "The Ecological Future of Cities," *Science*
     352, 6288 (2016): 936–38.
219 Drew Nelles, "There Goes the Neighbourhood," *Walrus* 12, 6 (2015): 40–47.
220 McDonnell and MacGregor-Fors, "The Ecological Future of Cities," 936–38.
221 Robert McCleery, "Urban Mammals," in *Urban Ecosystem Ecology,* ed. Jacqueline Aitkenhead-
     Peterson and Astrid Volder, Agronomy Monograph 55 (Madison, WI: American Society of
     Agronomy, Crop Science Society of America, Soil Science Society of America, 2010), 90.
222 Savard, Clergeau, and Mannechez, "Biodiversity Concepts and Urban Ecosystems"; Eyal
     Shochat, Susannah Lerman, and Esteban Fernández-Juricic, "Birds in Urban Ecosystems:
     Population Dynamics, Community Structure, Biodiversity, and Conservation," in *Urban
     Ecosystem Ecology,* ed. Jacqueline Aitkenhead-Peterson and Astrid Volder, Agronomy
     Monograph 55 (Madison, WI: American Society of Agronomy, Crop Science Society of
     America, Soil Science Society of America, 2010), 76.
223 Ingrid Stefanovic and Stephen Bede Scharper, eds., *The Natural City: Re-Envisioning the
     Built Environment* (Toronto: University of Toronto Press, 2012), 24.
224 Louv, *Last Child in the Woods.*
225 Peter James et al., "Exposure to Greenness and Mortality in a Nationwide Prospective Cohort
     Study of Women," *Environmental Health Perspectives* 124, 9 (2016): 1344–52.
226 T. Takano, K. Nakamura, and M. Watanabe, "Urban Residential Environments and Senior
     Citizens' Longevity in Megacity Areas: The Importance of Walkable Green Spaces," *Journal*

of Epidemiology and Community Health 56, 12 (2002): 913–18; Richard Mitchell and Frank Popham, "Effect of Exposure to Natural Environment on Health Inequalities: An Observational Populations Study," *Lancet* 372, 9650 (2008): 1607–1706; Patrick ten Brink et al., *The Health and Social Benefits of Nature and Biodiversity Protection* (London: Institute for European Environmental Policy, 2016); Payam Dadvand et al., "Risks and Benefits of Green Spaces for Children: A Cross-Sectional Study of Associations with Sedentary Behavior, Obesity, Asthma, and Allergy," *Environmental Health Perspectives* 122, 12 (2014): 1329–35.

227 Demuzere et al., "Mitigating and Adapting to Climate Change."

228 UN Human Rights Council, "Issue of Human Rights Obligations Relating to the Enjoyment of a Safe, Clean, Healthy and Sustainable Environment: Report of the Special Rapporteur," GA 40th Session, February 25–March 23, 2019, A/HRC/40/55.

229 Demuzere et al., "Mitigating and Adapting to Climate Change."

230 Zöe Schlanger, "Now Is the Time to Take Care of Your Lungs. Here's How," *New York Times,* March 27, 2020, https://www.nytimes.com/2020/03/27/climate/climate-pollution-coronavirus-lungs.html.

231 "Airborne Particles May Be Assisting the Spread of SARS-CoV-2," *Economist,* March 26, 2020, https://www.economist.com/science-and-technology/2020/03/26/airborne-particles-may-be-assisting-the-spread-of-sars-cov-2.

232 Birute Balseviciene et al., "Impact of Residential Greenness on Preschool Children's Emotional and Behavioral Problems," 11, 7 (2014): 6757–70.

233 Payam Dadvand et al., "Green Spaces and Cognitive Development in Primary Schoolchildren," *Proceedings of the National Academy of Sciences of the United States of America* 112, 26 (2015): 7937–42.

234 Robin Moore, "The Need for Nature: A Childhood Right," *Social Justice* 24, 3 (1997): 203–20.

235 Demuzere et al., "Mitigating and Adapting to Climate Change," 110.

236 Howard, *Garden Cities of Tomorrow,* 44.

237 Randolph T. Hester, *Design for Ecological Democracy* (Cambridge, MA: MIT Press, 2006), 335.

238 Spirn, *The Granite Garden,* 115.

239 Darko Radovic, "Introduction: Towards a Theory of Eco-Urbanity," in *Eco-Urbanity: Towards Well-Mannered Built Environments,* ed. Darko Radovic (London: Routledge, 2009), 15.

240 Hester, *Design for Ecological Democracy,* 323.

241 P. Bolund and S. Hunhammar, "Ecosystem Services in Urban Areas," *Ecological Economics* 29, 2 (1999): 293–301.

242 Cowichan Valley Regional District, "News Release: Dikes up and Ready for Stormy Weather in Duncan," 2014, http://www.cvrd.bc.ca/DocumentCenter/ View/63773.

243 "How Do Your Gardens Grow?," *Green Places* 75 (2011): 21–26.

244 Mel Armstrong, "River of Dreams," *Green Places* 73 (2011): 24–29, 24.

245 Armstrong, "River of Dreams," 24.

246 JoAnn Greco, "Hail to the Blue and the Green," *Planning* 76, 9 (2010): 12–16.

247 Ishikawa Mikiko, "Excavating the Lost Commons: Creating Green Spaces and Urban Water Corridors for Eco-Urban Infrastructure," in *Eco-Urbanity: Towards Well-Mannered Built Environments,* ed. Darko Radovic (London: Routledge, 2011), 102.

248 Warren Breckman, "A Matter of Optics," *Lapham's Quarterly* 3, 4 (2010): 180.

249 Tony Burton, "Planning Power to the People," *Green Places* 80 (2011): 31.

250 Pitman, Daniels, and Ely, "Green Infrastructure as Life Support."

251 Leila Scannell and Robert Gifford, "The Relations between Natural and Civic Place Attachment and Pro-Environmental Behavior," *Journal of Environmental Psychology* 30, 3 (2010): 289–97.

252 Richard C. Stedman, "Toward a Social Psychology of Place: Predicting Behavior from Place-Based Cognitions, Attitude, and Identity," *Environment and Behavior* 34, 5 (2002): 577.

253 Carter, in discussion with Brewer.

254 Carter, in discussion with Brewer.

255 Paul Cawood Hellmund and Daniel Somers Smith, *Designing Greenways: Sustainable Landscapes for Nature and People* (Washington, DC: Island Press, 2006), 160.

256 Paul Milbourne, "Growing Public Spaces in the City: Community Gardening and the Making of New Urban Environments of Publicness," *Urban Studies* 58, 14 (2021): 2901–19.

257 Emma Abbott, "Growing Together," *Green Places* 75 (2011): 28.

258 Jacklyn Johnston, "Gaining Public Support for Wildlife in the City," in *Green Cities,* ed. David Gordon (Montreal: Black Rose, 1990), 237.

259 Rachel Sebba, "The Landscapes of Childhood: The Reflection of Childhood's Environment in Adult Memories and in Children's Attitudes," *Environment and Behavior* 23, 4 (1991): 395–422.

260 Hester, *Design for Ecological Democracy,* 334.

261 J.R. Lyons, "Urban Ecosystem Management: Bringing Science and Policy Together," *Urban Ecosystems* 1 (1997): 77–83.

262 William McDonough, "A Field of Dreams: Green Roofs, Ecological Design and the Future of Urbanism," in *Green Roofs: Ecological Design and Construction,* ed. Earth Pledge (Atglen, PA: Schiffer, 2005), 12–15.

263 Beatley, *Biophilic Cities.*

264 Rudolf S. de Groot, Matthew A. Wilson, and Roelof M.J. Boumans, "A Typology for the Classification, Description and Valuation of Ecosystem Functions, Goods and Services," *Ecological Economics* 41, 3 (2002): 393–408.

265 New York City Comptroller, *Safeguarding Our Shores: Protecting New York City's Coastal Communities from Climate Change* (New York: New York City Comptroller, 2019).

266 Demuzere et al., "Mitigating and Adapting to Climate Change."

267 City of Surrey, *City of Surrey: Climate Adaptation Strategy,* 2013, https://www.surrey.ca/sites/default/files/media/documents/ClimateAdaptationStrategy.pdf.

268 Mirza and Shafqat, "Infrastructure Crisis."

269 New York City, *NYC Green Infrastructure Plan,* 9.

270 New York City, *NYC Green Infrastructure Plan,* 10.

271 Corry Buckwalter Berkooz, "Green Infrastructure Storms Ahead," *Planning* 77, 3 (2011): 19–24.

272 City of Philadelphia, *Clean City, Clean Waters: Program Summary* (Philadelphia: City of Philadelphia, 2011).

273 City of Philadelphia, *Clean City, Clean Waters.*

274 National Oceanic and Atmospheric Administration, "Biden Administration Announces Historical Coastal and Climate Resilience Funding," June 29, 2022, https://www.noaa.gov/news-release/biden-administration-announces-historic-coastal-and-climate-resilience-funding.

275 Ripple et al., "World Scientists' Warning," 8–12.

276 Kate Raworth, *Doughnut Economics* (White River Junction, VT: Chelsea Green, 2017).

277 Peter Victor, *Managing without Growth: Slower by Design, not Disaster* (Cheltenham, UK: Edward Elgar, 2008).

278 Niki Frantzeskaki, "Seven Lessons for Planning Nature-Based Solutions in Cities," *Environmental Science and Policy* 93 (2019): 101–11.

279 Frantzeskaki, "Seven Lessons"; Judy Bush and Andréanne Doyon, "Building Urban Resilience with Nature-Based Solutions: How Can Urban Planning Contribute?," *Cities* 95 (2019): https://doi.org/10.1016/j.cities.2019.102483.

280 Carter, in discussion with Brewer.

281 Kate Raworth, "Why It's Time for Doughnut Economics," *IPPR Progressive Review* 24, 3 (2017): 216–17.

282 Doughnut Economics Action Lab, "The Amsterdam City Doughnut: A Tool for Trans-formative Action," March 2020.

283 Center for the Advancement of the Steady State Economy, "Steady State Economy Defin-ition: Summary," https://steadystate.org/discover/steady-state-economy-definition/.

284 Brian Czech, "An Act of Congress for the Steady-State Timeline," *Daily News,* September 5, 2018, https://steadystate.org/act-of-congress-for-the-steady-state-timeline/.

285 Peter J. Taylor, Geoff O'Brien, and Phil O'Keefe, "Commentary," *Environment and Planning A* 47 (2015): 1023–27.

Chapter 5: Nature-Directed Stewardship in Cities

1 US Geological Survey, Watersheds and Drainage Basins, Water Science School, June 8, 2019, https://www.usgs.gov/special-topics/water-science-school/science/watersheds-and-drainage-basins.

2 John Potyondy et al., *Watershed Condition Framework: A Framework for Assessing and Track-ing Changes to Watershed Condition FS-977* (Washington, DC: US Department of Agriculture – Forest Service, 2011), 1–34.

3 Coast Information Team Secretariat, Cortex Consultants, "The Scientific Basis of Ecosystem-Based Management," 2001, 13.

4 Lance H. Gunderson, Craig R. Allen, and C.S. Holling, *Foundations of Ecological Resilience* (Washington, DC: Island Press, 2010), 3–4.

5 Gunderson, Allen, and Holling, *Foundations of Ecological Resilience,* 3–4.

6 Brian Walker and David Salt, *RESILIENCE Practice: Building Capacity to Absorb Disturbance and Maintain Function* (Washington, DC: Island Press, 2012), 4–5.

7 Walker and Salt, *RESILIENCE Practice,* 4–5.

8 Herb Hammond, *Seeing the Forest among the Trees: The Case for Wholistic Forest Use* (Vancouver: Polestar Press, 1992), 17.

9 Stuart Connop et al., "Renaturing Cities Using a Regionally-Focused Biodiversity-Led Multifunctional Benefits Approach to Urban Green Infrastructure," *Environmental Science and Policy* 62 (2016): 99–111.

10 Connop et al., "Renaturing Cities."

11 City of Vancouver, Vancouver Board of Parks, "Northeast False Creek Park Design," 2017.

12 USEPA, "Principles of Watershed Management," Watershed Academy, January 10, 2023, 6–11, https://cfpub.epa.gov/watertrain.

13 US Department of Agriculture, Forest Service, "Is All Your Rain Going down the Drain? Look to Bioretainment – Trees Are a Solution," Center for Urban Forest Research, Pacific Southwest Research Station, 2003, 1–4.

14 Gregory E. McPherson et al., "Surface Storage of Rainfall in Tree Crowns: Not All Trees Are Equal," *Arborist News,* June 2017, 30–33.

15 Gregory E. McPherson et al., "Urban Tree Database and Allometric Equations," General Technical Report PSW-GTR-253, Pacific Southwest Research Station, US Department of Agriculture, Forest Service, 2016.

16 McPherson et al., "Urban Tree Database and Allometric Equations."

17 E. Shaver et al., *Fundamentals of Urban Runoff Management: Technical and Institutional Issues* (Madison, WI: North American Lake Management Society, 2007), 4–76.

18 Shaver et al., *Fundamentals of Urban Runoff Management,* 4–77.

19 Richard Pinkham, *Daylighting: New Life for Buried Streams* (Old Snowmass, CO: Rocky Mountain Institute, 2000), 1–73.

20 Luna Khirfan, Megan Leigh Peck, and Niloofar Mohtat, "Digging for the Truth: A Combined Method to Analyze the Literature on Stream Daylighting," *Sustainable Cities and Societies* 59 (2020): 1–12.

21   Michael E. Soule and John Terborgh, *Continental Conservation: Scientific Foundations of Regional Reserve Networks* (Washington, DC: Island Press, Wildlands Project, 1999), 129–37.
22   Richard B. Primack, *A Primer of Conservation Biology* (Sunderland, MA: Sinauer Associates, 2000), 210.
23   Jerry F. Franklin and David B. Lindenmayer, "Importance of Matrix Habitats in Maintaining Biological Diversity," *Proceedings of the National Academy of Sciences of the United States of America* 106, 2 (2009): 349–50.
24   "Erosion Prevention and Sediment Control," Capital Regional District, January 10, 2023, https://www.crd.bc.ca/education/stormwater-wastewater-septic/green-stormwater -infrastructure/erosion-prevention-sediment-control.

CHAPTER 6: NATURE-DIRECTED STEWARDSHIP IN EAST VANCOUVER

Epigraph: Bob Sandford, "Learning from the Burning: Sustainability in the Wake of the Summer of 2018," Wings Over the Rockies Festival, May 6–12, 2019, abridged version *Canada's Bob Sandford is "The Winston Churchill of Water"* in *Partnership for Water Sustainability in British Columbia,* May 21, 2019, https://mailchi.mp/watersustainabilitybc.ca/bob -sandford-winston-churchill-water-994917?e=7cffcddo8c.
 1   Gordon Omand, "Study Explores Ancient Wetland-Gardening Site in British Columbia," *Globe and Mail,* December 21, 2016, http://www.theglobeandmail.com/news/british -columbia/study-explores-ancient-wetland-gardening-site-in-british-columbia/article 33409050/; Gordon Omand, "Clam Gardens Call into Question Hunter-Gatherer Past of B.C. First Nations," CBC News, May 10, 2015, http://www.cbc.ca/news/canada/british -columbia/clam-gardens-call-into-question-hunter-gatherer-past-of-b-c-first-nations-1. 3068709; Darcy Mathews, in discussion with Herb Hammond, July 9, 2016, in *Still Creek Watershed: Ecosystem-Based Stewardship Plan for Ecological Restoration,* Silva Forest Foundation, Herb Hammond, Chloe Boyle, and Emily Doyle-Yamaguchi (Slocan Park, BC: Silva Forest Foundation, 2018), 69–89.
 2   Frances Woodward, "The Influence of the Royal Engineers on the Development of British Columbia," *BC Studies* 24 (1974–75): 15.
 3   Woodward, "The Influence of the Royal Engineers," 15.
 4   Musqueam Band Council, *Musqueam Comprehensive Land Claim: Preliminary Report on Musqueam Land Use and Occupancy* (Vancouver: Musqueam Band Council, June 1984), in *Still Creek Watershed: Ecosystem-Based Stewardship Plan for Ecological Restoration,* Silva Forest Foundation Herb Hammond, Chloe Boyle, and Emily Doyle-Yamaguchi (Slocan Park, BC: Silva Forest Foundation, 2018), 69–89.
 5   Burnaby Community Heritage Commission, *Charting Change: An Atlas of Burnaby's Heritage into the New Millennium* (Burnaby: City of Burnaby 2002).
 6   Derek Pethick, *Vancouver Recalled* (Saanichton, BC: Hancock House, 1974).
 7   Woodward, "The Influence of the Royal Engineers," 15.
 8   Burnaby Community Heritage Commission, *Charting Change.*
 9   Pethick, *Vancouver Recalled,* 1–96.
10   Musqueam Band Council, *Musqueam Comprehensive Land Claim.*
11   Burnaby Community Heritage Commission, *Charting Change.*
12   Catherine Parsons, "Restoring a 'Paradise of Place': Exploring Potential for Urban Ecosystem-Based Management in the Still Creek Watershed, Vancouver BC," master's thesis (Simon Fraser University, 2015), http://summit.sfu.ca/item/15649.
13   Parsons, "Restoring a 'Paradise of Place.'"
14   Vancouver City Planning Commission, *Vancouver Planning Chronology: A Chronology of Planning and Development in Vancouver* (Vancouver: City of Vancouver, 2016), http://chronology.

vancouverplanning.ca/chronology/, in *Still Creek Watershed: Ecosystem-Based Stewardship Plan for Ecological Restoration,* Silva Forest Foundation, Herb Hammond, Chloe Boyle, and Emily Doyle-Yamaguchi (Slocan Park, BC: Silva Forest Foundation, 2018), 69–89.

15   Vancouver Town Planning Commission, *A Plan for the City of Vancouver, British Columbia, Including a General Plan of the Region* (Vancouver: Harold Bartholomew and Associates, 1928), https://archive.org/details/vancplanincgen00vanc.

16   Vancouver Town Planning Commission, *A Plan for the City of Vancouver.*

17   City of Burnaby, Greater Vancouver Regional District, and City of Vancouver, "From Pipe Dreams to Healthy Streams: A Vision for the Still Creek Watershed. Integrated Stormwater Management Plan for the Still Creek Watershed," City of Burnaby, 2006, http://www.burnaby.ca/Assets/From+Pipe+Dreams+to+Healthy+Streams.pdf.

18   City of Burnaby, Greater Vancouver Regional District, and City of Vancouver, "From Pipe Dreams to Healthy Streams."

19   Burnaby Community Heritage Commission, *Charting Change.*

20   Burnaby Community Heritage Commission, *Charting Change.*

21   Lower Mainland Regional Planning Board, "Official Regional Plan for the Lower Mainland Planning Area, 1966," Metro Vancouver Library, http://www.metrovancouver.org/about/library/LibraryPublications/Official_Regional_Plan_For_The_Lower_Mainland_Planning_Area_1966.pdf.

22   City of Burnaby, Greater Vancouver Regional District, and City of Vancouver, "From Pipe Dreams to Healthy Streams."

23   City of Burnaby, Greater Vancouver Regional District, and City of Vancouver, "From Pipe Dreams to Healthy Streams."

24   Andrew Ling (City of Vancouver), in discussion with Herb Hammond and Emily Doyle-Yamaguchi, September 16, 2016, in *Still Creek Watershed Ecosystem-Based Stewardship Plan for Ecological Restoration,* Silva Forest Foundation, Herb Hammond, Chloe Boyle, and Emily Doyle-Yamaguchi (Slocan Park, BC: Silva Forest Foundation, 2018), 69–89; Amy McDonald et al., "An Analysis of Laneway Housing in Vancouver," UBC School of Community and Regional Planning, n.d.

25   Kerr Wood Leidal – CH2M Hill, *Integrated Stormwater Management Strategy for Stoney Creek Watershed* (Burnaby: City of Burnaby, Environment and Waste Management Committee, 1999), 1–12.

26   Kerr Wood Leidal – CH2M Hill, *Integrated Stormwater Management Strategy,* 65–73.

27   Partnership for Water Sustainability, "Historical/Regulatory Context for 'Integrated Stormwater Management Plans in British Columbia,'" November 26, 2010, Partnership for Water Sustainability in BC, http://waterbucket.ca/gi/2010/11/26/historical-regulatory-context-for-integrated-stormwater-management-plans-in-british-columbia/.

28   City of Burnaby, Greater Vancouver Regional District, and City of Vancouver, "From Pipe Dreams to Healthy Streams."

29   Metro Vancouver, "Metro Vancouver 2040," strategy 2.2.

30   City of Vancouver, *Rain City Strategy* (Vancouver: City of Vancouver, 2019), 3.

31   Herb Hammond, *Maintaining Whole Systems on Earth's Crown: Ecosystem-Based Conservation Planning for the Boreal Forest* (Slocan Park, BC: Silva Forest Foundation, 2009), 34.

32   Del Meidinger and Jim Pojar, *Ecosystems of British Columbia* (Victoria: BC Ministry of Forests, 1991), 81–111.

33   Meidinger and Pojar, *Ecosystems of British Columbia,* 81–111.

34   Herb Hammond, Chloe Boyle, and Emily Doyle-Yamaguchi, *Still Creek Watershed: Ecosystem-Based Stewardship Plan for Ecological Restoration* (Slocan Park, BC: Silva Forest Foundation, 2018), 20.

35   Hammond, Boyle, and Doyle-Yamaguchi, *Still Creek Watershed,* 22.

36 US Department of Agriculture, Forest Service, "Is All Your Rain Going down the Drain? Look to Bioretainment – Trees Are a Solution (Center for Urban Forest Research, Pacific Southwest Research Station, Davis, CA, 2003, 1–4.

37 Sandra Strieby, "Comparing Conifers and Deciduous Plants," *Botanical Rambles, Washington Native Plant Society Blog,* July 3, 2013, https://www.wnps.org/blog/conifers-deciduous -trees?.

38 Strieby, "Comparing Conifers and Deciduous Plants."

39 Patrick Condon, "A Safe, More Enjoyable Street for Our New Times," *Tyee,* May 12, 2020, https://thetyee.ca/Analysis/2020/05/12/Vancouver-Could-Save-Money-On-Sewage -With-Swales/.

40 Still Moon Arts Society, "About Still Moon Arts Society," December 12, 2023, https:// stillmoonarts.ca/.

41 Hammond, Boyle, and Doyle-Yamaguchi, *Still Creek Watershed.*

42 Carmen Rosen (artistic director, Still Moon Arts Society), in discussion with the authors, July 2016.

43 Shawnigan Basin Society, "The Shawnigan Basin Society," January 13, 2023, https://www. shawniganbasinsociety.org/about.html.

CHAPTER 7: A PROCESS FOR INVITING NATURE HOME

Epigraph: Jane Jacobs, "The Greening of the City," *New York Times Magazine,* May 16, 2004, http://www.nytimes.com/2004/05/16/magazine/16ESSAY.html.

1 Sara T. Borgström et al., "Scale Mismatches in Management of Urban Landscapes," *Ecology and Society* 11, 2 (2006): 16, http://www.ecologyandsociety.org/vol11/iss2/art16/; Henrik Ernstson et al., "Scale-Crossing Brokers and Network Governance of Urban Ecosystem Services: The Case of Stockholm," *Ecology and Society* 15, 4 (2010): 1–17.

2 Johan Colding et al., "Incorporating Green-Area User Groups in Urban Ecosystem Management," *AMBIO: A Journal of the Human Environment* 35, 5 (2006): 237–44, 240.

3 Borgström et al. "Scale Mismatches in Management of Urban Landscapes," 16; Ernstson et al., "Scale-Crossing Brokers and Network Governance."

4 Jean-Pierre L. Savard, Philippe Clergeau, and Gwenaelle Mennechez, "Biodiversity Concepts and Urban Ecosystems," *Landscape and Urban Planning* 48 (2000): 131–42.

5 Peter Gisolfi, "Reclaiming Spoiled Landscapes: A New Way of Thinking about an Entrenched Problem," *Planning* 77, 2 (2011): 23–25, 24.

6 See, for example, Stephan Barthel, "Sustaining Urban Ecosystem Services with Local Stewards Participation in Stockholm (Sweden)," in *From Landscape Research to Landscape Planning: Aspects of Integration, Education and Application,* ed. Bärbel Tress et al., Wageningen UR Frontis Series, vol. 12 (Wageningen, Netherlands: Wageningen UR, 2006), 305–15; Colding, Lundberg, and Folke, "Incorporating Green-Area User Groups"; Henrick Ernstson, Sverker Sörlin, and Thomas Elmqvist, "Social Movements and Ecosystem Services: The Role of Social Network Structure in Protecting and Managing Urban Green Areas in Stockholm," *Ecology and Society* 13, 2 (2008): 39, http://www.ecologyandsociety.org/vol13/iss2/art39/; Ernstson et al., "Scale-Crossing Brokers and Network Governance"; Borgström et al., "Scale Mismatches in Management of Urban Landscapes," 16.

7 Cities Plus, *A Sustainable Urban System: The Long-Term Plan for Greater Vancouver* (Vancouver: Sheltair Group, 2003), 29.

8 Ernstson et al., "Scale-Crossing Brokers and Network Governance," 5.

9 Edward O. Wilson, *Half-Earth: Our Planet's Fight for Life* (New York: Liveright, 2016).

10 Marina Alberti, "Urban Patterns and Environmental Performance: What Do We Know?," *Journal of Planning Education and Research* 19 (1999): 151–63.

11 Carl Folke et al., "Biological Diversity, Ecosystems, and the Human Scale," *Ecological Applications* 6 (1996): 1018–24, 1020.

12 Christina von Borcke, "Landscape and Nature in the City," in *Sustainable Urban Design: An Environmental Approach,* ed. Randall Thomas and Max Fordham (London: Spon Press, 2003), 33–45.

13 Amy K. Hahs, Mark J. McDonnell, and Jürgen H. Breuste, "A Comparative Ecology of Cities and Towns: Synthesis of Opportunities and Limitations," in *Ecology of Cities and Towns: A Comparative Approach,* ed. Mark J. McDonnell, Amy K. Hahs, and Jürgen H. Breuste (Cambridge, UK: Cambridge University Press, 2009), 574–96.

14 Andrew S. MacDougall, Brenda R. Beckwith, and Carrina Y. Maslovat, "Defining Conservation Strategies with Historical Perspectives: A Case Study from a Degraded Oak Grassland Ecosystem," *Conservation Biology* 18, 2 (2004): 455–65, 455.

15 Anne R. Beer, "Greenspaces, Green Structure, and Green Infrastructure Planning," in *Urban Ecosystem Ecology,* ed. Jacqueline Aitkenhead-Peterson and Astrid Volder, Agronomy Monograph 55 (Madison, WI: American Society of Agronomy, Crop Science Society of America, Soil Science Society of America, 2010), 431–48.

16 Michael L. Rosenzweig, *Win-Win Ecology: How the Earth's Species Can Survive in the Midst of Human Enterprise* (Oxford: Oxford University Press, 2003), 7.

17 Ussif R. Sumaila et al., "Evaluating the Benefits from Restored Ecosystems: A Back to the Future Approach," paper presented at International Institute for Fisheries Economics and Trade 2000: Microbehavior and Macroresults, Oregon State University, July 10, 2000, 2.

18 Sumaila et al., "Evaluating the Benefits from Restored Ecosystems," 2.

19 Nancy Olewiler, *The Value of Natural Capital in Settled Areas of Canada* (Stonewall, MB and Toronto: Ducks Unlimited Canada and Nature Conservancy of Canada, 2004).

20 Kristina L. Nilsson and Clas Florgård, "Ecological Scientific Knowledge in Urban and Land-Use Planning," in *Ecology of Cities and Towns: A Comparative Approach,* ed. Mark J. McDonnell, Amy K. Hahs, and Jürgen H. Breuste (Cambridge, UK: Cambridge University Press, 2009), 556.

21 Ann L. Riley, "What Is Restoration?," in *The Sustainable Urban Development Reader,* ed. Stephen Wheeler and Timothy Beatley (London: Routledge, 2004), 184–89.

22 H.K. Burgess et al., "The Science of Citizen Science: Exploring Barriers to Use as a Primary Research Tool," Biological Conservation 208 (2017): 113–20; Caren B. Cooper et al., "Citizen Science as a Tool for Conservation in Residential Ecosystems," *Ecology and Society* 12, 2 (2007): 11.

23 City of Vancouver, "Greenest City Neighbourhood Small Grants," Neighbourhood Small Grants, https://neighbourhoodsmallgrants.ca/our-grants/greenest-city-grants/.

24 Hillary Rudd, Jamie Vala, and Valentin Shaefer, "Importance of Backyard Habitat in a Comprehensive Biodiversity Conservation Strategy: A Connectivity Analysis of Urban Green Spaces," *Restoration Ecology* 10, 2 (2002): 368–75; Rosenzweig, *Win-Win Ecology;* Mark A. Goddard, Andrew J. Dougill, and Tim G. Benton, "Scaling Up from Gardens: Biodiversity Conservation in Urban Environments," *Trends in Ecology and Evolution* 25, 2 (2010): 90–98.

25 Rosenzweig, *Win-Win Ecology,* 8.

26 Maleea Acker, in discussion with Herb Hammond.

27 Colding, Lundberg, and Folke, "Incorporating Green-Area User Groups," 242.

28 Henrik Ernstson, "Urban Transitions: On Urban Resilience and Human-Dominated Ecosystems," *AMBIO: A Journal of the Human Environment* 39, 8 (2010): 531–45, 531.

29 Barthel, "Sustaining Urban Ecosystem Services," 315.

30 J.R. Lyons, "Urban Ecosystem Management: Bringing Science and Policy Together," *Urban Ecosystems* 1 (1997): 77–83, 82.

31 Fern Alder, "Full Frontal," https://www.hardy-plant.org.uk/docs/publications/journal/33b/p11.pdf.

32 Timothy Beatley, *Biophilic Cities* (Washington, DC: Island Press, 2011), 30.

33 Marvin L. Rosenau and Mark Angelo, *The Role of Public Groups in Protecting and Restoring Habitats in British Columbia, with a Special Emphasis on Urban Streams* (Vancouver: Pacific Fisheries Resource Conservation Council, 2001).

34 Andrew Karvonen and Ken Yocom, "The Civics of Urban Nature: Enacting Hybrid Landscapes," *Environment and Planning A* 43, 6 (2011): 1305–22, 1307, 1310.

35 Ray Tomalty et al., *Ecosystem Planning for Canadian Urban Areas* (Toronto: ICURR Publication, 1994).

36 F. Stuart Chapin et al., "Design Principles for Social-Ecological Transformation toward Sustainability: Lessons from New Zealand Sense of Place," *Ecosphere* 3, 5 (2012): 16.

37 Tomalty et al., *Ecosystem Planning for Canadian Urban Areas.*

38 Mohsen Mostafavi, "Why Ecological Urbanism? Why Now?," *Harvard Design Magazine* 32 (2010): 124–35, 133.

39 Savard, Clergeau, and Mannechez, "Biodiversity Concepts and Urban Ecosystems."

40 Robert M. Searns, "The Evolution of Greenways as an Adaptive Urban Landscape Form," *Landscape and Urban Planning* 33 (1995): 65–80; Jack Ahern, "Greenways as a Planning Strategy," *Landscape and Urban Planning* 33 (1995): 131–55, 152.

41 Tomalty et al., *Ecosystem Planning for Canadian Urban Areas.*

42 Kacia Tolsma and Paige Hunter, *Advancing a Regional Green Infrastructure Network in Metro Vancouver* (Burnaby: Action on Climate Change Team, 2020), https://act-adapt.org/wp-content/uploads/2020/09/ACT_MV_2020_WEB-09.pdf.

43 Sybrand Tjallingii, "Green and Red: Enemies or Allies? The Utrecht Experience with Green Structure Planning," *Built Environment* 29, 2 (2003): 107–16; Marisa T. Mamede Frischenbruder and Paulo Pellegrino, "Using Greenways to Reclaim Nature in Brazilian Cities," *Landscape and Urban Planning* 76 (2006): 67–78.

44 R. Stanvliet et al., "The UNESCO Biosphere Reserve Concept as a Tool for Urban Sustainability: The CUBES Cape Town Case Study," *Annals of the New York Academy of Sciences* 1023 (2004): 80–104.

45 Beer, "Greenspaces, Green Structure, and Green Infrastructure Planning," 434.

46 David Korten, *Change the Story, Change the Future: A Living Economy for a Living Earth* (Oakland, CA: Berrett-Koehler, 2015).

Index

Note: "(f)" after a page number refers to a figure; NDS stands for nature-directed stewardship.

of our liberal society, of course. Expanding occupational choice has been part of the increasing differentiation of occupations, and freeing occupational choice from parental constraints and from gender and racial stereotyping has been part of the shift from family-based to school-based transmission of status.

When educational differentiation leads to different levels of employment, two new competencies become crucial for individuals trying to get ahead: knowledge of how the education system itself works and the appropriate paths to different occupations, and the ability to make appropriate choices at crucial junctures. Since some paths through the education maze lead nowhere, many students make "choices" that serve them poorly over the long run. In high school, students can fail to take gatekeeper courses like algebra, or may take a potpourri of courses but find themselves as high school seniors without college prerequisites. Working-class students (boys in particular) sometimes decide that the whole business of schooling is foolish, and display the hostility and resistance that earns them low grades or dismissal (Willis, 1977). Some black students may decide that school success means "acting white" and resist school learning (Fordham and Ogbu, 1986). At the postsecondary level, large numbers of "experimenters" in community colleges have little sense of what to study, while others change their major every semester or two; students in four-year colleges can also take long periods of time to "find themselves." In all these examples, the inability to make self-interested choices impedes educational progress, for reasons ranging from class and racial hostility to ignorance of options to an inability to make rational decisions even with full information (Grubb, 2002c). While knowledge of the system and the ability to make choices are crucial competencies, they are not often explicitly taught. Usually they are learned from family and friends, and are therefore as inequitably distributed as any other resource based on family background. Furthermore, guidance and counseling efforts in schools and colleges have been both weak and unequal, as we argued in Chapter 7. Our system of vocationalism is in this sense archetypically American: it provides a wide variety of options but requires that individuals make their own way among them. And this *combination* of differentiation and choice is critical: only with differentiated institutions and multiple ways of moving through them are false choices both likely and highly dangerous.

The contradictory effects of access, differentiation, and choice have been especially powerful for certain groups of students: women, African Americans and other minorities, and recent immigrants. The expansion of education in the early years of the twentieth century allowed more women to enter high school and then college; women now have higher educational attainment rates than men do. But they also face a system of schooling that reflects the gender differentiation in the labor force. Students exercising what seems to be individual "choice" have created gender-segregated forms of traditional vocational education, with boys in auto shop and metalworking, girls in retailing and home economics. Postsecondary occupational and professional education reflects the crowding of women into the "helping professions"—teaching, nursing, social work, therapeutic occupations—while technical and science-based programs are still dominated by men. While many efforts have been made to lure women into nontraditional employment, these have been only marginally successful given the power of gender norms both in the labor force and in vocationalized forms of schooling.

Similarly, the expansion of education and the elimination of de jure segregation have allowed minority Americans, particularly African Americans, to expand their levels of schooling relative to whites. In fact, much of the reduction in earnings differences between whites and blacks since World War II has been due to a narrowing of education differences, especially among women (Smith and Welch, 1986; Carnoy, 1994). But powerful differences persist, especially for low-income blacks and for Latinos, because of a confluence of factors including lower-quality schools, family influences on levels of schooling, and a lack of information about how schooling and employment work. As for women, programs promoting high school retention and college access have helped to moderate these differences, but they must contend with the many effects of family background without being able to do anything directly about inequality.

At the beginning of the twenty-first century, then, we have a system of schooling with much higher levels of access than a century ago, and with greater access than in almost all developed countries. There is surely greater equality of opportunity through education, at least compared with the nineteenth century, when there were very few school-based paths to higher status. The twentieth-century expansion of education facilitated rags-to-riches stories, including the advancement of working-class Jews in the 1920s and '30s; recent Asian groups, who have made it through diligent efforts in school and college; and a few welfare mothers and dropouts, who have clawed their way up through the second-chance system. The American dream of mobility through one's own efforts now operates largely through schooling (Hochschild and Scovronek, 2003). But overall, substituting school-based access to adult status for family-linked mechanisms has made little difference in mobility from generation to generation. High-status parents still tend to beget high-status children, to the same extent that they did before schools were important.[4]

A final consequence of differentiated occupations and differentiated education is that school attainment and related competencies are highly unequal. There is enormous variation among eighteen-year-olds, for example, some of whom have completed four or five college-level courses while others are still reading at elementary-school levels; there is still greater variation among thirty-year-olds, some of whom have completed as much as twenty years of formal schooling with public support while others are high school dropouts. The Programme for International Student Assessment (PISA) study of reading levels among fifteen-year-olds showed that the United States has among the highest levels of inequality among OECD countries. The International Adult Literacy Survey (IALS) found that more than one-fifth of American adults aged sixteen to sixty-five are at Level 1 in prose, document, and quantitative literacy scales—a level describing "persons with very poor skills"—with another fourth at Level 2, still below "a suitable minimum for coping with the demands of everyday life and work in a complex, advanced society."[5] The complaint that the United States is falling into a low-skills equilibrium from which it will be difficult to ascend—the fear of *America's Choice: High Skills or Low Wages!*—is not a complaint about the upper level of the labor force, educated in a postsecondary system envied by most other countries. It is a complaint about low skill levels at the bottom of the labor force, about the *inequality* of schooling and skills. In a country with extraordinarily high levels of economic inequality, we have also managed to create high levels of inequality in schooling and in related skills. The mechanisms associated with vocationalism are largely to blame.

Equality of Opportunity and the "Policies of Correction"

Another shift in ideals, obvious and yet subtle in its effects, took place as schooling became vocationalized. As the primary goals modulated from civic and moral purposes in the common schools, and from moral and intellectual purposes in higher education, to occupational preparation, the ideals behind schooling shifted from political conceptions to economic ones. But ideals of equality in the United States, much more powerful than in Europe with its aristocracies and hereditary privileges, have applied much more to *political* equality—to equality before the law, equality of social and legal stature, and voting rights—than they have to *economic* equality (Pole, 1978). Equality of access to the nineteenth-century common school was consistent with equality of political standing. Even though this political equality was marred in practice by the exclusion of women, African Americans, and Native Americans, the common-school ideal provided an argument for their inclusion in schooling, particularly as the rights of citizenship spread. But as schooling's goals moved into the economic realm around 1900, the question became whether the ideal of equality should be extended to *economic* equality, and this has been a much more difficult concept for Americans to embrace.

The only ideal of economic equality that has achieved any real acceptance in the United States has been equality of opportunity, a slippery and ambiguous concept. Equality of opportunity promises equity in the race for success, not equality in results—and certainly not in an economy like our present one, of growing inequality in earnings and employment. It stresses the need for individuals to take advantage of opportunities offered, to earn their position through diligence and hard work—in the twentieth century, through schoolwork rather than on-the-job experience—and it is therefore consistent with the older Protestant ethic of individual effort. In 1793 Noah Webster, author of America's first dictionary, described equality of opportunity in this country (Pole 1978, 118): "Here every man finds employment, and the road is open for the poorest citizen to amass wealth by labor and economy, and by his talent and virtue to raise himself to the highest offices of the State." Outcomes may be unequal, then, but there ought to be no differences owing to family background (contrary to Figure 8.1B) or other factors aside from diligence, thriftiness, native abilities, or moral character. This conception of equal opportunity has also become the dominant version of the American dream, the belief that anyone can succeed with some talent and sufficient work.

As schools changed from political to economic institutions, then, equity shifted from political equity to the murkier notion of equal opportunity. Equality of *educational* opportunity has presented a never-ending series of conceptual and evidentiary problems. Equality itself—whether measured by expenditures, other resources such as qualified teachers, or outcomes such as test scores or years of schooling completed—is relatively easy to measure. But since opportunity is an abstract quality, it is hard to know when equality of opportunity has been achieved. It has been easier to know when it does *not* exist, and so the dominant approach has been to challenge conditions that most obviously undermine educational opportunity.

Exclusion has been the most evident form of unequal opportunity, particularly in a vocationalized system where exclusion from schooling means preclusion from employment. Challenges to exclusion have therefore been prominent—notably in the long struggle over racially segregated education, where the Supreme Court in *Brown v. Board of Education* (1954) offered both political and vocational justifications: "Compulsory school attendance laws and the great expenditures for education both demonstrate our recognition of the importance of education to our democratic society . . . In these days, it is doubtful that any child may reasonably be expected to succeed in life if he is denied the opportunity of an education." Many other equity cases are challenges to exclusion, including the efforts of non-English-speaking students to gain access to bilingual education, the legislative battles to include students with disabilities, the movement to provide equal access for women to all programs and facilities, and the current reforms eliminating tracking.

Another obvious barrier to equal opportunity has been the underprovision of resources—funding, and then the resources (skilled teachers, effective curricula, and adequate facilities) that money can buy. Educators began worrying about the unequal distribution of resources shortly after 1900, starting with the "discovery" in 1905 by Elwood Cubberly that districts had differing capacities to finance schools. The state aid mechanisms that he promoted were elaborated throughout the century, with mixed results. Following the interest in equity in the late 1960s, a series of lawsuits were brought, starting with *Serrano v. Priest* (1973) in California, to challenge inequities in spending among districts. Those led in turn to legislative responses, some of which narrowed the distribution of revenues, although many failed to do so.[6] At the postsecondary level, the same concern over resources led to grants and loans for low-income students, as well as to the expansion of state-supported institutions. Low income nonetheless remains one of the most formidable barriers to access and, as we have seen in the work-family-schooling dilemma, to the ability to complete postsecondary programs. Unequal financing and resources have been the subject of many court cases and legislative battles, with some successes but little overall effect on educational outcomes.

Efforts to eliminate barriers to equal opportunity constitute a kind of negative approach, removing government-created roadblocks to equal access and resources. A more affirmative approach has asserted a governmental role in providing schooling that is actively favorable to some groups or individuals who would otherwise suffer from lower levels or lower quality of schooling.[7] Such compensatory policies, or "policies of correction," date at least from the early years of the nineteenth century, when charity schools were established for poor children. The common schools replaced philanthropic funding with public funding, with many of the same assumptions. As Henry Barnard, one of the founders of the public school system, wrote in 1851 (Katz, 1971, 10): "No one at all familiar with the deficient household arrangements and deranged machinery of domestic life of the extreme poor and ignorant . . . can doubt that it is better for children to be removed as early and as long as possible from such scenes and such examples and placed in an infant or primary school, under the care and instruction of a kind, affectionate, and skillful female teacher."

Ever since, the compensatory rationale has rested on the premise that some children may be unable to take advantage of opportunities because of their impoverished family background, their lack of preparation for schooling, or their unfamiliarity with the culture of schooling (Deschenes, Cuban, and Tyack, 2001). Compensatory practices have included early childhood education to prepare children for schooling; the Great Society programs of the 1960s, represented today in the No Child Left Behind Act; school reform efforts targeted at low-income students; the efforts to require special services for special education students; language programs for immigrant students; lunch and breakfast programs for students who might otherwise come to school hungry; and more limited efforts to provide various physical and mental health services. Lawsuits have argued that equal opportunity requires not the *same* levels of resources but *adequate* levels, considering the greater needs of low-income students, immigrant children (and those with limited English), and children with handicapping conditions (Minorini and Sugarman, 1999a; Clune, 1994).

In postsecondary education, affirmative action has been the most obvious and controversial policy of correction. Others have included various outreach and bridge programs to attract low-income and minority students and then to prepare them for college-level work. Many community colleges and four-year colleges also offer forms of compensatory education in special programs of counseling and tutoring for students identified by income or prior school performance, or in special learning communities aimed at students who are otherwise more likely to drop out—like the Puente programs in California for Latino students and the PACE programs for older adults.

The affirmative form of equal educational opportunity has several advantages, particularly the recognition that *equality* might not be *equity*—that removing all barriers to access and differences in public resources might not eliminate the effects of family background and private resources. But it is also plagued by several problems. One is that the compensatory rationale is inherently tinged by demeaning attitudes toward the poor, since it is impossible to escape the perception that their deficiencies are the root of educational problems. These attitudes have sometimes created compensatory programs that are ineffective or stigmatizing. In addition, in a society where inequalities are large and take many different forms, there is an almost infinite list of inequities that affect the ability of students to take advantage of educational opportunities. The ideal of equal opportunity can identify some of the most egregious inequalities, but it will always be an impossible target— and often a moving target, as the conditions of inequality change.

The most powerful limitation of all is that, in a vocationalized system of education in which the outcomes are effectively zero-sum, there is no reason for voters and taxpayers to support programs that benefit other people's children to the potential detriment of their own. An adequate system of school finance might require substantial additional funding for urban districts that have concentrations of low-income and minority students, and thus generate political resistance from middle-income taxpayers. Despite the popularity of Head Start, the funding to provide preschool for all eligible children has not developed, and funding for a broad range of services beyond lunch and breakfast programs has consistently foundered, despite calls for "full-service schools" (Dryfoos, 1994; USGAO, 1993). Outreach programs that provide some students with special services are often attacked by teachers and parents whose children don't get those services, reflecting the "politics of resentment" that opposes any departure from equal resources.

At the postsecondary level, low tuitions at state colleges have not only allowed more low-income students to attend but also have provided subsidies to middle-income families—so the obvious alternative (to economists) of high tuitions with high grants to low-income students (e.g., McPherson and Schapiro, 1991) has been consistently shot down by middle-class parents. Perhaps the most naked of these conflicts has been the struggle over affirmative action and admissions standards, where some students defined by race (African American, Latino, and Native American) might gain at the direct expense of others (white and Asian). Such policies of correction have been stridently opposed by those who stand to lose—as one might expect in a political system based on self-interest rather than principle.[8] Of course, none of this would matter much in a nonvocational system of education. What makes these battles so ferocious is that they involve access to the highest-status and best-paid employment (Bowen and Bok, 1998).

Vocationalism has therefore led to a conception of equity—equality of educational opportunity, in place of the common-school ideal of equal access and curriculum—that has been difficult to define and impossible to achieve. While campaigns to equalize access and resources have been widespread, the centrality of education to economic success has usually throttled those efforts, and in a zero-sum world the "policies of correction" have been especially embattled. Even as vocationalism has enhanced access and the promises of equity, it has made the achievement of equity through schooling more difficult.

Equity, the Welfare State, and Schooling

Education is not the only realm in which policies of correction have been articulated. Many other government mechanisms in the policies of the twentieth-century welfare state were created to overcome the inequalities associated with family background, including policies related to transfers and taxes, health care, nutrition, housing, and other resources. Understanding the limitations of government in the United States is therefore crucial to understanding what the educational system can and cannot do to decrease inequality.

For most of the nineteenth century, when citizens became alarmed about the burgeoning inequality in American cities, government played only a limited role in alleviating social problems. Support for families and children in need and for the unemployed was largely provided through private charity. Education for the poor, to prevent the moral decay of poor children and to contribute to public order, was initially a charitable enterprise. By and large, inequality and poverty took their own course, buffeted by waves of immigration and by economic cycles that were extremely deep by current standards, and there was little sense that government could intervene (Williamson and Lindert, 1980).

During the twentieth century the instruments of government that could alleviate poverty and inequality expanded, particularly in the period after 1900, in the 1930s, and in the 1960s—the mechanisms that analysts usually label the welfare state. One strand of the welfare state has focused on providing a "safety net" to the very poorest citizens: income support for the elderly, the disabled, low-income mothers (and a few fathers), and the unemployed; nutrition programs, including food stamps and school lunch and breakfast programs; public housing and housing vouchers; medical services for the elderly through Medicare and for the poor through Medicaid; some subsidy for child care; and tax benefits through the Earned Income Tax Credit (EITC) for low-wage workers. While the list of such programs is long, most of these supports are available to only the neediest recipients, or to some well-defined segment of the poor, such as mothers with small children. The practice in European welfare states of providing universal services—universal health coverage or child care, for example—has never been part of the limited welfare state in the United States, with its historic fear of overzealous government (Esping-Anderson, 1990). Furthermore, the most generous safety-net programs are linked to employment—Social Security, Supplemental Security Income (SSI), Unemployment Insurance, the EITC—so that parents with intermittent employment or young students trying to work their way through college are ineligible. Other programs—particularly Aid to Families with Dependent Children (AFDC) and now Temporary Assistance to

Needy Families (TANF) and food stamps, with their emphasis on Work First—have tried to maintain incentives to move out of welfare and into employment, and provide at best temporary "help to self-help." The so-called safety net in America is necessarily a minimal version of a welfare state, one that avoids undermining labor-market incentives, and it is constantly subject to cutting because it emphasizes support only for the neediest.

A second and even more controversial strand of the welfare state in this country has been its efforts to influence labor markets, for example through child labor laws, minimum wage legislation, limitations on working hours, health and safety conditions, the regulation of unionizing activities, and efforts to reduce gender and racial discrimination. Broader policies influencing employment have included monetary and fiscal policy designed to even out business cycles and promote full employment. But while the government's capacity to intervene expanded dramatically during the twentieth century, here too the American version of the welfare state has been limited, compared with other developed economies, because it has been hostile to anything that might undermine labor market incentives or supplant private jobs with public opportunities (Esping-Anderson, 1990, ch. 3; Estevez-Abe, Iversen, and Soskice, 2001). Despite rhetorical commitment to full employment, monetary policy has emphasized limiting inflation rather than unemployment. Fiscal policy to enhance employment through careful use of budget deficits and surpluses has all but vanished because of sustained budget deficits, first under Reagan and now with George W. Bush. Minimum wages have been consistently controversial, and have fallen considerably behind the rate of inflation. Efforts to regulate health and safety conditions through the Occupational Safety and Health Administration and to eliminate discrimination through the Equal Employment Opportunity Commission have been strenuously opposed by employers. Public employment has been tried only briefly in this country—once under the extreme conditions of the Great Depression and then again in the late 1970s—and it was quickly rejected both times. And so the interventions that in other countries bolster employment and incomes, or that could provide better employment opportunities to young people facing the work-family-schooling dilemma, are weak to nonexistent in the United States.

If we include in the welfare state all government activities intended to enhance the well-being of the population, a third strand surely includes education and job training—even though we rarely think of schooling as part of the welfare state.[9] Particularly as schooling became vocationalized, Americans have promoted education as the primary agency of social improvement, the solution to poverty, inequality, and social dislocation. The examples are legion:

- Advocates have consistently promoted early childhood programs as moderating the differences among children attributable to family and community. These efforts extend from the charity schools of the early nineteenth century to the day nurseries of the early twentieth century to Head Start and current efforts to establish universal preschool.

- Promoters of vocational education initially characterized it not only as a response to the need for higher skill levels but also as a cure for poverty and social dislocation. This idea has persisted in legislation directing that federal vocational education funds be spent for "special populations" including low-income and minority students.

- Early twentieth-century advocates for African Americans, such as Booker T. Washington and W. E. B. Du Bois, believed that education was critical to the future of their race. This argument continues to be renewed in many different education programs for racial minorities that stress education rather than eliminating employment discrimination or improving the low-skilled labor market.

- The War on Poverty of the 1960s was founded on educational remedies. In announcing the Elementary and Secondary Education Act of 1965, President Johnson declared that it would "help five million children of poor families to overcome their greatest barrier to progress—poverty" (Lazerson, 1987, 163–166); as Johnson restated the Education Gospel, "A youngster who finishes high school earns over $35,000 more during his lifetime than a school dropout earns. A college graduate earns over $100,000 more during his lifetime than a high school graduate. And beyond the benefit to the economy of more productive citizens is the simple fact that dropouts are the first casualties of our advancing technology."

- Short-term job training has been consistently promoted as a way to reduce unemployment and poverty, starting with the programs of the Great Depression, continuing with the manpower programs intended to correct technological unemployment and to reduce the welfare rolls during the 1960s.

• No Child Left Behind, the centerpiece of the George W. Bush education policy, is intended to eliminate achievement differences among students "so they're prepared for the demands of postsecondary education and the workforce," as Secretary of Education Rod Paige declared in 2002. A flyer from the Department of Education described "The Solution": "Attack the soft bigotry of low expectations and demand that schools close the achievement gaps." But evidently the solution does not include attacking other forms of bigotry (in employment and housing, for example) or demanding that health care policy or housing policy or Hollywood or welfare programs do their part to close those gaps.

In emphasizing how frequently Americans have converted major social and economic problems into educational issues, we do not mean to diminish the importance of schooling. Some claims for education as a way of reducing inequality have been valid. Both in the period after 1900 and during the Great Depression, many immigrant children achieved social mobility by graduating from high school and going on to college; the same is now true for many Asian American immigrants. The narrowing of earnings differentials between blacks and whites—and particularly between black and white women—has been due to steady increases in black educational attainment (Smith and Welch, 1986; Carnoy, 1994). The GI Bill after World War II opened professional opportunities to large numbers of working-class veterans. Women have moved into a broad array of professions through their access to higher education from the 1960s on, reducing the earnings and status gap between men and women. So the role of education in reducing inequality is powerful enough that it should remain a crucial part of any solution.

However, treating education as the exclusive avenue to increased equality is a terrible mistake. The centrality of educational solutions has simultaneously exaggerated expectations about what education can accomplish and limited more direct interventions in support of equity. As David Tyack and Larry Cuban (1995, 1) have written:

Reforming the public schools has long been a favorite way of improving not just education, but society. In the 1840s Horace Mann took his audience to the edge of the precipice to see the social hell that lay before them if they did not achieve salvation through the common school. In 1983 a presidential commission produced another fire-and-brimstone sermon about education, *A Nation at Risk*, though its definition of damnation (economic decline) differed from Mann's (moral dissolution). For over a century and a half, Americans have translated their cultural anxieties and hopes into dramatic demands for educational reform.

More recently, the ascent of free-market ideology and of political opposition to government interventions in markets has undermined other strands of the welfare state—the provision of a safety net, no matter how limited, and the regulation of labor markets—leaving education as the only arena in which equity can be legitimately pursued. Broader discussions of equality of opportunity, in theory encompassing multiple social and economic policies, have narrowed to discussions about equality only of *educational* opportunity.

Education as the main avenue to equity cannot succeed because formal schooling cannot possibly meet the challenge—particularly not in a country where inequality is so great. As we clarified at the end of Chapter 5, too many influences outside education affect how schools operate: disparities in cognitive abilities and values among little children as they start school; variation in access to health care, with chronically sick children missing too much school; differences in housing that force some families to move constantly and undermine the stability of their children's schooling; variation in the neighborhoods where children live, with too many in communities where gangs, crime, and violence add their own trauma as well as provide a wretched vision of the future; variation in families' ability to pay for reading material, travel, tutoring and private counseling, or to afford the escalating costs of college, or to support their children over the lengthening period of educational preparation. And vocationalism has ensured that the kinds of cognitive abilities and the values parents pass on to their children vary systematically among occupational groups, replicating differences among parents in yet another way. These multiple effects have left education in the worst of all possible worlds, committed to equity and now pressured to close the achievement and access gaps but without any control over underlying social and economic inequalities.

Unfortunately, the three strands of the American welfare state—providing a minimal safety net, limited efforts to shape labor markets, and providing educational opportunity through vocationalized schooling—undermine one another. Limited intervention in labor markets leaves substantial amounts of poverty and underemployment unaddressed, which in turn creates the politically impossible demand for more generous welfare programs. Restricted welfare programs make unemployment and underemployment more dangerous, increasing the pressure on government to "do something" during recessions—even if it's only providing symbolic and ineffective training or summer jobs programs. The stinginess of income support, housing, health care, and urban development programs all undermine the education of poor children. The lack of child care and of employment opportunities for young people exacerbates the work-family-schooling dilemma. The persistent inequalities in education accentuate the need for a more generous welfare state, since poverty and inequality continue from generation to generation. And the possibility that welfare policy, labor market regulation, and education policy might be coordinated is weakened by the scattering of authority in many government agencies and across federal, state, and local jurisdictions: education policy in the Department of Education, transfer policies in Health and Human Services, labor market efforts in the Department of Labor, monetary policy in the Federal Reserve Board, fiscal policy in agreements between the executive branch and Congress, and the dominant education policies in state and local governments although other programs are federal. Any hope of using coordinated policies to combat inequality is thwarted by the dominant conceptions of what government should do and by divisions in the government itself.

In many ways, then, the American welfare state is severely limited, particularly compared with the welfare state in comparable countries. More to the point, it has undermined the equity of even those education policies—the policies of the Education Gospel—for which there is substantial public support. The promotion of educational solutions to social and economic problems has made it difficult for us to look beyond education to resolve the inequalities of American society. In choosing how to engage in "policies of correction" to resolve inequality—whether to provide more effective education for the poor, or to equalize the family and community conditions of poor children through the welfare state—the American approach has been to do very little of either.

Creating the Foundational State

The conception of the welfare state is not only descriptive, encompassing various policies developed over the twentieth century, but also normative. It suggests that government *ought* to take responsibility for protecting the well-being of its citizens, particularly by ensuring that basic material needs are met, regulating the conditions of employment, providing support for education, and in other ways superceding the private market with public decisions. The value of the welfare state as a normative concept, however, has effectively been destroyed. The image of welfare has shifted from its positive connotation in supporting the common good to a negative association with the undeserving poor (Katz, 2001). Politically, its support has vanished, displaced by free-market ideologies and a self-centered individualism hostile to market intervention. The economic conditions that underlay the Great Society in the 1960s have been replaced by greater competitive pressures, again supporting free-market extremism.

Rather than trying to resurrect the welfare state, we propose the concept of a Foundational State, one that would create the foundations or preconditions necessary for a more equitable version of the Education Gospel. Many well-accepted policies are already part of the Foundational State, since they create the conditions necessary for the American form of liberal democracy to thrive: monetary and fiscal policy, regulatory policies including the regulation of financial markets, international trade policies, the legal system, the regulation of the political system, defense policy, the system of policing and social order. Free-market ideologues consistently forget how much social energy is necessary to maintain "private" markets in working order. Countries that abandon public supports for markets descend into gangster capitalism (as in Russia) or totalitarianism (as in many African countries) or into anarchy (as in Haiti), or into periodic thievery, as the United States experienced during the 1980s with the savings and loan and defense industry scandals, and more recently with the collapse of Enron,

WorldCom, and other enormous corporations. So the idea of the Foundational State is well established; its practices simply need to expand to other dimensions of policy that are just as crucial to the maintenance of a liberal democracy.

Our version of the Foundational State accepts the American commitment to markets, marketlike mechanisms, and individual effort ("labor and economy, talent and virtue"), though markets—including the quasi-markets in education and training—should work efficiently and equitably. It encompasses the deeply rooted belief in equality of opportunity (not just equality of educational opportunity). It includes the various tenets of the Education Gospel, the belief in both individual and social progress through education that has grown up over the twentieth century, including equity in education, without which equality of opportunity has little meaning in a vocationalized system.[10] These basic precepts of the Foundational State lead to at least three different kinds of activities in the realm of education, as well as other noneducation policies that we will examine in Chapter 9.

Correcting Inequitable Educational Practices

The Foundational State should reinforce the efforts to eliminate obvious barriers to opportunity, specifically differences in learning opportunities. At the elementary and secondary levels, these include the inequities in fiscal resources and effective real resources, like well-qualified teachers and stable teaching conditions, that are lacking in many urban schools. The efforts to de-track the curriculum, to create smaller schools and learning communities that can provide richer instructional environments (including the efforts we have labeled "education through occupations") all need to be reinforced. These reforms will require new resources, but the approach that we have labeled the "renewed" school finance (Grubb, Huerta, and Goe, 2003) insists both that resources be made more equal *and* that they be spent effectively, rather than assuming that more money alone will eliminate current inequalities in outcomes. Conversely, the Foundational State should ensure that new expectations, or curriculum standards, or testing requirements must always be accompanied by the resources and capacity-building necessary for all students, all teachers, and all schools to meet those expectations. The recent movements to develop higher learning standards, in both state accountability efforts and in the federal No Child Left Behind Act, have failed to meet this requirement because they set standards for greater equity in learning without enhancing the capacities of schools to teach those standards, and they establish exit exams without the resources to enable all students to pass the exams at equivalent rates—thereby dooming some students to a life of low-wage work. School reforms must provide more balanced resources and capacities along with accountability.

At the postsecondary level, our gravest concern about unequal opportunity remains the vast structure of inequality—the differentiation of postsecondary opportunities into community colleges, second-tier comprehensive universities, and elite public and private universities, with corresponding inequalities in overall resources and labor market destinations. Their unavoidable differentiation along occupational lines is part of the problem, but the problem is infinitely exacerbated by inequality in the resources provided for those differentiated opportunities. The postsecondary structure of inequality violates another conception of equal opportunity: the idea that governments should not support private privilege, whether that takes the form of support for corporations that reinforce inequality or support for higher education systems that favor high-income families. Andrew Jackson articulated this concept 160 years ago:[11]

> When the laws undertake to add to the natural and just advantages [of superior industry, economy, and virtue] artificial distinctions, to grant titles, gratuities and exclusive privileges, to make the rich richer and the potent more powerful, the humble members of the society—the farmers, mechanics and laborers—have a right to complain of the injustice of their Government . . . If it would confine itself to equal protection, and, as Heaven does its rains, shower its favors alike on the high and the low, the rich and the poor, it would be an unqualified blessing.

The enormous disparities among different postsecondary institutions are gross examples of unequal opportunities that "make the rich richer and the potent more powerful." If this country is to provide equality of opportunity, then, it must narrow the resource differentials among different institutions. One way would be to provide more support for the "humble members of society" who attend community colleges and second-tier universities, to enhance their completion rates and access to related occupational opportunities. Another would be to improve the second-chance system that serves the poorest individuals in greatest need of further education, through a variety of outreach efforts, support services, revised noncredit offerings in community colleges, and perhaps improved job training and adult education programs linked to mainstream education.

Eliminating inequalities of educational opportunity is a never-ending project, since the political battles are difficult and new inequalities are constantly created. Equal opportunity is not a clear and unambiguous goal, and it is not possible for us—or anyone else—to give a precise list of policies necessary to attain it. But the underlying ethos is the most basic element of the Foundational State, rooted in the long-standing American commitment to equal opportunity and in more recent vocational developments that have made schools and colleges central to occupational futures.

Creating Strong Markets in Education

While free marketeers have trumpeted the benefits of market mechanisms, unregulated markets don't always work as they are supposed to—as Americans found to their dismay in the deregulated atmosphere of the 1980s, and again in the corporate scandals at the start of this century. Similarly, unconstrained markets in education and training often work poorly, especially at lower levels of the education system with unsophisticated "consumers" and unprincipled providers. One duty of the Foundational State should therefore be to assure that markets do work as they are supposed to, whether they are energy markets or education markets. They should operate with full information about consequences; all consumers able to make rational and self-interested choices; all producers responding to appropriate incentives, rather than scheming against the interests of the public (as Adam Smith complained); the public consequences of private decisions fully considered; some competition among providers, motivated by the interests of consumers; and market-making mechanisms that allow consumers and providers to find each other.

The Foundational State should guarantee the efficiency and equity of quasi-markets in elementary and secondary education, to the extent that the public supports choice mechanisms. But our greatest concern with quasi-markets in education comes at the postsecondary level, where students face a wide variety of options in a relatively unregulated market. As we clarified in Chapter 7, quasi-markets in education are not objectionable where consumers are sophisticated and educational institutions are of high quality, as in elite universities. But where low-quality institutions are more interested in revenue and enrollment than in the quality of teaching, where potential consumers are unsophisticated, and where information about effects (including completion rates and future employment consequences) is scant, then free-market rhetoric is unjustified—for example, when it is used by proprietary schools, or advocates for vouchers in the Workforce Investment Act, or proponents of consumer sovereignty in One-Stop Centers. Therefore another task of the Foundational State should be to assure the quality of institutions—especially when they are public institutions like community colleges and comprehensive universities—and to enhance the sophistication of consumers. We think this now happens best in cases where licensing mechanisms and credentials are created through tripartite planning that includes education providers, employers, and representatives of incumbent workers. These conditions can be mimicked in professional as well as nonprofessional fields, particularly as ideals of professionalism are extended to new occupations.

The obligation to create "strong" markets extends to correcting one of the novel sources of inequality under vocationalism—differences in levels of knowledge about schooling and access to employment. While there has been a consistent small voice for strengthening guidance and counseling, this strategy has been well developed only in elite colleges with their attention to "student development" and to career and graduate school placement. In the interests of both equity and strong markets, more needs to be done at the high school level, where too many students lack any clue about why schooling might be important, and in postsecondary institutions like community colleges, where the number of experimenters seems excessive. The major tasks are to accept the need to help students through noninstructional services, to generate the resources required, and to develop more powerful ways of helping students learn to make decisions—going beyond simple trait-and-factor approaches and information dumps that now dominate career counseling. Otherwise the absence of informed decision making among students will continue to reinforce the inequalities and market imperfections created by vocationalism.

Correcting Differences in Family Resources

The inescapable truth is that schools and colleges are not very effective institutions for equalizing either income or occupational opportunity. Educational institutions have no influence on the conditions of inequality outside the schools that sometimes make their job so difficult. We've already pointed out that the limited safety net of the welfare state has been inadequate to correct the inequality of such resources. Our hope is that the conception of the Foundational State, asserting the need to create the foundations of a society that develops the capacities of all its citizens, can be more favorable to equalizing these resources.

The notion of the Foundational State clarifies which resources need to be equalized: those that are complementary to school achievement. At the elementary and secondary levels, these include universal preschool programs, so that students do not start their K–12 education with such disparities in preparation; health services, so that sick children do not fall behind in school; a decent housing policy, so that low-income students do not have their schooling interrupted by mobility related to housing; an urban development policy, so that no student is surrounded by decay and violence; family support mechanisms to reduce violence against children; and mental health and social services, to make available to low-income children the programs that middle-income parents seek when their children are depressed, angry, antisocial, attracted to drugs or alcohol, or otherwise unable to participate in normal developmental stages. The image of full-service schools providing an array of social programs to students (see Dryfoos, 1994; USGAO, 1993) is a compelling one, except that it should be funded by social welfare budgets rather than school budgets, and it should rely on the initiative of social welfare agencies—perhaps with school-based social workers as liaisons between the two—so as not to distract educators from their teaching and learning responsibilities (National Research Council, 2003, ch. 6).

At the postsecondary level, the resources that need to be equalized are also complementary to school achievement. In every examination of postsecondary enrollment, family income and other measures of family background have powerful effects on access and completion. Family background also influences intermediate variables like the quality of high schools, grades, test scores, and aspirations. In terms of completion, a persistent problem is the work-family-schooling dilemma, created in part by the extension of higher education to nontraditional students who lack parental income and moral support. The resolution of this dilemma obviously depends on providing adequate child care, family support centers, and better forms of income support for low-income postsecondary students. Other policies intended to enhance completion rates—academic support, counseling, and tutoring, for example—fall within the realm of educational responsibilities, but none will be effective without correcting the conditions of income and family demands outside of education.

Requiring that the Foundational State compensate for differences in family resources as well as foster equality of educational opportunity is an example of a "both-and" policy. It reflects John Dewey's warning against either-or statements and false dichotomies, as well as Harold Howe's (1993) declaration that "both policies"—both fixing schools and directly attacking poverty—"must be followed at the same time." Developing complementary policies will be difficult because of the politics of health and housing, of urban development and income support, and because governments are not structured to coordinate their programs. But we should not kid ourselves with rhetoric from the Education Gospel—about the "devastating waste of human potential and severe economic costs to our country" of failing to educate poor children—if we do not correct the social and economic conditions that make it impossible for some students to benefit from educational opportunities.

The advantage of articulating the Foundational State in place of the welfare state is that it clarifies that many preconditions are necessary for markets in general and education markets in particular to work well, for equality of opportunity to be realized, and for the fullest development of the Education Gospel to take place. If we as a society could create these foundations, then we would have both a more equitable and a more productive society. The forms of "help to self-help" and the capacities for "learning to learn" and lifelong education would be much more potent than they are now, when large numbers of individuals are undereducated and lack the competencies for a knowledge-based economy. The flexibility of educational institutions would be much greater if basic competencies could be assured among all students; and the labor force could be more responsive to changes than it is now, eliminating one potential barrier to economic growth. The policies of the Foundational State would complement one another rather than being antagonistic, as the different strands of the welfare state now are. And education reforms would be balanced with other social and economic policies, rather than bearing the entire burden of equal opportunity.

9

∿ Vocationalism and the Education Gospel in the Twenty-First Century

$\mathcal{B}$Y ALL OMENS, we are on the cusp of substantial change in the United States and in many other developed countries. After a century of now-familiar developments—the growth of enormous corporations, a labor force shift first to manufacturing and then to services, an increasingly national and now international economy, and the dominance of vocationalism at most levels of schooling—there are signals that some of this world may be superceded by another. One way to interpret the agonizing over the Knowledge Revolution and the extreme statements of the Education Gospel is that commentators are trying to understand these coming changes; they are describing not the world of the early twenty-first century but the world as it might look over the long haul. After all, the Knowledge Revolution has directly touched only a minority of jobs at this point, perhaps 1 to 5 percent of all nongovernmental workers, depending on how knowledge workers are defined—even though many more have been affected by less substantial changes like word processors and computerized machines. Some claims, such as the statement that college for all is "just common sense," are simply absurd when only 30 percent of job openings require any kind of postsecondary education. Many histrionic statements about our educational institutions are gross exaggerations—like the assertion that "the familiar ethic of scholarship has been ousted by just-in-time, immediate-gratification values of the marketplace," or headlines about the "academic-industrial complex," or the threat to universities made by Michael Milken, former junk-bond dealer: "You're in an industry which is worth hundreds of billions of dollars, and you have a reputation for low productivity, bad management, and no use of technology. We're going to eat your lunch."[1] Currently, scholarship and scholarly publications are expanding exponentially. The maligned proprietary universities have only 3 percent of postsecondary enrollments, and they do fill a niche unserved by conventional universities. But *if* current developments continue over this new century, then such transformations might come to pass—and so we interpret the excesses of the Education Gospel as anxious statements about the future, not as accurate descriptions of the present.

Large transformations have taken place before, of course, and historians have had a wonderful time separating the past into epochs of technological and social development: the Stone Age, the Bronze Age, the Iron Age, the ancient world of the classical civilizations, the Dark Ages and the medieval world, the Renaissance and the Enlightenment. For our relatively young country, the most important period after the initial stage of small-scale agricultural production and craft work was surely the Industrial Revolution, with the development of factory production based on a division of labor and on new forms of steam power. While innovations associated with the Industrial Revolution have continued, the communications revolution (or the second Industrial Revolution) began around 1890 to 1900, and brought various technological developments—electricity in place of steam, the telephone, radio, and then television, the automobile and then the airplane—facilitating the transfer of goods, people, and information across greater spaces, and enabling large national corporations to dominate our economic life.[2] Each of these stages took many decades to unfold; each of them transformed occupations, economic sectors, government policies, formal schooling, conceptions of life stages, and many other features of our society. And each stage continues to unfold. The transformations of the Industrial Revolution continue in our own period, now with computer-assisted methods, and the communications revolution continues to develop, with e-mail, cell phones, and the Web. Now the Knowledge Revolution may usher in a new stage, accompanied by organizational changes like "lean production" with more responsibilities for front-line workers, and international or transnational corporations moving capital, goods, jobs, and information around the globe. *If* such a fundamental transformation is about to usher in another long wave of change, it will not arrive fully formed but will instead develop gradually, as it extends its influence over different practices and institutions.

While substantial transformations will surely take place over the next century, many practices will endure. After all, the university—a venerable institution, more than 350 years old even in the United States—endured through the transformations of the century of vocationalism, though it evolved in crucial ways. The high school has persisted from the nineteenth century, though with substantial modification. The earlier ideals of political and moral education have continued, though they now have to share space with vocational goals. The ideas about vocationalism and the Education Gospel first articulated a century ago have largely the same forms now, even though the specific occupations and the particular skills required by economic change have evolved. Our major vocationalized institutions—the high school, the second-tier comprehensive university, the professionalized research university, the community college—will endure, partly because of the support of the Education Coalition and partly because the competitors that have emerged so far (job training, proprietary schools, and Web-based education) are generally inferior. Throughout this book our recommendations for reforming these institutions implicitly recognize that, since they will endure, we should be serious about making them as good as they can be.

Now that it is out of the bottle, the genie of vocationalism will be around for a good long time. New institutions within new niches may evolve—as the community college and the second-tier university developed during the past half century, and as proprietary universities may over the next century. But they will still follow familiar patterns of establishing and expanding vocational programs, of offering credentials with some value in the labor market, of reinforcing marketlike mechanisms, and of joining a recognizable system of vocationalized education. The problems endemic to vocationalism in all its forms—the conflict between public and private goals, the problems caused by the separation of schooling and employment, and the ways that vocationalism transforms and reinforces inequality—will continue and will need to be resolved, in ways we have suggested at the end of each chapter. Conversely, we doubt that any radically new type of institution will emerge to displace existing educational institutions. The failed efforts to develop short-term job training programs sponsored by a variety of organizations illustrates the difficulty of muscling in on the territory of established educational institutions, and we doubt that employers will develop any large-scale alternative to publicly sponsored schooling—even though we would like them to play a greater role. We may be wrong in our predictions—as social science so often is—but we think it historically more accurate to forecast major continuities with slow but cumulatively substantial transformations, rather than leaping to conclusions about cataclysmic change.

Being on the cusp of a substantial change creates a period not only of anxiety but also of possibility. As a society we can, if we understand the situation clearly, try to steer the change in desirable rather than undesirable directions. And so in this chapter we try to clarify what has been beneficial about vocationalism, to disentangle those elements from less desirable strands, and to describe the positive elements of both the Education Gospel and vocational practices. Then, since no conception of schooling should be divorced from other policies and practices in which it is embedded, we return to the nature of government, to the Foundational State, and to the noneducation policies necessary for the fullest version of the Education Gospel. We conclude with a statement of our highest ambitions for both schooling and work, since the two have been independently and jointly the focus of America's great hopes.

What's Right and What's Wrong with the Education Gospel

It's easy to poke fun at the excesses of the Education Gospel, but we should acknowledge that much of it is truly admirable. One obvious and easily overlooked aspect is that the Gospel places its faith in education as the salvation of a society—rather than, for example, geographic expansion or Manifest Destiny, colonialism or Lebensraum, specific industry sectors like plastics or computers, a hyperactive militarism, a free-market ideology, the detailed division of labor of the Industrial Revolution, or the corporate giantism of the communications revolution. Education has in so many times and so many places carried the hopes of civilization, and a vision that reinforces its value—especially when compared with some of the horrendous alternatives—is to be cherished. If nothing else, the current period of educational examination and reform that dates roughly from 1983 has caused politicians and taxpayers to pay attention to schooling, even if that attention has not always produced desirable results.

A second positive element is that the Education Gospel has consistently paid attention to the *public* dimensions of schooling—including its potential value in maintaining economic growth, in fostering international competitiveness, in promoting equity and social cohesion— rather than harping on individual benefits only, though most believers in the Gospel have had plenty to say about those as well. In a highly individualistic society it is heartening to see public dimensions taken seriously, even if the links—between education and growth, for example, or between education and competitiveness—are less direct than the pieties of the Education Gospel acknowledge.

A related feature is that it has justified the public expenditures necessary to expand schooling, no small feat in a country so stingy with public spending except for defense. A variety of benefits have came from the expansion of schooling. Most commentators around 1900 thought that additional schooling was preferable to working in low-wage, dead-end jobs, and further schooling now is still surely preferable for teenagers who would otherwise hang around the mall or be stuck in low-wage, dead-end jobs. Additional education, and particularly post-secondary education, has always carried the hopes not only of the aspiring middle class and the upwardly mobile working class, but also of those who see in education the way to rescue humanity from ignorance and barbarity. The emphasis on lifelong learning recognizes that human beings are not stagnant creatures but rather people who continue to learn throughout their lifetime. Even if the verbiage surrounding lifelong learning has sometimes been impenetrable, its essential insight has been highly consistent with humanist conceptions of continuous development. We may have qualms about educational inflation paired with exclusively instrumental values of schooling, but more learning has always been preferable to less, and the Education Gospel has justified that development for one and all, often at public expense.

Finally, the Education Gospel has promoted the essential core of vocationalism: the incorporation of occupational preparation into schools and colleges. Expanding the goals of educational institutions has been, in our view, a positive development: it makes them richer, denser enterprises, where students and teachers alike can establish connections with the political, moral, and economic aspects of society, where the vocational and the academic can be explored simultaneously, where students can come to understand their economic rights and responsibilities as surely as their political rights and obligations, where they can learn to be citizens knowledgeable about economic issues. The vocational goals of education become objectionable only when they displace prevocational purposes, a substitution that has been common in the sacred texts of the Education Gospel, like *A Nation at Risk* and the SCANS reports, with their near neglect of political and intellectual education. But the worst excesses of the Education Gospel and the narrowest forms of vocationalism should not blind us to the expansive possibilities in adding new purposes to old institutions.

Although the Education Gospel has had much to offer, it also contains a number of failings that need to be corrected. The most obvious is that it constantly exaggerates the pace of change. The enormous transformations in occupations, from agricultural labor to manufacturing occupations to service work to "knowledge" work, have taken place over two *centuries*. They will continue to unfold gradually, despite moments—like the dot-com boom of the late 1990s—that have gulled people into thinking that everything was changing right away. The exaggerations make us think of Chicken Little, a moral tale warning children (and grown-ups) not to mistake small events (a falling acorn) for imaginary catastrophes ("The sky is falling!" or "The barbarians have destroyed the university!") and thereby fail to identify the real villain— the fox, or the narrow version of vocationalism we caricature as HyperVoc.[3] A reasonable version of the Education Gospel would tone down the rhetoric of cataclysmic change and recognize that identifying the *direction* of change without exaggerating its *pace* is a worthy endeavor. And the villain isn't change itself but rather the wrong kind of change—which in this case we identify as the wrong kind of vocationalism.

Another failing of the current form of the Education Gospel is that it neglects history—not particularly surprising in a country without much historical recollection ("History is bunk," Henry Ford once said). Our prominent institutions have developed over long periods of time; they are relatively durable structures, unlikely to be blown away by the heavy breathing of catastrophizers. Specifically in the realm of education, elementary schools, high schools, and universities have evolved over two centuries, adding different elements but retaining much that was valuable from the nineteenth and even the eighteenth century. Even relatively new institutions—community colleges and second-tier, nonresidential universities—draw on these traditions, taking the form of comprehensive institutions, incorporating general education, aspiring to march up the academic hierarchy, and therefore responding to the same incentives and purposes that drive Harvard and Stanford and Berkeley. Our educational institutions are in this sense conserving and conservative institutions, which is why one strand of the Education Gospel critiques them for not responding quickly enough to changes around us. But conservatism has its value, particularly in periods of uncertainty, since it prevents us from responding wildly ("The sky is falling!") to small or temporary currents of change. A reasonable version of the Education Gospel would recognize, therefore, that schools and colleges have long histories, that they are accretions of changes, that old practices endure even when there are forces against them. By the same token, it would recognize that new programs and practices—the work-based learning of the School-to-Work Opportunities Act, short-term training to respond to business cycles and dislocations, the variety of SCANS skills—will be incorporated into existing institutions and made permanent only if they are reasonably congruent with existing practices *and* if there are sustained efforts to change, rather than simply rhetorical or piddling commitments.

The Education Gospel, like many other narratives useful in motivating public action, also has a strong tendency to simplicity and sloganeering.[4] The examples are legion: the naive version of human capital; the easy rhetoric about the Knowledge Revolution, without asking how much has changed; the promotion of college for all, in a period when most jobs don't require college; the concern with the school-to-work transition, without clarifying why that transition is often difficult; the constant repetition of "lifelong learning," a pretty slogan unclear about what needs to change; the statement that "all children can learn" and the title of the No Child Left Behind Act, which assume that equity can be achieved simply by thinking in different ways about low-performing children. Perhaps we should accept simplification and sloganeering as part of our political process, and then work to give rhetoric concrete meaning in individual schools and colleges. But a stronger alternative would be to elevate the discourse around education, to recognize the flaws in these simple slogans, and then to develop policies with more nuanced theories of action or conceptual underpinnings.[5] This would lead, for example, to increased concern about how a specific occupational or training program provides employment benefits, or how new credentials can attract the support of employers and providers. In the reform-oriented strand of the Education Gospel, a more realistic approach would recognize that substantial changes require *adequate* funding, *sustained* efforts, the retraining of instructors, and often other alterations (in facilities, for example, particularly for high-tech occupational programs)—in addition to a central vision. A less simplistic form of the Education Gospel could help us recognize the difficulties of enhancing work-based learning in a society where employers have abandoned much responsibility for work preparation; or of changing the pedagogy of occupational and professional education at levels of schooling that have been resistant to pedagogical change; or of narrowing the "achievement gap" in a country of shamefully high inequality and weak welfare policies.

The Education Gospel—as its name implies—has always been preoccupied only with education, emphasizing improvements in education rather than parallel changes in workplaces. It has extolled the contributions of education to economic growth, ignoring the roles of many other economic and political practices. As a solution to inequity, it has offered equality of educational opportunity, dismissing the contributions of other social and economic policies both to schooling itself and to equality of opportunity in its broadest sense. The focus on the power of education, noble as it may be, has ignored equally venerable rhetoric about the benefits of meaningful work, the centrality of political community, and the search for republican virtue. The Education Gospel in its current form is part of a grand vision of life in a great society, but it is incomplete.

Finally, most texts of the Education Gospel aren't particularly specific about the kind of vocationalism they assume. They usually do presume that schools and colleges (rather than employers) are the route to salvation, that educational institutions have primarily vocational purposes, that they can and should respond to the changes demanded by the Knowledge Revolution, and that they can include sufficient numbers of individuals to redirect the labor force. But there are many forms of vocationalism, as we stressed in Chapter 5. Some conceptions respond to student intentions while others stress special access to employment. Some narrow versions focus on specific skills, in opposition to broad versions with more generic and academic content; some emphasize conventional academic content while others incorporate a greater variety of skills. Some forms look like traditional low-level voc ed while others reflect high-level professionalism. Some variants (including some professional education) are "academic" in the pejorative sense of remaining distant from the world of work, while others incorporate significant amounts of work-based learning. And still other versions of vocationalism can be found in other countries, with important variations that come from their own histories and institutions. So the silence of the gospel about what kind of vocationalism might be appropriate isn't helpful for deciding how to respond.

A worthy version of the Education Gospel would acknowledge these limitations. It would avoid the current exaggerations and try to be more careful about the pace of change. It would work harder to recognize which changes are compatible with our history and which require sustained effort to incorporate into existing institutions. It would avoid sloganeering, particularly by being concrete about the practices entailed in phrases like "lifelong learning," "developing the skills of the twenty-first century," and smoothing the "school-to-work transition." It would not treat education as a panacea, despite the long history of doing so in this country, and it would acknowledge that education is often *part* of the solution to growth, or social stability, or equity, or unemployment, but that other areas of reform are both necessary and complementary. Finally, it would be more specific about the form of vocationalism that we require, lest we wind up with a narrow, anti-intellectual, inequitable, and small-minded version.

What's Right and What's Wrong with American Vocationalism

If we are on the cusp of a new period of development based on the technologies of the Knowledge Revolution and the reorganization of work and economic life, then what version of vocationalism might we want? What positive elements of our current version of vocationalism should we extend, and which negative elements do we want to eliminate? What do we want our educational institutions to do, and how might we share preparation for work with other institutions? How many of our social responsibilities can we load onto formal schooling, and how many must other institutions and policies bear? While answering these questions will ultimately be a political process, engaging large numbers of individuals and institutions in the deliberations, we can at least suggest some directions emerging from the best and the worst features of vocationalism.

The most encouraging aspect of vocationalism, both in general and in its American form, is that it has made formal schooling much more important. Enrollments have increased at all levels; at least in the United States, with its faith in education for democracy, the expansion of schooling has always been positive.[6] Many more occupations have been pulled into vocationalized schooling; and in many ways occupational preparation in formal schooling has been superior to traditional work-based learning and formal apprenticeships, which have suffered from endemic conflicts between production and learning, the tendency of employers to poach workers rather than train their own, the fragility of paternalistic relationships between masters and apprentices, and the inequities of family-based social mobility. But in some cases educational inflation seems to be taking place with no benefit either to the individual or to society. This happens when individuals get further schooling in the hope of improved employment but then fail to obtain the jobs they prepared for—when the criterion of *occupational intentions* is at odds with *related employment.* In other cases individuals continue their schooling because the dominant approach of vocationalism has eliminated alternative forms of preparation via experience, or apprenticeships, or informal preparation—even where schooling is a potentially poor substitute for the "school of experience." So educational expansion is often positive, but it has its dark side as well.

A second admirable feature of the U.S. form of vocationalism is that it has always promoted both public and private consequences—both national competitiveness and "getting ahead," both equity and the American dream of individual attainment. The inclusion of public goals has been central to maintaining public support for education and training, one of the few areas of social policy to loosen Americans' antipathy to taxation. But this version of vocationalism may become unstable when either public or private motives dominate. For example, traditional vocational education in high school was initially promoted for its public benefits, like eliminating skill shortages, increasing growth, and reducing social instability from the "wasted years." But having public benefits without private incentives to enter vocational education has led to coerced attendance, and to charges that voc ed is a dumping ground, that counselors cool out working-class and minority students in low-level vocational programs, and that welfare administrators force clients into ineffective job training and welfare-to-work programs. Conversely, when private incentives outrun public purposes, then it becomes difficult to justify government support. Currently, for example, there's considerable political support from middle-income parents and others in the Education Coalition for government higher-education subsidies, but it's hard to defend them for public reasons because the private benefits are substantial enough that most individuals will pay their own way; and the public benefits—economic growth, the promotion of democratic values and republican virtues, the maintenance of public order—seem to be small (as we argued in Chapter 6). A worthy form of vocationalism, then, should maintain an equilibrium of public and private purposes.

Vocationalism brought a different approach to the teaching of skills or competencies, its third admirable feature. It replaced apprenticeship, with its unavoidable conflict between production and educational purposes, with a form of preparation devoted entirely to education. It also facilitated the incorporation of new knowledge and new skills, including those based on research and advances in technology and work organization, in ways that on-the-job training often cannot. And vocationalism brought new subjects into the curriculum of schools and colleges, broadening conceptions of competence and bringing the outside world closer to the classroom than was true in the nineteenth century—a development that all critics of academic education consider positive. It has brought us closer to a vision of schooling incorporating multiple competencies or "intelligences" (Gardner, 1983), reflecting the perspective that virtually every human activity, including work, requires multiple abilities.

But the American form of vocationalism constantly threatens to become unbalanced in the competencies it teaches. In some cases—low-level voc ed and short-term job training are persistent examples—it has become too job-specific, particularly in a society of constant change; it fails to educate individuals for work over the longer run, and for continued learning on their own ("lifelong learning" and "learning to learn"). In other cases the academic slant of formal schooling has downgraded noncognitive competencies, important though they may be to many walks of life, and converted vocational and professional programs into academic exercises as remote from the world as was the nineteenth century's mental discipline. The version of vocationalism that seems most admirable to us is one that incorporates a variety of competencies or intelligences—cognitive *and* noncognitive abilities, general "academic" knowledge *and* generic occupational knowledge, conceptual or theoretical approaches *and* their application in different spheres including production—but leaves job-specific and firm-specific skills to be learned on the job. Accomplishing this balancing act is not easy, and the endless debates in professional schools reflect the social discussion necessary to create such an equilibrium. But it is a goal always to keep in mind, along with the procedures—including the planning associated with professionalism that involves employers, education providers, and professional associations—that might achieve this goal.

A fourth admirable feature of vocationalism is that, while it has taken many forms during the twentieth century, it has been the foundation for professionalism. To be sure, professionalism has always had a self-serving dimension in its efforts to regulate entry, just as unionism has sometimes been self-serving and exclusionary. But the ethos of professionalism provides several distinct advantages—quite apart from the status and earnings of the occupations for which it prepares students. The advantages include a celebration of knowledge and competence as the basis of special status, a search for ever-greater knowledge through additional schooling and continuing education, and mechanisms including meetings and journals to keep members up to date. Professional associations have often created career ladders that define mobility over time, as distinct from the lateral or random movement of nonprofessional and working-class jobs (including the job-hopping of contingent work). In many professions the need for external licensing exams has engaged employers, educational programs, and professional associations in defining licensing requirements and thus also professional programs, hiring standards, and student expectations. Such planning comes as close as anything in the United States to the tripartite planning conducted in European countries, in which the interests of all stakeholders are represented and a forum exists to balance the interests of all as well as to debate the competencies necessary for work over the long run. Professionalism has justified its special privileges with claims of public service, and that ethos can be strengthened by making it the price of access to professional privilege—for example, by requiring public service from doctors and lawyers, or public responsibility from engineers and architects, or ethical behavior backed by government oversight from the business professions. We view the expansion of professionalism over the twentieth century—from the high professions to semi-professions and now to many nascent or emerging professions—as a positive sign, an extension of the best form of vocationalism.

Vocationalism has also transformed the potential for equity in crucial ways, and its fifth positive element has been the replacement of apprenticeship mechanisms, controlled entirely by parents, with public schooling and public universities, where equity of access and resources might be subject to general debate. Unfortunately, the shift from work-based learning to formal schooling has not really led to greater equity, as we showed in Chapter 8, since vocationalism has contributed its own forms of inequality through differentiation, choice, and vocationalized conceptions of equity. While debating these issues in the public forum today is infinitely preferable to the nineteenth-century world, where inequity was beyond the reach of public improvement, the next steps will require a more equitable form of vocationalism. That in turn will require the range of developments we articulated in Chapter 8 as part of the Foundational State, including politically difficult policies of correction both within education and in other areas of policy.

A sixth admirable feature of vocationalism, at least in a liberal society where choice is sacred, is that it has expanded options in both schools and universities, reflecting in part the greater variety of occupations in the late nineteenth and twentieth centuries. This dimension of vocationalism led to the incorporation of new subjects and competencies, more dynamic and entrepreneurial educational institutions, and an education system more responsive to external demands—from students, the public, and employers—in place of an inward-looking system manipulated by education providers and professors (the "hollow men") to further their own interests. But while almost every American worships choice, the other elements of quasi-markets reinforced by vocationalism have not been as universally celebrated, such as the price-like and extrinsic incentives for students to learn in order to enhance earnings, the institutional motivation to increase enrollments, and the development of credentials as market-making mechanisms. Markets never work perfectly, despite what free marketeers claim, and all markets need to be appropriately regulated lest debacles like the savings and loans scandals of the 1980s and the collapse of Enron and WorldCom at the turn of the century continue. This is particularly the case with abstract and ill-defined "commodities" such as education, and we have consistently argued that quasi-markets in education need to be carefully structured. The form of vocationalism we prefer is one with appropriate regulation, particularly through public intervention to create sophisticated consumers and strong institutions and through public efforts (including professional mechanisms) to create credentials that work as they should to set consistent criteria for employers, students, and providers.

Overall, then, vocationalism ushered in substantial improvements over pre-vocational practices, particularly in expanding the roles of schooling, promoting both public and private goals, changing the nature of skill acquisition, reinforcing the development of professionalism, enhancing our collective ability to address equity, and expanding choices and the flexibility of educational institutions. But for all of these transformations there are both positive and negative consequences, as well as everything in between. The version we favor is one that gives a greater role to work-based learning, rather than one that relies on school-based learning only, with an equilibrium between public and private goals, with a broad range of general competencies, with professional standards and planning mechanisms, with equity assured through a variety of school and nonschool policies, and with markets carefully regulated.

IT IS EASY to outline a scenario in which the negative elements of vocationalism come to dominate the twenty-first century—a world we label HyperVoc. This is the scenario that the alarmists opposing the Education Gospel often describe, and some current trends, if left unchecked, would lead us to it.

In the world of HyperVoc, narrow work skills are all that matter, and a great deal of work has been routinized so that it can be carried out with prescribed skills—even for many professionals. The search among students for fast access to employment leads them to avoid all other "frills," including the arts, the humanities, and any version of general education. Employers seek specific skills narrowly tailored to their production needs, which they certify through firm-specific credentials (like Microsoft's MOUS or Cisco's CCNA credentials, but applied to many more occupations) or find by hiring contingent workers, since they can purchase any skills they need—including the professional skills of engineers and designers, lawyers and researchers—on the open market. Schools and colleges are limited to providing preparation for employer-dominated exams and the other specific skills of the turnkey employee. The well-rounded programs that colleges and universities used to offer—with appropriate academic coursework, a series of occupational courses of sufficient breadth, and coherent general education requirements—have disappeared because employers are unwilling to pay for them and students are unwilling to go through them.

Since education markets are unregulated, fly-by-night schools and Web sites regularly appear, make a bundle, and then disappear into the darkness, and outraged students try to get their high tuition back with the help of legions of education lawyers. Public institutions, especially the second-tier universities, are forced by competition to emulate these providers; they abandon all pretense of public responsibility and become dispensers of credential-preparation programs and narrow skills-oriented courses for increasing numbers of semiprofessions—advertising professionals, aluminum-siding professionals—motivated only by self-interest. Community colleges also provide credential-preparation programs and narrow skill training for workers; with public goals like equity and inclusivity fallen by the wayside, their second-chance role for poorly prepared students and experimenters is dismantled in favor of "economic development," or specific training for individual firms. The Harvards and Stanfords of the world still exist, of course, since wealthy parents understand the value of a broad education and a period of reflection for their precious children. But the differences between these few elite universities and most other institutions become greater and greater, inflating inequality enormously.

Aside from applied research aimed at improving the productivity of particular sectors, the research function is squeezed out of most universities, since research is increasingly funded by firms with proprietary interests. Professors like us—long the butt of attacks like those in the book *ProfScam*, complaining about our lack of productivity—have to teach a schedule more like that in high school, with six classes a day of students demanding relevance, high grades, low reading and writing requirements, entertaining lectures, and cool subjects, all for salaries not much higher than those of early childhood teachers (and much lower than those of aluminum-siding professionals). And grateful we must be for these crumbs; most instructors teach individual courses on contract, and universities hire instructors at auction for specific courses. Imagine the auctioneer, otherwise known as a University Human Resource Manager: "Two sections of Aluminum Siding 101, $2,010!!" or "One section of Business Ethics and Other Oxymorons, $870!!"

The world of HyperVoc is a ghastly place. Education is stripped of its power; work is de-skilled so that it can be performed with a minimal set of easily learned skills; students are narrow-minded and anti-intellectual drones; instructors become production-line workers; a few education providers find profit, both financial and intellectual, but hypercompetition and standardization squeeze most profit out of the system. Yet there is not a single feature of HyperVoc that does not already exist in some form, and this is why the alarmists fret about the potential effects of the Knowledge Revolution. We can already see what such a world would look like, and we should do everything in our collective power to prevent it from coming into existence. It will require strengthening the positive elements of vocationalism, and that, in turn, will require the expanded policies of the Foundational State.

Our Ambitions for Schooling, Work, and the Foundational State

If we take seriously the positive elements of the Education Gospel and want to reinforce the positive aspects of vocationalism rather than the excesses of HyperVoc, then we need to clarify the obligations of collective responsibility. In the previous chapter we argued for the elements of the Foundational State necessary to create an equitable version of vocationalism. But the requirements of the Foundational State extend beyond equity issues. They also include the policies necessary to avoid a world like HyperVoc and to reaffirm a broader version of vocationalism in which the development of human capacities is taken seriously.

Supporting Broad Forms of Vocationalism

Promoting the positive elements of the Education Gospel and vocationalism against the perils of HyperVoc requires supporting the development of broad human competencies and avoiding policies that tend to degrade them. Again, there are many ways of doing this, both in education policy and in the larger social, employment, and economic polities. Here we can only outline some of the potential directions.

Within education policy, this goal requires that public institutions assert the need for well-rounded programs, either occupational or academic, instead of allowing student "choice" to create havoc with coherent programs—as often occurs when colleges facilitate the process of "swirling," when students accumulate a grab-bag of unrelated credits from different institutions. In turn this requires educational institutions to make coherent programs compelling to students, for example by developing learning communities of related coursework, by creating coherent majors matched with work-based learning, and by clarifying the economic and intellectual benefits of completing such programs. Occupational programs that incorporate broader content should also benefit students even if they fail to find related employment. Such an approach would help restore public benefits—particularly moral and civic elements—to the high school as well as to colleges and universities. This might be accomplished through the integration of academic and occupational curricula when standard general education programs no longer seem to have much appeal, and by using the ethos of professionalism to promote other dimensions of public responsibility.

As part of creating broader programs and avoiding the descent into HyperVoc, it is also crucial to support the professional power of instructors at all levels, from K–12 to the university. The degradation of instruction results when high schools retreat to packaged curricula, multiple-choice tests, and idiot-proof teaching, and when second-tier universities and community colleges turn to part-time instructors solely for financial reasons. These instructors become replaceable cogs in a giant education machine, with limited responsibilities for teaching what becomes a standardized curriculum. Then the possibilities for powerful teaching—the kind that can integrate the general and the specific, that can incorporate flexible internships coordinated with classroom content, and that can provide the higher-order skills demanded by the Education Gospel—begin to leak away, replaced by short, specific modules, the harbingers of HyperVoc. The only antidote is to maintain the kind of autonomous professionalism for instructors at all levels that, we have argued, is the best form of vocationalism, rather than pretending that educational institutions can thrive when instructors themselves receive narrow forms of job training.

Broad forms of vocationalism also require a professionalism based on the kind of broadly defined credentials resulting from the collaboration of government, education providers, and professional associations. Conversely, governments should discourage the kinds of short-term, specific credential programs offered by individual firms, either by reducing public funding for them (including tax credits) or—as community colleges have recently done—by incorporating such specific training in broader certificate and associate-degree programs that combine both narrow vocational skills and broader "academic" competencies.

It would help avoid meaningless education inflation, we think, if some alternatives to school-based preparation could be developed, so that individuals did not feel forced to attend more school in order to enter an occupation. Alternative routes into employment could include apprenticeship methods and other experienced-based routes, though these should recognize and avoid the weaknesses of traditional apprenticeships; forms of alternating schooling and working that exploit the complementarities between them, as some co-operative education now does; preparation in other settings, such as community-based organizations, linked to and coordinated with formal schooling; and employment hierarchies within firms that allow employees to advance with additional preparation both on and off the job. There should also be room in this vision for short-term job training programs for the unemployed, dislocated workers, and others who have relatively short-term employment problems. However, these should provide meaningful educational opportunities and connections to both employment and further education—unlike Work First and current short-term training programs that are disconnected from future options—both as a model for enhancing rather than degrading competence and as an issue of equity. A Foundational State that supports broad conceptions of vocationalism also has the option of educative forms of public employment, following existing models like Youthbuild, again to support equity and to provide a mechanism for developing competencies while simultaneously meeting public needs.

The relatively extreme school-based preparation of American-style vocationalism would be moderated and complemented by all of these alternatives. Such efforts would help us move away from the narrowness of much firm-sponsored training, on the one hand, and the incompleteness of school-based learning, on the other. By now we have enough experience from the failures of the 1970s and 1990s to understand that such fundamental transformations require a clear vision, sufficient resources carefully directed toward that vision, cooperation from educational providers and employers alike, the development of educative work placements, and a substantial period of time.

Finally, we all need to revise our claims for education, because the exaggerated forms of the Education Gospel almost always lead to disappointment and frustration. This means that public figures and politicians and commissions need to moderate their rhetoric, difficult as that might be in the era of the sound bite. Simple claims for education should be replaced with a deeper understanding of what education and training can accomplish, and which goals require other social and economic policies as well. Only a realistic form of the Education Gospel that avoids the alarmism of Chicken Little can ever be achieved, and only a version of the Education Gospel applied broadly and equitably can help us avoid HyperVoc in large ghettoes of our economy.

Reforming Employment to Enhance Competence

But supporting the positive elements of the Education Gospel and American vocationalism, and defending against HyperVoc, requires more than education policy by itself can deliver. The basic promise of the Education Gospel has been to develop human competencies as a way of creating both individual wealth and the preconditions for economic growth, stability, and democracy. The problem is that many jobs in our economy are structured so that they don't encourage the development of serious competencies. The jobs of the youth labor market are virtually all low-skill, repetitive service jobs, and they present young people with an image of work in which even basic academic and personal competencies—never mind the complex abilities forecast for the twenty-first century—are all but irrelevant. The figures in Table I.1 reinforce that conception of the labor market, with about 70 percent of new jobs by 2010 requiring no more than a high school education, and about 75 percent requiring no more than modest on-the-job training.

These data hardly encourage college for all or even a serious emphasis on the "school of experience." The extent of overeducation documented in Chapter 7 and in Table 7.1, with perhaps 35 to 40 percent of those in the labor force overschooled for their positions, clarifies in a different way the tendency for formal schooling to outrun the demands of jobs themselves. A great deal of employment is not particularly educative, as generations of reformers have found when they have tried to develop work-based learning and have come up with too many deadening job placements. Educators and social commentators can fulminate all they want about the skills of the twenty-first century, but if employment patterns don't justify these claims, then schooling institutions and academic standards and commission reports just look silly. There is no reason for large numbers of students to develop those skills, and they might just as well enjoy themselves, or take hobby courses and life skills (or life adjustment) courses, or get credit for extracurricular activities like band and Strutters. This is how members of the employment community contribute to the degradation of the Education Gospel—not by failing to support it rhetorically or financially, but by failing to live up to its promises in their employment practices.

Therefore a key responsibility of the Foundational State is to create the preconditions for developing human competencies, not only by supporting the *supply* of the right kinds of education and training but also by stimulating the *demand* for these competencies. It should encourage employers to restructure jobs so that they are educative, discourage the de-skilling of work, and provide a model in public employment. While the political barriers to doing this are obvious, there are many approaches worth considering. Public employment, which meets worthwhile public needs as it employs individuals, can also provide high-quality training tied to both vocational and academic competencies. Examples like the Youthbuild program, which trains youths in construction skills while they rebuild inner-city housing, and the Youth Conservation Corps, which provides training while its members engage in environmental projects, can be expanded to other activities. Then they can be carefully linked with educational options, to prepare individuals for both subsequent employment and education (like programs advocating "college and careers" do). The New Hope program provides evidence for the success of this strategy, since giving community service jobs to a group of low-income individuals was found to increase employment, raise income, enhance parental skills, improve health, and reduce depression (Huston et al., 2003). In addition, greater sustained public support for cooperative education would link schooling and employment, and the process of negotiation between education providers and employers about the content of co-op placements would help to keep the quality of both schooling and employment high. Similarly, public support for efforts to professionalize occupations, especially through licensing requirements and tripartite planning, would enhance competencies and limit the tendency to de-skill jobs and subvert existing occupations.

Other options to reinforce demand-side policies and enhance the development of competence include efforts to combat employment discrimination, so that students no longer believe their educational efforts are unlikely to be rewarded—particularly women, who can now see their routes into "male" jobs circumscribed, and minority students with firsthand evidence of unfair hiring. Because the trend toward using temporary or contingent workers is detrimental to the development of educative jobs, public policy should discourage contingent work; it should, for example, reduce the economic incentives for converting full-time work into contingent work by requiring that contingent workers be paid the same benefits as regular employees, and it should use antidiscrimination efforts to prevent contingent work from being used disproportionately for jobs held by women and minority workers. In addition, the quality of employment might benefit substantially from publicly supported experiments with alternative forms of work organization, like worker cooperatives and team-based models that give more discretion and responsibility to frontline workers, partly as alternatives to contingent work (Pencavel, 2001; Applebaum and Batt, 1994). Monetary and fiscal policy committed to the preconditions for developing competence would support full employment because such conditions improve salaries and benefits, including training and working conditions, as ways of attracting a well-qualified labor force.

Policies to strengthen the bargaining power of workers could also improve the conditions of employment and aid the conversion of routine and noneducative jobs into more challenging positions that make greater use of the skills of the twenty-first century—or at least prevent workers' jobs from being de-skilled.[7] These policies should discourage "right to work" statutes and simplify organizing efforts, steps that might stem the steady slide in rates of unionism; raise minimum wages, which might drive out the least productive jobs from the economy; enforce labor regulations, including child labor laws and health and safety standards, to undercut the ability of employers to create low-quality and dangerous jobs; insist that labor standards be included in all international agreements so that employers cannot undermine employment by threatening to move to countries without such standards; and enact stricter plant closing legislation, again to undercut the ability of employers to threaten to move jobs.

Like the policies to eliminate barriers to equal opportunity in education, or to compensate for differences in family backgrounds, the effort to restructure employment opportunities for higher-order competencies is not a simple campaign whose remedies can be exhaustively delineated. These recommendations represent a long-run strategy that must develop over time, as conditions evolve and challenges emerge. They are also part of an effort to move to a "high-skills equilibrium" more consistent with the rhetoric of the Education Gospel, in place of the low-skills equilibrium—or, more precisely, the enormous range of skill and schooling levels—characteristic of the United States.

These are also policies intended to resurrect our grandest ambitions about both work and schooling. Work, we should remind ourselves, has played a central role in our society—indeed, in most societies we can think of. In its best forms, work has offered individuals a connection to the rest of society, creating a means of living within the company of others. It has been simultaneously a source of individual satisfaction and a root of personal identity. In some versions—particularly in the Protestantism of colonial America—work has also been a connection to the Divine and good works a route to salvation, a concept that lives on in the sense of work as a calling, work as a vocation rather than merely a job. From this perspective Paradise is not the Garden of Eden, where no work was necessary, but rather a world in which work takes meaningful forms. Particularly in a society in which people work as hard as Americans do (Schor, 1991), it's difficult to escape the centrality of work in people's lives.

Formal schooling has also played a central role in our society, from the Old Deluder law and the dame schools of the seventeenth century to the latest efforts to develop profit-making universities. Schooling has some of the same characteristics as work: it has provided both individual meaning and social purpose; it has promised to contribute to the development of society in an economic sense and also in moral, civic, and cultural ways. And education has consistently borne the hopes of immigrants in a nation of immigrants, the aspirations of those wanting entry into the mainstream of society, the ambitions for upward mobility. The power of the American dream, usually interpreted as the possibility of success through individual effort for anyone, of any background, has increasingly come through schooling rather than simple hard work, or the luck and pluck and moral character of Horatio Alger's heroes (Hochschild and Scovronek, 2003).

If both work and schooling have carried so much meaning in our society, one would think that school-based preparation for work would take on enormous value too. It should be something that children are taught to look forward to, as they put away their childish things and begin to take their places among adults, as valued members of society with contributions to make, responsibilities to uphold, rewards to receive, knowledge to learn and expand and pass on to others. Instead, schooling for work and vocational education have often been dirty words, connoting a narrow and mean form of preparation for routine and joyless work. It is all too easy to corrupt both schooling and work. When each is debased and then joined—when narrow forms of schooling prepare individuals for low-quality, low-status work, in short-term job training or traditional vocational education or the practices visible in our description of HyperVoc—then vocationalism takes the negative forms outlined earlier in this chapter. So the ambitions we as a society have had for work and schooling—and then for schooling as a way of preparing for work—can be realized only if both take broad and meaningful forms. This does not happen "naturally," or through laissez-faire practices including unregulated markets. Realizing the ambitions Americans have always had for work and for schooling requires the complex policies of the Foundational State, to construct appropriate forms of work as well as broad conceptions of education, and then to make sure that the two are consistent with each other through the linkage mechanisms we recommended in Chapter 7.

In these efforts, the developments of the Knowledge Revolution—*if* they materialize over the next century—have many attractive features. If knowledge-based forms of work become the basis for another long cycle of development—instead of a momentary dot-com blip—then the central requirements of work will become more consistent with the central features of schooling. This was not true in preindustrial societies dominated by traditional agriculture and handicraft. It certainly was not characteristic of the Industrial Revolution, when repetitive and essentially unthinking activity was the basis of most work. Nor has it been true of most employment associated with the communications revolution, where corporate size and enormous economies of scale generated a great deal of repetitious, semiskilled work. According to projections for the new knowledge society, however, work could become meaningful for much larger numbers of individuals through the expansion and exercise of human competencies, just the kind of abilities that formal schooling in its best forms teaches well. The consistency between schooling and work that has been missing in previous long waves of development might be easier to achieve because work could be widely reinvented.

But the *potential* for the Knowledge Revolution to make schooling and work more compatible is unlikely to be realized unless Americans remember how much social and political energy is necessary to make sure that our society moves toward a broad version of vocationalism. The Foundational State we have outlined requires a very different approach to politics and democracy than we have now. It provides a clear vision of the common good: a society in which human capacities are consistently and equitably developed, congruent with a realistic version of the Education Gospel and a broad conception of vocationalism. Other interests must then be subordinated to this conception—sometimes the prerogatives of employers, often the entrepreneurialism of educational institutions, sometimes the immediate choices of students or their parents, and certainly the tendency of policy makers to fix all problems through educational measures. The politics of the Foundational State cannot work like interest-group liberalism, in which any possible conception of the common good can be destroyed by the opposition of powerful interest groups, including corporations, or free-market ideologues, or proponents of one practice or another of narrow vocationalism, or middle-class parents supporting special privileges for their children only.[8] Instead it requires widespread acceptance of some fundamental principles that are more important than individual interests, principles that would in turn govern a variety of specific policies to prevent our descent into the pit of HyperVoc. The Foundational State also requires a "good government" approach to politics, one in which the electorate focuses on issues and solutions rather than personalities and entertainment, one that avoids the circus democracy we so often see, one that avoids lying by politicians and chicanery in economic policy (Krugman, 2003).

Perhaps we as a nation cannot develop the politics necessary for the Foundational State. But then we should stop prattling on about the "skills of the twenty-first century," the "common sense" of college for all, and the imperatives of the knowledge society including lifelong learning, because we cannot achieve any positive version of vocationalism without the policies of the Foundational State. If we believe in the rhetoric of the Education Gospel as it was developed over the past century, then we need to take the collective actions necessary for the continued development of broad competencies over the next century. Only then will we have forms of schooling and work, and schooling in preparation for work, that live up to the noblest ambitions of the Education Gospel.

Notes

Introduction

1. The etymological origin of *gospel* is "good tidings," consistent with the Education Gospel's upbeat message about education. We called this perspective the "new orthodoxy" or the "dominant narrative" until we came across Kwon's (2001) contention that "the idea of a knowledge-based economy is enthusiastically treated like a gospel among Korean people." Simultaneously Stuart Tannock pointed out the passing reference to the "training gospel" in Canada by Swift (1995). While Swift applies the phrase only to short-term job training, we intend for the phrase to cover both education and training.

2. See Immerwahr and Foleno (2000). On college for all see also Boesel and Fredland (1999), and Rosenbaum (2001).

3. James Ketelson, founder, "Project Graduation Really Achieves Dreams," available from Project GRAD in Houston, 1998.

4. For example, *A Nation at Risk* said virtually nothing about equity, and its conclusions were challenged by a counterreport, *Our Children at Risk*, by the National Coalition of Advocates for Children (1985).

5. The term *vocation* is the closest equivalent in English to the German *Beruf*, which better captures the centrality of all occupations (even low-skilled or low-schooled occupations) to identity and social status as well as economic benefits.

6. Massachusetts Commission on Industrial and Technical Education; see Lazerson and Grubb (1974), doc. 5, 78.

7. Markets have transformed everything they touch, even those institutions that seem most hostile to the individual advantage and accumulation that underlie capitalism, and there's no possibility that schooling could have escaped its influence. On the power of individualism to transform the institutions of family, community, religion, education, and politics, see Bellah et al. (1985). See also Grubb and Lazerson (1982, ch. 10) for a similar argument.

271

8. This and the following quotations are from Lazerson and Grubb (1974), docs. 7, 10, 13, and 14.

9. Vocationalism has also influenced middle schools and elementary schools, principally by emphasizing the most utilitarian subjects—reading, writing, and math—over the moral learning of the nineteenth century, and by changing the overall purpose of schooling from civic preparation to getting ahead. However, middle and elementary schools are more distant from and therefore less affected by the crucial movement into employment.

10. These figures come from the *Statistical Abstract of the United States, 1870–1970*, supplemented by the *Digest of Educational Statistics* and the *Statistical Abstract of the United States* for several years.

11. Policy in many countries is driven by narratives, or widely accepted "stories" about why certain programs are worthwhile. The creation of such narratives typically takes a considerable period of time and many participants. Established policy narratives like the Education Gospel, or human capital, are resistant to change, and subtle empirical evidence—the results that research can generate—is usually not enough to modify or complicate a policy narrative. See, e.g., Roe (1994).

12. Lazerson and Grubb (1974), doc. 16, 147; the Washington–Du Bois debate is described in this volume (12–13) and in Kliebard (1999), 13–21.

13. Based on Brint (2001), table 2. Brint's definition of the SPK sector is based on the proportion of employees with graduate degrees, not on an assessment of what role knowledge plays in work.

14. On long waves, see Wiebe (1967) and Bledstein (1978) for historical perspectives, and Freeman (1984, 1996) for two compendia of articles, many focused on economic cycles rather than broader social and economic developments. Mager (1987) describes shorter, fifty-year waves rather than the longer cycles we prefer.

15. This argument harks back to Lowi's (1969) claim that interest-group liberalism cannot plan and cannot redistribute effectively.

16. This suggests the opportunity to examine "varieties of vocationalism," parallel to the developing literatures on "varieties of capitalism" and "varieties of welfare states" (e.g., Hall and Soskice, 2001).

1. Transforming the High School

1. On the apprenticeship system in the eighteenth and nineteenth centuries, see Rorabaugh (1986); on the nineteenth and early twentieth centuries, see Douglas (1921). See also Hansen (1997), chs. 2 and 8, whose interpretation of apprenticeship is similar to ours.

2. Our historical explanation is consistent with the economic model of Estevez-Abe, Iversen, and Soskice (2001), who argue that specific skill instruction based in workplaces fails without certain regulatory policies.

3. The themes that follow draw heavily on Kaestle (1983); Kaestle (2000); Kliebard (1999); Kantor (1988); Labaree (1997); and Lazerson and Grubb (1974).

4. Kantor (1988) and Kliebard (1999, ch. 2) review the politics of the vocational education movement. For the views of the Education Coalition, see Lazerson and Grubb (1974), 69–136.

5. The claims of skill shortages provide an early example of exaggeration in

the Education Gospel. The evidence for shortages of skilled labor was mixed, since the division of labor in manufacturing substituted semiskilled machine tenders for skilled craftsmen. See especially Kliebard (1999) and Douglas (1921).

6. On home economics and scientific domesticity, see Rothman (1978) and Ehrenreich and English (1978). On clerical education, see Powers (1992), 114–119. See also Tyack and Hansot (1990) and Rury (1991).

7. See Deschenes, Cuban, and Tyack (2001) on the impulse to differentiate schooling as a solution to differences among students.

8. See Bestor (1953) and Ravitch (1983, ch. 2) on the rise and fall of life adjustment. A recent movement has replaced general education with either academic courses or programs integrating academic and occupational education; see Bottoms and Presson (1995) on the reforms of High Schools That Work.

9. On the decline of coherent vocational programs, see Grubb and McDonnell (1996). The definitive study of vocational course-taking reveals that while 96.5 percent of students in 1998 took some form of vocational course, only 25 percent were "concentrators" taking 3 or more credits in one area (down from 33.7 percent in 1982), and only 14.4 percent were "advanced concentrators" taking at least one advanced credit among the 3 (down from 24 percent in 1982); see Levesque (2003), fig. 11, 23.

10. On the lack of any "academic press" in vocational and general tracks, see Claus (1990); Powell, Farrar, and Cohen (1985) on the vertical curriculum; and Oakes (1985).

11. The criticisms of the 1970s include Panel on Youth (1974), National Panel on High School and Adolescent Education (1976), Timpane et al. (1976), National Commission on Youth (1980), and Carnegie Council on Policy Studies in Higher Education (1980). Large-scale critical studies of high schools include Powell, Farrar, and Cohen (1985), Goodlad (1984), and Boyer (1983), and critical historical studies include Angus and Mirel (1999) and Labaree (1997). Commission reports include *Breaking Ranks* (NASSP, 1996) and on-going work by the Carnegie Commission (e.g., Carnegie Council, 1989; Baldwin, 2000). See also National Research Council (2003), a recent study examining the lack of motivation and engagement in the high school.

12. The criticism that high schools lack any serious purpose dates back at least to Paul Goodman's (1956) scathing critique.

13. Evaluations have generally found vocational students earning wages no higher than those of comparable students in other tracks, except perhaps girls in commercial courses; see Gustman and Steinmeier (1982), Hu and Stromsdorfer (1979), Meyer and Wise (1981), Rumberger and Daymont (1984).

14. On the failures of the School-to-Work Opportunities Act, see esp. Hershey et al. (1998), Hershey (2003), Medrich et al. (2000), and Stull (2003). Most programs increased conventional career education and counseling, rather than establishing new forms of work-based learning. The optimists of the school-to-work movement see a residue of partnerships and awareness, a "constructive thread in the evolving fabric of American education," while the pessimists note the sharp decline in activity with the end of funding.

15. See esp. National Commission on Social Studies in the Schools (1989) and the massive *Civitas: A Framework for Civic Education* (Quigley and Buhmueller, 1991).

16. See the *Digest of Educational Statistics, 2001*, Table 103. See also Rumberger (2001) for a review of dropout issues and rates (especially fig. 1). Barton (2002) shows graduation rates increasing until the mid-1960s and dropping since then to about 75 percent. Goldin's (1998) series is similar, though she stresses that national figures mask substantial regional variation.

17. See also Hill, Foster, and Gendler (1990) on "high schools with character."

18. On "education through occupations" and evidence about its benefits, see National Research Council (2003), esp. ch. 7; Grubb (1995a); Grubb (1997a); Stern (1999); Stern, Dayton, and Raby (2001).

19. See Lee and Smith (2001) for evidence that small schools with 600–900 students and modifications in teaching methods improve achievement gains. See also National Research Council (2003).

20. On these and related reforms see National Research Council (2003), ch. 6; McCharen (1995); Grubb, Lara, and Valdez (2002). See also the Family Advocacy System included in First Things First and the teams in Comer schools (Comer, 1996).

21. On the concept of civic capacity, where the different segments of a community work cooperatively rather than in antagonistic ways, see Stone (1998). On a new round of so-called adequacy cases in school finance, see Minorini and Sugarman (1999a). On the lack of support services, see National Research Council (2003), ch. 6.

2. Professionalism in Higher Education

1. These figures come from *Historical Statistics of the United States, 1870–1970*, supplemented by the *Digest of Educational Statistics* and the *Statistical Abstract of the United States* for several years. The college enrollment rates come from *Digest of Educational Statistics*, 2001, table 184. The figures from the 1990s are from the National Educational Longitudinal Study of the class of 1988 (NELS88) data, calculated by Timothy Leinbach of the Community College Research Center, Columbia University.

2. See Eddy (1957), 25, 31; Veysey (1965), 13–14; Bledstein (1978), ch. 6.

3. "Inaugural Address of President Charles Richard Van Hise," *Science* 20 (Aug. 12, 1904), 193–205.

4. Figures earlier than 1910–1920 are unavailable, though they were surely quite low before the 1890s. These figures are based on degrees received; see Brint et al. (2002), fig. 1. They probably understate the extent of professional degrees, since some fields counted as academic—psychology, law and legal studies, visual and performing arts—could be considered professional. On professional education, see also Kett (1994).

5. See Geiger (2000b); Kett (1994); Bledstein (1978); and Sullivan (1995).

6. On professionalization see Larson (1977); Sullivan (1995); Cheit (1975).

7. *Digest of Educational Statistics, 2001*, tables 172–173.

8. The six-year completion rates are listed, along with predicted completion rates, in "Actual versus Predicted Institutional Graduation Rates for 1100 Colleges and Universities," *Postsecondary Education Opportunity* 58 (April 1997).

9. Dunham (1969, 28) provides a useful table showing the origins of state colleges and universities belonging to the American Association of State Colleges and

Universities: 59 percent originated as teachers' colleges, 14 percent as technical or agricultural colleges, 10 percent as multipurpose colleges, 8 percent as junior colleges, 6 percent as academies, and 3 percent as religious or YMCA institutions. There's virtually no research on these institutions, and no consensus about what to call them. Dunham described them as "colleges of the forgotten Americans"; Kantor, Gamson, and London (1997) defined them as "non-elite, unselective, and neither research institutions nor true liberal arts colleges" (2). See also Selingo (2002) and Wlodkowski, Mauldin, and Gahn (2001).

10. Examples include the Carnegie Foundation (1977); Gaff (1991); Westbury and Purves (1988); Orrill (1995) and (1997); Kantor, Gamson, and London (1997). Many of these critics bemoan the decline of liberal education without acknowledging the rise of professional goals.

11. These figures intend to remove noninstructional spending. Figures come from California Postsecondary Education Commission reports available at www.cpec.ca.gov/completereports/2003reports/03–08/.

12. Many professions have a journal devoted to teaching in the profession—for example, *Journal of Teaching in Social Work, Journal of Engineering Education, Journal of Nursing Education, Journal of Teacher Education, Journal of Legal Education, Journal of Management Education, Management Learning, American Medicine: The Journal of the American Medical Association*. On the pedagogy of occupational education, see Achtenhagen and Grubb (2001).

13. Tinto (1993) and his colleagues have popularized the idea that social integration—integration into the life of the campus, facilitated by smaller-scale communities—is important in enhancing retention. On the structure of learning communities, see Matthews (1994) and Smith (1991); for evidence about effectiveness, see Tinto, Goodsell-Love, and Russo (1994) and Tokina (1993).

14. Dunham (1969, 155) also argues that the state and regional universities should create unique roles for themselves instead of trying to emulate elite universities.

3. Dilemmas of the Community College

1. On the history of the community college see Brint and Karabel (1989), esp. chs. 2–4; Dougherty (1994), chs. 10–14. We also draw on Grubb (1996b) and Grubb and Associates (1999).

2. See Brint and Karabel (1989) on the "vocationalizing project," the advocates in favor of occupational education. Another group has insisted that community colleges remain academic and transfer-oriented; see Cohen and Brawer (1987) and Eaton (1994).

3. See Dougherty (1994), table 10-1. The estimate for 1992–93 comes from National Postsecondary Student Aid Survey (NPSAS) data reported in Tuma (1993). About 17 percent of community college students do not answer this question; they are presumably either "experimenters" unsure of their direction, avocational students, or remedial students.

4. Some colleges have established noncredit divisions that support the transition into education for second-chance students particularly well; see Grubb, Badway, and Bell (2003).

5. On "experimenters," see Manski (1989). See Grubb (1996b), ch. 2, for in-

terviews with community college students indicating their uncertainty about the value of college. For the reactions of instructors to experimenters see Grubb and Associates (1999), ch. 1.

6. Technical colleges have recently become comprehensive institutions in Minnesota, Indiana, South Carolina, and Louisiana; several technical colleges in Wisconsin's system have developed transfer programs, in effect creating comprehensive colleges.

7. For discussions about missions see Cohen and Brawer (1989), chs. 8–12; Dougherty (1994), ch. 15; Bailey and Averianova (1998). On economic development activities, see Grubb et al. (1997) and Dougherty and Bakia (1998).

8. Clark (1960), 68—85; the quotations from the *San Jose Junior College Handbook for Counselors, 1957—58* are on 73.

9. Our review of the evidence (Grubb, 1996b, ch. 2) concludes that advancement outweighs the effects of cooling out, and that most community college students would not have attended four-year colleges. See also Rouse (1995) and (1998), and Dougherty (1994, ch. 3).

10. On counselors' lack of power, see Grubb (2003), Worthen (1997), and Goto (1998).

11. See Gardner (1983) for one way of conceptualizing multiple abilities or "intelligences." The special issues in occupational teaching are analyzed in Achtenhagen and Grubb (2001).

12. See Gittell and Steffy (2000); Matus-Grossman and Gooden (2002); California Tomorrow (2002); and Woodlief, Thomas, and Orozco (2003), esp. ch. 3. The quotations are from the California Tomorrow report, 6. We are reasonably sure that the same dilemma affects many students in less-selective, second-tier comprehensive universities too, though there has been very little research about these students.

13. On ways to improve teaching and to make community colleges more hospitable to low-income students, see Grubb and Associates (1999), esp. chs. 8–9; Grubb (2001a); Grubb, Badway, and Bell (2003).

14. On the lack of critical perspectives, see Grubb and Associates (1999), ch. 3, and the interchange between Gregson (1997) and Grubb (1997b).

4. Second Chances in Job Training and Adult Education

1. For the history of job training, see National Academy of Sciences (1975); Lafer (2002). See also the argument of Tyack, Lowe, and Hansot (1984) that the links between the 1930s and the 1960s were slender.

2. On the political developments around AFDC and Temporary Assistance for Needy Families (TANF), see Katz (2001) and Lafer (2002), ch. 6.

3. On Work First, see Brown (1997); the legislator's quote is from "Michigan—Work First," www.ospr.nie.edu/street/long/michigan.htm.

4. By fall of 2002, only a few studies had appeared on the effects of welfare reform. Primus et al. (1999) found polarized results; Scrivener et al. (1998) found positive results but under favorable conditions including a predominantly white caseload, a high proportion of clients with high school diplomas, and a strong local labor market; Quint et al. (1999) found uneven efforts for the most disadvantaged recipients; Equal Rights Advocates (2000) found that the most disadvantaged recipients were being left behind; and the review by Blank (2000) indicated that the

most disadvantaged welfare recipients were made worse off. These studies were carried out before the worst of the post-2000 recession.

5. There is some evidence of "triage" outcomes under WIA: the most advantaged job seekers find employment on their own, the least advantaged have too many barriers to benefit from WIA's limited services, and those in the middle benefit the most. See Friedlander (1988); Gueron and Pauly (1991), ch. 4; Grubb (1996a), 63–68.

6. An experiment in Great Britain with vouchers for job training proved not to expand choice either for unemployed youth or for employers; see Hodkinson, Sparkes, and Hodkinson (1996). For the mixed effects of Career Management Accounts (CMAs), a program that costs substantially more than ITAs and has better-educated participants, see Public Policy Associates (1998).

7. WIA was due to be reauthorized in the fall of 2003, but the various drafts circulating in Congress amounted to little more than marginal tinkering. Similarly, the early drafts for TANF reauthorization have only toyed with its provisions and have kept the restrictions on education and training—for example, allowing at most three months of education in any twenty-four-month period to count toward work requirements. See the bulletins of the Workforce Alliance, www.workforce alliance.org/policy.wia_proposals.

8. Most JTPA programs cost around $2,500 per person. The expensive and experimental programs—New Chance with its mentors and complex support services costing $9,000; the residential Job Corps spending nearly $20,000 per student—have not been widely replicated. In 1995–96 community colleges spent an average of $6,733 per student, involving considerably more contact hours. Public four-year colleges in this country spent an average of $19,700, or almost $80,000 for a four-year program; the less selective public four-year colleges spent $13,403 per year and the most elite private universities spent about $37,200. See the *Digest of Educational Statistics, 1999*, tables 349–353.

9. For summaries of the evaluation literature see Grubb (1996a); LaLonde (1995); U.S. Department of Labor (1995); Fischer and Cordray (1996); O'Neill and O'Neill (1997); and Strawn (1998). Even the benefits reported are surely over-estimates, since they fail to consider substitution, where individuals from public training programs get jobs while other equally needy individuals fail to get the same jobs; see Lafer (2002) and Grubb and Ryan (1999), ch. 3.

10. For a census of federally supported adult education programs, see Young et al. (1994).

11. For the effects of the GED on employment, see Cameron and Heckman (1993), who find no effects, and Murnane, Willett, and Boudett (1995), who conclude that there are small effects but question whether these effects are worth the influence of the GED exam on the content of the programs. For evidence that the GED does not provide greater access to postsecondary education, see Quinn and Haberman (1986). (The GED test changed at the beginning of 2002, and it's possible that the consequences of earning this credential will change as well.) On the outcomes of adult education, see Grubb and Kalman (1994). See also the fourth report of the National Evaluation of Adult Education Programs, titled *Learner Outcomes and Program Results* (Young, Fitzgerald, and Morgan, 1994): very few outcome studies are cited, and the statistical analysis carried out is marred by many technical flaws.

12. On the ways community colleges can serve as bridges between training and

education, see Grubb (1996a), ch. 7, and Grubb (1996b), ch. 4. On "ladders" of opportunity, see Grubb et al. (1999), sec. 6. On the potential roles of CBOs, see Osterman and Lautsch (1996) and Roberts (2002).

13. Most of these examples are drawn from Grubb and Associates (1999), ch. 5. See also Tinto and Goodsell-Love (1995) on learning communities for basic skills instruction, and Matthews (1994).

14. On individuals finding their way into programs by accident, see Hull (1993); on the lack of information, see Grubb (1996b, ch. 2), and Schneider and Stevenson (1999), ch. 9.

5. *The American Approach to Vocationalism*

1. These figures come from the *Statistical Abstract of the United States, 1870–1970*, supplemented by the *Digest of Educational Statistics* and the *Statistical Abstract of the United States* for several years.

2. Different countries have had different approaches to vocationalism, though all developed countries and most transitional ones have oriented their schooling systems around preparation for vocations. A future project is an analysis of the various approaches to vocationalism, parallel to the literature on varieties of capitalism and varieties of welfare states (e.g., Hall and Soskice, 2001).

3. We don't mean to oversell this point. Evidently the grammar school expanded during the nineteenth century based on its civic roles, and early childhood programs expanded over the twentieth century based on the goals of supporting working mothers, developing the whole child, providing compensatory preparation for schooling, and accelerating school readiness.

4. See also Hansen (1997), ch. 8, comparing the United States with Germany.

5. See the international comparisons in table 40-1 of NCES (2003). In 1999 the United States had the highest spending per pupil in postsecondary education of any OECD countries: $19,220 compared with an average of $9,210. Its spending on postsecondary education as a fraction of GDP was 2.3 percent, trailing only Korea (2.4 percent); and the portion of total education spending that went for postsecondary education was 38 percent, second only to Canada (40 percent). See Hansen (1997), whose history of secondary vocational education also stresses the greater success of postsecondary occupational education.

6. See esp. the *Journal of Teaching in Social Work*.

7. We are indebted for this example to Professor Bill Charland, chair, Department of Art, Grand Rapids State University, Michigan. See also Tomkins (2002).

8. For a listing of baccalaureate fields, see NCES (2002), table 258.

9. The term *de-schooling* was popularized by Illich (1971), who proposed an apprentice-like system instead.

10. De-skilling does not reduce the education requirements of specific occupations but instead operates by slicing an occupation into several components and using less skilled or less *schooled* individuals in the new occupation.

11. We rely for our statements about registered apprenticeships on Robert Glover, University of Texas, Austin.

12. An extensive literature on the signaling value of educational credentials fails to ask how the information value is established; for a recent review, see Riley (2001).

13. On the weakness of the American state, see esp. the comparative work of Esping-Anderson (1990), as well as the data on employment and unemployment protection in Estevez-Abe, Iversen, and Soskice (2001), tables 4.1 and 4.2.

14. The definitive comparative data come from the Luxembourg Income Study. By one measure of inequality, the Gini coefficient varying from zero when income is equally distributed to 1.0 with maximal inequality, the most recent coefficient for the United States was .368 in 2000. Even other laissez-faire countries have lower levels of inequality: Australia (.311), Canada (.305), and the United Kingdom (.345). Countries with stronger welfare states have still lower levels of inequality: Austria (.266), Germany (.252), Denmark (.257), France (.288), Belgium (.224), Finland (.247), the Netherlands (.253), Norway (.238), Sweden (.252). Recent poverty figures for 2000 show 21.9 percent of U.S. children below 50 percent of median income, compared with figures like 15.7 percent in Canada, 15.4 percent in the U.K., and 15.8 percent in Australia, and figures of 10.2 percent in Austria, 8.7 percent in Denmark, 6.8 percent in Germany, 8.1 percent in the Netherlands, 5.2 percent in Norway, and 4.2 percent in Sweden. To find figures comparable to the U.S. we must look to truly undeveloped countries, like Mexico (27.7 percent) and Russia (23.7 percent). These figures are available at www.lisproject.org/keyfigures/povertytables.htm.

15. For other arguments along this line, see Lafer (2002) and Livingstone (1998) for Canada. There's a substantial literature in the United Kingdom on approaches to the demand side, reviewed in Lloyd and Payne (2002).

6. The Public and Private Benefits of Schooling

1. See also the argument of Labaree (1997) on the dominance of social mobility (an individual benefit, despite its name) over social efficiency and democratic equality, an argument resting on the distinction between the public and private goals of schooling developed in Grubb and Lazerson (1982), ch. 10.

2. Mann presented some evidence, including the fact that literate workers earned 18.5–27 percent more than nonliterate workers, but overall his data were inconclusive; Vinovskis (1970) criticizes Mann's methods. On "learning to earn" see Lapp and Mote (1915). The first efforts to examine different *kinds* of education, in the early 1940s, were largely negative, finding that students with high school vocational education had no clear advantage over those without such training, except for girls in commercial education (Menefee, 1942, discussed in Kliebard, 1999, 211–221).

3. Remarks by the President at San Jacinto Community College, Houston, Texas, Sept. 26, 1997; www.pub.whitehouse.gov.

4. These rough calculations come from *Census of the Population 1940* (Washington, DC: Government Printing Office, 1947), tables 21–22. Slightly different figures are contained in *Historical Statistics of the United States*, series 656—661. In addition, Goldin and Katz (1999) have calculated earlier returns to schooling using a sample from the Iowa State Census of 1915, finding high returns to both years of high school and years of college and helping to explain the growth of high schools.

5. The effects of variables other than schooling have sometimes been summarized in the "alpha coefficient"—the proportion of the simple wage or earnings differentials associated with schooling (from figures like those in Table 6.1) that can be explained by schooling alone, controlling for other variables. Leslie and

Brinkman (1988) conclude that the average value in thirteen studies was 79 percent, which they judge too low. More recently economists have concluded that the "ability bias" in estimating the effects of education may be offset by the bias caused by measuring educational attainment incorrectly; see Krueger and Lindahl (2001). Our own work in this particular vineyard has focused on returns to pre-baccalaureate education (Grubb, 1995b, 1997b, 2000a, and 2000b). For other reviews see Pascarella and Terenzini (1991), ch. 11; Bowles, Gintis, and Osborne (2001) have summarized results about personality and behavioral traits.

6. See also Cohn and Geske (1990), ch. 5, whose results suggest an increase in the rate of return during the 1970s and 1980s.

7. See, e.g., Gustman and Steinmeier (1982); Hu and Stromsdorfer (1979); Meyer and Wise (1981). Rumberger and Daymont (1984) found that students with employment related to their occupational field of study worked more than other students.

8. Of students entering public two-year colleges in 1995–96, 9.7 percent earned a certificate by June 2001, 15.7 percent earned an associate degree, and 10.5 percent completed a baccalaureate degree; however, 46.9 percent were not enrolled and had no credential, and 17.5 percent were still in school. By contrast, of those entering public four-year colleges, 53 percent had completed a baccalaureate degree within this five-year period, 17.3 percent were still in school, and 22.5 percent had no degree and were not enrolled (Berkner et al., 2002, tables 2.1-A, 2.2-A). However, nonselective four-year colleges have much lower completion rates, often in the range of 20 to 30 percent; see n. 8 of Chapter 2. See also Boesel and Fredlund (1999).

9. On the failures of School-to-Work, see n. 14 of Chapter 1. Most attempts to emulate the German system (described in Buechtemann, Schupp, and Solof, 1993) have failed to understand the institutional developments required, including government intervention in labor markets and strong unions and employer associations.

10. Murnane, Willett, and Boudett (1995) found small effects for the GED, vanishing with increased experience, and they acknowledged that this small gain might not be worth the pedagogical damage the GED does. Quinn (1993) argues that the rise of the GED after World War II caused a decline in adult high schools with better-developed curricula. See also Cameron and Heckman (1993), and Quinn and Haberman (1986) on the paltry effects of the GED on postsecondary enrollment.

11. Another tactic has been endogenous growth theory showing how growth can become self-sustaining, like Lucas's (1988) model emphasizing human capital. But theoretical models cannot help us distinguish empirically among many plausible candidates for x-factors.

12. Goldin (1998 and undated) and Goldin and Katz (1999) have constructed the historical argument that increases in schooling, specifically at the secondary level (at least until 1970), may be responsible for growth rates over the twentieth century as well as differences between the United States and European countries. However, from 1970 to the present, increases in human capital are surely the result of expanding postsecondary rather than secondary education. While their work offers the most thorough compendium of data on schooling increases, it suffers from the common flaw of emphasizing education while neglecting, and failing to measure the effects of, a greater variety of factors.

13. See also the critique of the growth claims for the United Kingdom in Wolf (2002). Krueger and Lindahl (2001) provide more technical analysis of the difficulties in using cross-section evidence.

14. See Mowery (1999), esp. the sections on university-based research in the computing industry (229–230), hard disk drives (312–317), chemicals (33–35), pharmaceuticals (364), semiconductors (274–275), steel (95), and biotechnology (388–395). The chapter on chemicals by Arora and Gambardella (1999) is particularly clear on the role of research universities in keeping U.S. firms ahead of European competitors.

15. In addition to Schor's (1991) analysis of how hard Americans work, a widely republished article by Ferguson (2003) has argued that the higher growth rates of the United States compared with Europe are due to the amount of time Americans work. This suggests that Weber's (1930) argument about the connection between work and the Protestant ethic is most powerful in the United States.

16. See www.teenpregnancy.org/whycare/default.asp and www.adcouncil.org/issues/High_School_Dropout_Prevention.

17. See Eccles and Grootman (2002), and *Youth Development* (2002).

18. See esp. Ogbu (1978), drawing on literature from the 1960s when the economic returns to schooling for blacks relative to whites were lower than they are now. Whether the perceptions of black youth are realistic is another question.

19. See Orr et al. (1994), exhibit 4.22; Quint et al. (1994), tables 3–6; Cave et al. (1993); Grossman and Sipe (1992); Walker and Vilella-Velez (1992). Grubb (1996a) reproduces many of these results in tables 4-13 and 4-14.

7. The Ambiguities of Separating Schooling and Work

1. On the School-to-Work Opportunities Act, see n. 14 of Chapter 1.

2. On counseling in high schools, see Grubb and Watson (2002); Krei and Rosenbaum (2001). For the community college level, see Grubb (2003).

3. E.g., while almost 900 community colleges (out of about 1,200 in the country) report having some co-op education, it reaches a small proportion of students in most institutions; see Stern et al. (1995) and Bragg, Hamm, and Trinkle (1995).

4. However, there seems to be an increase in the number of high schools creating career academies and other schools within schools following the philosophy of "education through occupations." Kirp (2003) has described some recent efforts to create modest linkages in high schools, through information-technology certificate programs using Microsoft or Cisco teaching packages.

5. See Villeneuve and Grubb (1996), esp. 20–22, contrasting firms who believe in "grow your own" approaches with those who use co-op programs as sources of low-cost labor.

6. See the enormous literature on licensing in the journals of specific professions. For a now-dated overview, see Shimberg et al. (1972); for the arguments against licensing, see Gross (1984) and Young (1987).

7. On various credentials and skill standards, see Carnevale (2000); Resnick and Wirt (1996); and the Web site of the National Skills Standards Board (NSSB), www.nssb.org; on voluntary efforts, see Wills (1993b) and Stacey (1999). On the failure of government-initiated standards and the NSSB, see Haimson and Hulsey (1999). Educators have found it difficult to use national skill standards because of

inconsistencies among state and national frameworks, a lack of technical assistance, and low levels of academic competence (Klein et al., 1997).

8. In 1996 in the United States, 6.1 million certificates were awarded, an upper limit on the number of private credentials; in contrast there were 9.7 million associate degrees, 22.5 million baccalaureate degrees, 11 million advanced degrees, and 42.4 million high school diplomas (Bauman and Ryan, 2001, table C). There may be a serious undercount of informal certificates, particularly from employer groups; see Carnevale (2000). However, interest in these private credentials has diminished substantially with the decline of the computer industry since 2000.

9. The concept of skill has been endlessly debated, particularly in sociology; see "Special Issue on Skills," *Work and Occupations*, Nov. 1990. The conception of individual skill is part of what Attewell (1990) calls the positive school, while skill as context-dependent is part of the ethno-methodological critique.

10. See esp. Forman and Steen (1995); Mathematical Sciences Education Board (1995, 1998). The concept of quantitative literacy, as a replacement for conventional "school" mathematics, is arguably better suited to both work preparation and democratic participation; see Steen (2001).

11. On learning communities, see Matthews (1994); Smith (1991); Grubb (1996b), ch. 5; Grubb and Associates (1999), ch. 7.

12. These competencies have been embedded in "document literacy"—measuring the ability to extract information from different types of documents—included in the National Adult Literacy Survey and the International Adult Literacy Survey. Articles by Irwin Kirsch and others published in the *Journal of Reading* in 1990 and 1991 discuss how to teach document literacy.

13. Rumberger (1981), table 8. See also Rawlins and Ulman (1974), Eckhaus (1964), Scoville (1966), and Berg (1970), ch. 3.

14. See Daly, Buchel, and Duncan (2000), table 1; the review in Hartog (2000), esp. tables 1–2; and the special issue of *Economics of Education Review* on over-education, vol. 19 (2000).

15. See the review of signaling by Riley (2001), esp. sec. 5.1. It has been difficult to confirm the existence of much signaling, possibly because schooling both increases competencies and signals ability, as in Riley's (1979) model.

16. The use of routine and uneducative work for work-based programs is a problem even in the highest quality co-op education; see n. 3 above and the descriptions of low-quality work placements in Greenberger et al. (1982), Moore (1981), and Stasz and Kaganoff (1998).

17. These are reviewed in National Research Council (2003), ch. 6, based on Grubb and Watson (2002). On the counseling in "education through occupations," see McCharen (1995) and Grubb (1995a); on Puente counselors, see Grubb, Lara, and Valdez (2002); on Comer schools, see Comer (1996).

8. The Evolution of Inequality

1. See again the figures from the Luxembourg Income Study, in n. 14 of Chapter 5.

2. The Coleman Report of 1966 and an enormous literature that followed it estimated statistically the relative importance of schooling resources versus family background, and school resources proved to have much weaker effects than family

background; Hanushek (1989) summarizes the school effects. For our reinterpretation of this debate, see Grubb, Huerta, and Goe (2003).

3. Deschenes, Cuban, and Tyack (2001) argue that one way of ascribing blame for students who do not do well has been to claim that schools are not differentiated enough, leading in turn to new forms of differentiation.

4. Collins (1979, ch. 7) summarizes the evidence, and blames this inequality on empty forms of credentialism. His solution—"credential abolitionism"—ignores both the politics of the Education Coalition and the difficulty of certifying learning in the American context through more formal assessment of work-related abilities.

5. On variation in the reading literacy scale, see Kirsch et al. (2002), tables 4.1, 4.15. On the mathematical reading scale, see OECD (2001b), table 3.1. For IALS data, see *Literacy in the Information Age* (2000), table 2.2.

6. For evidence about these varying effects, see Hickrod (1997); Murray et al. (1998); and USGAO (1997).

7. In Pole's (1978) examination of equality in the United States, three conceptions of equality of opportunity dominate: the prohibition of obvious barriers to opportunity, represented by Webster's formulation; the Jacksonian concern that public institutions not support private privilege; and the effort to develop "policies of correction," or compensatory policies.

8. See Lowi's (1969) contention that interest-group liberalism cannot redistribute—in this case, cannot distribute educational opportunities more equitably.

9. Virtually no treatment of the welfare state has included education; see, e.g., Esping-Anderson (1990), Piven and Cloward (1997), and Katz (2001), the latter written by an educational historian.

10. The concept of the Foundational State has some elements in common with Gilbert's (2001) enabling state, which also promotes marketlike mechanisms. But Gilbert views the enabling state as part of the "silent surrender of public responsibility," whereas we view the Foundational State as a normative concept to resurrect public responsibility.

11. Cited in Pole (1978), 145.

9. Vocationalism and the Education Gospel in the Twenty-First Century

1. See Kirp's (2000) review of several books on higher education, as well as Kirp (2003). See Lee (2003) on the academic-industrial complex, and Levine (2002) for the Milken quote and other dire predictions, such as the death of textbooks and newspapers.

2. On long waves, see n. 14 in the Introduction.

3. For grown-ups who have forgotten their nursery tales, Chicken Little mistakes a falling acorn for the sky falling, and with her friends (Cocky Locky, Henny Penny, and Loosey Goosey) she sets off in haste to tell the king. When promised a shortcut by Foxy Woxy, they are nearly led to the fox's lair to be gobbled up—a danger prevented at the last minute by the fortuitous appearance of the king's hunting dogs. A straightforward retelling cannot possibly capture the power of the original, however.

4. On the power of narratives, see n. 11 of the Introduction and Roe (1994).

5. Theories of action refer to the conceptions linking any action with desirable outcomes (Argyris and Schon, 1978; Malen et al., 2002). Legislation or a re-

form practice that lacks a valid theory of action can have positive results only by chance.

6. We can contrast this American belief with the greater European distrust of education for the masses lest they revolt against their superiors. The United States has distinctly different patterns of enrollment, with expansion in both secondary and postsecondary education starting much earlier and continuing over a longer period of time than in European countries; see Wolf (2002), fig. 6.2, for the postsecondary patterns in six countries.

7. Some of these proposals are mentioned by Lafer (2002, 223), who argues that short-term job training should not be a substitute for demand-side policies. See also Livingstone's (1998) argument that the demand for higher-order competencies is inadequate; his remedies—shareholder capitalism, stakeholder capitalism, and economic democracy—are different versions of the social ownership of capital.

8. See, e.g., Truman's (1951) early analysis of interest-group liberalism, where he sneers at the conception of the common good. Lowi (1969) has shown how difficult it is for interest-group liberalism to plan and to redistribute. The conception of democracy we articulate here is more Jeffersonian: "Only lay down true principles, and adhere to them inflexibly. Do not be frightened into their surrender by the alarms of the timid, or the croakings of wealth against the ascendancy of the people" (Padover, 1939, 53). See also MacPherson (1977) on developmental democracy and participatory democracy.

References

Achtenhagen, F., and W. N. Grubb (2001). Vocational and occupational education: Pedagogical complexity, institutional indifference. In V. Richardson, ed., *Handbook of research on teaching*, 4th ed., 176–206. Washington, DC: American Educational Research Association.

Adelman, C. (1992). *The way we are: The community college as American thermometer*. Washington, DC: Office of Educational Research and Improvement, U.S. Department of Education.

Alexander, B. (2002). Agencies say college-educated staff show results. *Youth Today* 11(6): 1, 14–17.

American Youth Policy Forum (2000). *High schools of the millennium*. Washington, DC: AYPF.

Angus, D., and J. Mirel (1999). *The failed promise of the American high school, 1890–1995*. New York: Teachers College Press.

Appelbaum, E., and R. Batt (1994). *The new American workplace: Transforming work systems in the United States*. Ithaca, NY: ILR Press.

Argyris, C., and D. Schon (1978). *Organizational learning: A theory of action perspective*. Reading, MA: Addison-Wesley.

Arora, A., and A. Gambardella (1999). Chemicals. In D. Mowery, ed., *U.S. industry in 2000: Studies in competitive performance*, 45–74. Washington, DC: National Academy Press.

Association of American Medical Colleges (1984). *Physicians for the twenty-first century*. Washington, DC.

Astin, A. (1998). The changing American college student: Thirty-year trends, 1966–1996. *Review of Higher Education*, 21(2): 115–135.

Attewell, P. (1990). What is skill? *Work and Occupations*, 17(4): 422–448.

Averett, S., and S. D'Allessandro (2001). Racial and gender differences in the returns to two-year and four-year degrees. *Education Economics* 9(3): 281–292.

Bacchetti, R. (1999). The most important reform objective: Staying power. *Education Week* 19(Nov. 10): 41.

Badway, N., and W. N. Grubb (1997). *A sourcebook for reshaping the community college: Curriculum integration and the multiple domains of career preparation*, vol. 1: *Framework and examples*. Berkeley: National Center for Research in Vocational Education.

Bailey, T., and I. Averianova (1998). *Multiple missions of community colleges: Conflicting or complementary?* New York: Community College Research Center, Teachers College, Columbia University.

Bailey, T., and Merritt, D. (1997). Industry skill standards and education reform. *American Journal of Education* 105(Aug.): 401–436.

Baldwin, J. (2000). *Creating a new vision of the urban high school*. New York: Carnegie Corporation.

Barley, S. (1993). *What do technicians do?* Unpublished paper, School of Industrial Relations, Cornell University.

Barley, S., and J. Orr (1997). *Between craft and science: Technical work in U.S. settings*. Ithaca: Cornell University Press.

Barnow, B., and C. King (2003). *The workforce investment act in eight states: Overview from a field network study*. U.S. Department of Labor, wdr.doleta.gov/owsdrr/papers/RIG_Interim_Report_7–8–03.pdf.

Barro, R. (1997). *Determinants of economic growth: A cross-country empirical study*. Cambridge, MA: MIT Press.

——— (2000). Inequality and growth in a panel of countries. *Journal of Economic Growth* 5: 5–32.

Barton, P. (2002). *The closing of the education frontier?* Princeton: Educational Testing Service, Policy Information Center.

Bauman, K., and C. Ryan (2001). *What's it worth: Field of training and economic status*. Current Population Reports, P70–72. Washington, DC: U.S. Census Bureau.

Becker, G. (1993). *Human capital: A theoretical and empirical analysis with special reference to education*, 3rd ed. Chicago: University of Chicago Press.

Bell, J., and M. Linn (1993). *Scaffolding novices in spatial reasoning and visualization for engineering*. Working paper. Berkeley: School of Education, University of California.

Bellah, R., et al. (1985). *Habits of the heart: Individualism and commitment in American life*. Berkeley: University of California Press.

Berg, I. (1970), with S. Gorelick. *Education and jobs: The great training robbery*. New York: Praeger.

Berkner, L., et al. (2002). *Descriptive summary of 1995–96 beginning postsecondary students: Six years later*. NCES 2003–151. Washington, DC: National Center for Education Statistics, U.S. Department of Education.

Berryman, S. (1995). Apprenticeship as a paradigm of learning. In W. N. Grubb, ed., *Education through occupations in American high schools*, vol. 1: *Approaches to integrating academic and vocational education*. New York: Teachers College Press.

Berryman, S., and T. Bailey (1992). *The double helix of education and the economy*. New York: Institute on Education and the Economy, Teachers College, Columbia University.

Bestor, A. (1953). *Educational wastelands: The retreat from learning in our public schools.* Urbana: University of Illinois Press.

Bird, C. (1975). *The case against college.* New York: David McKay.

Bishop, J. (1989). Why the apathy in American high schools? *Educational Researcher* 18(1): 6–10.

Blank, R. (2000). Fighting poverty: Lessons from recent U.S. history. *Journal of Economic Perspectives* 14(2): 3–19.

Bledstein, B. (1978). *The culture of professionalism: The middle class and the development of higher education in America.* New York: Norton.

Bloom, A. D. (1987). *The closing of the American mind.* New York: Simon and Schuster.

Bloom, H. S., et al. (1994). *The national JTPA study: Overview: Impacts, benefits, and costs of Title II-A.* Bethesda: Abt Associates.

Bloomfield, M., ed. (1915). *Readings in vocational guidance.* Boston: Ginn and Co.

Blum, R., C. McNeely, and P. Rinehart (2002). *Improving the odds: The untapped power of schools to improve the health of teens.* Minneapolis: Center for Adolescent Health and Development, University of Minnesota. www.allaboutkids.umn.edu.

Board on Science, Technology, and Economic Policy, National Research Council (1999). *Securing America's industrial strength.* Washington, DC: National Academy Press.

Boesel, D., and E. Fredlund (1999). *College for all: Is there too much emphasis on getting a four-year college degree?* Washington, DC: U.S. Department of Education.

Bottoms, G., and A. Presson (1995). Improving high schools for career-bound youth: Reform through a multi-state network. In W. N. Grubb, ed., *Education through occupations in American high schools*, vol. 2: *The challenges of implementing curriculum integration*, 35–56. New York: Teachers College Press.

Bowen, W, and D. Bok (1998). *The shape of the river: Long-term consequences of considering race in college and university admissions.* Princeton: Princeton University Press.

Bowles, S., and H. Gintis (1975). *Schooling in capitalist America.* New York: Basic Books.

Bowles, S., H. Gintis, and M. Osborne (2001). The determinants of earnings: A behavioral approach. *Journal of Economic Literature* 34(Dec.): 1137–1176.

Boyer, E. (1983). *High school: A report on secondary education in America.* New York: Harper and Row, for the Carnegie Foundation for the Advancement of Teaching.

——— (1990). *Scholarship reconsidered: Priorities of the professoriate.* Princeton: Carnegie Foundation for the Advancement of Teaching.

Bragg, D., R. Hamm, and K. Trinkle (1995). *Work-based learning in two-year colleges in the United States.* Berkeley: National Center for Research in Vocational Education.

Braverman, H. (1974). *Labor and monopoly capital: The degradation of work in the twentieth century.* New York: Monthly Review Press.

Breneman, D. (1994). *Liberal arts colleges: Thriving, surviving, or endangered?* Washington, DC: Brookings Institution.

Brint, S. (2001). Professionals and the "knowledge economy": Rethinking in the theory of postindustrial society. *Current Sociology* 49(4): 101–132.

———— (2002). The rise of the "practical arts." In S. Brint, ed., *The future of the city of intellect: The changing American university*, 231–259. Stanford: Stanford University Press.

Brint, S., and J. Karabel (1989). *The diverted dream.* New York: Oxford University Press.

Brint, S., et al. (2002). *Colleges and universities of the "practical arts": Correlates of a resurgent form.* Department of Sociology, University of California at Riverside.

Brown, A. (1997). *Work first: How to implement an employment-based approach to welfare reform.* New York: Manpower Demonstration Research Corporation.

Buechteman, C., J. Schupp, and D. Solof (1993). Roads to work: School-to-work transition patterns in Germany and the United States. *Industrial Relations Journal* 24(2): 97–111.

Burnside, C., and D. Dollar (2000). Aid, policies, and growth. *American Economic Review* 90(4): 847–868.

California Tomorrow (2002). A new look at California community colleges: Keeping the promise alive for students of color and immigrants. Unpublished report. Oakland: California Tomorrow.

Callahan, R. (1962). *Education and the cult of efficiency.* Chicago: University of Chicago Press.

Cameron, S., and J. Heckman (1993). The non-equivalence of high school equivalents. *Journal of Labor Economics* 11(1): 1–47.

Carnegie Council on Adolescent Development (1989). *Turning points: Preparing American youth for the 21st century.* New York: Carnegie Corporation.

Carnegie Council on Policy Studies in Higher Education (1980). *Giving youth a better chance: Options for education, work, and service.* San Francisco: Jossey-Bass.

Carnegie Foundation for the Advancement of Teaching (1977). *Missions of the college curriculum.* San Francisco: Jossey-Bass.

Carnevale, A. (1990). *Workplace basics: The essential skills employers want.* San Francisco: Jossey-Bass.

———— (2000). *Help wanted . . . credentials required: Community colleges in the knowledge economy.* Princeton: Educational Testing Service; Arlington, VA: American Association of Community Colleges.

Carnoy, M. (1994). *Faded dreams: The politics of race in America.* New York: Cambridge University Press.

Cave, G., et al. (1993). *JOBSTART: Final report on a program for school dropouts.* New York: Manpower Demonstration Research Corporation.

Cheit, E. (1975). *The useful arts and the liberal tradition.* New York: McGraw-Hill for the Carnegie Commission on Higher Education.

Clark, B. (1960). *The open door college: A case study.* New York: McGraw-Hill.

Clark, D. (1988). School/business partnerships are too much talk and not enough performance. *American School Board Journal* 175(8): 33, 44.

Claus, J. (1990). Opportunity or inequality in vocational education? A qualitative investigation. *Curriculum Inquiry* 20: 7–39.

Clune, W. H. (1994). The shift from equity to adequacy in school finance. *Educational Policy* 8(4): 376–394.

Cochran-Smith, M., and S. Lytle (1999). The teacher-research movement: A decade later. *Educational Researcher* 28(7): 15–25.

Cohen, A., and F. Brawer (1987). *The collegiate function of community colleges: Fostering higher learning through curriculum and student transfer.* San Francisco: Jossey-Bass.

—— (1989). *The American community college,* 2nd ed. San Francisco: Jossey-Bass.

Cohn, E., and T. Geske (1990). *The economics of education,* 3rd ed. Oxford: Pergamon.

Coleman, J., et al. (1966). *Equality of educational opportunity.* Washington, DC: Government Printing Office.

Collins, A., J. Brown, and S. Newman (1989). Cognitive apprenticeship: Teaching the craft of reading, writing, and mathematics. In L. Resnick, ed., *Knowing, learning, and instruction: Essays in honor of Robert Glaser,* 453–494. Hillsdale, NJ: Erlbaum.

Collins, R. (1979). *The credential society: An historical sociology of education and stratification.* New York: Academic Press.

Comer, J. (1996). *Rallying the whole village: The Comer process for reforming education.* New York: Teachers College Press.

Commission on Admission to Graduate Management Education (1990). *Leadership for a changing world: The future role of graduate management education.* Los Angeles: Graduate Management Admission Council.

Commission on National Aid to Vocational Education (1914). *Report on national aid to vocational education.* 63rd Cong., 2nd sess., U.S. House of Representatives, doc. no. 1004.

Commission on the Skills of the American Workforce (CSAW) (1990). *America's choice: High skills or low wages!* Rochester, NY: National Center on Education and the Economy.

Cook-Gumperz, J. (1986). Literacy and schooling: An unchanging equation? In *The social construction of literacy.* New York: Cambridge University Press.

Counts, G. (1932). *Dare the schools build a new social order?* John Day Pamphlets no. 11. New York: John Day Co.

Crandall, J. (1981). A socio-linguistic investigation of the literacy demands of clerical workers. Ph.D. diss., Department of Linguistics, Georgetown University.

Cremin, L. (1961). *The transformation of the school.* New York: Knopf.

—— (1989). *Popular education and its discontents.* New York: Harper and Row.

Cuban, L. (1990). Reforming again, again, and again. *Educational Researcher* 19(1): 3–13.

—— (1993). *How teachers taught: Constancy and change in American classrooms, 1880–1990,* 2nd ed. New York: Teachers College Press.

Cuban, L., and D. Shipps (2000). *Restructuring the common good in education: Coping with intractable American dilemmas.* Stanford: Stanford University Press.

Cubberly, E. P. (1934). *Readings in public education in the United States.* Boston: Houghton Mifflin.

Cummings, W., and P. Altbach, eds. (1997). *The challenge of eastern Asian education: Implications for America.* Albany: State University of New York Press.

D'Amico, R. et al. (1999). *An evaluation of the self-service approach in one-stop career centers* (Contract No. G-5966–6–00–87–30). Washington, DC: U.S. Department of Labor.

Daly, M., F. Büchel, and G. Duncan (2000). Premiums and penalties for surplus and deficit education: Evidence from the United States and Germany. *Economics of Education Review* 19: 169–178.

Darrah, C. (1996). *Learning and work: An exploration in industrial ethnography.* New York: Garland.

Deil-Amen, R., and J. Rosenbaum (2001). How can low-status colleges help young adults gain access to better jobs? Applications of human capital versus sociological models. Unpublished paper, Department of Sociology, Northwestern University.

Denison, E. (1967). *Why growth rates differ: Postwar experience in nine western countries.* Washington, DC: Brookings Institution.

—— (1985). *Trends in American economic growth, 1929–1982.* Washington, DC: Brookings Institution.

Deschenes, S., L. Cuban, and D. Tyack (2001). Mismatch: Historical perspectives on schools and students who don't fit them. *Teachers College Record* 103(4): 525–547.

Devenport, W., and M. Hebel (2001). Laboratory curriculum: A turnkey approach. *Community College Journal* 72(12): 17–22.

Dewey, J. (1916a). Vocational education. *New Republic* 6(Mar. 11): 159–160.

—— (1916b; 1966). *Democracy and education: An introduction to the philosophy of education.* New York: Free Press.

—— (1938). *Experience and education.* New York: Macmillan.

Diekhoff, G. M. (1988). An appraisal of adult literacy programs: Reading between the lines. *Journal of Reading* 31(7): 624–630.

Dougherty, K. (1994). *The contradictory college: The conflicting origins, impacts, and futures of the community college.* Albany: State University of New York Press.

Dougherty, K., and M. Bakia (1998). The new economic development role of the community college. Occasional Paper. New York: Community College Research Center, Teachers College, Columbia University.

Douglas, J. (2000). *The California idea and American higher education: 1850 to the 1960 Master Plan.* Stanford: Stanford University Press.

Douglas, P. (1921). *American apprenticeship and industrial education.* Studies in History, Economics, and Public Law, vol. 95, no. 2. New York: Columbia University.

Dreeben, R. (1968). *On what is learned in school.* Reading, MA: Addison-Wesley.

Dryfoos, J. (1994). *Full-service schools: A revolution in health and social services for children, youth, and families.* San Francisco: Jossey-Bass.

Dunham, E. A. (1969). *Colleges of the forgotten Americans: A profile of state colleges and regional universities.* Carnegie Commission on Higher Education. New York: McGraw-Hill.

Dutile, F. N., ed. (1981). *Legal education and lawyer competency: Curricula for change.* Notre Dame: University of Notre Dame Press.

Eaton, J. (1994). *Strengthening collegiate education in community colleges.* San Francisco: Jossey-Bass.

Eccles, J., and J. A. Grootman (2002). *Community programs to promote youth development.* Washington, DC: National Academy Press.

Eckaus, R. (1964). Economic criteria for education and training. *Review of Economics and Statistics* 46(May): 181–190.

Eddy, E. D. (1957). *Colleges for our land and time: The land-grant idea in American education.* New York: Harper.

Ehrenreich, B., and D. English (1978). *For her own good: 150 years of experts' advice to women.* Garden City, NJ: Anchor Books.

Elson, W., and F. Bachman (1910). Different courses for elementary schools. *Educational Review* 39: 359–362.

Equal Rights Advocates (2000). *The broken promise: Welfare reform two years later.* San Francisco: ERA.

ERIC Clearinghouse on Educational Management. (1990). *The role of business in the schools.* The Best of ERIC on Educational Management, no. 102. ED321391.

Erikson, E. (1959; 1980). *Identity and the life cycle.* New York: Norton.

Esping-Anderson, G. (1990). *The three worlds of welfare capitalism.* Princeton: Princeton University Press.

Estevez-Abe, M., T. Iversen, and D. Soskice (2001). Social protection and the formation of skills: A reinterpretation of the welfare state. In P. Hall and D. Soskice, eds., *Varieties of capitalism: The institutional foundations of comparative advantage,* 145–183. Oxford: Oxford University Press.

Etzioni, A. (1969). *The semi-professions and their organization: Teachers, nurses, social workers.* New York: Free Press.

Fearfull, A. (1996). Clerical workers, clerical skills: Case studies from credit management. *New Technology, Work, and Employment* 11(1): 55–65.

Ferguson, N. (2003). How Weber's "Protestant Ethic" explains U.S. edge over Europe. *International Herald Tribune,* June 9, 9.

Fischer, R., and D. Cordray (1996). *Job training and welfare reform: A policy-driven synthesis.* New York: Russell Sage.

Fordham, C., and J. Ogbu (1986). Coping with the "burden of 'acting white.'" *Urban Review* 18(3): 176–206.

Forman, S., and L. Steen (1995). Mathematics for life and work. In I. Carl, ed., *Prospects for school mathematics: Seventy-five years of progress.* Reston, VA: National Council of Teachers of Mathematics.

Frank, A., H. Rahmanou, and S. Savner (2003). *The workforce investment act: A first look at participation, demographics, and services.* Update no. 1. New York: Center for Law and Social Policy.

Freeman, C. (1984). *Design, innovation, and long cycles in economic development.* London: Frances Pinter.

——— (1996). *Long wave theory.* Cheltenham, UK: Edward Elgar.

Freeman, R. (1976). *The over-educated American.* New York: Academic Press.

Friedlander, D. (1988). *Subgroup impacts and performance indicators for selected welfare employment programs.* New York: Manpower Development Research Corporation.

Friedlander, D., and G. Burtless (1995). *Five years after: The long-term effects of welfare-to-work programs.* New York: Russell Sage.

Gaff, J. G. (1991). *New life for the college curriculum: Assessing achievements and furthering progress in the reform of general education.* San Francisco: Jossey-Bass.

Gallager, M. (2003). *Higher education financing in Australia.* Paris: Organization for Economic Cooperation and Development.

Gardner, H. (1983; rev. 1993). *Frames of mind: The theory of multiple intelligences.* New York: Basic Books.

Geiger, R. (2000a). The era of multi-purpose colleges in American higher education, 1850–1890. In R. Geiger, ed., *The American college in the nineteenth century*, 127–152. Nashville: Vanderbilt University Press.

——— (2000b). The rise and fall of useful knowledge. In R. Geiger, ed., *The American college in the nineteenth century*, 153–168. Nashville: Vanderbilt University Press.

Gilbert, N. (2001). *Transformation of the welfare state: The silent surrender of public responsibility*. Oxford: Oxford University Press.

Gilpin, K. (2002). Turning a profit with higher education. *New York Times*, Oct. 20, BU7.

Gittell, M., and T. Steffy (2000). Community colleges addressing students' needs: A case study of LaGuardia community college. New York: Howard Samuels State Management and Policy Center, City University of New York.

Goldin, C. (1998). America's graduation from high school: The evolution and spread of secondary schooling in the twentieth century. *Journal of Economic History* 58: 345–374.

——— (1999). *A brief history of education in the United States*. Historical Paper 119. Cambridge, MA: National Bureau of Economic Research.

——— (undated). The human capital century and American leadership: Virtues of the past. Unpublished paper, Department of Economics, Harvard University.

Goldin, C., and L. Katz (1999). *Education and income in the early twentieth century: Evidence from the prairies*. National Bureau of Economic Research Working Paper.

Goodlad, J. (1984). *A place called school: Prospects for the future*. New York: McGraw-Hill.

Goodlad, J., and T. McMannon, eds. (1997). *The public purpose of education and schooling*. San Francisco: Jossey-Bass.

Goodman, P. (1956). *Growing up absurd: Problems of youth in the organized system*. New York: Random House.

Gorn, E. R. (1998). *The McGuffey Readers: Selections from the 1879 edition*. Boston: Bedford/St. Martin's.

Goto, S. (1998). The threshold: Basic writers and the open door college. PhD diss., School of Education, University of California, Berkeley.

Gott, S. P. (1988). Apprenticeship instruction for real-world tasks: The coordination of procedures, mental models, and strategies. In E. Rothkopf, ed., *Review of Research in Education* 15: 97–169. Washington, DC: American Educational Research Association.

——— (1995). Rediscovering learning: Acquiring expertise in real-world problem-solving tasks. *Australian and New Zealand Journal of Vocational Education Research* 3: 30–68.

Green, J. (2001). *High school graduation rates in the United States*. New York: Center for Civic Innovation, Manhattan Institute.

Greenbaum, J. (1979). *In the name of efficiency: Management theory and shopfloor practice in data-processing*. Philadelphia: Temple University Press.

Greenberger, E., and L. Steinberg (1986). *When teenagers work: The psychological and social costs of adolescent employment*. New York: Basic Books.

Gregson, J. (1997). A critical response to Grubb. *Journal of Vocational Education Research* 22(2): 123–133.

Groot, W., and H. M. Van den Brink (2000). Over-education in the labor market: A meta-analysis. *Economics of Education Review* 19: 149–158.

Gross, S. J. (1984). *Of foxes and hen houses: Licensing and the health professions.* Westport, CT: Quorum.

Grossman, J. B., and C. L. Sipe (1992). *Summer training and education program (STEP): Report on long-term impacts.* Philadelphia: Public/Private Ventures.

Grubb, W. N., ed. (1995a). *Education through occupations in American high schools,* vol. 1: *Approaches to integrating academic and vocational education;* vol. 2: *The challenges of implementing curriculum integration.* New York: Teachers College Press.

Grubb, W. N. (1995b). Response to comment. *Journal of Human Resources* 30(1): 222–228.

——— (1995c). *The returns to education and training in the sub-baccalaureate labor market: Evidence from the survey of income and program participation, 1984–1990.* Berkeley: National Center for Research in Vocational Education.

——— (1996a). *Learning to work: The case for reintegrating job training and education.* New York: Russell Sage.

——— (1996b). *Working in the middle: Strengthening education and training for the mid-skilled labor force.* San Francisco: Jossey-Bass.

——— (1997a). Finding common ground: A brief response. *Journal of Vocational Education Research* 22(2): 133–139.

——— (1997b). The returns to education in the sub-baccalaureate labor market, 1984–1990. *Economics of Education Review* 16(3): 231–246.

——— (1999). Lessons from education and training for youth: Five precepts. In *Preparing youth for the twenty-first century: The transition from education to the labour market,* 363–386. Paris: Organization for Economic Cooperation and Development.

——— (2001a). *From black box to Pandora's box: Evaluating remedial/developmental education.* Occasional Paper, Community College Research Center, Teachers College, Columbia University. www.tc.columbia.edu/ccrc/papers/grubb2.pdf.

——— (2001b). Second chances in changing times: The roles of community colleges in advancing low-skilled workers. In R. Kazis and M. Muller, eds., *Low-wage workers in the new economy,* 283–306. Washington, DC: Urban Institute Press.

——— (2002a). Learning and earning in the middle, part I: National studies of pre-baccalaureate education. *Economics of Education Review* 21: 299–321.

——— (2002b). Learning and earning in the middle, part II: State and local studies of pre-baccalaureate education. *Economics of Education Review* 21: 401–414.

——— (2002c). *Who I am: The inadequacy of information in the information age.* Paris: Organization for Economic Cooperation and Development. www.oecd.org/dataoecd/32/35/1954678.pdf.

——— (2003). "Like, what do I do now?" The dilemmas of guidance and counseling. Draft chapter. Community College Research Center, Teachers College, Columbia University.

Grubb, W. N., and Associates (1999). *Honored but invisible: An inside look at teaching in community colleges.* New York: Routledge.

Grubb, W. N., N. Badway, and D. Bell (2003). Community college and the equity agenda: The potential of non-credit education. In K. Shaw and J. Jacobs, eds.,

Community college: New environments, new directions. Annals of the American academy of political and social science 586: 218–240.

Grubb, W. N., L. Goe, and L. Huerta (forthcoming). The unending search for equity: California policy, the "new" school finance, and the *Williams* case. *Teachers College Record.*

Grubb, W. N., L. Huerta, and L. Goe (2003). *Straw into gold, resources into results: Spinning out the implications of the "renewed" school finance.* Earlier version available as Research Series 01–1. Berkeley: Policy Analysis for California Education, Graduate School of Education, University of California.

Grubb, W. N., and J. Kalman (1994). Relearning to earn: The role of remediation in vocational education and job training. *American Journal of Education* 103(1): 54–93.

Grubb, W. N., C. Lara, and S. Valdez (2002). Counselor, coordinator, monitor, mom: The roles of counselors in the Puente program. *Educational Policy* 16(4): 547–571.

Grubb, W. N., and M. Lazerson (1982). *Broken promises: How Americans fail their children.* New York: Basic Books. Reprinted in 1988 with a postscript, "Let Them Eat Ketchup: The Plight of Children in the 1980s." Chicago: University of Chicago Press.

Grubb, W. N., and L. McDonnell (1996). Combating program fragmentation: Local systems of vocational education and job training. *Journal of Policy Analysis and Management* 15(2): 252–270.

Grubb, W. N., and S. Michelson (1974). *States and schools: The political economy of public school finance.* Lexington, MA: Lexington Books.

Grubb, W. N., and P. Ryan (1999). *The role of evaluation for vocational education and training: Plain talk on the field of dreams.* London: Kogan Page.

Grubb, W. N., L. Tredway and A. Furco (2003). Principals as researchers and analysts: New challenges for school leadership programs. Paper presented at the annual meeting of the American Educational Research Association, Chicago.

Grubb, W. N., and C. Watson (2002). Engagement and motivation in high school: The multiple roles of guidance and counseling. Paper prepared for the National Research Council, Committee for Increasing High School Students' Engagement and Motivation to Learn.

Grubb, W. N., et al. (1989). *Innovation versus turf: Coordination between vocational education and Job Training Partnership Act programs.* Report to Congress, the Secretary of Education, and the Secretary of Labor. Berkeley: National Center for Research in Vocational Education.

Grubb, W. N., et al. (1997). *Workforce, economic, and community development: The changing landscape of the entrepreneurial community college.* Mission Viejo, CA: League for Innovation in the Community College.

Grubb, W. N., et al. (1999). *Toward order from chaos: State efforts to reform workforce development systems* (MDS-1249). Berkeley: National Center for Research in Vocational Education.

Gueron, J. M., and E. Pauly (1991). *From welfare to work.* New York: Russell Sage.

Gustman, A. L., and T. L. Steinmeier (1982). The relation between vocational training in high school and economic outcomes. *Industrial and Labor Relations Review* 36(1): 73–87.

Gutmann, A. (1987). *Democratic education.* Princeton: Princeton University Press.

Haimson, J., and L. Hulsey (1999). *Making joint commitments: Roles of schools, employers, and students in implementing national skill standards*. Princeton: Mathematica Policy Research.

Hall, P., and D. Soskice, eds. (2001). *Varieties of capitalism: The institutional foundations of comparative advantage*. Oxford: Oxford University Press.

Hamilton, S. (1990). *Apprenticeship for adulthood: Preparing youth for the future*. New York: Free Press.

Hampel, R. (1986). *The last little citadel: American high schools since 1940*. Boston: Houghton Mifflin.

Hansen, H. (1997). Caps and gowns: Historical reflections on the institutions that shaped learning for and at work in Germany and the United States, 1800–1945. PhD diss., University of Wisconsin, Madison.

Hanushek, E. A. (1989). The impact of differential expenditures on school performance. *Educational Researcher* 18(May): 45–62.

Harberger, A. (1998). A vision of the growth process. *American Economic Review* 88(1): 1–32.

Harper, D. (1987). *Working knowledge: Skill and community in a small shop*. Chicago: University of Chicago Press.

Hartog, J. (2000). Over-education and earnings: Where are we, where should we go? *Economics of Education Review* 19: 131–147.

Hecker, D. (2001). Occupational employment projections to 2010. *Monthly Labor Review* 124(11): 57–84.

Heckman, J. (1999). Policies to foster human capital. Working paper 7288. Cambridge, MA: National Bureau of Economic Research. www.nber.org/papers/w7288.

Herr, E., and S. Cramer (1992). *Career guidance and counseling through the life span: Systematic approaches*, 4th ed. New York: HarperCollins.

Hershey, A. (2003). Has school-to-work worked? In W. Stull and N. Sanders, eds., *The school-to-work movement: Origins and destinations*, 79–100. Westport, CT: Praeger.

Hershey, A., et al. (1998). *Expanding options for students: Report to congress on the national evaluation of school-to-work implementation*. Princeton: Mathematica Policy Research.

Hickrod, A. (1997). The effect of constitutional litigation on educational finance: A further analysis. In W. Fowler, ed., *Selected papers in school finance, 1995* (NCES 97–536). Washington, DC: National Center for Education Statistics.

Hill, P., G. Foster, and T. Gendler (1990). *High schools with character*. R-3944-RC. Santa Monica: RAND.

Hirsch, E. D. (1987). *Cultural literacy: What every American needs to know*. New York: Vintage.

Hochschild, J., and N. Scovronik (2003). *The American dream and the public schools*. New York: Oxford University Press.

Hodkinson, P., A. Sparkes, and H. Hodkinson (1996). *Triumphs and tears: Young people, markets, and the transition from school to work*. London: David Fulton.

Holmes Group (1986). *Tomorrow's teachers*. East Lansing: School of Education, Michigan State University.

Howe, H. (1993). *Thinking about our kids*. New York: Macmillan.

Hu, T.-W., and W. W. Stromsdorfer (1979). Cost-benefit analysis of vocational education. In T. Abramson, C. K. Tittle, and L. Cohen, eds., *Handbook of Vocational Education Evaluation*. Beverly Hills: Sage.

Hull, G. (1993). Critical literacy and beyond: Lessons learned from students and workers in a vocational program and on the job. *Anthropology and Education Quarterly* 24(4): 373–396.

Huston, A., et al. (2003). *New hope for families and children: Five-year results of a program to reduce poverty and reform welfare*. New York: Manpower Development Research Corporation.

Illich, I. (1971). *De-schooling society*. New York: Harper and Row.

Immerwahr, J., and T. Foleno (2000). *Great expectations: How the public and parents—white, African, and Hispanic—view higher education*. New York: Public Agenda Foundation.

Javart, J., and S. Wandner (2002). Use of intermediaries to provide training and employment services: Experiences under WIA, JTPA, and Wagner-Peyser programs. In C. O'Leary, R. Straits, and S. Wandner, eds., *Job training in the United States: History, effectiveness, and prospects*. Kalamazoo: W. E. Upjohn Institute for Employment Research.

Johanek, M., ed. (2001). *A faithful mirror: Reflections on the college board and education in America*. New York: College Entrance Examination Board.

Jones, B. (1984). *Sleepers, wake! Technology and the future of work*. Melbourne: Oxford University Press.

Jones, C. (2000). *Sources of U.S. growth in a world of ideas*. Department of Economics, Stanford University. www/stanford.edu/ chadj.

Jorgenson, D., and B. Fraumeni (1992). Investment in education and U.S. economic growth. *Scandinavian Journal of Economics* 94(supplement): 51–70.

Kaestle, C. (1973). *The evolution of an urban school system: New York City, 1750–1850*. Cambridge, MA: Harvard University Press.

——— (1983). *Pillars of the republic: Common schools and American society, 1780–1860*. New York: Hill and Wang.

——— (2000). Toward a political economy of citizenship: Historical perspectives on the purposes of common schools. In L. McDonnell, P. M. Timpane, and R. Benjamin, eds., *Rediscovering the democratic purposes of education*. Lawrence: University of Kansas Press.

Kantor, H. (1988). *Learning to earn: School, work, and vocational reform in California, 1880–1930*. Madison: University of Wisconsin Press.

Kantor, S. L., Z. F. Gamson, and H. B. London (1997). *Revitalizing general education in a time of scarcity: A navigational chart for administrators and faculty*. Boston: Allyn and Bacon.

Katz, M. (1971). *Class, bureaucracy, and schools: The illusion of educational change in America*. New York: Praeger Publishers.

——— (2001). *The price of citizenship: Redefining the American welfare state*. New York: Holt.

Kerr, C. (1991). The new race to be Harvard or Berkeley or Stanford. *Change* 23(3): 3–8.

——— (2002). Shock wave II: An introduction to the twenty-first century. In S. Brint, ed., *The future of the city of intellect: The changing American university*, 1–22. Stanford: Stanford University Press.

Kett, J. (1994). *The pursuit of knowledge under difficulties: From self-improvement to adult education in America, 1750–1990*. Stanford: Stanford University Press.

King, C., et al. (2000). Training success stories for adults and out-of-school youth: Past effects and lessons for the future. In B. Barnow and C. King, eds., *Improving the odds: Increasing the effectiveness of publicly funded training*. Washington, DC: Urban Institute Press.

Kirp, D. (2000). The new U. *The Nation*, April 17, 25–29.

——— (2003). *Shakespeare, Einstein, and the bottom line: Higher education goes to market*. Cambridge, MA: Harvard University Press.

Kirsch, I., et al. (2002). *Reading for change: Performance and engagement across countries*. Paris: Organization for Economic Cooperation and Development.

Klein, S., et al. (1996). *Skill standards: Concepts and practices in state and local education*. Berkeley: MPR Associates for the Office of Vocational and Adult Education, U.S. Department of Education.

——— (1997). *Apply the standards: Using industry skill standards to improve curriculum and instruction*. Berkeley: MPR Associates.

Klerman, J., and L. Karoly (1994). Young men and the transition to stable employment. *Monthly Labor Review* 117(8): 31–48.

Kliebard, H. (1999). *School to work: Vocationalism and the American curriculum, 1876–1946*. New York: Teachers College Press.

Knock, G. H. (1985). Development of student services in higher education. In M. J. Barr and L. A. Keating, eds., *Developing effective student services programs*. San Francisco: Jossey-Bass.

Kogan, D., et al. (1989). *Improving the quality of training under JTPA*. Berkeley Planning Associates and SRI International for the U.S. Department of Labor.

Krei, D., and J. Rosenbaum (2001). Career and college advice to the forgotten half: What do counselors and vocational teachers advise? *Teachers College Record* 103(5): 823–842.

Krueger, A., and M. Lindahl (2001). Education for growth: Why and for whom? *Journal of Economic Literature* 34(Dec.): 1101–1136.

Krug, E. (1969). *The shaping of the American high school 1880–1920*. Madison: University of Wisconsin Press.

Krugman, P. (2003). The tax-cut con. *New York Times Magazine*, Sept. 14, 54–62.

Kusterer, K. C. (1978). *Know-how on the job: The important working knowledge of "unskilled" workers*. Boulder: Westview.

Kwon, D. B. (2001). Adult education in Korea. Unpublished paper, College of Education, Korea University, Seoul.

Labaree, D. (1997). Public goods, private goods: The American struggle over educational goals. *American Educational Research Journal* 34(1): 39–81.

Ladner, J. (1995). *Tomorrow's tomorrow: The black woman*. Lincoln: University of Nebraska Press.

Lafer, G. (2002). *The job training charade*. Ithaca: Cornell University Press.

LaLonde, R. (1995). The promise of public sector training programs. *Journal of Economic Perspectives* 9(2): 149–168.

Landau, R. T., T. Taylor, and G. Wright (1996). *The mosaic of economic growth*. Stanford: Stanford University Press.

Lapp, J., and C. Mote (1915). *Learning to earn: A plea and a plan for vocational education*. Indianapolis: Bobbs-Merrill.

Larson, M. S. (1977). *The rise of professionalism: A sociological analysis*. Berkeley: University of California Press.

Lave, J., and E. Wenger (1991). *Situated learning: Legitimate peripheral participation.* New York: Cambridge University Press.

Lazerson, M. (1987). *American education in the twentieth century: A documentary history.* New York: Teachers College Press.

———— (1998). The disappointments of success: Higher education after World War II. *Annals of the American Academy of Political and Social Science* 559: 64–76.

Lazerson, M., and Grubb, W. N. (1974). *American education and vocationalism: A documentary history, 1870–1970.* New York: Teachers College Press.

Lazerson, M., U. Wagener, and N. Shumanis (2000). What makes a revolution: Teaching and learning in higher education, 1980–2000. *Change* 32(3): 18–19.

Lee, F. (2003). Academic industrial complex. *New York Times,* Sept. 6, 14, 15.

Lee, V., and J. Smith (2001). *Restructuring high schools for equity and excellence: What works.* New York: Teachers College Press.

Leslie, L., and P. Brinkman (1988). *The economic value of higher education.* New York: American Council on Education and Macmillan Publishing.

Levesque, K. (2003). *Trends in high school vocational/technical coursetaking: 1982–1998.* NCES 2003–025. Washington, DC: U.S. National Center for Education Statistics.

Levesque, K., et al. (2000). *Vocational education in the United States: Toward the year 2000.* NCES 2000–029. Washington, DC: U.S. Department of Education, Office of Educational Research and Improvement.

Levin, H. (1980). Educational vouchers and social policy. In J. Guthrie, ed., *School finance: Policies and practices,* 235–263. Cambridge, MA: Ballinger.

Levin, H., and R. Rumberger (1987). Educational requirements for new technologies: Visions, possibilities, and current realities. *Educational Policy* 1(3): 333–354.

Levine, A. (2002). College education will soon be whole new experience. *Honolulu Advertiser,* Jan. 16. thehonoluluadvertiser.com/2000/jan/16/ opinion6.html.

Levine, D. (1986). *The American college and the culture of aspiration, 1915–1940.* Ithaca: Cornell University Press.

Levine, L. (1996). *The opening of the American mind: Canons, culture, and history.* Boston: Beacon.

Lewin, T. (2002). For students seeking edge, one major just isn't enough. *New York Times,* Nov. 17, 1, 22.

Lindley, B., and E. Lindley (1938). *A new deal for youth: The story of the national youth administration.* New York: Viking.

Literacy in the Information Age. (2000). Final Report of the International Adult Literacy Survey. Paris: Organization for Economic Cooperation and Development; Ottowa: Statistics Canada, Ministry of Industry.

Livingstone, D. W. (1998). *The education-jobs gap: Unemployment for economic democracy.* Boulder: Westview.

Lloyd, C., and J. Payne (2002). Developing a political economy of skill. *Journal of Education and Work* 15(4): 365–390.

Lowi, T. (1969). *The end of liberalism: Ideology, policy, and the crisis of public authority.* New York: Norton.

Lucas, R. (1988). On the mechanics of economic development. *Journal of Monetary Economics* 22: 3–42.

Lucas, S. (1999). *Tracking inequality: Stratification and mobility in American high schools.* New York: Teachers College Press.

Ludmerer, K. (1983). *Learning to heal: The development of American medical education.* New York: Basic Books.

——— (1999). *Time to heal: American medical education from the turn of the century to the era of managed care.* New York: Oxford University Press.

Lynd, R., and H. Lynd (1929). *Middletown: A study in American culture.* New York: Harcourt, Brace, and World.

MacCrate R. (1992). *Legal education and professional development—An educational continuum.* Report of the Task Force on Law Schools and the Profession: Narrowing the Gap. Washington, DC: American Bar Association Section of Legal Education and Admissions to the Bar.

MacGregor, J. (1991). What differences do learning communities make? *Washington Center News* 6(1): 4–9.

MacPherson, C. B. (1977). *The life and times of liberal democracy.* Oxford: Oxford University Press.

Macro, B., et al. (2002). *Understanding the role of intermediaries under WIA.* Interim Report to the U.S. Department of Labor. Oakland: Berkeley Planning Associates.

Mager, N. (1987). *The Kondratieff waves.* New York: Praeger.

Malen, B., et al. (2002). Reconstituting schools: "Testing" the "theory of action." *Educational Evaluation and Policy Analysis* 24(2): 113–132.

Manlove, J. (1998). The influence of high school dropout and school disengagement on the risk of school-age pregnancy. *Journal of Research on Adolescents* 8(2): 187–220.

Manski, C. (1989). Schooling as experimentation: A reappraisal of the college dropout phenomenon. *Economics of Education Review* 8(4): 305–312.

Marcus, J. (2002). An unknown quality: Olin College students, faculty and administrators create an innovative new university from scratch. *National Crosstalk* 20(2): 1, 14, 15.

Mathematical Sciences Education Board, National Research Council. (1995). *Mathematical Preparation for the Technical Workforce.* Washington, DC: National Academy Press.

——— (1998). *High school mathematics at work: Essays and examples for the education of all students.* Washington, DC: National Academy Press.

Matthews. R. S. (1994). Enriching teaching and learning through learning communities. In T. O'Banion et al., *Teaching and learning in the community college,* 179–200. Washington, DC: American Association of Community Colleges.

Matus-Grossman, L., and Gooden, S. (2002). *Opening doors: Students' perspectives on juggling work, family, and college.* New York: Manpower Development Research Corporation.

McCharen, B. (1995). Guidance and counseling: An essential component for effective integration. In W. N. Grubb, ed., *Education through occupations in American high schools,* vol. 2: *The challenges of implementing curriculum integration,* 151–155. New York: Teachers College Press.

McGrath, E., and C. Russell (1958). *Are liberal arts colleges becoming professional schools?* New York: Teachers College, Columbia University.

McPherson, M., and M. Schapiro (1991). *Keeping college affordable: Government and educational opportunity.* Washington, DC: Brookings Institution.

Medrich, E., et al. (2000). School-to-work progress measures: A report to the National School-to-Work Office for the period July 1, 1997–June 30, 1998.

Washington, DC: National School-to-Work Office, U.S. Departments of Education and Labor.

Menefee, S. (1942). *Vocational training and employment of youth.* Research Monograph 25, Works Progress Administration. Washington, DC: Government Printing Office.

Meyer, R. H., and D. A. Wise (1981). High school preparation and early labor market experience. In R. B. Freeman and J. L. Medoff, eds., *Youth joblessness and unemployment.* Chicago: University of Chicago Press.

Minorini, P., and S. Sugarman (1999a). Educational adequacy and the courts: The promise and the problems of moving to a new paradigm. In H. Ladd, R. Chalk, and J. Hansen, eds., *Equity and adequacy in education finance: Issues and perspectives,* 175–208. Washington, DC: National Academy Press.

—— (1999b). School finance litigation in the name of educational equity: Its evolution, impact, and future. In H. F. Ladd, R. Chalk, and J. S. Hansen, eds., *Equity and adequacy in education finance: Issues and perspectives,* 34–71. Washington, DC: National Academy Press.

Mishel, L., J. Bernstein, and J. Schmitt (2001). *The state of working America 2000/2001.* Ithaca: Cornell University Press.

Moore, D. T. (1981). Discovering the pedagogy of experience. *Harvard Educational Review* 51(2): 286–300.

Mowery, D., ed. (1999). *U.S. industry in 2000: Studies in competitive performance.* Washington, DC: National Academy Press.

Murnane, R., and F. Levy (1996). *Teaching the new basic skills: Principles for educating children to thrive in a changing economy.* New York: Free Press.

Murnane, R., J. Willett, and K. P. Boudett (1995). Do high school dropouts benefit from obtaining a GED? *Educational Evaluation and Policy Analysis* 17(2): 133–148.

Murray, S., W. Evans, and R. Schwab (1998). Education finance reform and the distribution of education resources. *American Economic Review* 88(4): 798–812.

National Academy of Sciences (1975). *Knowledge and power in manpower.* Washington, DC: National Academy Press.

National Association of Secondary School Principals (NASSP) (1996). *Breaking ranks: Changing an American institution.* Reston, VA.

National Center for Education Statistics (NCES) (2002). *The digest of education statistics 2001* (NCES 2002–13). Washington, DC.

—— (2003). *The condition of education 2003* (NCES 2003–67). Washington, DC.

National Center for Public Policy and Higher Education. (2002). *Measuring Up 2002: The state-by-state report card for higher education.* San Jose, CA.

National Coalition of Advocates for Children (1985). *Barriers to excellence: Our children at risk.* Boston: National Coalition of Advocates for Students.

National Commission on Excellence in Education (NCEE) (1983). *A nation at risk: The imperative for education reform.* Washington, DC: Government Printing Office.

National Commission on Secondary Vocational Education (1985). *The unfinished agenda: The role of vocational education in the high school.* Washington, DC: U.S. Department of Education.

National Commission on Social Studies in the Schools (1989). *Charting a course: Social studies for the 21st century.* Washington, DC: National Council for the Social Studies.

National Commission on the High School Senior Year (2001). *Raising our sights: No high school senior left behind.* Princeton: Woodrow Wilson National Fellowship Foundation.

National Commission on Youth (1980). *The transition of youth to adulthood: A bridge too long?* Boulder: Westview.

National Education Association (1918). *Report of the commission on the reorganization of secondary education.* U.S. Office of Education Bulletin no. 35. Washington, DC: Government Printing Office.

National Governors' Association (1986). *Time for results.* Washington, DC.

National Panel on High School and Adolescent Education (1976). *The education of adolescents.* Washington, DC: Government Printing Office.

National Research Council (2003). *Engaging schools: Fostering high school students' motivation to learn.* Washington, DC: National Academies Press.

Nelsen, B. (1997). Work as a moral act: How emergency medical technicians understand their work. In S. Barley and J. Orr, eds., *Between craft and science,* 154–184. Ithaca: Cornell University Press.

Newman, F. (1985). *Higher education and the American resurgence.* Princeton: Carnegie Foundation for the Advancement of Teaching.

O'Neil, E. H., and Pew Health Professions Commission (1998). *Recreating health professional practice for a new century.* San Francisco: Pew Health Professions Commission.

Oakes, J. (1985). *Keeping track: How schools structure inequality.* New Haven: Yale University Press.

Odden, A. (2001). The new school finance. *Phi Delta Kappan* 83(1): 85–91.

Ogbu, J. (1978). *Minority education and caste: The American system in cross-cultural perspective.* New York: Academic Press.

O'Neil, E. H., and Pew Health Professions Commission (1998). *Recreating health professional practice for a new century.* San Francisco: Pew Health Professions Commission.

O'Neill, D., and J. O'Neill (1997). *Lessons for welfare reform: An analysis of the AFDC caseload and past welfare-to-work programs.* Kalamazoo: W. E. Upjohn Institute for Employment Research.

Organization for Economic Cooperation and Development (OECD) (2001a). *Education policy analysis: Education and skills.* Paris.

———— (2001b). *Knowledge and skills for life: First results from PISA 2000.* Paris.

Orr, L. L., et al. (1994). *The national JTPA study: Impacts, benefits, and costs of Title II-A.* Bethesda: Abt Associates.

Orrill, R., with B. A. Kimball (1995). *The condition of American liberal education: Pragmatism and a changing tradition.* New York: College Entrance Examination Board.

Orrill, R., ed. (1997). *Education and democracy.* New York: College Board.

Osterman, P., and B. Lautsch (1996). *Project QUEST: A report to the Ford foundation.* Cambridge, MA: MIT Sloan School of Management.

Padover, S. (1938). *Democracy by Thomas Jefferson.* New York: Greenwood.

Panel on the General Professional Education of the Physician (1984). *Physicians for the twenty-first century: A report of the panel on the general professional education of the physician.* Washington, DC: American Association of Medical Colleges.

Panel on Youth of the President's Science Advisory Committee. (1974). *Youth: Transition to adulthood.* Chicago: University of Chicago Press.

Parsons, F. (1909). *Choosing a vocation.* Boston: Houghton Mifflin.

Pascarella, E., and P. Terenzini (1991). *How college affects students: Findings and insights from twenty years of research.* San Francisco: Jossey-Bass.

Pencavel, J. (2001). *Worker participation: Lessons from the worker co-ops of the Pacific Northwest.* New York: Russell Sage.

Pentland, B. (1997). Bleeding edge epistemology: Practical problem solving in software support hotlines. In S. Barley and J. Orr, eds., *Between craft and science,* 113–128. Ithaca: Cornell University Press.

Perkins, D. N., and G. Salomon (1988). Teaching for transfer. *Educational Leadership* 46(1): 22–32.

Perkinson, H. (1991). *The imperfect panacea: American faith in education, 1865–1976* 3rd ed. New York: McGraw-Hill.

Peterson, P. (1983). "Commissionitis" in higher education. *Brookings Review* 4 (Winter/Spring): 21–26.

Piven, F. F., and Cloward, R. (1997). *The breaking of the American social compact.* New York: New Press.

Pole, J. R. (1978). *The pursuit of equality in American history.* Berkeley: University of California Press.

Porter, W., and L. McKibbin (1988). *Management education and development: Drift or thrust into the 21st century?* New York: McGraw-Hill.

Powell, A., E. Farrar, and D. Cohen. (1985). *The shopping mall high school: Winners and losers in the educational marketplace.* Boston: Houghton Mifflin.

Power, C. (1985). Democratic moral education in the large public high school. In M. Barkowitz and F. Oser, eds., *Moral education: Theory and application.* Hillsdale, NJ: Erlbaum.

Powers, J. B. (1992). *The "girl question" in education: Vocational education for young women in the progressive era.* Philadelphia: Falmer Press.

President's Commission on Higher Education (1947). *Higher education for American democracy.* New York: Harper.

Primus, W., et al. (1999). *The initial impacts of welfare reform on the incomes of single-mother families.* Washington, DC: Center on Budget and Policy Priorities.

Public Policy Associates (1998). *Career management account: Demonstration project evaluation final report.* Lansing, MI.

Putnam, R. (2000). *Bowling alone: The collapse and revival of American community.* New York: Simon and Schuster.

Quigley, C. N., and C. Buhmueller (1991). *Civitas: A framework for civic education.* Calabasas, CA: Center for Civic Education.

Quinn, L. (1993). *The test that became an institution: A history of the GED.* Milwaukee: Employment and Training Institute, University of Wisconsin.

Quinn, L., and M. Haberman (1986). Are GED certificate holders ready for postsecondary education? *Metropolitan Education* 2(Fall): 72–82.

Quint, J. C., J. S. Musick, and J. A. Ladner (1994). *Lives of promise, lives of pain.* New York: Manpower Demonstration Research Corporation.

Quint, J. C., et al. (1994). *New chance: Interim findings on a comprehensive program for disadvantaged young mothers and their children.* San Francisco: Manpower Development Research Corporation.

Quint, J. C., et al. (1999). *Big cities and welfare reform: Early implementation and ethnographic findings from the project on devolution and urban change.* San Francisco: Manpower Development Research Corporation.

Ratcliff, T. (1995). The evolution of student affairs and its implications for community colleges. Paper, School of Education, University of California, Berkeley.

Ravitch, D. (1983). *The troubled crusade: American education 1945–1980.* New York: Basic Books.

Rawlins, V. L., and L. Ulman (1974). The utilization of college-trained manpower in the United States. In M. Gordon, ed., *Higher education and the labor market,* 195–235. New York: McGraw-Hill.

Reich, R. (1991). *The work of nations: A blueprint for the future.* New York: Simon and Schuster.

Resnick, L. (1987). Learning in school and out. *Educational Researcher* 16(9): 13–20.

———, ed. (1989). *Knowing, learning, and instruction.* Hillsdale, NJ: Erlbaum.

Resnick, L., and Wirt, J. (1996). *Linking school and work: Roles for standards and assessments.* San Francisco: Jossey-Bass.

Reuben, J. (1996). *The making of the modern university: Intellectual transformation and the marginalization of morality.* Chicago: University of Chicago Press.

Riley, J. (1979). Testing the educational screening hypothesis. *Journal of Political Economy* 87(5), pt. 2: S227–S252.

——— (2001). Silver signals: Twenty-five years of screening and signaling. *Journal of Economic Literature* 39: 432–478.

Roberts, B. (2002). *The best of both: Community colleges and community-based organizations partner to better serve low-income workers.* Philadelphia: Public/Private Ventures.

Rodgers, D. T. (1978). *The work ethic in industrial America, 1850–1920.* Chicago: University of Chicago Press.

Rodrik, D. (1997). *TFPG controversies, institutions and economic performance in East Asia.* Working Paper 5914. Cambridge, MA: National Bureau of Economic Research.

——— (2000). *Institutions for high-quality growth: What they are and how to acquire them.* Working Paper 7540. Cambridge, MA: National Bureau of Economic research.

Roe, E. (1994). *Narrative policy analysis: Theory and practice.* Durham: Duke University Press.

Rorabaugh, W. J. (1986). *The craft apprentice: From Franklin to the machine age in America.* New York: Oxford University Press.

Rosenbaum, J. (2001). *Beyond college for all: Career paths for the forgotten half.* New York: Russell Sage.

Rosenstock, L. (1991). The walls come down: The overdue reunification of vocational and academic education. *Phi Delta Kappan,* Feb., 434–439.

Rosenstock, L., and A. Steinberg (1995a). City works: Redefining vocational education. In J. Oakes and K. H. Quartz, eds., *Creating new educational communities.* Chicago: National Society for the Study of Education.

——— (1995b). Beyond the shop: Reinventing vocational education. In M. Apple and J. Beane, eds., *Democratic schools.* Arlington, VA: American Society for Curriculum and Development.

Rothman, S. (1978). *Women's proper place: A history of changing ideals and practices, 1870 to the present.* New York: Basic Books.

Rothstein, R. (2002a). *Out of balance: Our understanding of how school affects society and how society affects schools.* Chicago: Spencer Foundation.

———— (2002b). Linking infant mortality to schooling and stress. *New York Times,* Feb. 6, A20.

Rouse, C. (1995). Democratization or diversion: the effect of community colleges on educational attainment. *Journal of Business and Economic Statistics* 13(2): 217—224.

———— (1998). Do two-year colleges increase overall educational attainment? Evidence from the states. *Journal of Policy Analysis and Management* 17: 595—620.

Rudolph, F. (1962; 1990). *The American college and university: A history.* Athens: University of Georgia Press.

Rumberger, R. (1981). *Over-education in the U.S. labor market.* New York: Praeger.

———— (2001). *Why students drop out of school and what can be done.* Santa Barbara: School of Education, University of California, Santa Barbara. www.civilrights project.harvard.edu/research/dropouts/.

Rumberger, R. W., and T. N. Daymont (1984). The economic value of academic and vocational training acquired in high school. In M. E. Borus, ed., *Youth and the Labor Market,* 157–191. Kalamazoo: W. E. Upjohn Institute.

———— (1993). The economic returns to college major, quality, and performance: A multilevel analysis of recent graduates. *Economics of Education Review* 12(1): 1—19.

Rumberger, R., and K. Larson (1998). Student mobility and the increased risk of high school dropout. *American Journal of Education Research* 107: 1–35.

Rury, J. (1991). *Education and women's work: Female schooling and the division of labor in urban America, 1870–1930.* Albany: State University of New York Press.

Ryan, P. (2001). The school-to-work transition: A cross-national perspective. *Journal of Economic Literature* 39(1): 34–92.

Ryken, A. E. (2001). *Content, pedagogy, results: A thrice-told tale of integrating work-based and school-based learning.* PhD diss., School of Education, University of California, Berkeley.

Scarselletta, M. (1997). The infamous "lab error": Education, skill, and quality in medical technicians' work. In S. Barley and J. Orr, eds., *Between craft and science,* 187–209. Ithaca: Cornell University Press.

Schneider, B., and D. Stevenson (1999). *The ambitious generation: American teenagers, motivated but directionless.* New Haven: Yale University Press.

Schor, J. (1991). *The overworked American: The unexpected decline of leisure.* New York: Basic Books.

Scoville, J. (1966). Education and training requirements for occupations. *Review of Economics and Statistics* 48(Nov.): 387–392.

Scrivener, S., et al. (1998). *Implementation, participation patterns, costs, and two-year impacts of the Portland (Oregon) welfare-to-work program.* Washington, DC: U.S. Department of Education.

Secretary's Commission on Achieving Necessary Skills (SCANS) (1991). *What work requires of schools: A SCANS report for America 2000.* Washington, DC: U.S. Department of Labor.

Selingo, J. (2002). Mission creep? More regional colleges start honors programs to raise their profiles and draw better students. *Chronicle of Higher Education* 47(May 31): A19–A21.

Shaw, K., and S. Rab (2003). Work-first federal policies: Eroding access to community colleges for Latinos and other low-income populations. Unpublished paper, College of Education, Temple University.

Shimberg, B., et al. (1972). *Occupational licensing: Practices and policies.* Washington, DC: Public Affairs Press.

Simon, R., D. Dippo, and A. Schenke (1991). *Learning work: A critical pedagogy of work education.* New York: Bergin and Garvey.

Smith, B. (1991). Taking structure seriously: The learning community model. *Liberal Education* 77(2): 42–48.

Smith, J. P., and F. Welch (1986). *Closing the gap: Forty years of economic progress for blacks* (Report R-3330). Santa Monica: Rand.

Smith, V. (1993). Phantom students: Student mobility and general education. *AAHE Bulletin* 45(10): 10–13, 7.

Stacey, N., ed. (1999). *Competence without credentials.* Office of Educational Research and Improvement, U.S. Department of Education.

Stasz, C., and T. Kaganoff (1998). Work-based learning: Student perspectives on quality and links to school. *Educational Evaluation and Policy Analysis* 20(1): 31–46.

Steen, L., ed. (2001). *Mathematics and democracy: The case for quantitative literacy.* Princeton: National Council on Education and the Disciplines, Woodrow Wilson National Fellowship Foundation.

Steinberg, A. (1998). *Real learning, real work: School-to-work as high school reform.* New York: Routledge.

Steinberg, L. (1996). *Beyond the classroom: Why school reform has failed and what parents need to do.* New York: Simon and Schuster.

Stern, D. (1999). Improving pathways in the United States from high school to college and career. In *Preparing youth for the 21st century: The transition from education to the labour market,* 155–214. Paris: Organization for Economic Cooperation and Development.

Stern, D., C. Dayton, and M. Raby (2001). *Career academies: Building blocks for reconstructing American high schools.* Career Academy Support Network, School of Education, University of California, Berkeley.

Stern, D., et al. (1995). *School-to-work: Research on programs in the United States.* Bristol, PA: Falmer Press.

Stevenson, H. (1992). *The learning gap: Why our schools are failing and what we can learn from Japanese and Chinese education.* New York: Summit.

Stone, C. (1998). Civic capacity and urban school reform. In C. Stone, ed., *Changing urban education,* 250–276. Lawrence: University Press of Kansas.

Strawn, J. (1998). *Beyond job search or basic education: Rethinking the role of skills in welfare reform.* Washington, DC: Center for Law and Social Policy.

Stull, W. (2003). School-to-work in schools: A overview. In W. Stull and N. Sanders, eds., *The school-to-work movement: origins and destinations,* 3–25. Westport, CT: Praeger.

Sullivan, W. (1995). *Work and integrity: The crisis and promise of professionalism in America.* New York: Harper Business.

Swift, J. (1995). *Wheel of fortune: Work and life in the age of falling expectations*. Toronto: Between the Lines.

Terman, L. (1922). *Intelligence tests and school reorganization*. Yonkers, NY: World Book Co.

Timpane, M., et al. (1976). *Youth policy in transition*. R-2006-HEW. Santa Monica: Rand.

Tinto, V. (1993). *Leaving college: Rethinking the causes and cures of student attrition*, 2nd ed. Chicago: University of Chicago Press.

Tinto, V., and A. Goodsell-Love (1995). *A longitudinal study of learning communities at LaGuardia Community College*. ERIC Document ED 380 178. Washington, DC: Office of Educational Research and Improvement, U.S. Department of Education.

Tinto, V., A. Goodsell-Love, and P. Russo (1994). *Building learning communities for new college students: A summary of research findings of the collaborative learning project*. Washington, DC: Office of Educational Research and Improvement, U.S. Department of Education.

Tokina, K. (1993). Long-term and recent student outcomes of freshman interest groups. *Journal of the Freshman Year Experience* 5(2): 7–28.

Tomkins, C. (2002). Can art be taught? *New Yorker*, Apr. 15, 44–49.

Topel, R. (1999). Labor markets and economic growth. In O. Ashenfelter and D. Card, eds., *Handbook of Labor Economics*, vol. 3, 2944–2984. Amsterdam: Elsevier Science.

Truman, D. (1951). *The governmental process: Political interests and public opinion*. New York: Knopf.

Tuma, J. (1993). *Patterns of enrollment in postsecondary vocational education and academic education*. Prepared for the National Assessment of Vocational Education. Berkeley: MPR Associates.

Tyack, D., and L. Cuban (1995). *Tinkering toward Utopia: A century of public school reform*. Cambridge, MA: Harvard University Press.

Tyack, D. B., and E. Hansot (1990). *Learning together: A history of co-education in American schools*. New Haven: Yale University Press.

Tyack, D., R. Lowe, and E. Hansot (1984). *Public schools in hard times: The Great Depression and recent years*. Cambridge, MA: Harvard University Press.

U.S. Department of Commerce (1999). *21st century skills for 21st century jobs*. Washington, DC: Government Printing Office.

U.S. Department of Labor (1995). *What's working (and what's not): A summary of research on the economic impacts of employment and training programs*. Washington, DC.

U.S. General Accounting Office (USGAO) (1993). *School-linked human services: A comprehensive strategy for aiding students at risk of school failure*. GAO/HRD-94-21. Washington, DC.

—— (1995). *Multiple employment training programs: Major overhaul needed to create a more efficient, customer-driven system*. Washington, DC.

—— (1997). *School finance: State efforts to reduce funding gaps between poor and wealthy districts*. Washington, DC.

—— (2003). *Workforce investment act: One-stop centers implemented strategies to strengthen services and partnerships, but more research and information-sharing is needed*. GAO-03-725. Washington, DC.

Veysey, L. (1965). *The emergence of the American university*. Chicago: University of Chicago Press.

Viadero, D. (2002). Holding up a mirror: Teacher-researchers use their own classrooms to investigate questions. *Education Week* 21(June 12): 32–35.

Villeneuve, J. (2000). Composing a life: Community college students and project-based learning in a multimedia program. PhD diss., School of Education, University of California, Berkeley.

Villeneuve, J. C., and W. N. Grubb (1996). *Indigenous school-to-work programs: Lessons from Cincinnati's co-op education*. Berkeley: National Center for Research in Vocational Education.

Vinovskis, M. (1970). Horace Mann on the economic productivity of education. *New England Quarterly* 43: 550—571.

Walker, G., and F. Vilella-Velez (1992). *Anatomy of a demonstration: The summer training and education program (STEP) from pilot through replication and post-program impacts*. Philadelphia: Public/Private Ventures.

Weber, M. (1930). *The Protestant ethic and the spirit of capitalism*. New York: Scribner.

Weinrauch, J. D., M. Stevens, and R. Carlson (1997). Training requirements for professional certification of manufacturers' representatives. *Industrial Marketing Management* 26: 509–518.

Westbury, I., and A. G. Purves, eds. (1988). *Cultural literacy and the idea of general education*. Chicago: National Society for the Study of Education.

Whalley, P., and S. Barley (1997). Technical work in the division of labor: Stalking the wily anomaly. In S. Barley and J. Orr, eds., *Between craft and science*, 23–52. Ithaca: Cornell University Press.

Wiebe, R. (1967). *The search for order 1877–1920*. New York: Hill and Wang.

Williamson, J., and P. Lindert (1980). *American inequality: A macroeconomic history*. New York: Academic Press.

Willis, P. (1977). *Learning to labor: How working-class kids get working-class jobs*. Farnborough, UK: Saxon House.

Wills, J. (1993a). *An Overview of skill standards systems in education and industry*. Washington, DC: Institute for Educational Leadership.

——— (1993b). *Industry-driven skill standards systems in the United States*. Washington, DC: Institute for Educational Leadership.

Witt, A., et al. (1994). *America's community colleges: The first century*. Washington, DC: Community College Press.

Wlodkowski, R., J. Mauldin, and S. Gahn (2001). *Earning in the fast lane: Adult learners' persistence and success in accelerated college programs*. Center for the Study of Accelerated Learning, School for Professional Studies, Regis University. www/luminafoundation.org/Publications.

Wolf, A. (2002). *Does education matter? Myths about education and economic growth*. London: Penguin.

Woodlief, B., C. Thomas, and G. Orozco (2003). *California's gold: Claiming the promise of diversity in our community colleges*. Oakland: California Tomorrow.

Woodward, C. M. (1887). *The manual training school*. Boston: D. C. Heath.

Worthen, H. (1997). Signs and wonders: The negotiation of literacy in community college classrooms. PhD diss., School of Education, University of California, Berkeley.

Young, M., N. Fitzgerald, and M. Morgan (1994). *Learning outcomes and program results*. National Evaluation of Adult Education Programs, Fourth Report. Arlington, VA: Development Associates, Inc., for the Office of the Under Secretary, U.S. Department of Education.

Young, M. B., et al. (1994). *National evaluation of adult education programs*. Contract no. LC90065001. Washington, DC: U.S. Department of Education.

Young, S. D. (1987). *The rule of experts: Occupational licensing in America*. Washington, DC: Cato Institute.

Youth Development: Issues, Challenges, and Directions (2002). Philadelphia: Public/Private Ventures.

Zeichner, K., and S. Nofke (2001). Practitioner research. In V. Richardson, ed., *Handbook of Teaching on Research*, 298–330. Washington, DC: American Educational Research Association.

Zuboff, S. (1988). *In the age of the smart machine: The future of work and power*. New York: Basic Books.

Index

Abilities, 16, 26, 50; industrial intelligence, 8–9, 37, 117; cognitive, 76, 200–203, 256; occupational, 94–95; noncognitive, 200–203, 256; lore, 201; shortcuts, 201; tacit knowledge, 201; visual, 201; multiple intelligences, 255. *See also* Skills

Academic standards, 15–16, 31, 42, 46, 50, 62–63

Academic subjects, 199–200; in high schools, 7, 13–15, 29–31, 35, 38, 41–43, 46–49, 51–55; in liberal arts colleges/universities, 58–60, 64, 66, 68, 132, 137; in community colleges, 85–86, 89, 104–105

Academic tracking, 40–41, 44–45, 132, 139

Access to college, 30, 47, 98, 102, 132, 218–219, 223–225, 257

Accountability movement, 30, 50–51, 139, 239

Achievement gap, 252

Adelman, C., 99

Admissions tests, 62–63, 73, 135–136, 138, 148

Adult education, 25–26, 90–91, 131, 136–137; as second-chance opportunity, 120–124; ways to reconstruct, 124–128

Advanced placement courses, 44, 49

Advertising Council, 176

Affirmative action, 66, 73–74, 148, 221–222, 229–230

Africa, 237

African Americans, 223, 281n18; early vocational education for, 12–13, 17, 44, 233; racial discrimination, 22, 44, 46, 127, 149, 152–154, 177, 232–234; and slavery, 35; as high school dropouts, 50, 163; attending community colleges, 73, 90; and work-family-schooling dilemma, 98; employment discrimination, 177, 233; access to education, 218–219, 224; and policies of correction, 226, 230; equity issues, 234

Agricultural training, 10, 16, 58–60

Aid to Families with Dependent Children, 110, 231

Alexander, B., 146

Alger, Horatio, 16, 267

Altbach, P., 170

American Association of State Colleges and Universities, 274n9

American Bar Association, 75

American Culinary Foundation, 145

American dream, 4, 12, 43, 55–56, 74, 89, 217, 225–226, 254, 267

American Enterprise Institute, 112

American Federation of Labor, 37

American Hotel-Motel Association, 145

American Mountain Guides Association, 145

American Welding Society, 193